HARPER'S
ENCYCLOPEDIA OF
BIBLE LIFE

HARPER'S ENCYCLOPEDIA OF BIBLE LIFE

Madeleine S. and J. Lane Miller

A completely revised edition of the original work by

BOYCE M. BENNETT, Jr.
DAVID H. SCOTT

1817

Published in San Francisco by
HARPER & ROW, PUBLISHERS
New York, Hagerstown, San Francisco, London

HARPER'S ENCYCLOPEDIA OF BIBLE LIFE, *Third Revised Edition.* Copyright © 1978 by Harper & Row, Publishers. All rights reserved. Printed in the United States of America. No part of this book may be used or reproduced in any manner whatsoever without written permission except in the case of brief quotations embodied in critical articles and reviews. For information address Harper & Row, Publishers, Inc., 10 East 53rd Street, New York, N.Y. 10022. Published simultaneously in Canada by Fitzhenry & Whiteside Limited, Toronto.

Designed by Jim Mennick

Library of Congress Cataloging in Publication Data

Miller, Madeleine Sweeny, 1890–1976
THE HARPER ENCYCLOPEDIA OF BIBLE LIFE

Third rev. ed.
Previous editions published under title: Encyclopedia of Bible life.
Bibliography: p. 11 22 33 44 56 78 90 0
Includes index.
1. Bible—Dictionaries. I. Miller, John Lane, 1884–1954, joint author. II. Bennett, Boyce M. III. Scott, David H. IV. Title.
BS440.M5   1978   220.3   78–4752
ISBN 0-06-065676-X

Contents

ILLUSTRATIONS   ix

ABBREVIATIONS OF THE BOOKS OF THE BIBLE   xv

PREFACE   xvii

I. THE WORLD OF THE BIBLE   1

The Land of the Bible   2
The History Covered by the Bible   8
The Bible As a Book   12
The Old Testament   14
The New Testament   19
The Unique Nature of the Bible   22

II. HOW THE PEOPLE OF THE BIBLE LIVED   25

HOMES   25
Cave-Homes   25
Tents   27
Houses   33

FOOD   40
Hospitality   41
Everyday Foods   43
Food in Jesus' Teachings   46
"At the King's Table"   47

CLOTHING   48
Everyday Apparel   49
Clothing in Mosaic Law   52
Traditional Styles and Innovations   53
Clothing in New Testament Times   53
Jesus' Attitude toward Clothing   54

JEWELRY   55

Pearls   57
Jewels Crafted of Metals and Other Materials   58
Amulets   60
Egyptian Jewelry   61
Israel and the Decorative Arts   63

MEDICINE   65

Medicine in Egypt   66
Medicine in Mesopotamia   67
Medicine in Israel   68
Ointments, Perfumes, and Cosmetics   74

FAMILY EVENTS   89

The Birth of a Child   90
Circumcision   95
Marriage   98
Death   103

RELIGIOUS EVENTS   108

The Sabbath   109
The Pilgrimage Festivals   112
The Other Feasts   117

III. HOW THE PEOPLE OF THE BIBLE WORKED   121

THE LIFE OF THE NOMAD   121

Kinds of Nomads   121
Basics of Seminomadic Life   128
The Institutions of Nomadism   133
Life of a Typical Nomad Family   138
The Shepherd   141

THE LIFE OF THE FARMER   144

The Beginnings of Agriculture in Ancient Palestine   146
Types of Agriculture in the Ancient Near East   148
The Geography and Climate of Ancient Palestine   151
Land Use and Crops   157
History of Farming in the Biblical Period   161
The Life of an Israelite Farmer   168

THE PROFESSIONAL LIFE   188

Priests and Levites   190
Prophets   198

Magicians and Diviners   204
Pharisees and Sadducees   206
The Essenes   208
Teachers and Rabbis   209
Scribes   213
Engineers and Architects   216
Merchants   223
Sailors   226
Craftsmen   227
Musicians   230
Mourners   231
Prostitutes   232

THE CIVIL LIFE   233

The Structure of Biblical Society   234
The Civil Institutions of Biblical Society   236
The Administrative Organization of the Israelite Monarchy   252
Civil Institutions During the Period of Foreign Rule   265

THE MILITARY LIFE   269

Warfare During Israel's Tribal Period   269
Soldiering under David   280
The Weapons of David's Army   296
Solomon's Military Building Program   307
The Military Life During the Divided Kingdom   310
A Soldier in the Armies of Omri and Ahab   325
The Roman Presence   329

THE INDUSTRIAL LIFE   357

The Construction Industry   358
The Pottery Industry   363
The Metal Industry   373
The Textile Industry   376
The Jewelry Industry   380
The Fishing Industry   383
Miscellaneous Industries   385

IV. APPENDIX

SUGGESTIONS FOR FURTHER READING   390
INDEX OF SCRIPTURAL REFERENCES   397
INDEX OF NAMES AND SUBJECTS   411

Contributors

I. THE WORLD OF THE BIBLE

    Background   Boyce M. Bennett, Jr.

II. HOW THE PEOPLE OF THE BIBLE LIVED

    Homes   David H. Scott

    Food   James Cassidy

    Clothing   James Cassidy

    Jewelry   David H. Scott

    Medicine   David H. Scott

    Family Events   David H. Scott

    Religious Events   Boyce M. Bennett, Jr.

III. HOW THE PEOPLE OF THE BIBLE WORKED

    The Life of the Nomad   David H. Scott

    The Life of the Farmer   William P. Anderson

    The Professional Life   William P. Anderson

    The Civil Life   William P. Anderson

    The Military Life   David H. Scott

    The Industrial Life   William P. Anderson

IV. APPENDIX

    Bibliography   William P. Anderson

    Index   David H. Scott

Illustrations chosen, arranged and captioned by Boyce M. Bennett, Jr.

Illustrations

1. Israel, the land bridge between Egypt, Mesopotamia and Anatolia 3
2. Rain and the rain shadow in Israel 5
3. The average mean rainfall in Israel 6
4. Rain, crops and festivals throughout the year (*based on an idea originally conceived by John Wilkinson*) 7
5. Periods of biblical history on a time line 10
6. The arrangement of the Old Testament Books in the English Bible 13
7. The arrangement of the New Testament Books in the English Bible 14
8. The Old Testament Books of the Hebrew Bible 15
9. Comparison of the arrangement of the Books of the Hebrew and English Old Testaments 17
10. Cave shelter in the Wilderness of Judea 26
11. Modern cave dwelling near Jerusalem 27
12. Modern Bedouin tent 28
13. Division of a tent into two "apartments" 29
14. Large residence in an ancient Israelite village (from *Everyday Life in Old Testament Times*, by E. W. Heaton, illustrated by Marjorie Quennell; New York: Charles Scribner's Sons, 1956; used by permission) 34
15. Modern mud-brick house 35
16. Straw bed in typical Old Testament house 36
17. Reconstructed Old Testament house 37
18. Stove and cooking pot in reconstructed Old Testament house 38
19. Typical lamp from the period of the Israelite monarchy 38
20. The roof of a modern mud-brick house 39
21. A community baker in modern Jerusalem 44
22. Water jar and drinking jug from period of the Israelite monarchy 45
23. Dates on a date-palm tree 46

24. Nomadic clan entering Egypt, from the tomb of Beni-Hasan (from Heaton, *Everyday Life*, used by permission)   50

25. The Black Obelisk (from Heaton, *Everyday Life*, used by permission)   51

26. The colobium, New Testament period garment   55

27. Jewelry from the period of the Israelite monarchy   58

28. A scarab in a swivel-ring setting   59

29. Representation of a fertility goddess   60

30. Design from an ivory carving at Megiddo (from Heaton, *Everyday Life*, used by permission)   64

31. Ivory found at Megiddo (from Heaton, *Everyday Life*, used by permission)   65

32. A foot bath from Samaria (from Heaton, *Everyday Life*, used by permission)   86

33. Entry into the "Tombs of the Sanhedrin"   106

34. A tomb in the so-called Tomb of the Kings, Jerusalem   107

35. An ossuary from the Chalcolithic Period   107

36. The opening to a first-century tomb in the "Tomb of Kings"   108

37. Bedouin woman with her camels   122

38. Camels in the desert near Jericho   122

39. Camels eating cactus in the desert   122

40. Sheep and goats grazing   123

41. Arabs at the sheep market in modern-day Hebron   124

42. Wild asses roaming the Judaean Desert   124

43. The Negev desert   126

44. A whirlwind on the desert horizon   126

45. The desert of Jeshimon   127

46. Typical sheep in modern Israel   130

47. Goat of the kind found in Israel today   132

48. A modern Arab shepherd   141

49. The separation of sheep from goats on an early Christian sarcophagus   145

50. The green oasis of Jericho   151

51. Hill farming   152

52. A wadi (dry stream bed)   155

53. A cistern cut from bedrock   156

54. Grove of olive trees in Galilee   159

55. Unripened grapes on the vine   160

56. A fig tree   160

57. Pomegranates on the bush   161

58. Branch of an almond tree in blossom   162
59. Nabataean cistern in the Negev desert   165
60. Millstones from Pompeii   167
61. Modern refugee village near Jericho   170
62. Courtyard of a reconstructed house from the period of the Israelite monarchy   171
63. The sleeping room in a reconstructed house   172
64. Storage jars in a reconstructed house   173
65. A yoke of oxen plowing   175
66. Pottery and tools from the Iron Age I period of the Israelite monarchy   176
67. Iron tools from the Iron Age I period (from Heaton, *Everyday Life*, used by permission)   176
68. Seed sown by hand   177
69. Reaping the wheat harvest (from Heaton, *Everyday Life*, used by permission)   180
70. Arab boy on a threshing-sledge   181
71. Arab woman sifting the chaff   182
72. A saddle-quern for grinding grain (from Heaton, *Everyday Life*, used by permission)   183
73. Pair of millstones   187
74. An incense altar from the Iron Age I period   192
75. The priestly breastplate   193
76. The Temple of Solomon   195
77. The altar of burnt offering at Solomon's temple (from Heaton, *Everyday Life*, used by permission)   195
78. The vestments of the High Priest   197
79. Clay tablets with cuneiform writing   210
80. Mosaic floor at partially-restored Beit Alpha synagogue   212
81. The partially restored synagogue at Capernaum   212
82. The top of the ark in the synagogue at Chorazin   213
83. Israelite scribe with his scribal kit (from Heaton, *Everyday Life*, used by permission)   214
84. An ancient writing board   214
85. The subterranean water system at Hazor   218
86. The subterranean water system at Gibeon   219
87. The subterranean water system at Megiddo   219
88. Cave into which the water from the Spring Gihon runs   220
89. Hezekiah's Tunnel   220
90. Part of the temple platform built by Herod the Great   221

91. Part of the grand staircase leading from the lower city to the Temple of Herod   222

92. Part of the aqueduct which led water into Caesarea during the Roman period   222

93. A portion of the aqueduct constructed by Pontius Pilate   223

94. Part of the *suq* in Jerusalem   224

95. Seeds and nuts for sale in the *suq*   225

96. The ancient port of Joppa, or Jaffa   227

97. A reconstructed potter's wheel   228

98. Loom weights on a reconstructed loom   229

99. Musical instruments from the Bible (from Heaton, *Everyday Life*, used by permission)   232

100. The Jezreel Valley near Mount Gilboa   240

101. The designs of the Solomonic gates at Hazor, Megiddo and Gezer   242

102. The remains of the Solomonic gate at Gezer   243

103. The Plain of Jezreel or Esdraelon   249

104. Megiddo seen from the northeast   250

105. The plain north and east of Megiddo, seen from the city ruins   250

106. Model of reconstructed Megiddo   251

107. Reconstruction of Megiddo's ancient gate (from Heaton, *Everyday Life*, used by permission)   251

108. Ninth-century Israelite wall at Samaria   255

109. Designs from the ivories found at Samaria (from Heaton, *Everyday Life*, used by permission)   256

110. The "storehouse" found at Hazor   263

111. Inscription with Pontius Pilate's name on it found at Caesarea   267

112. The "sickle sword" (from *The Art of Warfare in Biblical Lands*, by Yigael Yadin, 2 vols.; New York: McGraw-Hill Book Company, 1963; used by permission)   274

113. Mace and ax (from Yadin, *Art of Warfare*, used by permission)   275

114. Spears and shields used in the Egyptian army (from Naville, E.: *The Temple of Deir el Bahari*, III–IV, London, 1898, p. LXIX, used by permission)   276

115. The individual pieces of a composite bow (from Yadin, *Art of Warfare*, used by permission)   277

116. Chariot of the XVIIIth Dynasty in Egypt (from Yadin, *Art of Warfare*, used by permission)   289

117. The battle between Ramses III and the Philistines, seen on the relief at Medinet Habu (from Wrezinski, W.: *Atlas zur altägyptischen*

Kulturgeschichte, Leipzig, ii, 1935, p. 113–114, used by permission)   297

118. A Sherden with round shield and straight sword (from Yadin, *Art of Warfare*, used by permission)   298

119. Spears (from Yadin, *Art of Warfare*, used by permission)   299

120. Javelins (from Yadin, *Art of Warfare*, used by permission)   299

121. Arrowheads (from Yadin, *Art of Warfare*, used by permission)   301

122. An Egyptian slinger (from Yadin, *Art of Warfare*, used by permission)   303

123. Typical Assyrian helmet (from Yadin, *Art of Warfare*, used by permission)   304

124. Scales of armor (from Yadin, *Art of Warfare*, used by permission)   305

125. The city of Lachish (from Heaton, *Everyday Life*, used by permission)   306

126. An Assyrian war chariot (from Yadin, *Art of Warfare*, used by permission)   316

127. Assyrian slingers (from Heaton, *Everyday Life*, used by permission)   316

128. Warriors, from a relief in the palace of Sargon, Khorsabad (from Botta, P. E. & Flandin, E.: *Monuments de Ninive*, ii, Paris, 1849, p. 145, used by permission)   317

129. Types of shields (from Yadin, *Art of Warfare*, used by permission)   318

130. Attack of a city by the Assyrian army (from Heaton, *Everyday Life*, used by permission)   319

131. Assyrian battering ram (from Yadin, *Art of Warfare*, used by permission)   320

132. The siege of Lachish (from Layard, A. H.: *The Monuments of Nineveh*, London, ii, 1853, p. 20, used by permission)   324

133. The remains of a Roman encampment   339

134. Uniform of a Roman soldier   351

135. Pyramid of ballistae   351

136. Captives making bricks (from Heaton, *Everyday Life*, used by permission)   359

137. Modern Arab stonemason   360

138. Phoenician merchant vessel (from Heaton, *Everyday Life*, used by permission)   362

139. Pottery wheel   363

140. Raw clay   366

141. Modern potter wedging the clay   367

142. Shaping the clay by hand   368

143. Indenting the clay to shape the vessel   368

144. Forming the sides of the vessel   369
145. The shaped bowl   369
146. Single shaped piece of clay to form several small vessels   370
147. Cutting the vessels from the clay   371
148. Egyptian women at a horizontal loom (from Heaton, *Everyday
     Life*, used by permission)   380
149. Open fish market in modern Jerusalem   385
150. Glassware from the Roman period   388

Abbreviations of the Books of the Bible

Genesis	Gen.	Daniel	Dan.
Exodus	Exod.	Hosea	Hos.
Leviticus	Lev.	Joel	Joel
Numbers	Num.	Amos	Amos
Deuteronomy	Deut.	Obadiah	Obad.
Joshua	Josh.	Jonah	Jon.
Judges	Judg.	Micah	Mic.
Ruth	Ruth	Nahum	Nah.
1 Samuel	1 Sam.	Habakkuk	Hab.
2 Samuel	2 Sam.	Zephaniah	Zeph.
1 Kings	1 Kings	Haggai	Hag.
2 Kings	2 Kings	Zechariah	Zech.
1 Chronicles	1 Chron.	Malachi	Mal.
2 Chronicles	2 Chron.	Matthew	Matt.
Ezra	Ezra	Mark	Mark
Nehemiah	Neh.	Luke	Luke
Esther	Esth.	John	John
Job	Job	Acts	Acts
Psalms	Ps.	1 Corinthians	1 Cor.
Proverbs	Prov.	2 Corinthians	2 Cor.
Ecclesiastes	Eccl.	Galatians	Gal.
Song of Solomon	S. of S.	Ephesians	Eph.
Isaiah	Isa.	Philippians	Phil.
Jeremiah	Jer.	Colossians	Col.
Lamentations	Lam.	1 Thessalonians	1 Thess.
Ezekiel	Ezek.	2 Thessalonians	2 Thess.

1 Timothy	1 Tim.	1 John	1 John
2 Timothy	2 Tim.	2 John	2 John
Titus	Tit.	3 John	3 John
Philemon	Philem.	Jude	Jude
Hebrews	Heb.	Revelation	Rev.
James	Jas.	1 Maccabees	1 Macc.
1 Peter	1 Pet.	2 Maccabees	2 Macc.
2 Peter	2 Pet.		

Preface

WHEN THE *Encyclopedia of Bible Life*, by Madeleine S. and J. Lane Miller, first appeared in 1944, it was a pioneering book for the general reader in the field of life in biblical times. The intention of that first edition was to present in non-technical language the elements of the day-to-day existence of the people of the Bible. Since 1944, the amount of information which has been unearthed through archaeological and other scholarly work has been enormous, necessitating a total revision of the original work. The original intention, however, has been retained. This current revision appears in non-technical language as did the original. It is meant to be of help to the layman rather than the scholar.

This encyclopedia has been divided into three parts. Part One presents the geographical, historical, and literary background against which the day-to-day existence of biblical people must be seen. Such a background is necessary if we are to understand the unspoken assumptions and presuppositions of biblical people about "the way things are." Part Two is concerned with the question, "How did the people live?" This part is interested in the ordinary details of everyday life. Part Three asks the question, "What did the people do for a living?" and is concerned with the lives of particular kinds of people who followed particular vocations or professions. These categories are somewhat arbitrary since what people did for a living sometimes determined the way they lived. But, on the whole, such a distinction can be useful.

It was with pleasure that the authors of this revision accepted the invitation of Harper's current religious book publisher, Clayton E. Carlson, to revise this encyclopedia so that it would include the newest information which had been obtained about biblical life styles. The major portion of the revision was done jointly by Boyce M. Bennett, Jr., Th.D., David H. Scott, and William P. Anderson, Ph.D. Later we procured the collaboration of James Cassidy, Jr. for several of the sections.

Many of the drawings are by Dr. Bennett, and most of the photographs are his also. Credits for the other illustrations, selected by Dr. Bennett, are given in the list of illustrations.

We trust that the *Encyclopedia of Bible Life* in its new form will prove to be as informative, stimulating, and useful to a general readership as was its prototype.

BOYCE M. BENNETT, JR.
DAVID H. SCOTT

New York, N.Y.
December 10, 1977

❧ I. The World of the Bible

FOR MANY people, reading the Bible is like visiting a foreign country. The ways of this foreign country are strange; its customs are different; its language takes some getting used to; and the countryside is unfamiliar. Travel is supposed to be broadening, but *informed* traveling can be much more than that. The traveler who goes to a foreign country prepared with a handful of maps, a booklet explaining the foreign currency, a short summary of the history of the country, and a list of "useful phrases" will find the trip not only much more broadening but much more fun. The chances of getting lost will be fewer, and the true essence of the country will be discovered. More important still, upon returning home the traveler will also find that life has been enriched and renewed in ways never expected before the venture.

Such preparation is even more valuable for reading the Bible. It is not necessary, or wise, to read everything in this encyclopedia at once before undertaking the Bible itself. Sometimes it is better to look up specific information as the need to know it arises. But sometimes a preliminary overall view assists in any detailed study. That is the purpose of this encyclopedia —to present the reader with facts that can make Bible study a very rewarding and enriching experience.

How did the people in the Bible live? What did they do for a living? Answers to these two basic questions are offered in this book because the Bible never attempts to do this for us. The Bible was not written to introduce us to an ancient people with seemingly strange ways. It was written to introduce us to the ways of God Himself. But we live so far away from the people of the Bible, both in distance and in time, that we are puzzled and confused by certain elements that were neither puzzling nor confusing to the writers themselves or to their earliest readers. Admittedly, the Bible

can sometimes appear deep and difficult to understand, dealing as it does
with the ultimate questions of life, which are never answered simply. But
the difficulty may arise from a lack of information on customs of the times.
The central message of the Bible need not be obscured because of this. It is
hoped that this encyclopedia will avoid such a disastrous result by focusing
on the ordinary aspects of biblical life. By helping to clear away false issues,
the essential issues of the Bible will appear as they really are.

A word concerning what this book does *not* intend to be:

It is not a book of geography. Knowledge of the place where Bible
events happened is important, and some insight will be provided into the
various geographical factors that influenced Bible life and the writing of
the Bible. But the primary purpose is not geographical.

It is not a book of biblical history. The time span covered by the Bible
and the major events of that period are included. But a detailed history will
not be found here.

It is not an introduction of the Bible as literature. Discussions of some
of the elements that went into the making of the Bible as a book will be
illuminating. But a thorough analysis of the individual books must be
sought in the respective commentaries.

Finally, it is not a book primarily on the theology of the Bible. That
does not imply, however, that this Encyclopedia is unrelated to theology.
Many, if not most, of the theological statements of the Bible were delivered
in a kind of verbal imagery that reflects the everyday life of the writers'
contemporaries. To be unfamiliar with this everyday life is to experience
difficulty in understanding the theological point being made. Thus the need
for a book concerned with the ordinary questions of "How did the people
in the Bible live?" and "What did they do for a living?"

The questions, although interesting because they involve a culture so
unlike our own, point up the real purpose of this encyclopedia: not to make
an anthropological study of an ancient and fascinating people, but rather
to let the Bible speak for itself to those of us far removed from the original
setting.

THE LAND OF THE BIBLE

The importance of Israel in influencing the future world is in great contrast to the actual territorial size of the ancient country. Maps of ancient
Israel showing the boundaries of the twelve tribes suggest a country of considerable size. It is a surprise to most students to learn that Israel was about
the size of the state of Vermont. The phrase "from Dan to Beersheba" is
frequently used in the Bible to indicate the full length of the country, as if
it were big, but this north-south extent measures only about 150 miles. Natu-

ral geographical features prohibited much territorial spread: the Mediterranean Sea to the west, the vast deserts to the east and the south, and the mountains to the north. Israel therefore never had the potential of becoming a large power like her neighbors.

Another geographical reality that kept Israel from becoming a powerful nation was the fact that Palestine was a land bridge between the vast centers of civilization in Egypt to the south and Mesopotamia and Anatolia (modern Turkey) to the north (Fig. 1). Important geographical features enabled these areas to become great powers: Egypt had the Nile River, Mesopotamia had the Tigris and the Euphrates Rivers, Anatolia had natural defenses and mineral resources in her vast mountains. Without any such natural advantages, Palestine furthermore had a huge disadvantage for any people attempting to build a significant nation in its territory: it was situated directly on the easiest route between the great powers. There was no alternative route, for the Mediterranean Sea and the Arabian Desert both provided

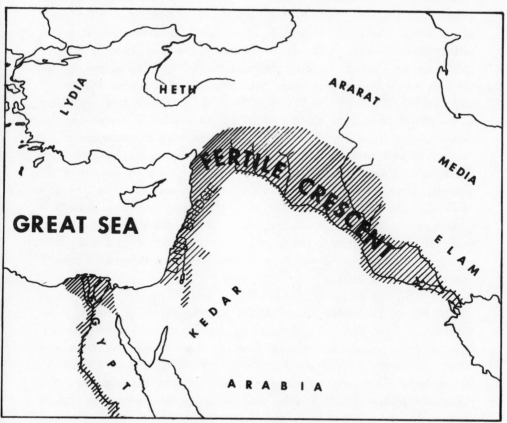

1. Israel acted as a land bridge between Egypt, Mesopotamia, and Anatolia.

difficulties in transportation which were prohibitive for most ancient armies and discouraging for merchants. Hence Israel's strategic situation as a land bridge. It followed logically that its possession was of extreme importance to any expanding empire. Consequently, the land of the twelve tribes of Israel has been fought over more than most other areas of the world.

Many countries of the size of Palestine consist of one basic type of landscape or terrain. In contrast to those, Palestine's landscape is varied, from high mountains to flat plains and sub-sea level rifts and valleys, from desert conditions to conditions permitting intensive agriculture. If the Israelites ever were a homogeneous people, the varied landscape of the Promised Land soon produced regional differences among them, depending on the geography of their settlement. The inhabitants who lived on the borders of the Negev desert, for instance, had to adapt to a quite different kind of terrain from those who lived in the hill country of Ephraim, or those who settled in agriculturally rich Transjordan.

Furthermore, in most countries with both barren deserts and lush agricultural areas, the transition between desert land and sown land (hereafter referred to as "desert" and "sown") is fairly gradual. Not so with Israel. In some places, for example just east of Jerusalem, the desert changes abruptly into the sown. One can stand on the Mount of Olives in Jerusalem and see the edge of the desert as it comes from the Jordan Valley up the eastern slopes of the mountains. On the other hand, the transition from Jerusalem to the desert toward the south takes about 20 miles. The reason for this difference is that Jerusalem lies at the top of the ridge of mountains which runs north and south. The prevailing moisture-bearing winds come from the Mediterranean Sea, and as they are forced to rise upward because of the mountains in their eastward journey across the countryside, they lose their moisture content in the form of rain (Fig. 2). East of Jerusalem and the N–S mountain ridge on which it sits, the westerly winds descend into the Jordan Valley rift, but they have lost their moisture; the rainfall stops and the land in a few miles becomes desert. It is the absence or insufficiency of rainfall that creates such a desert.

The critical factor in the weather is that Israel is on the border of two climate zones: the Mediterranean climate and the Sahara–Arabian climate. Consequently, any change in topography causes a decided change in climate. The difference between the two climate zones is not evident in the summer when both have the same temperatures, the same dryness, and the same lack of clouds. Only in the winter does the difference become apparent, with the Mediterranean climate bringing rain, while the Sahara–Arabian climate remains dry. Low-pressure weather systems move over the Mediterranean Sea and pick up moisture in the journey from west to east toward Israel.

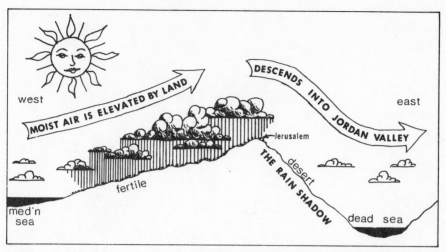

2. The prevailing wind in Israel is from west to east. The moist air above the Mediterranean Sea is pushed upward by the mountains, and rain results. When the air descends into the Jordan Valley, rain is prohibited and a "rain shadow" results.

Jesus said, "When you see a cloud rising in the west, you say at once, 'A shower is coming'; and so it happens" (Luke 12:54). However, winds which originate not from the humid area of the Mediterranean Sea but from the dry areas to the south do not pick up moisture, and no rain can result from their passage over the southern part of Israel. So Jesus also said, "And when you see the south wind blowing, you say, 'There will be scorching heat'; and it happens" (Luke 12:55). This weather pattern explains why the annual amount of rainfall in the country increases remarkably from south to north, from about 2 inches to 22 inches per annum (Fig. 3). This rainfall pattern was also true in ancient times. The farther north one went, the more productive, the more prosperous, the land became.

All life in the ancient Near East depended upon the abundance of the winter rains. Otherwise the crops would fail and famine result, and the springs which supplied water for humans and animals during the rainless summer months would also run dry. Drought was one of the greatest dangers to life. The importance of water to the people is indicated by the frequent use of water as a figurative image throughout the Bible.

Where the annual rainfall was less than 10 or 12 inches, agriculture, as it was practiced during the biblical period, was not usually possible. Of course there might be enough rain in an occasional year to produce a crop, but this might happen in only three out of every ten years in regions averaging 10–12 inches annually. Farmers who settled in relatively permanent buildings could not succeed or survive in this kind of uncertainty, and such transitional

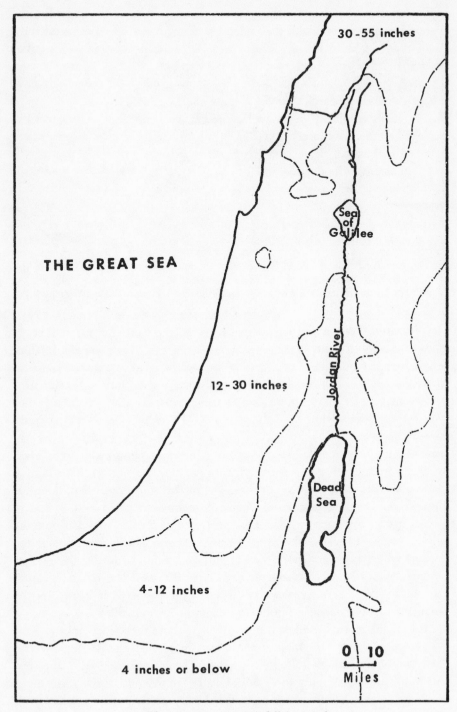

3. The average mean rainfall in Israel.

areas between the desert and the sown were inhabited by nomads. In a year when the rains failed, they would pick up their belongings and move with their flocks to better areas. These nomadic folk would sow seed in marginal lands each year near their tents in the hopes of raising a crop, but if the rains did not materialize, they could still live off their flocks until better rains for crops returned to their region.

Another peculiarity of Israel's weather (in Western eyes) is that the winter months are those in which crops grow. With us the winter season is thought of as the "dead" season because the temperature is low and vegetation either dies or is dormant. Our vegetation does not come alive until the spring, when the growth cycle begins and lasts until winter returns. In Israel, however, the "dead" season is during the summer, when there is no rain and the intense heat dries out the vegetation. The intermittent winter rains which usually begin in mid–October and end in mid–March revive the dormant vegetation (Fig. 4).

Barley and wheat must be sown at the beginning of the rainy season. They are harvested shortly after the end of that season. The religious celebration of Passover in the spring, coinciding with the harvest of barley, and the Feast of Pentecost seven weeks later, coinciding with the harvest of

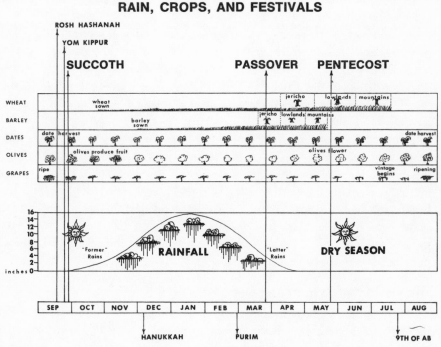

4. Rain, crops, and festivals throughout the year.

wheat, reflected the specific agricultural facts of life of the land.

But religious festivals were not the only element of Hebrew life affected by seasonal factors. War was normally confined to the months from June to October. Thus the statement "in the spring of the year, the time when kings go forth to battle . . ." (2 Sam. 11:1) becomes more meaningful, for only in the spring, after the harvests, were farmers free to fight. Furthermore, only in the spring does the dry season begin; only then does swampy land dry out. So, in Bible times, only then could rivers be crossed easily, and in fact most of them dried up each summer. Roads were no longer muddy and the implements of war could be transported more easily. Also, in the spring, after harvesttime, it would be possible to locate a defeated enemy's grain storage and confiscate it, thereby weakening the enemy for the next twelve months. Winter was not for war; the rain made it too difficult.

So it was that the geographical location of the people of Israel influenced not only the way they lived but also the way they thought. With their inability to become a large world power because of their country's function as a land bridge, they had ultimately to conclude that either their God was not so powerful as the gods of the larger nations, or that God's power was greater than their national boundaries. They chose the latter alternative; they were in effect forced to regard God no longer as a tribal deity, but in larger, more universal terms.

Also influenced by their physical setting was their religious language. The pressing need of water made water the symbol of a person's greatest spiritual need. Jesus said, "Every one who drinks of this water will thirst again, but whoever drinks of the water that I shall give him will never thirst; the water that I shall give him will become in him a spring of water welling up to eternal life" (John 4:13–14).

Throughout most of the Bible there is evidence of the important but subtle role geography played in the shaping of the biblical material. Once the discerning reader recognizes and clarifies the geographical realities, the message originally intended by the Bible poets, wise men, prophets, and historians can be heard in a context bearing a good resemblance to that understood by the ancient Israelites themselves. Then false issues can be seen to be just that, and the real issues of the spiritual message can be faced more accurately for what they are.

THE HISTORY COVERED BY THE BIBLE

The question of how many centuries the Bible covers immediately poses the problem of what the word "covers" means. Obviously, the Bible starts at the beginning of creation and continues into the 1st century A.D., which covers a very large time segment. If the question, instead, is concerned with how many centuries are covered by the historical events that are described in the Bible, the answer is easier (Fig. 5). Most scholars have agreed that the Patriarchs, the founding fathers of Israel, can be dated in the Middle Bronze Age at the beginning of the second millennium B.C.—possibly in the 19th or 18th centuries B.C. In other words, the stories of Abraham, Isaac, and Jacob have their setting in this very early period. Furthermore, the customs described in Gen. 12–50 fit in well with the customs, known from archaeological data, that were current at the time.

One must not be too confident in asserting that the Patriarchs lived in the 19th and 18th centuries B.C., because of insufficient evidence to support specific dates. Assume, for example, that Joseph went into Egypt in the 18th century B.C., and his brothers soon followed because of the great famine in Palestine during that period; then the time span between the end of the book of Genesis and the beginning of the book of Exodus is very long indeed. The book of Exodus states that there arose a Pharaoh that did not know Joseph—hardly a surprising statement, since most scholars date the Exodus in the 13th century B.C. This would mean a jump forward, between the time of Joseph in the 18th century B.C. and the Exodus in the 13th century B.C., of four or five centuries.

However much scholars may differ about the dating of the Patriarchs, that of the Exodus from Egypt and the conquest of the land of Canaan by the Israelites is much more certain. Such archaeological remains as the stele of Merneptah, the earliest known monument that mentions Israel, indicate that Israel did exist toward the end of the 13th century B.C. If so, then the Exodus and Conquest must be dated some time earlier. The traditions concerning the events of the Exodus are contained in the book of Exodus. After the Israelites are described as having crossed the "Sea of Reeds" (so stated in the Hebrew, as opposed to the "Red Sea" of the English text), they arrive at Mount Sinai and there form themselves into a people bound to their God by a covenant. The traditions surrounding the events in the Sinai peninsula en route to the land of Canaan are contained in the books of Leviticus, Numbers, and Deuteronomy.

Moses is the dominating leader throughout this period. By the end of Deuteronomy, Moses has led the people to attack the land of Canaan, which they describe as the Promised Land. Moses is an old man who dies, and the leadership passes to Joshua.

The traditions telling of the Conquest of Canaan by the Israelites are contained in the book of Joshua and the beginning chapter of the book of Judges. Joshua is principally concerned with how the land was taken and how it was settled. Judges deals with the way in which the land was governed for approximately two centuries after the Conquest, namely the 12th and the

PERIODS OF BIBLICAL HISTORY

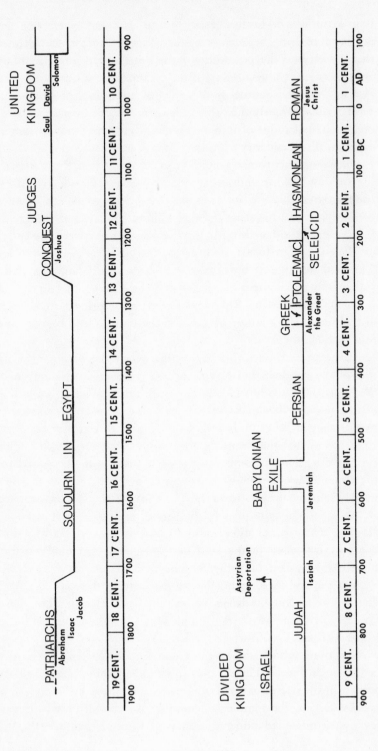

5. Periods of biblical history on a time line.

11th centuries B.C. Twelve "judges" ruled during this period, but their title might more aptly be "deliverers," since they were charismatic rulers who were raised into the position of leadership by delivering their people from their enemies at crucial times.

The book of 1 Samuel deals with the events of the latter half of the 11th century B.C., primarily the rise to power of a man named Saul. In many ways he was the last judge of the period of the Judges as well as the first king of Israel. Saul's ascendancy came at a time when the young country was facing its greatest threat from surrounding peoples, especially the Philistines.

Saul lost his life fighting the Philistines, and the kingdom eventually became that of David. David unified the kingdom split by Saul's death, and during his reign it reached its zenith in territorial expansion and influence. The rise of David to kingship is recorded in the latter part of 1 Samuel, and David's reign forms the substance of 2 Samuel. At the end of David's life Solomon, his son by Bathsheba, became king, and it fell to Solomon to build the first temple in Jerusalem.

Solomon shaped his kingdom and his royal city on a magnificent scale, and he became a genuine Oriental potentate. Consequently, the upkeep of the court became extremely burdensome on a small nation. Upon his death, when the people asked his son Rehoboam to lighten their financial and forced-labor burdens, he refused. Thereupon the kingdom split once again, becoming the kingdom of Israel in the north and the kingdom of Judah in the south. Jeroboam became king of the northern kingdom, while Rehoboam remained king of Judah in the south.

The story of Solomon is found in 1 Kings, which continues to trace the stories of the northern and the southern kingdoms to about the middle of the 9th century B.C. Moving into 2 Kings, we see that the northern kingdom maintained its existence for about 200 years. Then it fell before the onslaught of the Assyrians, who, in order to suppress potential insurrection, deported many of the Israelites and resettled them in various parts of Mesopotamia. The fall of the capital of the northern kingdom, Samaria, occurred in 722 B.C. The surviving kingdom of Judah was able to exist, and sometimes barely to survive, for slightly longer than another century. Finally, the southern kingdom was overcome by the Babylonians, and the people were carried off into exile in Babylon.

This crucial event in Israel's history occurred in 587 B.C. when Jerusalem was taken by Nebuchadnezzar, the temple was destroyed, and all the leading people were exiled. These exiled Jews were allowed to return in 539 B.C. because of the decree of Cyrus the Persian, successor of the Babylonian kings, and by 520 B.C. the temple had been built. Known now after the Exile as Jews, they remained under Persian rule through the 5th century and into the 4th century B.C., until Alexander the Great began his series of Asiatic conquests in 333 B.C. Little Judah remained under Greek rule until 301 B.C., when it fell under the rule of the Ptolomies of Egypt, a rule which lasted to the end of the 3rd century B.C. At the beginning of the 2nd century B.C. the Palestinian area came under the control of the Seleucid kings of Syria, and remained there until in 167 B.C. The Jews, led by the Maccabees, revolted against this Hellenistic governance and achieved independence. Under a family of kings known as Hasmonean, the Jews maintained independence until the Romans under Pompey arrived in 63 B.C. Palestine, later cut up into several provinces for administrative purposes, remained under Roman control throughout the New Testament period and beyond the last events and writings of the young Christian Church.

THE BIBLE AS A BOOK

Although the Bible covers many centuries, it is more than just a book of ancient history. It is a whole library of different kinds of literature, written by various men over a long period of time. Unless this basic fact is kept in mind, the reader tends to approach the reading and study of the Bible with the wrong presuppositions.

There are several things one must know in order to use a library effectively, the first being the arrangement of the books. The most obvious division of the English Bible is between the Old and the New Testaments. The Old Testament contains the history and literature of the people of ancient Israel, who saw themselves as having entered into a covenant (a testament) with God. Similarly, the New Testament is concerned with the events and writings of the early followers of Jesus, who saw themselves as having entered into a *new* covenant with God.

The arrangement of the Old Testament of the English Bible is basically threefold (Fig. 6). The large first division consists of books which deal with the history of Israel as seen through the eyes of the Israelites themselves—Genesis through Esther, 17 books in all. The smaller second division contains the 5 "poetic" books, Job, Psalms, Proverbs, Ecclesiastes, and Song of Solomon. The third division includes the 17 prophetic books from Isaiah through Malachi.

A brief look at this arrangement will show the great emphasis on history in the Old Testament. Such an emphasis is not found in the literature of any other culture contemporaneous with ancient Israel. While various materials in the first 17 books would not be classified as history (for example, the Leviticus chapters dealing with the laws of Israel), the primary concern is historical. The last 17 books, the prophetic section, though not of the same narrative style as the first 17 books, are just as much concerned with history,

History	Poetry	Prophecy
Genesis	Job	Isaiah
Exodus	Psalms	Jeremiah
Leviticus	Proverbs	Lamentations
Numbers	Ecclesiastes	Ezekiel
Deuteronomy	Song of Solomon	Daniel
Joshua		Hosea
Judges		Joel
Ruth		Amos
1 Samuel		Obadiah
2 Samuel		Jonah
1 Kings		Micah
2 Kings		Nahum
1 Chronicles		Habakkuk
2 Chronicles		Zephaniah
Ezra		Haggai
Nehemiah		Zechariah
Esther		Malachi

6. The arrangement of the Old Testament Books in the English Bible.

setting forth as they do the insights of the prophets who saw God at work in current historical events. This is the basic theme of the Old Testament—that God set about to reveal His real nature to mankind through historical events. Even though historical events may be guided by God, they do not reveal His activity unless someone is able to perceive that revelation. The perception and proclamation of that revelation were the task of the prophets.

Biblical writers also saw the revealing activity of God in nature as well as in history, but more important still, they perceived that behind both kinds of revelation lay a divine plan which was to lead to the redemption of all mankind. In Abraham and his descendants all the families of the earth would be blessed (Gen. 12:3). The Bible portrays God as having chosen a small and insignificant group of people, the Hebrews, later called "Israel" and still later called "Jews," to be His instrument to accomplish this plan. The plan itself does not come to its fruition until the New Testament.

If the Old Testament contains, at least from a strictly human viewpoint, the most valued literature of ancient Israel, the New Testament contains the literature of the early Christians who thought of themselves as the "New Israel" (Fig. 7). The books are divided into gospels (Matthew, Mark, Luke, and John), history (the book of Acts), Epistles (the 21 letters written by Paul and various other early Christians), and an apocalypse (Revelation). While the number of books that seem to be concerned with history in the New Testament is not so large as that of the Old Testament,

Gospels	History	Epistles	Apocalypse
Matthew	Acts	Romans	Revelation
Mark		1 Corinthians	
Luke		2 Corinthians	
John		Galatians	
		Ephesians	
		Philippians	
		Colossians	
		1 Thessalonians	
		2 Thessalonians	
		1 Timothy	
		2 Timothy	
		Titus	
		Philemon	
		Hebrews	
		James	
		1 Peter	
		2 Peter	
		1 John	
		2 John	
		3 John	
		Jude	

7. The arrangement of the New Testament Books in the English Bible.

the emphasis on God's having acted decisively in history is, if anything, even more emphatic. The Gospel of the New Testament (a word derived from the Anglo-Saxon "Godspel," meaning "good news") is that in Jesus the Christ God acted in history in such a way that redemption was offered to all mankind. In Christ all the families of the earth had been truly blessed.

THE OLD TESTAMENT

Since Hebrew was the language spoken by the people of Israel while they were in Palestine until about the 5th century B.C., most of the Old Testament was written in Hebrew. Around the 5th century B.C., however, Aramaic became the common language of the ancient Near East, and even though Hebrew remained the distinctive language for worship and religious study, the Jews began to use Aramaic as an everyday language. This fact explains why a small portion of the Old Testament came to be written in Aramaic (Ezra 4:8–6:18; 7:12–26; Jer. 10:11; Dan. 2:4–7:28). Translations from the original Hebrew and Aramaic have had to be made from earliest times for those who did not understand the languages.

The Hebrew Bible was and still is arranged in a different order from our English Bible. It was divided into three sections: the Torah, the Prophets,

Torah	Former Prophets	Latter Prophets	Writings
Genesis	Joshua	Isaiah	Psalms
Exodus	Judges	Jeremiah	Job
Leviticus	1 Samuel	Ezekiel	Proverbs
Numbers	2 Samuel	Hosea	Ruth
Deuteronomy	1 Kings	Joel	Song of Songs
	2 Kings	Amos	Ecclesiastes
		Obadiah	Lamentations
		Jonah	Esther
		Micah	Daniel
		Nahum	Ezra
		Habakkuk	Nehemiah
		Zephaniah	1 Chronicles
		Haggai	2 Chronicles
		Zechariah	
		Malachi	

8. The Old Testament Books of the Hebrew Bible.

and the Writings (Fig. 8). This would be only an interesting but unimportant fact if the order did not also give us a rough indication of the period in which the books were written. The first division, the Torah, contains Genesis, Exodus, Leviticus, Numbers, and Deuteronomy. These 5 books comprise the Law in Judaism, and even today the Torah is considered by Jews to be the most sacred part of the Old Testament. The Torah was the first section to be accepted as canonical. The term "canon" is derived from a Semitic root meaning "reed" or "cane." It was eventually associated with a "measuring cane" and thus came to mean the limit or standard by which one determined what was authoritative and inspired scripture and what was not. The exact date of the canonization of the Torah is unknown, but it was thought of as Scripture at least by the middle of the 3rd century B.C. Even so, these books must have carried great authority for a much longer period before that.

The second division of the Hebrew Bible, the Prophets, is subdivided into (a) the Former Prophets: Joshua, Judges, 1 and 2 Samuel, 1 and 2 Kings, and (b) the Latter Prophets: Isaiah, Jeremiah, Ezekiel, Hosea, Joel, Amos, Obadiah, Jonah, Micah, Nahum, Habakkuk, Zephaniah, Haggai, Zechariah, and Malachi. The date of the acceptance of the Prophets as a canonical part of Hebrew scripture is uncertain, but it must have taken place at least before the first part of the 2nd century B.C.

The third division of the Hebrew Bible is that of the Writings: Psalms, Job, Proverbs, Ruth, Song of Solomon, Ecclesiastes, Lamentations, Esther, Daniel, Ezra, Nehemiah, 1 and 2 Chronicles. These Writings (among many others in existence) were accounted by the Jews as canonical toward the end of the 1st century A.D.

A careful check of this list will show that the books of Ruth, 1 and 2 Chronicles, Ezra, Nehemiah, and Esther, which are in the "Historical" section of the English Bible, were originally in the "Writings" section of the Hebrew Bible. This indicates that they were, on the whole, written at a later date than the Torah and the Prophets. Furthermore, the books of Lamentations and Daniel are in the "Prophecy" section of the English Bible, but they were originally in the "Writings" section of the Hebrew Bible (Fig. 9). Despite the fact that Lamentations is not prophecy but poetry, it was nevertheless inserted after Jeremiah in the English Bible because early translators believed that Jeremiah was its author. The book of Daniel is placed in the "Prophetic" section of the English Bible, but had originally been in the "Writings" section of the Hebrew Bible. Its style, however, is recognized by most scholars today as being that of apocalyptic literature (a term used to describe a kind of literature, frequently arising in times of persecution, that sees a cosmic struggle between good and evil in the world) rather than that of prophetic literature. Apocalyptic literature arose after the Jews began to believe that the prophetic period had completely ended. Consequently, many scholars believe that its origin is to be placed in a much later period than was previously supposed, probably during the persecution of the Jews under Antiochus Epiphanes, the foreign Syrian king who tried to stamp out Judaism (175–164 B.C.).

Before the writing of the New Testament, the only "Bible" that the early Christians had was the Old Testament. Even though the "Bible" of Jesus and the Apostles was probably the Hebrew Old Testament, most scholars believe that Paul and the early Christians used Greek translations of the Hebrew books. The Hebrew Bible had been translated by Jewish scholars into Greek in Egypt some time in the last few centuries before Christ so that the many Greek-speaking Jews who had migrated to that area could read their own scriptures. Tradition says that there were seventy-two translators, which explains the title Septuagint (Sep-too-a-jint), a Greek word meaning "seventy." This word has come to be used to describe the whole Old Testament in its Greek form, but it is more properly used to denote the Pentateuch, or Torah (the first five books of the Old Testament). By New Testament times, Greek had largely superseded Aramaic as the common language of the Near East, and this explains why the early Christians used the Greek writings in preference to the Hebrew. The Jews of Palestine, however, continued to speak Aramaic primarily, though many were undoubtedly able to speak Greek as well.

When the Jews finally came to agreement as to what was to be considered

THE HEBREW BIBLE

Torah	Former Prophets	Latter Prophets	Writings
Genesis	Joshua	Isaiah	Psalms
Exodus	Judges	Jeremiah	Job
Leviticus	1 Samuel	Ezekiel	Proverbs
Numbers	2 Samuel	Hosea	Ruth
Deuteronomy	1 Kings	Joel	Song of Songs
	2 Kings	Amos	Ecclesiastes
		Obadiah	Lamentations
		Jonah	Esther
		Micah	Daniel
		Nahum	Ezra
		Habakkuk	Nehemiah
		Zephaniah	1 Chronicles
		Haggai	2 Chronicles
		Zechariah	
		Malachi	

THE ENGLISH BIBLE

History	Poetry	Prophecy
Genesis	Job	Isaiah
Exodus	Psalms	Jeremiah
Leviticus	Proverbs	Lamentations
Numbers	Ecclesiastes	Ezekiel
Deuteronomy	Song of Solomon	Daniel
Joshua		Hosea
Judges		Joel
Ruth		Amos
1 Samuel		Obadiah
2 Samuel		Jonah
1 Kings		Micah
2 Kings		Nahum
1 Chronicles		Habakkuk
2 Chronicles		Zephaniah
Ezra		Haggai
Nehemiah		Zechariah
Esther		Malachi

9. A comparison of the arrangement of the Books of the Hebrew and English Old Testaments.

canonical Holy Scripture, many of the writings which the early Christians, and indeed the Jews of that period, had accounted as Holy Scripture were not included in the list. There were several criteria which seemed to have been used in deciding which of the books then currently in circulation should be accounted as canonical. Since the Torah had long been in a position of great authority, none of the books under consideration should contradict anything in the Torah. By the first century A.D. the Jews had already begun to believe that prophetic inspiration had started with Moses and ended forever at the time of Ezra. Consequently, if a book seemed to have been written at any time after that period, it would not qualify as canonical. Furthermore, if a book had *originally* been written in Greek, it was automatically excluded, as was any book written outside Palestine. Once these principles were adopted, a number of the books which had in fact been thought of as Holy Scripture by the Greek-speaking Jews had to be rejected. The Christians, however, saw no reason to accept the decisions of the Jews, and they continued to use the Greek writings as a part of their Bible. Some of the passages in the Greek were, in fact, used by Christians to refute the arguments of the Jews against Christianity, and, as a consequence, in A.D. 130, the Jews under the leadership of Rabbi Akiba condemned the Greek translation for ordinary religious use. The Christians continued to include these disputed books in their manuscripts of the Old Testament until the time of the Reformation when Luther put them between the Old Testament and the New Testament in a separate section called the Apocrypha (a Greek word meaning "hidden"). Since the 19th century many Protestant editions of the Bible have omitted this section.

Most modern people are so accustomed to reading from the printed page that they forget how relatively recent is the invention of printing. Before Gutenberg printed the first Bible in the 15th century A.D., all books were copied by scribes in manuscript form. This copying could be done in two ways. A single scribe would copy directly from a manuscript before him, thus producing a single copy at a time. Or a scribe would dictate the manuscript before him to a group of scribes, thus producing more manuscripts in the same amount of time. Despite great care, it is very easy to make errors while copying a book. Scribes inevitably made occasional errors as they copied books century after century. An undetected mistake in a manuscript would be perpetuated in all others copied from it. A large number of copies containing a similar mistake is called a "family of manuscripts" because they all resemble the original from which they were derived. But they will also carry their own distinctive errors. Consequently, the translator of an ancient manuscript which has been copied for any length of time will find slight variations in the text as he goes from one manuscript to another. These variations are called textual corruptions. When a scholar begins to translate, he must compare all available manuscripts and then try to reconstruct the "family history" of the manuscripts in order to decide the most probable original reading.

Unfortunately, for many years the oldest known manuscripts of the Hebrew Old Testament dated back only to the middle of the Christian era; but after the discovery of the Dead Sea Scrolls in 1947 in caves in the Judean Wilderness, not far from the ruins of a Jewish sectarian community, much more ancient parts of every book of the Old Testament except Esther have been recovered in scroll form. These scroll-manuscripts have turned out to be a thousand years older than any Old Testament manuscripts hitherto in our possession.

One of the conclusions that can be drawn from analysis of the Dead Sea Scrolls is that in the 1st century B.C. and the 1st century A.D. there were several divergent texts of the Hebrew Old Testament, including the one later known as the Masoretic text. This text seems to have been accepted as the standard text as early as the 2nd century A.D. Then from the 7th to the 11th centuries A.D. a group of Jewish scholars called the Masoretes (whose task it was to preserve the "tradition or "*masorah*" as accurately as possible) edited the text with great care, and it is from this text that our English Old Testament is translated. Even in the edited text, however, the Hebrew is often obscure because of very early textual corruptions. Fortunately, it is sometimes possible to determine the meaning of the confused Hebrew by examining the earliest translations of it into other languages to find out how those long-ago translators understood the text they were using. But translation, even with a perfectly straightforward text, is never an easy task, for in the process of translation the nuances of meaning and feeling carried in the original language are all too easily lost. Today, however, we have, in our major mid-20th century translations, much better renderings of the ancient texts, and much truer reflections of the meaning of the great majority of knotty passages than we had in the days when virtually the only English translations were the King James and the Douay-Rheims (Catholic) versions.

THE NEW TESTAMENT

In the 1st century A.D. Greek had long since become the common language of the eastern end of the Mediterranean Sea. Most Jews in Palestine, however, still spoke Aramaic as their primary language. Jesus taught his disciples in Aramaic, and his sayings were probably transmitted orally in Aramaic for some time. But Greek was understood by many more people, and so the New Testament was written in Greek. Several Aramaic phrases made their way into the New Testament, to testify to its Aramaic background. It is entirely possible that we have the actual words spoken by Jesus, as opposed to the translation of them, in such sayings as *Talitha cumi* (Mark 5:41) and *Eloi, Eloi, lama sabach-thani* (Mark 15:34).

In contrast to the Old Testament, which took almost a thousand years to be written, the New Testament was written within a century. Jesus himself left no written account of his life or teachings. All the records we have were written by his followers. The earliest records in the New Testament are the letters of Paul. The "Bible" of the early Christian Church was the Old Testament in the Greek translation. It is highly doubtful if Paul had any idea that his letters were anything more than pastoral counsels on contemporary problems dispatched to churches he had founded or was interested in—let alone any idea that his letters would be read and studied for centuries to come. In fact, he has many passages which are very personal in nature and speak to specific situations in the early churches. Quite naturally, letters from such an important figure were read and reread in the various churches, and copies of them were sent to other churches. They must have been read in the context of Christian worship at an early stage.

Meanwhile, since the eyewitnesses to Jesus' ministry were dying off, there was a growing need for the written presentation of the various oral traditions about the life and teachings of Jesus. Most scholars believe that of the four gospels in the New Testament the gospel of Mark was the earliest to have been written. Mark is primarily concerned with recording the major events in the life of Jesus. He provides a kind of outline of the ministry of Christ. The gospels of Matthew and Luke seem to have used Mark's gospel as a framework, but with additional material, such as the sections that deal with Jesus' infancy and formally arranged discourses that preserve some of his teachings—types of materials which do not appear in Mark. Both Matthew and Luke also have material not found in any of the other three gospels. Obviously, the recollections of the Christian eyewitnesses varied from locality to locality, depending on the witness of the Apostles from whom they heard the Good News. Thus the four gospels are a collection of traditions about Jesus, conditioned by the milieu in which they appeared.

While Mark seems concerned primarily to present the events in the life of Jesus in a chronological order, Matthew adds an emphasis on Jesus' teaching about right and wrong, the ethical life. He also takes pains to illustrate how Jesus was the fulfillment of what several Old Testament prophets had called the Messiah, or the Christ. Luke, on the other hand, being a physician and a Gentile (a non-Jew), emphasizes not only Jesus' teachings but also the healing ministry of Jesus and his relation to the Gentiles.

Since the first three gospels take a common approach in presenting the Gospel of Jesus Christ, they are often called the synoptic gospels—meaning literally, they can be "seen together." The gospel of John does not follow the basic outline of any of these, but instead is written in a quite different, often meditative, and deeply theological style. The primary aim of the first four books of the New Testament, rather than being singly or together a biography of Jesus as we understand the term today, seems to be to proclaim the Good News about Jesus as illustrated by events in his life, death, and resurrection, as each writer understood them.

The gospel of Luke is actually a two-volume work, the second volume being the book of Acts. The history of the early church was traced in this volume up until the time just prior to the martyrdom of Paul. Besides the four gospels, the book of Acts, and the letters of Paul, various other letters by early Christians are included in the New Testament. The last book of the Bible is Revelation, the apocalyptic style and content of which indicate that it was written in a time of severe persecution, just as the book of Daniel in the Old Testament must have been.

As with the Old Testament, we do not have any of the original manuscripts of the New Testament as they came from the hands of the authors. In contrast to the Old Testament, however, a larger number of manuscript copies are extant, thus enabling scholars to determine the most probable original text. Unfortunately, because of the great need for manuscripts for the growing number of churches, many of the early scribes who copied the New Testament were more interested in the quantity of manuscripts they reproduced than in the quality of their reproduction, so the problem is somewhat more complex. Nevertheless, with the use of early translations into other languages and the best early manuscripts in Greek, scholars are able to arrive at the most probable original text. Since many ancient manuscripts are available for the New Testament, we possess much more evidence for what the original texts must have been than for any other ancient literature.

The 27 books that comprise our New Testament were, of course, not the only literature written by the early Christians. Many more books never became a part of the New Testament. Some of the books were the products of groups of people, such as the Gnostics, who had deviated seriously from what later became accepted as normative Christianity, and so the need arose for an authoritative list of canonical books. From the beginning the majority of Christians were in agreement on the list that included most of the books of our present New Testament, just as they were agreed about excluding those books so obviously contrary to what had become normative belief and teaching. But there was an area in between these two extremes where honest opinions differed. Among the last books to be accepted as canonical by a majority of the Christian authorities were Hebrews, James, 2 Peter, 2 and 3 John, Jude, and Revelation. Other writings such as 1 and 2 Clement, the

Epistle of Barnabas, the Shepherd of Hermas, and the Didache were accepted by some regional elements of the Church at one time or another, but they were eventually excluded from the canon.

A further need for a canon arose when the Christians gradually ceased to use the scroll as a vehicle for transmitting their literature. The scroll had limitations to its use, especially the amount of text it could contain because of its restricted length. An excessively long scroll was too cumbersome. Hence the tendency to copy one work to a scroll, or at least no more than a few short works. However, with the common use of the codex much more material could be put into one handy binding. The codex consisted of folded sheets of vellum or papyrus stitched together in a form similar to our modern book. When this process became popular, the question arose as to which books should be included in a volume that would be regarded as Holy Scripture. After much discussion and debate in the 3rd century A.D., the matter was officially decided by church councils in the 4th century A.D. Athanasius of Alexandria, in A.D. 367, seems to have been the first person to list the present 27 books as canonical.

A more poignant element also entered into the need for establishing a canon. During the persecution of the early Christians by the Romans, one of the means used to stamp out this religion which was so disturbing to the rulers was to compel the Christians to surrender their holy books to be destroyed. The Christians, who believed that it was a serious sin to commit apostasy in this manner, had to know what was to be regarded as Holy Scripture and what was not. They would therefore not be compromising their faith in handing over certain writings to the Roman soldiers, and would be in other instances.

Even more than any authoritative pronouncement from any one person or any official council was the authentic internal witness to the faith of the early Christian Church that made the present books of the New Testament canonical.

THE UNIQUE NATURE OF THE BIBLE

Besides the external factors of the Bible, such as its arrangement, the languages in which it was written, the types of literature found there, and how the books became accounted authoritative, there are more important questions that must still be raised. In what sense is this collection of literature different from any other collection of ancient literature? The obvious answers to such a question recognize that the Bible has done more than any other body of writings to influence and form Western culture. But a further, more difficult question is raised: What is it in the Bible that has made it such an important influence?

The Bible's influence could be said to be great because it is great literature, and all really great literature influences the people who come into contact with it. But both Jews and Christians have always gone a large step beyond that. They have called the Bible the "Word of God" and claimed that it was "inspired." What is meant by these phrases has been differently defined according to the beliefs of the person making the claim. Some would say that the Bible is inspired in the sense that any great book is inspired—that is, an inspired book is the work of a person of great talent who had an "inspiration" and put it in literary form. This definition speaks strictly from the human viewpoint; it is humanistic. It argues the Bible was written as all literature is written—that is, by men.

A view opposing this humanistic one is held by those who claim that the Bible is the Word of God, that the books of the Bible are in fact not only the Word of God but the "words" of God. This definition emphasizes the divine viewpoint as opposed to the human element of this literature. Still others would claim that important elements in both statements are needed to express the real nature of the Bible. They would not, on the one hand, assert that the Bible is a collection of the "words" of God, thereby ignoring the human element that went into the making of the Bible. But, on the other hand, totally unacceptable to them is the assertion that the Bible is inspired only in the same sense that a poet is inspired when he writes a masterpiece, since not enough emphasis is placed on the guidance of God.

Each person who reads and studies the Bible with any seriousness will be drawn to one or another of these definitions, depending upon one's own background, education, and experience. Indeed, it is possible that one may find his position changing the more one ponders and meditates upon these writings. It has always been so. And the reason is that the Bible not only deals with the ultimate questions about Man: Who am I? Where did I come from? Where am I going? It also deals with the ultimate questions about God: What is God like? What has God done in the past? What relationship is there between God and Man? Between God and me?

The biblical writers believed that these questions had very real answers, ones they experienced in their own lives. Thus, for example, Amos felt compelled to prophesy, and Jeremiah felt it imperative to rewrite his prophecies when King Jehioakim burned the first copy. An invaluable part of reading and studying the Bible is the contact with men who believed that they had a genuine grasp upon Ultimate Reality, God Himself. But what is more important, had they been able to use our sophisticated terminology, they would have claimed that Ultimate Reality had a genuine grasp upon them and their lives. Not only did these men see God working on the broad canvas of history, using kings and nations and battles to accomplish His purpose, but they also saw God at work on the smaller canvases of their own portraits. If God truly reveals Himself in history, then God truly reveals Himself in life, and each person's life was that person's own history. The consequent value of Bible reading goes beyond an antiquarian interest in how people thought and acted. It furnishes insights into the nature of God, the nature of Man—and above all, the nature of a specific person, namely, the individual reader. It even goes one giant step further: It reveals how the life of the reader, with its inevitable dilemmas, can be brought into a true harmony with Ultimate Reality—through Jesus Christ.

❧ II. How the People of the Bible Lived

HOMES

CAVE–HOMES

Cave-homes almost certainly antedated the use of either tents or houses by the people resident in Palestine. The relatively soft limestone found in large portions of Palestine, combined with climatic conditions that aided its erosion and the formation of caves through heavy seasonal rains, provided Stone Age men with innumerable cave-shelters, especially along the courses of most of the perennial streams and wadis in the hill country. Even with primitive hammers and chisels, the man of prehistory in Palestine could chip off the inside walls of a cave and transform a shelter into a home. If his family grew, he could make additional chambers, passageways, and food storage areas. The extent to which this type of home was used in Palestine has only recently come to be appreciated.

For the earliest periods of Palestinian culture, the caves northwest of the Sea of Galilee at Mugharet ez-Zuttiyeh, those at Wadi Khareitun between Bethlehem and the Dead Sea, and those at Wadi el-Mugharah in the Mount Carmel range have added a whole new chapter to our understanding of civilization in Palestine (Fig. 10). And many more cavesites could be cited, but they are not "biblical." If it is true, as has been said, that in 3500–3000 B.C. almost every cave along the wadis leading to the Dead Sea was occupied, it is also clear that these people—whoever they were—were neither the biblical Canaanites nor the Israelites, and their cave-home life—or the reason for it—had largely disappeared by the time Abraham brought his flocks into Palestine. But the caves of course remained to serve as places of seasonal residence, temporary refuge, and burial.

10. A cave shelter along the course of a wadi in the Wilderness of Judea.

As a home, the entrance was through a hole in the wall of the hillside, from which crude steps led down onto the floor of the interior. This entrance was often barricaded by a stone wall. Prowling animals or human enemies respected such a defense, especially when at night torches burned at the entrance itself. One of the greatest attractions of cave-dwellings to the owner was the sense of rocky security they gave him and his family (Fig. 11).

Cooking was done at a rough stone hearth positioned near the "front door" so that the smoke might escape. The inner recesses of the cave were not popular for family use. They were too eerie, but they were useful as storage places for grains, meat, and fish.

The Old Testament speaks of no families living in caves, except in emergency, as in the story of Lot (Gen. 19:30). Other famous biblical uses of caves as dwellings are connected with Elijah's flight to a cave on Mount Horeb (1 Kings 19:9), and with David's hiding in the cave of Adullam (1 Sam. 22:1). When once Palestinian man had come out of his cave-home in favor of a house, he returned to cave-dwelling only in time of an enemy invasion, or perhaps in the course of an attack by his own people on enemy territory. The Midianites drove at least some Israelites into caves by their oppressive raids (Judg. 6:2) and the Philistines by the weight of their inva-

11. A modern cave dwelling located a short distance from the city of Jerusalem.

sion (1 Sam. 13:6). In the time of Jezebel the loyal prophet Obadiah hid 100 prophets of the Lord in a Mount Carmel cave.

The only biblical people who continued to use cave-homes and improve upon them after other Semites had moved on to tents and houses were the Horites and their successors in the land southeast of the Dead Sea, the Edomites. Inhabitants of the rose-red, rock-cut city of Petra, Edom's great city, continued to occupy their unique troglodyte (cave-dwelling) city down through the period of Roman rule. But by the first century B.C. Petra was a highly successful and sophisticated city, whose wealth came from its strategic location which dominated a trade-route intersection of caravan trains. Petra in fact amassed wealth comparable with that of the so-called "desert port" far to the north, Palmyra, which was on another great east-west and north-south trade crossing on the northern edge of the Arabian Desert.

TENTS

The dwelling places of the biblical Israelites were at first tents and later houses. But tents were never entirely discarded. Long after the Israelites had ceased to be roving herders and had settled down in walled cities or in small agricultural villages, many of them returned to their well-loved tents during the summer harvest season. The delights of tent life revived deep memories of the life of their ancestors. Indeed, some Israelites remained in tents year-round, and were shepherds long after the Conquest. But by far the greater part of them adopted the home style of their Canaanite neighbors and lived in houses, in cities (i.e., walled places), towns, or villages.

In appearance the typical tent of an Israelite family probably varied little from the long, flat tent of the modern Arab grazer of flocks, which is slightly higher in the center than at the ends (Fig. 12). Though originally made of the skins of animals, the more developed tent of the period after the Conquest was made of hand-woven goat's hair, and was dark brown or black in color. The material was woven in strips about three feet wide, which were sewn together and supplied with reinforcing strips, leather loops sewn onto the cover to which guy ropes were tied, and other fittings to assist in raising it and making it secure.

Goat's hair is both heat- and water-resistant, and it shrinks itself taut after its first wetting. New tents had to be made with an allowance for a predictable amount of shrinkage. Weaving usually followed goat-shearing time, when enough hair was available to make possible a worthwhile production. Old tents were at this time patched with care and patience. In early Bible times the women of every family wove the tent cloth on homemade looms. In later times the weaving of tent cloth became a more specialized craft and trade, carried on by families that passed on the arts and skills involved to the next generation, and ultimately by guilds of weavers. The Apostle Paul was the most famous maker of tent cloth in the Bible.

Tent poles, as many as were needed, depending on the overall dimensions

12. A typical modern Bedouin tent.

of the tent, were cut to fit from branches of trees, and were transported from site to site with the folded-up tent. The care and raising of the tent was primarily women's work, and the organization of life within it entirely so.

A typical family tent probably had three poles, about 7 feet high, in a row across the center of the tent, and two parallel rows of three slightly shorter poles on the two sides. The tent was stretched out over these poles, and cords or guy ropes were fastened at one end to leather loops that were sewn to the tent material, and at the other end to wooden pegs driven firmly into the ground to hold the covering in place and to give the tent structure a degree of tautness and stability in a breeze. Camping enthusiasts of today raise tents in a very similar manner, by getting underneath the spread-out tent and raising the center poles, then the side poles. One side of the tent was probably sewn into the tent's construction, and the other three sides were either removable for ventilation or could be folded back.

Normally such a tent was divided into two "apartments" by a fabric curtain or reed screen that hung on the center pole of each of the rows of poles. The women and children probably occupied the back half of the tent, and the front would have been reserved for the men and used for hospitality (Fig. 13). If the head of a tent-dwelling family were wealthy, he might provide a separate tent for his wife and perhaps another for her maidservants. Providing additional tents was more practical than expanding the size of the first tent.

13. A modern Bedouin tent, divided into two "apartments."

By definition a tent is a portable habitation or dwelling place. It suited a people who were in a seminomadic state of life, moving periodically—with the seasons, or as emergencies decreed—from oasis to oasis, or from highland to lowland, wherever sustenance could most easily be found. To the Israelites, to be portable meant that tent, poles, and furnishings had to be packed on the backs of asses, for only the Midianites and the true Bedouin of Arabia had domesticated the camel, and that probably only about the time of the Conquest. By a housewife's standards today, the furnishings of an Israelite tent—however commendably portable—were exceedingly primitive.

Tent Furnishings

A "bed" was a coarse straw mat, which could be rolled up during the day and used as a "chair" or tucked away in a corner of the tent. A "table" was simply a piece of leather spread on the dirt floor. (A goatskin will provide a surface measuring about 3 x 4 feet of usable space, plus appendages, and properly finished, its slick surface can easily be wiped clean.) The "stove" consisted of a few stones gathered at the site and placed just outside the entrance of the tent; in rainy weather the "stove" was placed under the cover of the tent, and the smoke and smells were allowed to escape as they might. If the family were to remain at one site for a long enough period, a hemispherical-shaped oven might be constructed from moist clay. Fire was inserted through a small opening near the ground, and pottery vessels were put on the round opening at the top to be heated.

The housewife's utensils consisted of a small stone grain mill or a mortar and pestle; a copper pot or two; a few earthen bowls and water jars; bags made of goatskins; "bottles" also made of goatskins, which could be drawn tight at the top, not unlike a modern laundry bag with drawstrings; two or three small pottery lamps; and a small assortment of crude knives, forks, and spoons. Gen. 18:1–15 provides an excellent picture of tent life as lived by the Israelites.

For protection from intruders, tents were usually pitched in groups, all members of one family (in the larger sense of all persons who recognized the authority of a "head of a family") clustering together. For relief from the heat, shade from the sun for part of the day was almost a necessity. Another desirable condition was exposure to the refreshing west-to-east winds that blew in during the later afternoon in many parts of Palestine.

For such a tent-dwelling people it was only natural that their first worship center was described as "the tent of meeting," otherwise known as the Tabernacle, in the back portion of which rested (when the Israelites were not on the move) the sacred Ark which held the stone tablets of the Law (Exod. 40:18–35).

Tents in Scripture

Abraham, traditional founder of the Hebrew people, had been born in a city of relatively comfortable, well-built, two-storied houses—Ur of the Chaldees, on the Euphrates River as it neared its entrance into the Persian Gulf. Abraham lived in no mean city, indeed, in a very sophisticated city, before he voluntarily became a wanderer for God, a sojourner by faith "in the land of the promise, as in a foreign land, living in tents . . . for he looked forward to the city which has foundations, whose builder and maker is God" (Heb. 11:9–10). When Abraham set out on his religious quest, like the Pilgrim Fathers who left their comfortable 17th-century English homes for the American wilderness, he pitched his tents and built his altars to the Lord time and again, as he became a very rich herdsman of sheep and cattle.

Tree-shaded sites for his tents were sought after; and if wells, too, were adjacent, in a not well-watered land, greatly contested was the privilege of pitching camp there. A generation after Abraham, "the herdsmen of Gerar quarreled with Isaac's herdsmen, saying, 'The water is ours'" (Gen. 26:20). Clearly, a good camping ground was something vastly different from wilderness wastes. Isaiah, wishing to picture the complete desolation to which Babylon would be reduced, declared that it would be so utterly demolished that "no shepherds will make their flocks lie down there," not even Arabs (Isa. 13:20).

Long after the Hebrews generally had ceased to dwell in tents they continued to use tent imagery in their religious writings and in their daily conversation. The nomadic origin of Israel could never be completely forgotten. Imagery based on tent life is found in Ps. 78:55; 104:2; Song of Sol. 1:5, 8; Isa. 33:20; 40:22; Jer. 10:20. The appeal of the sect of the Rechabites (see below) was to the nomadic tent-dwelling ideal (Jer. 35:6 ff.). The seductiveness and idolatry of domesticated city life was consistently attacked by all the prophets. In the later years of the nation it was as if there were a conflict within Israel's soul between the lures of an urbanized, Canaanitish life and the stark realities of tent life in the old seminomadic days.

That "tent" meant "home" to many Israelites many years after tent-dwelling had been largely outgrown is obvious from numerous Old Testament verses, such as Judg. 20:8; 1 Sam. 13:2; 1 Kings 12:16; Isa. 38:12; Jer. 4:20.

A word might be said, too, about a tent-dwelling, seminomadic society as a breeding place of democratic ideals, or perhaps better, as a society in which communal values and their preservation were a necessity: loyalty to family and clan; a closeness to the realities of life; a sure and swift code of justice; a shared standard of living; an absence of pretensions, of "putting on airs"; a sense of protectiveness toward those less fortunate. Clearly—on the basis of Judg. 8:23, 9:8 ff.; 1 Sam. 8:10 ff.; 12:1 ff.—democratic ideals were strong among the Israelites in the first centuries after the Conquest. As the writings of Amos and Micah especially show a few centuries later, however, Israelite society became quite different and even corrupted. The democratic ideals had been eroded. The gradual watering down, by time and circumstances, of the original tent-dwelling character and societal values of earlier generations of Israelites had taken its toll.

Rechabites

A discussion of this ultra-conservative sect is appropriate at this point because their ideology and rule of life reflect the essence of nomadism.

It is considerably easier to set forth the beliefs of the Rechabites than it is to determine when they made their first appearance and who was their founder. Their chief tenets and prohibitions are stated in Jer. 35:6–10. The Rechabites were convinced that the Lord was best served by Israel's remaining strictly inside the nomadic way of life as lived by their ancestors in the days before Israel's encounter with the Canaanites, whose urban-agricultural society the Rechabites despised. Assimilation and syncretism were anathema. The Rechabite rule of life included: living in tents, not houses; living as nomadic shepherds, not as sedentary farmers; drinking no wine (desert dwellers have never known viticulture or wine-drinking).

The number of Rechabites at the time of Jeremiah's symbolic use of them as faithful adherents to their principles, in contrast with Judah's faithlessness to hers, was probably small, for Jeremiah gathered them in but one chamber in the Temple complex (Jer. 35:2–4). Here they seem to be a Judahite sect.

Earlier, at the time of Jehu's uprising and his slaughter of the house of Omri, the Rechabites seem to be a nomadic sect in the Northern Kingdom, and their leader, Jonadab (also called Jehonadab), an eager supporter of Jehu, as that regicide pursued his bloody course. In this hatred of any perceived impurities in the worship of the Lord of Israel and in the consequent hatred of Ahab, Jezebel, and all the trappings of Baalism, in this longing for a return to the desert days and desert ways before the Canaanite society and Phoenician influences had threatened to assimilate Israel, the Rechabites of Jehu's time were walking in the steps of Elijah and Elisha. Jehu clearly welcomed Jonadab's support by his gesture of taking him up into his chariot (2 Kings 10:15–17) as he pressed his purge of "foreign" elements and influences from Israel.

Very little indeed is known of the Rechabites as a group after the exile in Babylon. For a discussion of the slim evidences and the theories of their later existence, see the article, RECHAB, in *Interpreter's Bible Dictionary*.

As to the origins of the Rechabites, a key verse in the problem is Jer. 35:6: "We will drink no wine, for Jonadab, the son of Rechab, our father,..." Who is the father (i.e., the founding father), Jonadab or Rechab? In verse 19 Jeremiah says "Jonadab your father." (If Jonadab was the father, then the sect sprang up in the time of Elijah-Elisha.) On the other hand, how did the patronymic designation, Rechabites, become fixed if Rechab was not the founder? And when Jonadab is referred to as "son of Rechab," was a direct father-son relationship intended, or was Rechab a more distant ancestor, as "father" so often means in the Old Testament?

The search for other biblical references to Rechab leads merely to the discovery that the same "Rechab" appears only in the phrases "son of Rechab" and "sons of Rechab."

A clue apparently unrelated to those mentioned above is found in 1 Chron. 2:55: "The families of the scribes that dwelt at Jabez: ... These are the Kenites who came from Hammath, the father of the house of Rechab." Some scholars find significance in the mention of Kenites here, for this was an unusual nomadic people who allied themselves with the Judahites and dwelt on desert lands bordering Judah (Judg. 1:16; 1 Sam. 15:6, etc.). Could Jonadab have had as ancestors such Kenites as Heber and his wife Jael, who used a tent-peg to dispatch the Canaanite general, Sisera? But "Hammath" in v. 55 provides difficulties, for the name is otherwise known only as a town in northern Naphtali.

The origins of the Rechabites, therefore, remain in obscurity.

HOUSES

The types of housing the Israelites inherited from the Canaanites were simple and functional, and in major respects they remained unchanged throughout the span of biblical history (Fig. 14; *see also* Fig. 61). For the average Israelite, home was a small boxlike structure with walls made of mud bricks, sealed by one or more layers of mortar and whitewash (Fig. 15). The bricks, molded out of soft clay mixed with straw, were set out in the hot sun and allowed to dry a few days before the bricklayers set them in place. Though walls of this sun-dried brick were normally vulnerable to erosion by wind and rain, in some cases they were known to survive for centuries, as at Solomon's key seaport and mining town of Ezion-geber, which was encircled by walls of sun-dried brick standing 12 feet wide at the base and 25 feet high. For greater stability, houses were sometimes built on foundations of kiln-baked brick, whose rocklike durability had been discovered by the early Babylonians: "'Come, let us make bricks and burn them thoroughly.' And they had brick for stone, and bitumen for mortar" (Gen. 11:3).

14. A large residence in an ancient Israelite village.

Ancient bricklayers also learned to increase the strength of a wall by arranging the bricks in intricate patterns of headers and stretchers. ("Headers" are bricks laid with their ends in the face of a wall; "stretchers" have their sides laid in the face of the wall.)

Throughout the period of the Old and New Testaments mud bricks remained the basic building material in the towns and villages of the low-lying plains. For those who lived in the central highlands of Israel, however, more solid structures could be built from the abundant supply of loose stones. Though a well-to-do man might employ the services of a stonecutter, most had to settle for walls of uncut, ill-fitting stones held together with mortar.

Whether made of stone or mud brick, and whether situated in a rural hamlet or a fortified city, the house of the average Israelite was characterized chiefly by its modest dimensions and—by modern standards at least—an extreme lack of comfort. The earliest doors were probably of wattle or woven cloth—long since vanished—and were gradually supplanted by more durable (and burglar-resistant) wooden doors hung on hinges of wood or leather. Normally they could not be opened until a wood or metal bar was pulled back from its socket on the inside, and many were equipped with rudimentary wooden locks using two- or three-pegged keys.

The Threshold

The stone sill, or threshold, by which visitors entered from the street, was especially sacred. Laid across the doorposts was the lintel, upon which Israelites were instructed by law to sprinkle blood with a bunch of hyssop

15. Mud bricks have been laid on top of each other and bound together with mud mortar in this modern mud-brick house. They are then covered on the outside with a mud plaster.

at the Passover season. This ritual was reminiscent of the first passing-over of the angel of death before the Exodus from Egypt (Exod. 12:22). As well, the door of every worshipful Hebrew had affixed to its post a small metal or wooden box containing on parchment the words of Deut. 6:4–9: "Hear, O Israel: The Lord our God is one Lord; and you shall love the Lord your God with all your heart, and with all your soul, and with all your might. And these words which I command you this day shall be upon your heart; and you shall teach them diligently to your children, and shall talk of them when you sit in your house, and when you walk by the way, and when you lie down, and when you rise. And you shall bind them as a sign upon your hand, and they shall be as frontlets between your eyes. And you shall write them on the doorposts of your house and on your gates." The tubelike amulet containing these words is called the "mezuzah."

For family and visitors alike, it would have been a serious breach of etiquette to wear sandals inside the house. They were removed at the door, even the opening of a tent, as the dusty shoes of worshipers are removed today at mosques.

A Typical Floor Plan

Inside, the visitor would likely find a single, badly lighted room, perhaps 10 feet square, that served as living room, dining room, kitchen, bedroom, and even as part-time stable for the family's few sheep, goats, and chickens. The floor was usually dirt or clay, made hard and smooth with use. Sometimes the earth was plastered with a compound of lime and mud, and a few of the luckier households had permanent, washable floors made up of close-fitting limestone slabs. In some houses a section of the floor was equipped with a raised platform, perhaps 18 inches high, where food could be prepared and the family could eat and sleep without constant intrusions by their animals. On the lower level of such houses, mangers of wood or stone were provided for the animals, and to accommodate the platform, ceilings were often 9 to 12 feet high. (For the floor plan of a somewhat wealthier farmer's house, see section THE LIFE OF THE FARMER.)

House Furnishings

The average Israelite family had neither the space nor the money for much furniture. Beds consisted of straw mats similar to those which had been used in Israel's tent-dwelling days; these were laid out side by side on the floor each night (Fig. 16; *see also* Fig. 63). Family members normally slept with their clothes on, covering themselves with the cloaks they had worn during the day. Houses of wealthier families might have couches or divans which doubled as beds at night—occasionally reaching the height of luxury, as in the palace of the Persian king Ahasuerus, which boasted "couches of gold and silver on a mosaic pavement of porphyry, marble, mother-of-pearl and precious stones" (Esth. 1:6).

16. The straw bed of a typical Old Testament house (from a reconstruction in the Ha-Aretz Museum, Tel Aviv, Israel).

Tables and chairs were likewise reserved for the well-to-do. In most houses the "dinner table" was similar to that used in the tent—no more than a mat or animal skin spread on the floor—and even simple three-legged stools were not owned by everyone (Fig. 17).

Cooking was done on a small clay stove fueled by charcoal or dry twigs. Usually placed on the lower level next to the raised platform, the stove was rounded at the back with one or more small holes for draft and an opening in front to receive fuel (Fig. 18). A cooking pot, generally of clay or brass, rested directly on top. Since most houses had nothing like a modern fireplace or a chimney, the only means of ventilation was through the doorway and one or two small windows. Often no more than narrow slits placed high up in the wall—to discourage intruders—the windows were sometimes equipped with wooden shutters or latticework, glass panes being as yet unknown.

Even at midday, little sunlight could enter through such windows. The main source of illumination—however meager—was the family's small oil lamp (Fig. 19). Molded from clay into a flat saucerlike shape, these ubiquitous lamps (found everywhere archaeologists dig in Palestine) typically had a narrow lip at one end where the wick was placed, with a pool of olive oil in the center. Later designers, particularly during the Greek period, turned up the edges more and more, until the lamp was closed, leaving only a center hole to receive the oil and a tiny spout where the wick burned.

17. A reconstructed Old Testament house with the "table" laid for a meal (from the Ha-Aretz Museum, Tel Aviv, Israel).

18. The stove and cooking pot of a reconstructed Old Testament house (from the Ha-Aretz Museum, Tel Aviv, Israel).

19. A typical lamp from the period of the Israelite monarchy.

These lamps were greatly utilized by Israelite families; even in the poorest homes one was kept burning day and night. This was not an extravagance but a practical matter: it was an easier way to start a fire for cooking, the only alternative being a laborious friction-producing device called a fire drill. More importantly, it was a defense against the fears long associated with the night—fears of thieves, of enemy armies, and particularly of the evil spirits believed to inhabit the nocturnal world. "Every one who does evil hates the light," said the author of the fourth Gospel, "and does not come to the light, lest his deeds should be exposed" (John 3:20). Hence the injunction in Proverbs that a good wife never lets her lamp go out at night (31:18). The dim, flickering oil lamp, whether set upon an elegant bronze lampstand, an overturned bushel, or a niche carved into the wall, was valued as a kind of symbolic beacon that "gives light to all in the house" (Matt. 5:15).

The Roof

Without question, the favorite part of an Israelite's house, the principal refuge from its dim, cramped living quarters, was the roof. Unchanged in design for many centuries, the roof was supported by heavy wooden beams resting on top of the walls. Across the beams—sycamore in poor houses, cedar or cypress in rich ones—smaller beams were laid. Over these were placed layers of brush, reeds, mud, grass, and clay, leveled off with a roller that was kept handy for use after heavy rains (Fig. 20). Such rustic construction made it

20. The roof of a modern mud-brick house with layers of brush, reed, mud, grass, and clay to keep out the rain.

possible to open up the roofs of the average or typical house without much difficulty, a fact that had occasional advantages. When the friends of a paralyzed man in Capernaum were prevented by a crowd from bringing him into a house where Jesus was staying, "they removed the roof above him; and when they had made an opening, they let down the pallet on which the paralytic lay" (Mark 2:4).

Reached by a stone staircase attached to one of the exterior walls, or else by a simple wooden ladder, the roof served a variety of purposes—so many, in fact, that Hebrew law included a specific safety requirement: "When you build a new house, you shall make a parapet for your roof, that you may not bring the guilt of blood upon your house, if any one fall from it" (Deut. 22:8). Women could do many of their household chores there—weaving at their looms, cleaning out grain, and baking their flat loaves of bread. It was an ideal place as well for drying out figs, dates, flax, and the family wash.

The roof was also a popular place to relax during the cool of the evening, to escape the noise and dust of the street. There friends could gather to socialize and gossip, or a man could go alone to pray as Peter did at the house of Simon the tanner in Joppa (Acts 10:9). Indeed, the housetops of Jerusalem were commonly used for pagan worship in the time of Jeremiah, who prophesied destruction for "all the houses upon whose roofs incense has been burned to all the host of heaven, and drink offerings have been poured out to other gods" (Jer. 19:13).

During the summer months many families set up temporary booths of branches and reeds on their roofs to use as sleeping areas for themselves or visitors. One such guest room was built by "a wealthy woman" in Shunem in preparation for a visit by Elisha (2 Kings 4:10): "Let us make a small roof chamber with walls, and put there for him a bed, a table, a chair, and a lamp, so that whenever he comes to us, he can go in there." More permanent shelters of wood or stone were often built atop large houses, thereby converting the roof into a full-time second floor. Perhaps the most famous chamber of this type was the "large upper room furnished" (Luke 22:12) where Jesus and his disciples gathered for their last supper together in Jerusalem.

FOOD

> . . . the Lord your God is bringing you into a good land, a land of brooks of water, of fountains and springs, flowing forth in valleys and hills, a land of wheat and barley, of vines and fig trees and pomegranates, a land of olive trees and honey, a land in which you will eat bread without scarcity . . . Take heed lest you forget the Lord your God . . . when you have eaten and are full. . . .
>
> —Deut. 8:7–12

As in most eras and societies, no subject reaches closer to the heart of everyday life in biblical times than that of food. Old Testament Israel, like the rest of the ancient Near East, was chiefly a rural, agricultural society. Its people were dependent on the land, cultivating their fields, orchards, and vineyards, and tending their flocks for a living.

His two months are (olive) harvest—(Sept.–Nov.)
His two months are planting (grain)—(Nov.–Jan.)
His two months are late planting—(Jan.–Mar.)
His month is hoeing up of flax—(Mar.–Apr.)
His month is harvest of barley—(Apr.–May)
His month is harvest and feasting—(May–June)
His two months are vine–tending—(June–Aug.)
His month is summer fruit—(Aug.–Sept.)

Trans. by W. F. Albright, *Bulletin of the American Society for Oriental Research* #92, December 1943.

Further, as all reverent Israelites understood that God provided their land and sustenance, it was only fitting that the three major religious festivals were linked to the agricultural cycle. They developed, in fact, from three similar festivals that had long been celebrated by the Canaanites. Passover, the springtime commemoration of the deliverance from Egypt, coincided with the beginning of the grain harvest. The Feast of Weeks, two months later, marked the completion of the grain harvest. And in early autumn the Feast of Booths, recalling Israel's years in the wilderness, was observed during the jubilant grape harvest (*see* Fig. 4).

It is scarcely surprising, then, that the Bible abounds in references to the cultivation and consumption of food—not only those celebrating its abundance but also those that speak in fear and sorrow of its scarcity. For in reality the average Israelite did not live far above the level of bare subsistence; even in the best of times, hunger was never further away than the next crop failure or the next war. When Jeremiah rebuked his wayward hearers, he threatened them in terms of a nation which would come from afar: "They shall eat up your harvest and your food . . . your flocks and your herds; they shall eat up your wines and your fig trees" (Jer. 5:15–17). More optimistically, Isaiah prophesied a golden age when even men who had no money to spend would secure food and drink "without money and without price" (55:1).

HOSPITALITY

From the beginning, the concept of hospitality was a central part of Hebrew life, as indeed it was throughout the Fertile Crescent. The early Babylonians made a special virtue of hospitality, and the Canaanites were so concerned with it that they subsidized local gods to protect strangers in their midst. Likewise, it was customary in Egypt to extend aid to needy travelers. A noteworthy passage on the subject from the Egyptian Book of the Dead closely anticipated the words of Jesus in Matt. 25:35-36. "I have given bread to the hungry man," runs the Egyptian document, "and water to the thirsty man, and apparel to the naked man, and a boat to the ship-wrecked mariner." It was also traditional in both Egypt and Syria to make a threshold covenant with a guest by smearing on the doorsill blood from a newly killed animal.

The importance of these customs to the Hebrews was evident from the earliest patriarchal times, and there was no more hospitable gesture than to offer food and drink to a visitor. One example of such courtesy occurs in the story of Isaac's betrothal to Rebekah (Gen. 24). To prevent the choice of a Canaanite wife by his son, Abraham dispatched his servant to his old homeland in northwestern Mesopotamia. The servant was found by Laban at the well, watering his camels, and was addressed as an honored guest: "Come in, O blessed of the Lord; why do you stand outside? For I have prepared a house and a place for the camels." So the man came into the house; and Laban ungirded the camels, and gave him straw and provender for the camels, and water to wash his feet and the feet of the men who were with him. Then food was set before him to eat" (24:31-33).

An even more striking incident was alluded to by the author of Hebrews when he advised, "Forget not to show love to strangers; for thereby some have entertained angels unawares" (13:2). When Abraham was encamped by the oaks of Mamre, near Hebron, he saw three men approaching and readily put himself at their disposal: " 'Let a little water be brought, and wash your feet, and rest yourselves under the tree, while I fetch a morsel of bread, that you may refresh yourselves'. . . . And Abraham hastened into the tent to Sarah, and said, 'Make ready quickly three measures of fine meal, knead it, and make cakes.' And Abraham ran to the herd, and took a calf, tender and good, and gave it to the servant, who hastened to prepare it. Then he took curds, and milk, and the calf which he had pre-pared, and set it before them; and he stood by them under the tree while they ate" (Gen. 18:4-8).

By the same token, gifts of food were commonly offered as a sign of gratitude or friendship. One such story (1 Sam. 25) involved Abigail, wife of the "churlish and ill-behaved" herder Nabal. Learning that her wealthy husband had refused a request for food from David's soldiers—though they had willingly protected Nabal's shearers—she on her own initiative decided to repay the kindness: "Then Abigail made haste, and took two hundred loaves, and two skins of wine, and five sheep ready dressed, and five measures of parched grain, and a hundred clusters of raisins, and two hundred cakes of figs," and brought them to David's camp. (Nabal died shortly thereafter and, fittingly enough, the beautiful widow became David's wife.)

In a similar incident, the servant Ziba declared his allegiance to David during Absalom's revolt by bringing him "two hundred loaves of bread, a hundred bunches of raisins, a hundred of summer fruits, and a skin of wine" (2 Sam. 16:1). Conversely, when people refused to give food to bands of hungry soldiers, they risked the kind of retribution suffered by Succoth and Penuel at the hands of Gideon (Judg. 8:16–17).

Others forced to travel long distances were well advised to bring along as much food as they could carry. During their wanderings between Egypt and Canaan, Moses' followers soon used up the scanty supplies in their pouches and found themselves yearning for the abundant meat stews, vegetables, and fruit guaranteed even to poor laborers in the Nile Delta. Indeed, only the quail and manna miraculously given them each day stood between the Israelites and starvation.

Most wayfarers were not able to rely on such divine intervention, however, and so made other provisions. Camel drivers in particular were careful to include ample amounts of food in their baggage—bread, cheese, olives, pressed fig cakes, and other relatively nonperishable items. There were inns along the major roads, of course, but they required money, and not every traveler was able to take advantage of this opportunity. As was evident in the stories of the Good Samaritan and the Nativity, no ancient rite of hospitality motivated the keeper of a lodging place.

EVERYDAY FOODS

Compared with people living in rural parts of the United States and Canada today, the living standard of the average Israelite was low, yet the choice of foods available to him was surprisingly varied and nourishing. The mainstay of the diet was coarse barley bread, generally baked at home each day. This was one of the housewife's most important and most time-consuming chores. The barley first had to be ground into meal, either with a mortar and pestle or between two flat stones, then mixed with water and salt to make a dough. Though unleavened bread was simpler to prepare—and was required during Passover and other religious festivals—yeast was usually added to make the mixture rise. The dough was then molded into flat loaves and baked in a small earthenware oven—or, where possible, sent to the community baker (Fig. 21). On special occasions cakes and pastries were also made, with honey or fruit for flavoring (sugar being as yet unknown in the Near East). Confections were also made with a blend of honey, dates, almonds, or pistachio nuts and gum arabic.

21. A community baker in modern Jerusalem.

Another unavoidable chore was providing a daily supply of fresh water for drinking and cooking. Some fortunate households had their own cisterns, but most had to rely on a community spring or well where the water was drawn by hand with a leather bucket and carried home by the mother or daughter in an earthenware pot balanced on her head. In times of drought water became so precious that enterprising merchants would appear in the streets of the towns and cities to sell water. They were able to command handsome prices until the next heavy rainfall (Fig. 22).

This scarcity also encouraged the use of milk, mainly from goats, as an everyday beverage, as well as for making butter and a variety of cheeses. Indeed, there is evidence of an extensive dairy business as far back as early Babylonian times, as illustrated by a famous inlaid "milking scene" recovered from Ur of the Chaldees showing men at work in a milking shed. In addition, the consumption of wine was a universal pleasure in Bible lands—enough so to warrant frequent warnings in the Old Testament about excessive drinking. Though most commonly made with grapes, wine was also produced from pomegranates and possibly from dates. One other time-honored intoxicant, beer, was popular among the Philistines and Egyptians but is not mentioned in the Bible as having been used by the Hebrew people.

For most Israelites, meat was a special treat, reserved for holidays, weddings, and other important occasions. Their animals were too valuable as sources of wool and milk—and of such labor as plowing and carrying—to

22. A jar of water and a drinking jug from the period of the Israelite monarchy (from the Ha-Aretz Museum, Tel Aviv, Israel).

be slaughtered for their meat. The consumption of meat was also governed by Deuteronomic law, which classified various animals and birds as clean or unclean. Sheep, goat, and oxen were approved, for example, while swine and camel were proscribed—though neighboring peoples ate them readily. In any case, no Hebrew was to eat an animal that had died of natural causes or had been killed by another animal. Chickens and their eggs were also enjoyed—at least after the exile period—as were fish from the Jordan, the Sea of Galilee, and occasionally the Mediterranean—sometimes eaten fresh but usually pickled or dried and salted to prevent spoilage.

Along with bread, vegetables constituted the major portion of the Israelite's diet. Stews with beans, lentils, and peas were probably the most common family meal, flavored with onions, leeks, garlic, or some other aromatic seasoning. Lettuce, beets, and cucumbers might also be found on the menu, and diverse spices were brought into Palestine over the ancient caravan routes up the Arabian Red Sea coast, or from India overland to Syria, and thence south.

The family's evening meal was likely to end with one of a number of fruits—usually figs, melons, dates, or pomegranates (Fig. 23). Fresh figs, in an era that did not know sugar, were especially prized for their sweetness; hence Hosea's image of the Israelites in Egypt as the "first fruit on the

23. Dates growing on a date-palm tree.

fig tree" (9:10), and Jeremiah's comparison of those in exile, the "first-ripe figs," with those remaining in Judah, "the bad figs which are so bad they cannot be eaten" (24:1–10). The most important fruit harvests were those of olives and grapes. The grapes were sometimes eaten in their natural state or dried into raisins, but were more often used to make wine. Similarly, olives were harvested and pressed for their oil, which was one of the most valuable commodities in the ancient world used by every household for cooking and as fuel in lamps.

FOOD IN JESUS' TEACHINGS

The words and deeds of Jesus dealing with food provide an insight into the ways of his fellow Galileans, and into the customs of the Greco-Roman world of which Palestine was a part. Jesus used images that his least-educated listener could grasp, and food was one subject familiar to all. His teachings on the virtues of charity and hospitality were epitomized in such passages as this: "I was hungry and you gave me food, I was thirsty and you gave me drink, I was a stranger and you welcomed me, I was naked and you clothed me . . ." (Matt. 25:35–36). Likewise he described his mission in simple words —"My food is to do the will of him that sent me" (John 4:34)—characterizing himself as "the bread of life" and telling his audience, "he who comes to me shall not hunger, and he who believes in me shall never thirst" (John 6:35).

Again, Jesus used images of everyday food when he described his friends as "the salt of the earth," and later when he advised them that their actions were like the fruits by which the quality of a tree was judged (Matt. 7:16–20).

Several of the dinner scenes in which Jesus took part also served to illustrate his teachings, as well as contributing toward our understanding of social customs in 1st-century Palestine. At the feast given by the tax collector Matthew at Capernaum, Jesus deliberately took the opportunity to break bread with the "publicans and sinners." "When the Pharisees saw this, they said to his disciples, 'Why does your teacher eat with tax collectors and sinners?'" To which Jesus replied simply, "Those who are well have no need of a physician, but those who are sick" (Matt. 9:11–12).

On another occasion he dined with a ruler of the Pharisees and gave the guests a pointed lesson in table manners: "When you are invited by any one to a marriage feast, do not sit down in a place of honor, lest a more eminent man than you be invited by him; and he who invited you both will come and say to you, 'Give place to this man,' and then you will begin with shame to take the lowest place. But when you are invited, go and sit in the lowest place, so that when your host comes he may say to you, 'Friend, go up higher' . . . for everyone who exalts himself will be humbled, and he who humbles himself will be exalted." At the same time, Jesus also spoke to them of true hospitality: "When you give a feast, invite the poor, the maimed, the lame, the blind, and you will be blessed, because they cannot repay you. You will be repaid at the resurrection of the just" (Luke 14:8–14).

Finally, at the last supper in Jerusalem, Jesus used the occasion to confirm his new covenant with the disciples, symbolically replacing the Israelite's original covenant with the Lord: ". . . as they were eating, Jesus took bread, and blessed, and broke it, and gave it to the disciples and said, 'Take, eat; this is my body.' And he took a cup [of wine], and when he had given thanks he gave it to them, saying, 'Drink of it, all of you; for this is my blood of the covenant, which is poured out for many for the forgiveness of sins'" (Matt. 26:26–28).

"AT THE KING'S TABLE"

When you sit down to eat with a ruler, observe carefully what is before you;
. . . Do not desire his delicacies, for they are deceptive food.

—Prov. 23:1–3

Royal meals in biblical times were almost always shared by numerous people—relatives, advisers, vassals, and others—and the king's table was generally the focal point of political affairs. When David, having been warned of Saul's anger, did not appear at his usual place at the royal table, the king realized that his plot to kill David had been foiled. Immediately after that, the rupture between Saul and Jonathan was made final when the son "rose from the table in fierce anger and ate no food . . . for he was grieved for David" (1 Sam. 20:34). Later, when David became king, he repaid his friend's loyalty by offering hospitality to Jonathan's son Mephibosheth: "Do not fear; for I will show you kindness for the sake of your father . . . and you shall eat at my table always" (2 Sam. 9:7).

Apart from political connotations, a royal meal was well worth attending strictly on its own merits. When Solomon held court in his cedar-trimmed palace in Jerusalem, the banquet table was nothing short of breathtaking. Even the Queen of Sheba, accustomed as she was to opulence, was stunned at the sight of Solomon's golden tableware. The proportions of such a feast can be surmised from the king's food quota—levied from his subjects—for a single day: "thirty cors [188 bushels] of fine flour, and sixty cors [about 370 bushels] of meal, ten fat oxen, and twenty pasture-fed cattle, a hundred sheep, besides harts, gazelles, roebucks, and fatted fowl . . . Barley also and straw for the horses . . ." (1 Kings 4:22–23, 28).

In the following centuries the rulers of Israel and Judah presumably dined on a similar scale, at least during periods of prosperity. The menu also grew diverse and exotic as time passed, until by Herod's day a kingly banquet might include such delicacies as jellyfish and mushrooms for appetizers, and main courses of flamingo tongues, wild boar, and lobster with truffles.

CLOTHING

> Then the eyes of both were opened, and they knew that they were naked;
> and they sewed fig leaves together and made themselves aprons.
>
> —Gen. 3:7

No sooner had Adam and Eve eaten the forbidden fruit and become conscious of good and evil, than they felt compelled to cover their naked bodies. Thus the idea of clothing was born, Genesis tells us, and down through the ages of biblical history it held a uniquely important place in Hebrew life. By the time of the Patriarchs, clothing was not simply something a person wore to hide his or her body or protect it from the elements. It was a means, like jewelry and cosmetics, to satisfy one's basic urge for decoration and self-expression, a visible advertisement of one's wealth and social status. "The Lord's glory is man," said a commentator in the Midrash, "and man's ornament is his clothes." Indeed, nothing—not even food and drink—was more highly valued by the Israelites. The prize offered by Samson for solving his riddle was not money or precious gems, but "thirty linen garments and thirty festal garments" (Judg. 14:12), and during the Conquest Achan was tempted as much by "a beautiful mantle from Shinar" as he was by a small fortune in silver and gold (Josh. 7:21). Likewise, General Naaman of the Syrian army offered "two changes of raiment" along with two bags of silver to Elisha's servants, and Sisera's mother hopefully daydreamed about "spoil of dyed stuffs embroidered, two pieces of dyed work embroidered for my neck . . ." (Judg. 5:30).

Even less glorified apparel was of considerable value, simply because of the time and effort involved in making it. In the early days most households were obliged to produce their own attire, starting out with nothing but sheep's fleece or flax from the field. The raw material then had to be cleansed, carded, spun, and woven by the women of the family—as Samuel's mother did, producing a new mantle each year for her son. In later times, particularly in the larger towns and cities, much of this work was taken over by specialized tradesmen—weavers, dyers, tailors, and the like (see section, THE PROFESSIONAL LIFE).

EVERYDAY APPAREL

Although the Bible contains numerous references to clothing, our knowledge of the subject is limited by the vagueness of the terms used to describe various articles. The same Hebrew word, for example, might be translated in different passages as "coat," "cloak," "robe," or simply "garment." Fortunately, the biblical text has been supplemented by the discoveries of various paintings and memorial tablets, bearing illustrations of Israelites and other peoples from the ancient Near East.

In Israel and most neighboring countries everyday attire seemed to fall into three or four general categories. For laborers working in the hot sun, the basic unit of clothing was a simple loincloth made of wool, sackcloth, or animal skin. It could either be worn loose, like a skirt, or pulled between the legs and tucked in at the waist. (So far as we know, modern-style underwear was unknown to people of that time.) This loincloth, or waistcloth, was a forerunner of the nearly universal tunic—worn by both men and women— a close-fitting, shirtlike article usually made of wool or linen. One kind of tunic, depicted in the famous Egyptian tomb painting at Beni-hasan (Fig. 24), was worn over one shoulder and reached slightly below the knees. Other styles had short or long sleeves and extended anywhere from the knees to the ankles. The typical tunic was probably white or off-white, since dyed material was more expensive, but the better ones came in a variety of hues.

The tunic was held in at the waist by a girdle or belt, usually a folded length of wool cloth. The girdle was where men kept their money and other valuables, and where soldiers carried their swords. As with a loincloth, the

24. A nomadic clan entering Egypt in the age of the Patriarchs (from the tomb of Beni-Hasan).

bottom of the tunic could also be folded up into the girdle for easier movement—hence men going into battle were exhorted to "gird up their loins."

Normally, the tunic was covered by a loose-fitting cloak or mantle, draped over one shoulder in the manner of a Roman toga. Most were made of heavy wool and also served as rugs to sit on and as blankets at night. (Ancient Israelites would have been as perplexed by pajamas as by underwear; they slept in the same clothes they wore during the day.) On the 9th century B.C. so-called "Black Obelisk" of Shalmaneser III, King Jehu and other submissive Israelites are depicted wearing such cloaks as they pay homage to the Assyrian ruler (Fig. 25).

A "mantle of distinction" made from animal's hair was also the proper attire for kings and prophets, especially on important occasions. David wore one when the ark was transferred to Jerusalem, and seers from Samuel to John the Baptist were similarly attired at crucial moments. Herod put on his "royal robes" to make a public oration, and a soldier's mantle was draped over Jesus' shoulders after his arrest in a mocking allusion to royalty. Related to this kind of mantle was the ephod worn by Levite priests and others, a simple white robe made of high quality linen.

The Israelites' standard footwear was a pair of simple leather sandals or shoes, probably of the type seen in the Beni-hasan painting (Fig. 24). This was apparently one of the few articles of clothing not highly prized. In a colloquial saying of the time, a pair of shoes signified something of relatively small value, and to be barefoot (except in times of mourning or on holy ground, when it was customary) was a sign either of extreme poverty or humiliation, as in the case of war prisoners.

There is little mention of hats or other headgear in the Bible, and none at all before the Exile. Some sort of turban was worn by priests, and soldiers protected themselves with helmets, but most Israelite men evidently went bareheaded except on special occasions. The Hebrews seen on the "Black Obelisk" (Fig. 25) wear cloth caps, a mark of high rank, and on other monuments some figures wear simple headbands. It was apparently more

25. The Black Obelisk, showing King Jehu kneeling before the Assyrian king, Shalmaneser III.

common for women to use headwear of some type—turbans, scarves, and sometimes veils concealing the face. In New Testament times, in fact, it was customary for Jewish women to keep their heads covered after marriage, a style that distinguished them from most other women in the Roman Empire.

The book of Leviticus prescribed (19:27) that "You shall not round off the hair on your temples or mar the edges of your beard"—an ancient heathen practice for mourning the dead—and one of the requirements for such Nazirites as Samson and Samuel was that they never take a razor to their hair, but instead let it grow long, as an offering to God. Other Israelites were not forbidden to cut their hair, of course, but through most of the Old Testament period long hair was admired on men and women alike. Absalom cut his hair only once a year, and the amount he cut reportedly (2 Sam. 14:26) weighed two hundred shekels—or about five pounds! Interestingly, by the New Testament era that custom had changed, at least in the young Christian community. To the Corinthians (1 Cor. 11:14-15) Paul wrote that "if a woman has long hair, it is her pride," but he insisted that for a man to wear long hair was unnatural and degrading.

CLOTHING IN MOSAIC LAW

As with hairstyles—and so many other aspects of everyday life—clothing had a variety of religious and social implications in ancient Israel. The book of Deuteronomy specified three regulations on the subject. One of them forbade men and women to wear each other's garments, and another barred the use of any article made of both wool and linen. Both of these reflected a general Mosaic prohibition against mixing things together that God had intended to be separate—planting two crops on the same field, for example, or interbreeding different species of cattle. The third rule stated that "You shall make yourselves tassels on the four corners of your cloak with which you cover yourself" (Deut. 22:12). The tassels were meant to serve as a reminder of the Lord's commandments, and in the New Testament era both Jews and Christians wore them, in contrast to the pagan majority of the Roman world.

In addition, the book of Leviticus included clothing in its numerous rules on ceremonial cleanliness. A garment that came in contact with an unclean animal or any other impure object had to be washed out promptly and thoroughly, and clothing that bore traces of leprosy was subject to a lengthy examination by a priest. It was also stipulated that "the leper who has the disease shall wear torn clothes and let the hair of his head hang loose" (Lev. 13:45).

TRADITIONAL STYLES AND INNOVATIONS

Perhaps the most obvious characteristic of the Israelites' attitude toward clothing was a rešistance to change. In a wide range of cultural matters theirs was a conservative society, jealously guarding its own traditions against the influences of other nations. "You shall not do as they do in Egypt," the Lord had told Moses, "and you shall not do as they do in the land of Canaan, to which I am bringing you" (Lev. 18:3). Though the common people seldom had enough money or leisure time to worry about such things, the worldly aristocrats of Israel and Judah had a keen interest in cultural trends from abroad—much to the chagrin of the prophets. It must have been one such change in fashion that prompted Zephaniah's outburst against "the officials and the king's sons and all who array themselves in foreign attire" (1:8). Similarly, Isaiah catalogued the haughty extravagance with which the women of Jerusalem adorned themselves: "In that day the Lord will take away the finery of the anklets, the headbands, and the crescents; the pendants, the bracelets, and the scarfs; the headdresses, the armlets, the sashes, the perfume boxes, and the amulets; the signet rings and nose rings; the festal robes, the mantles, the cloaks, and the handbags; the garments of gauze, the linen garments, the turbans, and the veils. Instead of perfume there will be rottenness; and instead of a girdle, a rope; and instead of well-set hair, baldness; and instead of a rich robe, a girding of sackcloth . . ." (3:18–24).

More than seven centuries later the same theme was echoed in the First Epistle of Peter, in which Christian women were exhorted to seek inward beauty and virtue, rather than relying on "the outward adornment with braiding of hair, decoration of gold, and wearing of robes" (3:3).

Despite the Israelites' traditional resistance to new styles of clothing, gradual changes inevitably occurred. As in other societies down through history, fashions that were considered outlandish or worse when they first appeared often came to be accepted within a period of one or two generations. The "foreign attire" decried by Zephaniah around 630 B.C. was most likely of Persian origin, typified by a coat with sleeves, trousers, boots, a cloak, and a felt hat. This was the basic mode of dress across the Persian empire for centuries, and it was probably adopted by many Jews by the time of their return to Palestine during the reign of Cyrus in 538 B.C.

CLOTHING IN NEW TESTAMENT TIMES

Following Alexander's conquest of the Near East in the 4th century

B.C., the Greek influence in clothing (and many other aspects of life) became consistently stronger. Under Jerusalem's Hasmonean dynasty of the 2nd and 1st centuries B.C. Hellenic styles of dress, architecture, education, and entertainment became a way of life, particularly among the aristocratic elite. To be sure, Judah's acceptance of these new fashions was not total: when Jason became high priest in 175 B.C. and attempted to popularize a Greek hat, for example, he encountered general opposition (2 Macc. 4:12). There is little doubt, however, that by the New Testament period Greek-style clothing was widely worn by the people of Palestine—including Jesus and the apostles.

The main item in this wardrobe was the *colobium*, a long, close-fitting tunic with openings for the head and arms (Fig. 26). Sometimes it was not sewn together but made from one piece of cloth—hence the brief dilemma of the soldiers who wanted to divide up Jesus' clothing at the Crucifixion. "They took his garments and made four parts, one for each soldier. But his tunic was without seam, woven from top to bottom; so they said to one another, 'Let us not tear it, but cast lots for it to see whose it shall be.'" (John 19:23–24). By the beginning of the 2nd century many tunics of this kind were decorated with two colored stripes running from the shoulder down to the hem.

Over the tunic was worn a cloak with the prescribed tassels, frequently described as "borders" or "fringes," attached at the four corners. One of the miraculous cures in Jesus' ministry directly involved this piece of clothing: "And behold, a woman who had suffered from a hemorrhage for twelve years came up behind him and touched the fringe of his garment . . . . And instantly the woman was made well" (Matt. 9:20–22).

JESUS' ATTITUDE TOWARD CLOTHING

Is not life more than food, and the body more than clothing?

—Matt. 6:25

Jesus in his teachings generally downgraded the importance his countrymen placed on their attire. One exception was his parable of the marriage feast, in which a man who did not wear a suitable wedding garment was cast out of the festivities—a grim prediction of what would happen to those who did not respond appropriately to their invitation to enter God's kingdom.

Elsewhere, however, Jesus spoke of clothing in much the same tone as he spoke of other material possessions. On one occasion he criticized the scribes and Pharisees for calling attention to themselves and their piety through their clothes—"they make their phylacteries broad and their fringes long" (Matt. 23:5). In another instance he told a crowd, "He who has two

26. The colobium, a garment worn in New Testament times.

coats, let him share with him who has none" (Luke 3:11), and declared that anyone who clothed the naked was giving clothes to God as well.

Finally, much of Jesus' message was summed up in a discourse on clothing during his Sermon on the Mount: "And why are you anxious about clothing? Consider the lilies of the field, how they grow; they neither toil nor spin; yet I tell you, even Solomon in all his glory was not arrayed like one of these. But if God so clothes the grass of the field . . . will he not much more clothe you, O men of little faith? . . . seek first his kingdom and his righteousness, and all these things shall be yours as well" (Matt. 6:28–33).

JEWELRY

Jewels in the narrow sense consist of stones which, because they are rare or intrinsically beautiful, or have been made so by cutting and dressing, polishing and engraving, are sought after for purposes of personal adornment. These "stones" may be divided into "gems" or "precious stones," such as diamonds, emeralds, and rubies, and "semiprecious stones," such as agate, amber, amethyst, and onyx.

There is no evidence of any precious stones being found in the Palestine-Syria region, nor for their wide use outside of members of royal families.

Even in lands where, in the ancient world, diamonds might be found, there was no technique for cutting such hard material and thereby setting it off to best advantage; diamond-cutting is a modern art developed in Europe. It is doubtful also if Bible people knew emeralds as we know them today. More likely what English-language Bibles call "emerald" was a turquoise or perhaps green feldspar. The Hebrew words for certain gems and semi-precious stones are not understood, and in some cases, therefore, their translation (as with "emeralds" and "bdellium") is more guesswork than fact.

Regardless of the nature of their jewelry and the availability of precious stones in the Bible world, Bible peoples, like all other peoples from the beginning of civilization, were motivated to acquire and wear jewels. The desire to adorn oneself with something beautiful, attention-attracting, and valuable either intrinsically or because of its workmanship seems always to have been universal. This desire was as true of men in Bible times as of women. Men also, as today, liked to deck out their women in jewelry and finery to show their own success in acquiring material things. And this desire to display one's wife wearing precious stones could be satisfied by the Israelites, if wealthy, by dealing with Phoenician or Arab merchants who acquired them in Mesopotamia and Egypt, which did have gem deposits, and whose people also knew how to work them into highly desirable merchandise. (Some jewels probably came into the biblical world from African regions south of Egypt and from India.)

Besides their use for adornment and as gifts, gems and semiprecious stones were regarded by men of property—then as today—as a prudent investment—that is, of a constant value over the long haul, marketable, and easily stowed away or transported. One additional attraction of jewels to biblical people has disappeared with the passage of time: the belief in the magical properties and benefits to the owner of certain jewels.

Precious stones tended to gather in the royal household as a result of the custom of giving a king a present on his accession, or upon being appointed to an administrative position in the royal government, of which the king was the absolute master. Kings also acquired jewels through their share in the booty of a defeated enemy. Precious gems, some of which could not perhaps be worked into a form that got the most out of them when given a solitary setting (as in a plain ring), could be used with great impressiveness in necklaces for a king and his wife and his mother; in royal crowns, insignia, and robes; in the robes and insignia of the high priest; and inset in jewel and cosmetic boxes, thrones, and door panelings in the palace. (For the jewels of the high priest's ephod, see section, THE PROFESSIONAL LIFE, "Ritual and Sacrifice.")

Militarily successful kings who had jewels in excess of immediate use-fulness simply deposited them in the palace treasury. According to 1 Chron. 27:25, one Azmaveth, son of Adiel, was overseer of the treasures of King David.

In the necklaces of Bible times gold or silver fillets hung on the front side of a ring or chain of the same material; into this fillet as many jewels were worked as the person could afford or had available. The necklaces, when worn by a male, also bore any symbol of his authority.

PEARLS

Pearls in the Old Testament continue to baffle scholars. In archaeological excavations to date no pearls have been found at Old Testament levels of occupation. The Hebrew word for "pearl" is unknown. The word in the Hebrew text at Job 28:18 is *peninim*, the meaning of which is unknown. The King James translators guessed that this might mean "pearls" and trans-lated the verse: "No mention shall be made of coral or of *pearls*, for the price of wisdom is above rubies." The American Standard Bible reads: "Coral and *crystal* are not to be mentioned; and the acquisition of wisdom is above that of pearls." The RSV offers: "No mention shall be made of coral and *crystal*; the price of wisdom is above pearls." Even more guesswork about the mean-ing of *peninim* is found at other places where it appears in the Hebrew: Prov. 3:15; 8:11; 20:15; and 31:10. Among the major modern translations some elect to use "coral" or "red coral"; some "rubies"; some "pearls"; while some equivocate with "jewels" or "precious stones." Neither the ASV nor the RSV uses, at the locations of *peninim* in Proverbs, the translation "crystal" they used in Job 28:18. These variations reflect the true state of contemporary ignorance about the meaning of several Hebrew words referring to jewels.

But scholars find no reason why pearls should not have been known in Palestine once the United Kingdom of David and Solomon began to enjoy international trade; for mollusks, in which pearls are found, were known to maritime peoples both for food and for industrial uses. However, the Greek world apparently did not know pearls until after Alexander had pushed his empire to the Persian Gulf; perhaps the same was true in Palestine. Pearls are still obtained along the Arabian coastline, especially in the Persian Gulf, and also in the Indian Ocean, notably at Ceylon.

During New Testament times pearls were commonly known and highly prized in Palestine. Jesus mentioned them twice (Matt. 7:6; 13:45). In 1 Tim. 2:9 women are urged to "adorn themselves modestly and sensibly in seemly apparel, not with braided hair or gold or pearls or costly attire, but by good deeds as befits women who profess religion." Many scholars regard

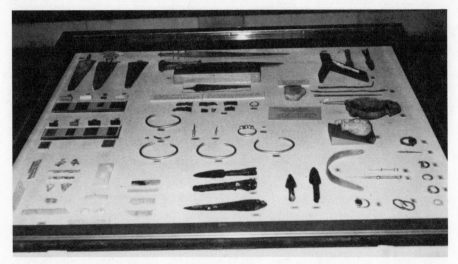

27. Examples of jewelry from the period of the monarchy in Israel (in the Rockefeller Museum, Jerusalem, Israel).

this pastoral letter as directed to Christian churches in largely Greek Asia Minor, perhaps at Ephesus. In any case the verse reflects a society in which wealth was not rare.

In Israel, in Old Testament times, the gap between what the king and his consort possessed in their jewel boxes and treasuries, and the few bits of decoration owned by a husband and wife among "the people of the land," was comparable with the difference in possessions of a ruler of a modern oil-rich Arab nation and a wage earner in his oil fields.

JEWELS CRAFTED OF METALS AND OTHER MATERIALS

Instead of the categories of "precious" and "semiprecious stones" a more realistic, closer-to-life division of the subject of jewelry in the Bible is into (a) professionally crafted items using precious metals, and (b) pieces crafted by local artisans out of more common materials, for everyday use by common people (Fig. 27).

True gems, and even semiprecious stones, were just too difficult to acquire to figure very significantly in the life of "the people of the land," as distinct from the royal household. Far less difficult were gold and silver in metal form, for these were used as a medium of exchange before coined money was developed by the Persians and the Greeks. Gold and silver could be made into attractive gifts of jewelry by metalsmiths and experts in engraving and the decorative arts. Bracelets were extremely popular with both men and women (Gen. 24:22; Ezek. 16:11; 23:42), men usually preferring to wear

28. A scarab mounted in a swivel ring setting.

them on their upper arms (2 Sam. 1:10). Ankle rings, too, were fashionable (Isa. 3:16, 18). Before David's conquest of the Philistines, iron and iron-making were unknown to the Israelites, and for a while iron bracelets or armlets had a vogue. For the poor a wide range of bronze bracelets was available, many of the unclosed design, with decorative knobs at the ends—a style universally popular today.

Among common people throughout the land rings would certainly be owned, of metals of differing values, as with bracelets. Rings were worn by some women in the nose and also on toes. A small landowner or craftsman would probably own a seal ring made of a semiprecious stone, with a scarab engraved on one side of a swivel-set stone, and some kind of identifying mark or insignia on the other. The man would wear the ring—scarab side out—so that he always had his seal with him if he had to issue a receipt or put his mark on the document of a transaction. These scarab seals varied from the simple to the ornate (Fig. 28).

Beads, commonly made of rock crystal, amber, shells, and agates of two or three colors, were widely owned and used by women. They could also be more handsomely put together of more expensive semiprecious stones, such as lapis lazuli (commonly called "sapphire" in the early English Bibles), carnelian, onyx, and jasper. Amethyst beads would be very luxurious.

All stones, from the valueless to the semiprecious, had rounded, convex shapes, were pierced if used as beads, and were dressed and polished to be made smooth to the touch. Engravers, by deft cutting of designs into the stones, could expose another color, and perhaps two, in each stone's multi-layered structure, thus enhancing their attractiveness.

Gold nets for hair would be owned and used by the more fortunate wives of wealthy landowners, district administrators of the king, generals of the army, and palace officials. These, too, probably owned cosmetic cases, simple or fancy. Gold and silver drinking cups, brought out for special occasions, would be owned by upperclass families.

29. A representation of a fertility
goddess.

AMULETS

Despite the Mosaic prohibition against making graven images of anything, *amulets* were probably as widely owned and carefully kept as bracelets, beads, and rings. These small images have been found whenever
archaeologists have dug in city-sites in Palestine, and they date from all
biblical centuries. Some of them represented male or female gods—often
Egyptian deities—or were simply nude female figures, perhaps representing
the Asherah-Astarte goddess of Israel's Canaanite and Phoenician neighbors
(Fig. 29). But there was no limit to what might be represented: a crescent
for a moon deity; cats, monkeys, and other animals; a heart-shape has often
been found. The use of amulets was much less connected with the religion
of Israel than it was with folk superstition. Everywhere the Israelites lived—
Paddan-aram, Canaan, Egypt, the desert—they found themselves among
people who accepted the wearing of amulets as the way human beings drove
off evil spirits.

Amulets were most often colored either red or blue; some scholars believe these may have been "magic" colors, as they are in modern Arab folklore. As with beads, and from whatever material they had been fashioned, they
were perforated to be strung and worn around the neck or hung from a
bracelet. However, some were attached over the doorways of houses, and
others were placed beside the bodies of deceased loved ones as they were laid
in their final resting place. On long trips the neck of the ass, mule, or camel
being used was draped with one or more amulets on a string. They were
meant to ward off evil spirits; and perhaps more positively, scholars con-

jecture they were to insure good fortune or to guarantee some advantage to the traveler.

Amulets were a low form of jewel in terms of their material, for even the best seem to have been made of semiprecious stones, such a carnelian, while many of them were fashioned from such odds and ends as animal teeth and small bones.

EGYPTIAN JEWELRY

"Solomon made a marriage alliance with Pharaoh king of Egypt; he took Pharaoh's daughter and brought her into the city of David."

So 1 Kings 3:1 records what was perhaps Solomon's most successful piece of international diplomacy. The name of the princess is unknown, and of the Pharaoh uncertain. However, the Pharaoh, as a dowry for his daughter, captured the ancient Canaanite stronghold city of Gezer, on the western border of Ephraim, and presented it to Solomon (1 Kings 9:16). Solomon built his Egyptian wife her own house in his palace complex.

What kind of jewelry would the princess have brought to Solomon's court?

Egypt was a land famous for gem deposits (some fifteen stones are known to have been mined there), and her craftsmen in precious metals and stones were highly skilled. For at least 3,000 years before Solomon's time—excavations have shown us—Egyptian jewelry had been unrivaled except for a while by the Sumerians at the other end of the Fertile Crescent. We may assume that the princess from Egypt was richly provided, and that the other wives and ladies at court were probably envious.

Egyptians were prodigal in their use of gold, covering it even with inlays of stones or enamel. The best-known example of this extravagance is in the solid-gold coffin of Tutanhk-amun and his mask of gold inlaid with gems and enamel. Gold was known long before silver in Egypt. In fact silver, which came principally from Asia Minor, was called "white gold" by Egyptian jewelers. Egyptians dug their gold from the eastern desert and along wadis such as Wadi 'Alaki, where its shining nuggets and gleaming particles attracted the attention of men long before they knew how to write of their findings.

Along with gold, the Egyptians were avid collectors and wearers of all the chief semiprecious stones, most notably turquoise from mines in the Sinai Peninsula and feldspar ("emeralds") from Africa south of Egypt. Lapis lazuli (incorrectly translated "sapphire" by King James's scholars), jasper, amethyst, carbuncle, and chalcedony would also be among the jewels of the princess.

Absent from her jewel box would be diamonds, rubies, true emeralds, and true sapphires, for these most precious stones were either unknown to the ancient Near East (not found in the region) or could not be cut, dressed, and set by the jewelers of the era because of their hardness.

But the princess would have other treasures beyond the imaginings of the typical Israelite bride: sacred amulets, beads, necklaces, and scarab rings almost without number—what might be called elegant "costume jewelry." Some of these might be of plain metals, or of ivory, bone, and fine wood. Others might be glazed with the vitreous substance used by Egyptian jewelers to coat all of the above-named objects. Egyptian glaze produced clear, deep-blue tones, secured from copper by a long process.

A higher form of vitreous glaze was enamel, really a melted glass, mixed with gum and painted onto a backing of gold or silver. It was fired to hardness at a lower temperature than would fuse the metal itself. Used to surface Egyptian jewelry, enamel produced rich and long-lasting effects.

The princess would surely have owned some inlaid pieces, for inlay work was a favorite device of Egyptian jewelers, who made tiny framework designs of upstanding metals and filled them with semiprecious stones, enamel, or faience.

Faience was the foundation substance of most of the Egyptian religious jewelry. It was a kind of plastic material, made by grinding up quartz and other materials, to form in pottery molds tiny forms of animal-gods, which were then treated to a high glaze.

A princess of Egypt would have acquired, as she grew up, a fabulous number of amulets—the small magical charms such as girls have almost always worn on bracelets, but with a more definite religious meaning. They might be fashioned of a semiprecious stone such as carnelian or lapis lazuli. Sometimes solid gold was used, but most often they were of glazed faience, blue, green, gray, or tan in color. They were frequently made in the shapes of principal god-emblems: birds, bulls, cows, cats, dogs, falcons, jackals, fish, crocodiles, lions, and lizards. Each stood for a particular god. The jackal, for example, stood for Anubis, a god protecting the dead. The bull was the deity Apis, worshiped at Memphis with high honors. The horned cow, with a solar disk between its horns, was identified with Hathor, goddess of love, music, and dancing. A falcon's head, topped by a sun disk, was the symbol of Ra, sun-god of Heliopolis; and so on, through the pantheon of Egyptian deities.

Equally impressive would be the princess's collection of bracelets and anklets. Her collection would have included (often in matching ensembles) those made of heavy, solid bands of gold; others of shell, ivory, crystal beads, and bone; of leather, resin, and alabaster. Often they were trimmed with plaques of crocodile skin. Flexible types in her collection would have been composed of beads of electrum (an alloy of gold and silver, light yellow in color), lapis, pale carnelian, and green glass with a large lapis scarab bearing the cartouche of the royal house of Egypt.

Could she be a princess of Egypt and not own a gold hairnet, a gold-banded tiara, a broad neck collar, and a breastplate or two? It seems unlikely. The broad collar, called the *usek*, was known in Egypt as early as c. 2500 B.C. By the time of Solomon's marriage (c. 960 B.C.) it was typically made of semiprecious stones alternating with rows of faience beads. It had insets of scarabs, and a golden clasp in the form, for example, of falcon heads. The rows of faience beads in such collars were made to imitate dates, flowers, or plant leaves.

We may also reasonably speculate that the Egyptian princess who became Solomon's wife was given by her Pharoah-father a pectoral, a jeweled breastplate that hung on a neck chain, not dissimilar from that found in the tomb of Princess Sit Hat-Hor Yunet, daughter of Pharaoh Senwosret II (c. 1887–1849 B.C.). The frame of this rare "find" is of gold, inlaid with precious stones, with the cartouche (or seal) of the king in the center. Two well-executed falcons, symbolizing the god Horus, look intelligently at each other from either end, across the beetle-shaped cartouche. Right and left of this scarab are *ankhs*, or keys of life. There are sun disks of the god Ra above the falcons' heads, and at the bottom, center, is a delicate little seated figure, suggesting immortality. The art details of this pectoral are worked out in fragments of turquoise, lapis lazuli, carnelian, and garnet—all inlaid on gold.

When Solomon's Egyptian wife appeared at a state dinner in her full complement of jewelry of her native land, she must have been dazzling!

ISRAEL AND THE DECORATIVE ARTS

The Israelites were not innovators in the field of decorative arts. Quite the contrary. The prohibition of the Law against making any "graven image" (Exod. 20:4)—a precaution against idolatry—precluded the development of painting, sculpture, and other forms of representational art. Yet there were some artists in Israel's earlier period (see Exod. 31:2–6). The kings of later Israel must have had artists too.

The Israelites, as we have seen, did not mine jewels, nor did they innovate in crafting metals into ornaments or in carving wood or ivory. They were consumers—to a large degree limited by their very modest standard of living —but not producers.

Along the western border and across the northern portion of Israel's land ran one of the world's most historic trade routes. It was impossible for the small country to remain unaffected by the commerce, the kinds of goods, and the style of the goods being transported on the Great Trunk Road from

Egypt to Syria and on to Babylon, Nineveh, and other cities in Mesopotamia, or in the opposite direction. Like almost all other people, the Israelites, from princes to paupers, were fascinated by jewels and ornaments, longed to acquire them, and decked themselves out in them once they did so. Their love of jewels is reflected in the writings of poets such as the author of Job (28:12–19) and of the Song of Solomon (e.g., 1:10–11; 5:14–15), and of prophets such as Isaiah (3:16, 18–24), Ezekiel (16:10–14), and Hosea (2:13). Abraham sent off his servant, in search for a wife for Isaac, well provided with gifts of jewelry for the woman he selected, for the man who would have to approve the match, and for the woman's mother (Gen. 24:53). But excavated Israelite cities have not yielded much in the form of finely crafted and valuable jewelry in comparison with the harvest found in Egyptian and Mesopotamian sites.

Rather untypically among excavated Israelite cities, Megiddo, not far from Tyre and strategically situated at the point where the Great Trunk Road passes through the Carmel Mountain range to enter the Plain of Esdraelon en route to Damascus, has yielded some outstanding finds in jewelry, especially in ivory carvings (Figs. 30, 31). This city exchanged hands several times in the two thousand years of Bible history, and its geographical situation, athwart the mainstream of trade in the Near East and close to Tyre, made it one of Israel's most cosmopolitan cities. At Megiddo, Israelites and Canaanites mingled with Phoenicians and Aegean islanders, with Egyptian craftsmen, Hittites, and Mesopotamians, and Arab merchants and camel drivers. No doubt thousands of Israelite soldiers, posted for a season at this pivotal military center, carried back to the home towns from which they had been drafted stories of ivory furniture they had seen in the military gover-

30. Design found on ivory carving at Megiddo.

31. A piece of ivory found at Megiddo which is dated around 1200 B.C.

nor's house, or of new-style earrings, pins, beads, bracelets, and scarab rings in swivel settings (Fig. 28) they had seen in the market stalls of Phoenician and Arab traders, or saw their general's wife wearing.

Would they not describe to their open-mouthed brothers the camel loads of elephant tusks they had seen at Megiddo, en route to Tyre for carving and inlaying purposes; and to their sisters the gleaming boxes they had seen for holding ointments, cosmetics, pins of all sorts, and jewels?

Just as the styles of women's clothing in the Western world were greatly influenced by Parisian designers, the styles for jewelry in the Near East were set by Egyptian and Babylonian jewelers in the Old Testament period—later by the Greeks. The Phoenicians especially were the transmitters of the Egyptian and Babylonian styles, occasionally improving upon the artfulness of their designs before passing them on to countries off the Egypt-Babylonian axis. Palestinian cities like Megiddo and Lachish and Hazor, which were on major north-south and east-west trade routes, were perhaps more significant as ports of entry into Israel of new jewel uses or designs, of crafted, decorated ivory screens, panels, inlaid furniture, and fine art objects than was Jerusalem, which in respect to Near Eastern trade was a somewhat provincial, off-the-main-track city, however important it was to the Israelites otherwise.

MEDICINE

In coming to an understanding of medicine as practiced in the lives of biblical people, readers brought up in the culture of the Western world, to whom the wonders of the medical sciences are almost commonplace, need first to picture an utterly different scene. For nearly all of the Bible period, medicine was closely associated with magic; in fact it is sometimes difficult to determine where one ends and the other begins. Primitive peoples—predecessors of those we meet in the Bible—held a demonic theory of the origins of disease; that is, disease was caused by hostile magic invading one's body and gaining a hold there, or by a person's breaking a taboo. In either case, since magic, sorcery, taboo, witchcraft, and the like were in the realm of religion, the practice of medicine was a function of the priesthood.

And to a very large degree, medicine remained in priestly hands in Bible lands until Greek medical practice penetrated the Fertile Crescent countries in the wake of the conquests of Alexander the Great.

MEDICINE IN EGYPT

In the third millennium B.C., in the period known as the Old Kingdom (c. 2850–2050), not long before the time of Abraham, Egypt seems to have known what may properly be called professional physicians—the first such in the world. But their professionalism was limited: they were repositories of traditional lore about useful "home-remedy" treatments; they had an organized pharmacopoeia consisting of useful herbs, unguents, and other substances; and they had a collection of anatomical observations acquired from the Egyptian practice of embalming the bodies of the dead, from battlefield surgery and treatment of wounds, and from mid-wifery.

From the period of the Middle Kingdom (c. 2050–1750) have come papyri which indicate there was a medical school. Among the contents of these papyri is a pharmacopoeia including some vegetable substances which are still in good medical repute. To these were added, by way of prescription for internal use, various outlandish items, such as ground donkey teeth, often foul-smelling, which one associates with the concoction of a witch's brew. At its best Egyptian medicine can be praised only for perceiving dimly that abetting the healing processes of nature was the soundest medical principle, and for a degree of diagnostic ability. Nevertheless, continued close ties to magic prevented any further development of medicine in Egypt throughout the Old Testament period. So long as the demon theory of the cause of diseases was held, the priesthood, as the expert and proper identifiers of the demon involved and the possessors of the appropriate incantations or methods of exorcism, controlled the future of this science.

The Egyptian god of healing was Imhotep, who started out as a human being and ended up as a god. As a human, Imhotep was minister to Pharaoh Djoser (also spelled *Zoser*) (c. 2850 B.C.). For Djoser he created the first large-scale monument made entirely of hewn stone, known as the Stepped Pyramid, forerunner of the still greater pyramids of Gizeh. Imhotep was also renowned as a scribe and a sage, and may also have been a physician. Not at all unnaturally for a people who regarded their Pharaoh as a god, they deified this most exceptional human being, Imhotep, about one thousand years later. However, the origin of Egyptian medicine was attributed to the god Apis of Memphis. Isis, sometimes depicted in the art of the late dynasties as a nursing mother, was "a healing deity of the highest rank," especially for children, who were adorned with her amulets to protect them from evil spirits.

The Edwin Smith Surgical Papyrus, now in the possession of the New York Academy of Medicine, dates probably from the period when the Hyksos were ruling Egypt (c. 1720–1550 B.C.), but it is a copy of an original written in the Pyramid Age (2850–2500 B.C.), and has been attributed to Imhotep. The Smith Papyrus is 15 inches high and rolls out to a length of 15 feet 3½ inches. It begins with treatments for injuries to skull and brain, and works downward to other parts of the body. We do not know whether this papyrus was a physician's handbook, or outlines of a medical professor's lectures, or some careful student's notebook. It has been surmised that the doctor-compiler followed the army and there studied and treated casualties. In any case, this priceless document, prepared when surgery was creating its terminology, has raised our appreciation of the skill of at least a few surgeons in ancient times when it came to treating serious head wounds such as a compound skull fracture. Its author was history's first empirical therapist of whom we have any knowledge.

MEDICINE IN MESOPOTAMIA

Lagging behind Egypt in building any empirical basis for medicine were the Mesopotamian city-states. In all matters of health the peoples of this region were intensely superstitious. The demonic origin of illness was firmly believed in, so that those skilled in the arts of exorcism were in constant demand. Since all forms of learning were concentrated in the priestly precincts surrounding the temples, and given the prevailing theory of diseases, from the priestly ranks inevitably came the exorcist-physicians. Among the Babylonians and Assyrians the relation between priestly sacrificial rites and exorcism was very close.

For a region with highly developed skills in mathematics and astronomy, the medical science was surprisingly primitive. Egypt has provided evidence that physicians practiced surgery, but not so with Mesopotamia. The Code of Hammurabi (a bit later than the time of Abraham) has a section that gives status to doctors, deals with medical malpractice, and sets down a tariff of prices for various services. But other medical texts, found through excavations, do not enable scholars to identify the drugs, herbs, and vegetable and mineral substances that comprised the physician's pharmacopoeia, or to determine whether anything resembling a science of diagnosis or prescription existed. The evidence suggests that there was not, and that exorcism and ritual practices were the chief reliance. Only a very few simple diseased conditions were treated in nonmagical (i.e., natural) ways; also battle wounds, burns, broken bones, and birth complications.

With the advantage of our hindsight we can see that the Mesopotamian priest-physician—whether he knew it or not—typically employed a three-part technique. First, he determined the exact nature of the spirit in possession of the patient; second, he expelled that spirit by the employment of the appropriate magical formulas and incantations in his repertory; and third, he prescribed a healing medicine or compound or regimen to help the person recover from the spirit-caused damage to his body.

The patron deity of exorcism was Ea, one of the chief "old gods," whose realm was the waters which were conceived to surround the earth. He was associated also with curative springs. It is noteworthy that Ea was also the patron of magic. The medical role of Ishtar, the Babylonian fertility-goddess, was related to childbearing and associated ills. The goddess Gula, once a goddess of death, later became the patroness of physicians. Shamash, the sun-god, prominently worshiped in Larsa and Sippar, was thought to help prolong life. However, there was no stability in the pantheon, for "young gods" kept appearing as new city-states, each with its own local deity, became politically prominent and anxious to promote its god to major rank, which sometimes required the "retirement" of formerly high-ranking gods and reshuffling of roles among the others. When Babylon became the most powerful element in the empire, for example, its god Marduk was elevated by his now-powerful priest-theologians into the ranks of the truly cosmic gods—Anu, Enlil, and Ea—and Ea was "kicked upstairs" to become Marduk's father. The same happened to Asshur when, later, Assyria became the head of this Mesopotamian empire composed of city-states.

In no cases of illness did an exorcist-physician make a "house call"; the patient was led or carried into the temple precincts. Incantations and exorcistic rituals intended to establish domination over the malignant evil present in the patient formed the major part of the physician's treatment. This was aided by the use of herbs, caper, mandrake, garlic, and other vegetable substances, which by some physicians were rightly or wrongly thought to have *curative* powers, but which to most were prescribed because they contained *magical* qualities. Knowing which incantation and which item in his pharmacopoeia possessed the right magic for the case in front of him was the Mesopotamian physician's chief claim to fame and his chief justification. We do know of one exception to this reliance on magic and religious tradition: there is evidence that castor oil was used empirically—that is, the results of its use, in various quantities and for various types of symptoms had been observed and remembered and passed along, so that by some physicians at least it was prescribed intelligently.

MEDICINE IN ISRAEL

The nature of the God of Israel made a difference in the way Hebrews regarded illness, and therefore its treatment. Whereas the Mesopotamians, more strongly than the Egyptians, believed in the demonic character of disease, the Hebrews regarded disease as an affliction sent by the one omnipotent Lord, usually a punishment. This belief is exemplified in many Old Testament verses: Exod. 12:12; 1 Sam. 5:6; 2 Chron. 26:20 are but a few instances. To the Hebrews, it followed that disease and ill health were signs that a person, or one's parents, had sinned, and so was being punished by the Lord. In Deut. 32:39, the Lord says, "I kill and I make alive; I wound and I heal." If sudden death, illness, and disease were due to the direct action of the Lord, then recovery to good health was a sign that the Lord had forgiven. It was the Lord one was dealing with. Hence the Hebrews, like the Mesopotamians but for a different reason, turned to the priest in cases of an illness, for it was the priest, not the doctor, who could help one to make things right for the sufferer with God. King Asa of Judah refused to accept the wisdom of this: "He did not seek the Lord, but sought help from physicians" (2 Chron. 16:12); for his mistake, the Chronicler implies, his disease became even more severe, and soon "Asa slept with his fathers."

To the Hebrew people as well as to their prophets, priests, and writers, there was a positive, observable connection between good health and a life lived acceptably to the Lord. The effect of the acceptance of this connection was to minimize the role of the physician and to elevate that of the priest and the other holy men, the prophets. It also strengthened adherence to the Law and promoted prayer and repentance. Perhaps it's no exaggeration to say that the typical Old Testament attitude of Hebrews toward disease was that the only reliable treatment consisted of fasting and sacrifice, repentance, and prayer for forgiveness. This is evidenced in several Psalms, especially 32:3–5, 38:1–11, and Hezekiah's prayer, Isa. 38:1–6. David fasted and prayed for his dying son by Bathsheba (2 Sam. 12:16–23).

Some scholars believe that the development of medicine was further inhibited in Israel by additional factors peculiar to Hebrew culture. First, the dead body of a human being was regarded as an object of horror, and contact with a corpse caused "uncleanness," which could be removed only by elaborate purification rituals (Num. 5:2–3; 6:7; 19:1–22). Hence learning about the degenerative biological processes attendant upon death through autopsy or post-mortem examination of corpses was closed off to the presumed experts on diseases, the priests. Secondly, the Hebrews had a unique aversion among Near Easterners for shedding blood, which was sacred—an aversion that inhibited the development of even minor surgical methods. Third, the Hebrews wrapped in mystery and reverence the biological beginnings of human life, as Gen. 4:1, Job 10:9–11, and Ps. 139:13–16, read in succession, demonstrate. Because of this attitude the Hebrews simply did not ask themselves, until Greek ideas began to permeate Palestine toward the end of the Old Testament period, how a human life could be generated, nor perform any investigative operations on the bodies of dead pregnant women.

While the prevailing Old Testament view of sickness among the spiritual leaders and the more fortunate and literate classes was that it was a punishment from God for sin, among ordinary Hebrews there remained a considerable belief in the diabolic work of demons. Living side-by-side with Canaanites, who saw evil spirits everywhere and had a large repertoire of incantations, charms, and rituals to use against them, it was easy for many Hebrews to conform. Indeed, the Hebrews themselves, prior to settling in Palestine, may have believed in magic for the treatment of disease as much as did the Canaanites and Mesopotamians. The fiery serpent (Num. 21:8-9) is an example of the belief in the magical properties of an object created to perform sympathetic magic, which is based on the principle that like affects like; in this case, a serpent image heals serpent bites. The Old Testament clearly and consistently denounces the practice of magic and magicians of all sorts: Exod. 22:18; Lev. 19:26, 31; 20:6, 27; and Deut. 18:10-11 are plain-spoken examples. But the magical treatment of diseases and afflictions never died out in Israel, as such verses as Isa. 3:2-3, 2 Chron. 33:6, and Ezek. 13:18-20 demonstrate. Even Elisha practiced it (2 Kings 4:22-37). The demonic theory of the cause of disease persisted in Israel because of the lack of anything remotely resembling our modern professional medicine, with its scientific basis; because of the unsatisfactory explanation of the official view that the all-governing God brought both illness and health; and because people suffering from mental disorders, plagues, and assorted fevers were constantly visible in daily life and did indeed seem to be "possessed."

Old Testament Diseases

The medical knowledge of the writers of the Old Testament books is so primitive that it is difficult to determine beyond reasonable doubt what diseases are meant by the Hebrew terms underlying our English translations. Nor do the symptoms, as they are described, help us much. There is some agreement among modern scholars and medical authorities, however, that the following diseases were found in Palestine in Bible times:

malaria (especially in the steamy Jordan Valley)
typhoid fever
paratyphoid
all diseases connected with the milk of animals
dysentery

enteric fevers (due to diseases of the alimentary canal and various para-
sitic worms)
leprosy
ringworm
erysipelas
boils
tuberculosis
pneumonia
smallpox
bubonic plague and other epidemic diseases
scurvy
eye diseases (conjunctivitis, congenital blindness, etc.)
diseases of newborn infants
epilepsy
dropsy
gout
poliomyelitis
palsy
sunstroke

There is considerable doubt that biblical "leprosy" was the same as
the disease now called "Hansen's disease," caused by a specific microorgan-
ism, and marked by patches of discoloration and thickening of the skin,
and by loss of sensation. According to Dr. Paul W. Brand, a modern authority on Hansen's disease, the disease *zara 'ath*, the Hebrew term used in
Lev. 13 and translated "leprosy," is "certainly quite different from leprosy
as it is known today." Dr. Brand believes that *zara 'ath* covers more than
one disease, "probably fungus conditions, ringworm, and perhaps psoriasis."
King Uzziah and the Syrian general Naaman were distinguished victims of
biblical *zara 'ath*, but the latter was cured by Elisha and the waters of the
River Jordan.

The problem over "leprosy" exemplifies the general problem of determining in a medically precise way what the Hebrew or Greek terms and the
symptoms described meant. In Mark 3:1–5, the "withered hand" that Jesus
cured on a sabbath may well have been caused by poliomyelitis, but we
can by no means be certain. Some conjecture that King Jeroboam (1 Kings
13:4) was seized by hysterical paralysis. The plague among the Philistines
(1 Sam. 5) after their capture of the Ark was almost certainly bubonic
plague. In addition to fevers and chills, the characteristic symptom of this
horrible, rat-spread epidemic disease is the appearance of buboes, inflamed

swellings of the lymph glands, especially in the groin. The Hebrew word for this symptom was translated "emerods" in KJV, but today is consistently translated "tumors." The Philistines returned the Ark, thinking perhaps that its resident God had caused the plague among them. But it is interesting to note that the gift that accompanied the Ark on its return home was some kind of representation, made of gold, of five golden tumors and five mice. Here is another example of the reliance on the sympathetic magic discussed above; but what is more interesting is that the Philistines seem to have made a medical connection between mice (or rats) and the plague that was ravaging their cities. These plagues moved along the traveled trade routes, carried by the diseased rats that accompanied shipments of food. Those peoples who lived far off the major commercial roads had a much better chance of survival than those living in the crowded, commercial, unsanitary cities.

Bubonic plague may also have been the disease that mysteriously destroyed Sennacherib's Assyrian army (2 Kings 19:35). Since there was no knowledge of the causes of disease, there was no defense against such a plague except an immunity built up in a person from a previous attack. In the absence of any medical understanding, it is no wonder that the Hebrews, with their religion, attributed devastating plagues to "the hand of the Lord." No wonder, too, that they sometimes listened to their Canaanite neighbors and acquired amulets to keep about their person, to head off dread diseases.

Old Testament Hygiene

The Book of Leviticus consists largely of legislation that seeks to establish a divine order of society in Israel. One of these legislative passages comprising the sacred Law, whose proper observance would provide the people with an approach to God for their salvation, deals with matters of hygiene or communal health (Lev. chs. 11–15), or what might be called principles of personal and social hygiene. In this regard the Hebrews were a unique people in antiquity. Having repudiated to a large degree the use of magic in the treatment of diseases, and thereby advancing the practice of medicine one large step, the Hebrews substituted the notion of a personal spiritual relationship between the suffering person and God. But there was also room in the Hebrew approach for examining disease from an empirical and practical standpoint. Chapters 11–15 contain regulations with regard to food, sanitation, infectious diseases, etc. It may be reading too much into these regulations to state that behind Leviticus lay a concern for public health; it is more likely that the hygienic aspects were a by-product of the religious concept of purification before approaching the Lord in ritual worship, and, by extension, of dedicating one's life to God.

In this connection it is noteworthy that the pig was a sacred, sacrificial animal in Canaanite worship. Everything about Canaanite worship was an abomination to Israel's spiritual leaders. So in the prohibition against eating pork we have much more certainly a taboo based on anti-Canaanite prejudice than a hygienic rule against eating a meat that is sometimes wormy. On the other hand, the separation from society of sufferers from certain diseases had a useful hygienic purpose, and the purification period prescribed for women after childbirth certainly abetted her recovery of strength.

The enforcement of all the laws of purification was left to the priests, and in the case of "leprosy" the rules were closely observed (Matt. 8:4).

Midwifery

Perhaps the persons in Israel medically most capable—at least in their one area of specialty—were the midwives. While they are not often mentioned in the Old Testament, there are two enlightening incidents (Exod. 1:15-19 and Gen. 38:27-30) in which they figure prominently, and the likelihood is that midwives were always present at a full-term birth at home—unless the parturition was unexpected and speedy—and are mentioned infrequently only because they were taken for granted.

A midwife may be looked upon as an early public health or visiting nurse. As early as the captivity in Egypt (Exod. 1:15-21), midwives had status. Some scholars hypothesize that there was a guild of Hebrew midwives, and that Pharaoh's order to them to kill Hebrew male babies on birth ran counter to their code of professional ethics. Verse 19 suggests that these Hebrew women assisted Egyptian mothers also. This passage also mentions the "birthstool," a kind of low, tilted seat that supported the mother in her final stages of labor.

The second illuminating incident in which a midwife figures significantly is the birth of twins to Tamar (Gen. 38:27-30). The interlocking of the bodies of the infants, described in vss. 28-29, would not have resolved itself naturally; the midwife's skill was required to turn the bodies within the mother's womb so that the birth could proceed naturally. In the process the baby whose hand appeared first was delivered second, and Tamar suffered some sort of perineal laceration in the process.

The art of midwifery is a very old one, based on the desire of one woman to help another woman in the usually very painful and exhausting process of parturition. Once a woman has helped another in childbirth, the knowledge gained is stored in memory. Further childbirths bring her further pragmatic experience. She becomes expert in the postnatal procedures and develops a sense of the necessity for cleanliness. She cuts the umbilical cord, helps the infant to take its first breath, washes the infant and rubs it in salt (Ezek.

16:4), removes any uterine sebaceous material from the mother and gives her a saltwater douche, cleans the mother and refreshes her with whatever warm beverage she has been taught by her predecessors to use. In Israel also the baby was wrapped in "swaddling" cloth. One midwife would tell another about her latest patient, until finally a body of knowledge based on firsthand experience was built up and passed along to the next generation of midwives, who learned also at first by watching and assisting.

The poets and prophets of Israel wrote of the experience of childbirth figuratively to express the pain and agonies the enemies of Israel would suffer (e.g., Ps. 48:6; Isa. 13:8; 42:14), or Israel itself as the Lord punished His people (e.g., Jer. 6:24; 22:23).

OINTMENTS, PERFUMES, AND COSMETICS

The distinction between an ointment and a perfume is one which the ancient world (and the Bible) never clearly drew. Explanation of biblical ointments and perfumes gets off on a better tack if the approach is by way of the principal ingredients and their principal uses. This approach also helps to make the first point: that ointments (including such virtual or partial synonyms as oils, unguents, salves, creams, and pomades) and perfumes (including incense) can be given separate discussions only with considerable repetition.

When ointments and perfumes are discussed in tandem it becomes evident that perfumes for the ancients covered a much larger slice of life than they do for us and were far more necessary to them. As the uses of these substances and compounds become clearer, the interlocking in biblical times of the sacred and the profane, the almost hand-in-hand relationship of religion and what we today call medicine and personal hygiene, also comes into focus.

Olive Oil

The chief harvest products of Palestine were grain (wheat and barley), wine, and oil. These three are constantly bracketed in the literature of Israel, as in Joel 2:18-19: "The Lord answered and said to his people, 'Behold, I am sending to you grain, wine, and oil, and you will be satisfied.'" By oil was meant olive oil, obtained by crushing the fruit of the olive trees which were widely cultivated in Palestine.

The versatility of olive oil is demonstrated by its many and important uses. Burned in lamps, it provided light for homes (Exod. 25:6; Matt. 25:3), and the finest grade, "pure beaten oil," was prescribed for the perpetual light in the sanctuary (Exod. 27:20). For cooking it was a staple ingredient (1 Chron. 12:40; Ezek. 16:13); probably it was used with many more foods than are suggested in the Bible (Num. 11:8, 1 Kings 17:12). Kings were anointed with olive oil (1 Sam. 10:1; 16:1, 13; 1 Kings 1:39; 2 Kings 9:1, 6); so were priests (Lev. 8:30) and prophets (Isa. 61:1). Shields, too, were anointed; scholars are divided as to whether this was an act symbolic of their dedication to the Lord, or a practical act to preserve the leather and help it deflect the weapons of the enemy (2 Sam. 1:21; Isa. 21:5). Though they washed their hands regularly before meals, the Israelites washed their bodies less than the Egyptians, and when they did they usually followed a washing with a gentle rubbing of the skin with olive oil to restore the natural body oils to the skin. Such a bath and cosmetic care of the body were required when terminating periods of ritual uncleanness or mourning (2 Sam. 12:20; 14:2). Anointing the hair was a method of cleaning and grooming (Ps. 23:5, Matt. 6:17). Only royalty and the wealthy could enjoy bathing in an artificial pool or a running stream on their property; indoors these same fortunate ones would be bathed standing, by servants who poured water from jars over them. After such a bath the body was anointed with olive oil to replace the natural oils of the skin.

Jacob twice offered libations of oil to the Lord (Gen. 28:18; 35:14), but after the patriarchal period this form of sacrifice is not mentioned; we find instead that oil is prescribed for use on the cereal offerings, either mixed with the flour or poured over the top (Lev. 2:1–7).

To anoint the head of a guest at a dinner party was an act of hospitality (Ps. 23:5; Luke 7:46). To bathe another's feet was an act of kindness and humility (John 13:5).

Least publicized, yet a most beneficient use of olive oil, was as an emollient. Palestine is a hot country during the summer (June 15 to September 15), and the weather varies hardly at all from day to day. The calm of a typical summer morning allows the temperature to leap upward toward its daily maximum not long after sunrise, and that daytime "high" remains for seven or even nine hours before relief is brought by the afternoon breezes from the Mediterranean. The air is dry, and evaporation is intense. Beth-shan in the Jordan Valley, one of the worst places for summer heat, has a six-month period with average maximum temperatures above 86°F. and a June 15–September 15 average high of about 95. This is hard weather for the skin of human beings. Olive oil (and other ointments, if one could afford them) applied before, during, or after exposure, preserved the skins of those who had to labor in the outdoors during the summer.

Thus, in addition to its ritual and secular uses, olive oil from ancient times was medicinally significant. It was a home remedy for injuries and hurts: burns, wounds, and abrasions of the sort that occur in the ordinary course of events among people who for the most part earned their living close to the soil. Olive oil is biostatic and it does not spoil. It keeps bandages from sticking to the wound. It thus promoted healing. Olive oil was an ointment in itself. Its standing medicinally is reflected in Isaiah's description (1:5-6) of sick Israel: "The whole head is sick,/and the whole heart faint./ From the sole of the foot even to the head,/ there is no soundness in it,/ but bruises and sores/ and bleeding wounds;/ they are not pressed out, or bound up,/ or softened with oil."

To the Israelites all the associations of olive oil were happy ones. When they wanted to concoct an ointment with a more exotic or stronger odor, or with greater healing powers, the people of the land most often used reliable olive oil as its base. In Mesopotamia the basic vegetable oil was sesame oil, made from the beans of an East Indian plant also called benne. Castor oil, extracted from castor beans and known to us as a cathartic, was another vegetable oil of the Middle East, one used by poorer folk.

In early Egyptian medical practice, if we may generalize from the evidence provided in the Edwin Smith Papyrus, the basic ingredients of the standard wound-healing ointment were a grease (animal or vegetable) and honey, in the proportion of 2 to 1, mixed with lint. The lint may have been any of a number of vegetable fibers, easily come by in a land that produced both flax and cotton. Lint is still used in surgical dressings. The grease used in the Egyptian poultices was often animal fat, obtained from oxen, ibises, and other animals native to the country. Honey is positively antibacterial: it kills bacteria within hours or days, in large part mechanically, by drawing the water out of their cells. Even diluted by two-thirds, honey prevents bacterial growth. The lint served to hold the ointment in place.

Mineral substances were not prominent in the *materia medica* of the ancient world. But the antiseptic qualities of copper compounds, especially copper acetate (verdigris), lead, and alum, in ground-powder form, were discovered in Egypt for use externally, especially in the treatment of wounds and the protection of eyes from bacteria carried by insects, especially flies. Later the Romans worked out a formula for the wound-dressings of soldiers, using large doses of copper acetate and lead oxide, mixed with oil and vinegar.

Resins, Gums, and Balsams

The odors of death, disease, diseased flesh, and mere bodily uncleanness were almost inescapable wherever men and women lived in community in the biblical world. The answer seemed to be to cover over the bad, the repellant, with the good, the alluring odors of ointments, incense, and perfumes.

This was the motivating source of the search for substances that could obliterate those odors with bad connotations and supply instead delightful, even heavenly, odors. It seems quite possible to many scholars that burning incense to the Lord (and to the various gods of other Fertile Crescent nations, of Greece, and of Rome) developed from the idea that a smell that pleased men would also please divinity. In any case, plant products with a positive, pleasure-inducing odor became almost a necessity of life. Olive oil, for all its usefulness, was not aromatic. Fortunately the lands of the Bible were homeland to a variety of shrubs and trees that yielded resins, gums, and balsams with positive qualities of odor and that lent themselves to mixing with spices and other perfuming ingredients to provide a wide range of olfactory pleasures. Some of these plants exuded fluids that could easily be smelled and gathered. Perhaps their discoverers also noticed that the resinous fluids performed a healing function in the life of the plant, and extrapolated from that observation the notion that they would heal the wounds of human beings. Indeed, curiously it worked out that these good-smelling oleoresins were also good-acting medicinally. Thus their incense-and-perfuming qualities and their medicinal properties were developed side-by-side.

Frankincense and Myrrh

The wise men from the East brought the infant Jesus "gold, frankincense, and myrrh" (Matt. 2:11)—all "treasures" of apparently equal merit. All were gifts worthy of a king.

Gold needs no describing. The other two, frankincense and myrrh, are gum-resins, that is, a mixture of gum and resin. Both are natural organic substances, and both are exudations from a plant. Today gums are used in the manufacture of mucilage, glue, and other adhesives; resin in varnishes and medicines. The chief variety of the plant from which frankincense was obtained (*Boswellia Carterii*) is shrublike in appearance, normally about 8 feet tall. *Balsamodendron myrrha*, a scrawny tree but with a central trunk, is regarded as the species that provided biblical myrrh.

Today there is no trade to speak of in these products. Their several ancient uses have been superseded by new products or methods. Our modern knowledge of these ancient treasures is therefore the result of the piecing together of fragments of information from ancient writers whose works have survived, from the journals of pioneer travelers in the regions of South Arabia and East Africa bordering on the Red Sea and the Gulf of Aden, and from the studies of biblical archaeologists with a specialized skill in the botany of the region that supplied the spice merchants.

During biblical times the exact source of frankincense and myrrh was a secret closely guarded by the rulers and merchants of southern Arabia and northeast Africa. Tall tales of the dangers that accompanied the gathering of these materials were concocted to dissuade the Greeks and the Romans, especially, from sending military expeditions to search for and seize the sources of an immensely lucrative trade. Today the provenance of frankincense and myrrh is well established: plateau and plains country in South Arabia, and in modern Somalia on the eastward-protruding "horn of Africa" that lies across the Gulf of Aden from the Arabian peninsula. In South Arabia, frankincense was found chiefly in the province of Dhofar, in what is now the most easterly portion of South Yemen. Myrrh was found farther west, in regions known as Hadhramaut, Qataban, and Saba (or Sheba), whose queen visited Solomon. The African location of frankincense was a strip of the coast between Zeila (just east of modern Djibouti) and Heis—a strip wide enough to include the inland Somalian plateau. Myrrh in Somalia was found in a similar strip extending eastward almost to the Indian Ocean. The two strips overlapped each other for perhaps 40 or 50 miles.

It should be noted here that South Arabia was a quite different social world from the vast desert portions of Arabia to the north. There was sufficient rainfall along the southwestern and southerly perimeters of the peninsula to support an agricultural, sedentary, and town-dwelling society. The Arabs of the region had long before Solomon's time given up nomadic life and institutions. Archaeology has demonstrated that South Arabians were masters of water entrapment and irrigation for agricultural purposes. Excavation at the site of one of their better known cities, Timnah, has shown, for example, that this commercial city was four times as large in area as Megiddo of Old Testament fame. And just as the Phoenicians were masters of Mediterranean ocean traffic, so were the South Arabians masters of international and intercultural trade plying out of their ports—Musa, Eden (modern Aden) and Canneh, to name but three—trade based on their commercial exploitation of frankincense and myrrh to India, the Persian Gulf states, Egypt, Palestine, Syria, and on into the Greco-Roman world. On return voyages from India these Arabian merchants filled the holds of their ships with the spices of India and Ceylon for their own consumption or for transshipment via camel caravan into the commercial marts of the burgeoning West. The domestication of the camel c. 1500 B.C. (a still disputed date) had made possible long-distance journeys over desert lands where water for pack animals was scarce, and the South Arabians were the major beneficiaries. They delivered most of their much-wanted goods to biblical lands by means of camel caravans following the so-called Incense Route, in a northerly direction, via Ma'in, Yatrit, and Dedan, into Edom, where some merchants might have gone due north on the King's Highway to Damascus and others west to Gaza and the Great Trunk Road to Egypt. As the caravans threaded their way along, they were forced to pay transit duties at the borders of every state or tribal territory they crossed. These levies were a significant factor in the high prices of frankincense and myrrh. Probably the taxes Solomon was laying on Sheba's produce were prominent among the topics Sheba's queen discussed with the Israelite monarch. However, the trade in frankincense and myrrh predated these rulers by at least 1,500 years, for in c. 2500 B.C. Egypt is known to have imported vast amounts of myrrh from South Arabia. (Both frankincense and myrrh—the latter especially—were used in embalming.)

Frankincense and myrrh were obtained by "tapping" the bark of the plants, not with a plug as in maple sugar operations, but by cutting the bark and peeling it off for several inches. Several such cuts could be made on one tree simultaneously. (The bark of myrrh tends to crack open almost spontaneously.) The gum-resins of both plants lie just beneath the bark, in small canals and cavities. When the plant is wounded by high winds spontaneously, or intentionally by man, this fluid exudes in an apparent effort to cover the open wound and thus to protect the plant. Frankincense in this fluid state is a milky color; it is translucent and aromatic. It will darken in color, to a yellow-green or brownish shade. Myrrh is red-brown. In both cases the gum-resins start to harden upon exposure to the air, and lumps of the stuff are formed. Left to harden for 3 or 4 months, some of these lumps fall on the ground and can be picked up; those left on the tree can easily be sliced off the branch or trunk of the plant and the harvest stored in a warehouse pending the fulfillment of an order. Both frankincense and myrrh—by now having become barely opaque under exposure to air— were shipped in this lumpy but firm state in bags. The pieces were ground into powder by the retailer.

Frankincense and myrrh burn readily, frankincense with a sooty smoke, myrrh with a barely noticeable smoke. When set aflame, the smoke of each carries its own distinctive odor: frankincense is judged to be more aromatic and myrrh more pungent. Myrrh is "bitter" only to the taste. But in use as incense neither was allowed to burn in flames, which consumed the materials too quickly. Properly handled, frankincense and myrrh merely smouldered, yielding their pleasant aromas at an economical rate of combustion and with much less smoke. They were totally consumed and were thus regarded as the perfect gift to the gods, who received every grain, man retaining nothing.

The major uses of frankincense and myrrh were three: as incense for use in religious centers and in homes, as a component of healing ointments in the medical practice of biblical times, and as a base for cosmetics and personal perfumes.

By derivation, "incense" means literally "that which is lit" or "burned," and also by derivation, the aroma of "incense" is "perfume," which means "by smoke." The "frank" of "frankincense" comes from French *franc*, meaning "free," "pure."

The burning of incense as a perfume was an ancient oriental custom. Though some scholars hold that the earliest use of incense was in a religious context, the weight of the evidence is that it was introduced from secular life into the religious rites of non-Israelites and Israelites alike on the theory that what smelled good to humans would be pleasing to the gods or the Lord of Israel also. Therefore incense was burned to propitiate the gods. There was another practical and insistent reason for burning incense in religious rites: a place where animals were constantly sacrificed would soon smell like a slaughterhouse without incense to counteract and cover up the sickening odors of burning flesh. In countries where the cremation of human corpses was sometimes practiced—e.g., Phoenicia—the need for incense burners strategically placed around the crematories was obvious. Either frankincense or myrrh was the major ingredient in the incense burned in Near Eastern religious rites. In Israel, frankincense (along with stacte, onycha, and galbanum in equal parts) was specified for the holy incense to be burned at the Tabernacle (Exod. 30:34–38), a recipe that was to be restricted to sacred uses. Frankincense alone is specified for burning with the cereal (grain or meal) offerings of first fruits (Lev. 2:15–16).

So many small incense burners have been found in home sites excavated by archaeologists, especially in the Iron Age at, e.g., Megiddo, Gezer, Shechem, Tell Beit Mirsim, but also in the Bronze Age, as at Hazor, that it is now clear that incense was regularly burned by all families who could afford it. Home-burning of incense would be for a secular purpose, such as counteracting the odors of a family living in crowded quarters, often cheek-by-jowl with domestic animals.

Medically, frankincense was also more important than myrrh in the *materia medica* of Old Testament peoples and the later Greco-Roman world. From the surviving writings of the Roman encyclopedist Celsus (first century A.D.) and others, we know that frankincense was recommended and used, in various formulas with other materials, to stop bleeding, to heal and clean wounds and abet suppuration, to mend cracked skulls, to cure ulcers and abscesses, to reduce hemorrhoids, and to cure assorted internal pains. However, myrrh medically held a strong position as the best resinous element in wound-salves developed by Egyptian doctors for Pharaoh's soldiers, as evidenced in a medical document known today as the Smyth Papyrus that dates to c. 1650 B.C. The Greek medical books that have survived recommend myrrh almost constantly as the resin to use in compounding healing salves. In Roman medicine myrrh is the frequent recommendation for application to wounds and old scars. What the ancient doctors didn't know was that myrrh is bacteriostatic—that is, it inhibits the growth of bacteria, not all types of bacteria, but those commonly found in wounds, such as *staphylococcus aureus*. Furthermore, resins are antiseptic and do not themselves decay. Thus myrrh helped the body win its battle against infection, most especially gangrene. The ancient doctors learned by observation alone that myrrh on wounds proved effective, and once that lesson had been learned it was never forgotten.

Balm

The word "balm" is a general word for any aromatic, resinous exudation from various trees or shrubs that is used medicinally. The word is a doublet for "balsam." Precisely what resin is meant the six times "balm" occurs in the Bible has not been determined. Some of the biblical references (Gen. 37:25; 43:11) imply a balm that was indigenous to Palestine. Jeremiah 8:22 speaks of "balm of Gilead." If Gilead is to be understood as the specific geographical source of biblical balm, then there are difficulties over the identification, for there is no known tree in Gilead today that produces a resin with the medicinal properties attributed to "balm." Some scholars prefer to leave out of consideration all Palestinian trees and shrubs in favor of *Balsamodendron opobalsamum*, which was native to S. Arabia, but which in biblical times very possibly was grown in several localities along the Jordan River valley where tropical conditions prevailed, including those regions of Gilead where the Jabbok and Nimrim rivers join the Jordan.

Other Ingredients

Aloes is known in the Bible only as an aromatic substance imported for burning as incense and for the manufacture of perfumes. Strictly speaking, *aloes* is the plural form of *aloe*, and an aloe is any of a genus of plants so-named, some of whom (African) yield a drug used pharmaceutically, others (East Indian) a fragrance. In the Bible *aloes* is construed as if it were singular. The source of biblical aloes was probably a tree native to India and Southeast Asia, *Aquilaria agollocha*, commonly known as eagle-wood. Another possibility is white sandalwood, *Santalum album*, from the same region of Asia. The wood of the inner cores of the trunks and main branches of these trees is permeated with fragrant, highly aromatic oleo-resins. In powdered form, aloes were easily blended with oils and resins or packaged in sachets. The Hebrew word translated "aloes" in Num. 24:6 is regarded by scholars as an error, and should probably refer to oaks—clearly a dignified native tree is implied.

Nicodemus brought a mixture of myrrh and aloes for use in preparing the body of Jesus for interment (John 19:39). The Jews did not embalm their dead, but they did wrap a corpse in strips of linen heavily sprinkled with deodorants and disinfectants. Aloes was also much used as a household deodorant.

Bdellium

This substance is probably a gum or resin (Num. 11:7); yet Gen. 2:12 suggests it is a precious stone.

"Holy Oil"

The "holy oil" for anointing rituals at the Temple was composed of four imported products—myrrh in a liquid form now known as balsam of Mecca, cinnamon, aromatic cane ("calamus"), and cassia—blended with the domestic olive oil (Exod. 30:22–25).

Frankincense and myrrh have been described above. *Cinnamon* was the bark of an evergreen tree native to Ceylon (*Cinnamomum zeylanicum*). Though cinnamon was used to give an aroma to wines, there is no record that cinnamon bark was used as a spice in cooking until the ninth century A.D. Its fruits, when boiled, yielded a fragrant oil. *Cassia* was the bark of a related tree, *Cinnamomum cassia*; it came from Ceylon, India, and Malay. The tree is native even farther east in North Vietnam and southern China. Cassia with its rougher bark was regarded as inferior to cinnamon. Ships from South Arabia would carry frankincense and myrrh to Persia (modern Iran), India, and Ceylon on their outward-bound voyage, and bring back cinnamon, cassia, aloes, nard, and galbanum on the return trip. These long voyages were accomplished without much danger once the mariners had learned to use the seasonal winds of the Indian Ocean, which blow eastward for a period each year and then reverse themselves.

Aromatic Cane ("Calamus")

This substance was a fragrant reed used as a perfume. In Ezekiel 27:19 calamus is said to come from Uzal, a town in Arabia of uncertain identification. Aromatic cane is generally regarded as belonging to the several species of reeds that yield sweet-scented volatile oils known as "India grass oils," native to India.

"Holy Incense"

The "Holy incense" was made of equal parts of stacte, onycha, galbanum, and frankincense.

Stacte is mentioned but once in the Bible, at Exod. 30:34. With no certainty, biblical scholars regard its source as either the storax tree, *Styrax officinalis,* or the opobalsamum, *Commiphora opobalsamum.* Its original form was as a gum exudation of trees. Stacte is a Greek word meaning literally "that which drips."

Onycha also is without certainty as to its nature or its source. Perhaps the most favored theory is that this ingredient of the incense burned at the Temple was a powder made from the operculum, the closing flaps or muscles, of a mollusk found in Red Sea waters.

Galbanum was an aromatic gum resin imported from Persia and perhaps India also. Its source is thought to be a plant, *Ferula galbaniflua,* allied to the giant fennel, *Ferula communis.* If the identification is correct, the stem and root of this tall perennial herb yield an amber-colored gum that, when burned, has a strongly fragrant odor.

The fourth component, *frankincense,* has been described above. By the time of Herod's Temple, seven additional perfumes had been added to the original mix: myrrh, cinnamon, cassia, aromatic cane, nard, saffron, and costus oil.

Nard (KJV, "spikenard," from the spikelike shape of the root and stem of this herb plant) is a perennial herb, *Nardostachys jatamansi.* It is native to the Himalaya Mountains. Today nard is a perfume used in India and other Asian countries.

Saffron was and is a spice extracted from the aromatic styles and thread-like stigmas of the flowers of certain crocuses, especially the *Crocus sativas,* which are dried and compressed into small cakes. *Crocus sativas* may have been cultivated in Palestine during biblical times; it is grown today in nearby countries.

Costus oil is obtained from an annual herb, costus root, found in Kashmir, which yields a volatile oil used in perfumes.

The previous paragraphs of this chapter have described the materials out of which the biblical apothecaries and the perfumers compounded their healing ointments and medicines, their anointing oils, their incense, perfumes, deodorants, and beautifying creams. Women may have been used to prepare materials for blending (1 Sam 8:13). The purposes to which the ultimate products were put were sometimes sacred, sometimes profane, occasionally both. "Oil and perfume make the heart glad," wrote the author of Prov. 27:9. This surely was the view of the common man, as well as of kings, princes, and the aristocracy. ". . . And the house was filled with the fragrance of the ointment," comments John (12:3) in a simple phrase that captures the potency, the pleasure, and the magic of the nard with which Mary anointed the feet of her Master at a dinner party in Bethany.

Ingredients for Cosmetics

There has never been a time in recorded history when cosmetics have not been used, and by males as well as females. Tattooing, scarring the body, filing the teeth, staining the skin with henna, dyeing the hair blue, are cosmetic acts only a step or two more primitive than pencilling the eyelids, rouging the cheeks, and painting the fingernails. A cosmetic is nothing more than something to beautify a person, according to the standards of the day.

When the Bible moves firmly into a historical framework, as it does with the Israelites in Egypt before the Exodus, cosmetics that bear comparison with those of our modern era were well established among the Egyptians. Out of the development of ointments for healing and incense for ritual purposes had come creams and pomades of various sorts to protect the body against the sun, to cleanse the tissues and tone the muscles, especially of the face and neck, arms and hands. These cosmetic oils and creams were highly perfumed, for the Egyptians loved strong scents. The Egyptians bathed more frequently than the other ancient peoples, and afterwards they applied, or had a servant apply, oils and creams to the entire body. The Mesopotamians and the Semites generally washed their bodies only for a special occasion, and anything resembling a facility for bathing was found only in the homes of the rich.

The composition of the Egyptian creams cannot be determined. It is thought that, for cosmetic purposes especially, the Egyptians, more frequently than the other Bible peoples, used animal fats instead of oils and resins as the basic ingredient: ox fat, goose fat, sheep fat, ibis fat, and the like. The perfumes of the Bible did not know musk, ambergris, or civet— the base of modern perfumes. Among the natural perfuming substances added to the base of animal fats were bitter almonds, cedar, citron, ginger, heliotrope, peppermint, rose, rosemary, and sandal. Among the spices mentioned previously as ingredients of ointments for healing and anointing purposes, calamus, cinnamon, and cassia were of course available to the perfumer, and so were the aromatic resins. Milk and honey were often used.

In the late centuries before Christ the great center of the perfuming trade was Alexandria. In Alexandria grew also an industry that provided the Near East with the containers for ointments and perfumes—jars, bottles, boxes, and bags, including sachets—made from alabaster (the finest), metal, stone, glass, and clay, in all sizes from the giant pottery jug for ordinary cosmetic bathing oil to a dainty scent bottle to adorn a lady's dressing table.

Before the time of Moses the Egyptians know how to macerate herbs in water and boil them until all their perfumes had been driven off in steam, only to be caught in fat-steeped cloths positioned above the boiling pot. Various strong-scented flowers were made to yield their perfumes into hot fat or oil. Certain flowers and seeds yielded an essence when crushed.

The botanical composition of the common perfumes of Palestine is not known. The phrase "vineyards of Engedi" in S. of S. 1:14 suggests one possible domestic source of ingredients for cosmetics; these vineyards may have been royal property. The rock rose, many species of which are found in Palestine, bears flowers in profusion which yield the fragrant resinous gum called *ladanum*, which was used in many perfume mixes. Probably other frequent ingredients were members of the mint family. The purpose of common perfume was to mask or obliterate bad odors; a large portion of the total volume of perfume bought was for household use as a deodorant. Many small incense burners made of stone and dating from the Persian period have been found in homes excavated by Palestinian archaeological expeditions. The late Dr. W. F. Albright concluded that these were not used primarily for cultic purposes, but for fumatory and for cosmetic purposes, especially after the return from Exile. As a fumigant the resinous smoke of perfumed incense attacked flies, fleas, and mosquitoes by upsetting their breathing mechanisms. When a woman wished to make herself more attractive, or simply wished to remove the odors of her workday, she lit a cosmetic-type incense and stood bending over the burner, holding a robe over her upraised arms to help trap the rising scents, as under a small tent. In this fashion the pleasing aroma of the perfume permeated her body and hair, as well as her robe. Perhaps in some such way Esther and the other maidens in the harem of Ahasuerus beautified themselves (Esth. 2:12).

Foot-washing

The Jews made much of foot-washing. Several times in the Old Testament (Gen. 18:4; 19:2; 24:32; 43:24; Judg. 19:21; 1 Sam. 25:41) the offer of a foot bath to a person who had completed a journey was an act of hospitality, no doubt much appreciated by the traveler who had come over the dusty country roads or filthy city streets of Palestine. Washbasins for foot-washing frequently turn up in Palestinian excavations (Fig. 32) and the Psalmist twice used this utensil as a figure for Moab (Ps. 60.8; 108:9), indicating that the washbasin was a familiar object. Soap was not used in biblical Palestine; foot-washing was done with water occasionally followed by oil applied with a cloth, especially on ceremonial occasions.

Washing Clothes

Fullers, cleaning fabrics and clothing, used either lye (Job 9:30), which

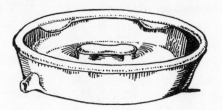

32. A foot bath from Samaria with foot rest in the center.

was probably a mixture of natron, alkalis, and fats, or a gentler alkali ("soap," Jer. 2:22; Mal. 3:2), a soluble salt (potassium carbonate) obtained from the ashes of *borith*, a soapwort, the bruised leaves of which had been discovered to be detergent.

Hairdressing

The Assyrians and Babylonians perfumed their beards, and some Jews after the Exile probably did likewise. The male Jew wore his hair long, and his beard also, but not without an occasional grooming by the local barber. The Hebrews were forbidden by their Law to shave their heads entirely (Lev. 19:27), and priests were enjoined not to make tonsures upon their heads (Lev. 21:5). These prohibitions probably were in reaction to the practices of the priests of the pagan cults of the people among whom the Israelites settled in the Promised Land. To the prophets, artificial baldness was a figure of impending doom (e.g., Isa. 15:2; Jer. 48:37; Mic. 1:16). Shaving the head was acceptable only under special circumstances as a sign of mourning (Job. 1:20); at the termination of a Nazirite vow, so that the hair could be dedicated to the Lord (Num. 6:9, 18); and when leprosy had been found on the head (Lev. 13:33; 14:8-9). Long hair was much admired (2 Sam. 14:25-26; S. of S. 5:11). The proscription of cutting the hair on the temples of males is still observed by strict Jews.

Nothing definite is known about the hairstyling of Jewish women: they do not appear in the monumental and funerary art that has survived, as do Egyptian, Greek, and Roman women. Dignified Roman matrons wore their hair in a high mass on the crown. A niece of Caesar Augustus is depicted with a row of curls atop her forehead and a beaded fillet above the curls, apparently used to keep the hairdo in place. Greek women often pulled their hair back in a knot, with a braid across the top of the head in front. Both Roman and Greek women dyed their hair, black or blonde, and wore wigs of human hair, as needed or desired. To what extent such styles from the Greco-Roman world penetrated Palestine we do not know—

probably very little. Biblical writers certainly deplored the excessive ornamentation of the hair (Isa. 3:24; 1 Pet. 3:3).

Egyptian women are shown wearing cones of ointment on the tops of their heads, which would melt and anoint their hair, faces, and necks as the dinner party or entertainment proceeded. This may have been widely practiced throughout lands of the Bible, for the worldly author of Ecclesiastes wrote: "Let your garments be always white; let not oil be lacking on your head."

Women's Make-up

In the field of cosmetics for purposes of beautification only, the Egyptians were the innovators. Ultimately the Romans, including men, became the most conspicuous users of perfume to the point where Horace, Seneca, and Pliny scolded their contemporaries, and Juvenal gibed that Roman men in Nero's reign thought themselves unprepared for a battle if they did not have, at the ready, cosmetics, perfumes, and a looking glass. In the lands along the Fertile Crescent, however, what we today call make-up, except for hair grooming, was used largely by women. Rouge, powder, and hair dye are not mentioned in the Bible. The scholarly consensus is that they were used by some wealthy Hebrew women who were exposed to foreign influences, but that they never achieved widespread use as they did in Egypt and Mesopotamia.

Eye paint. The eye paint used by women of the Bible was originally a mineral ingredient, mixed with water or a gum dissolved in water, to form a paste. At first no fats, oils, or resins were used. Galena, a lead sulphide, gave a black color. (The Arabic word for galena was "kohl.") Malachite, a copper compound, gave a brilliant green color. The popular fashion in Egypt was to paint the upper eyelid black and the lower one green. Galena had originally been used to treat various eye infections, and the copper compound was a common ingredient in Egyptian medicines. As cosmetics became more sophisticated and less medically oriented, galena and malachite were supplanted by the green resin of conifers and blackening materials such as burned almond shells and soot.

Another distinctive fashion in Egyptian eye make-up was to paint a bold black line just above the eyebrows and a narrower line along the eye lashes and the edges of the eyelids. At the outer corners of the eyes this line was extended to the edge of the surrounding socket of bone. The effect was to make the eyes larger, more noticeable, and alluringly almond-shaped. The various familiar modern representations of Queen Nefertiti exhibit most strikingly the effect of this eye-paint style.

The ingredients of eye paint were bought separately at the perfumer's shop, and were kept in linen or leather pouches, or in shells. Excavations of Palestinian towns have turned up many stone (limestone or slate) palettes found in the rubble of what had once been homes. Archaeologists have determined that these palettes were designed for the grinding and mixing of eye-paint ingredients. The paste mixed by the user was then applied with a "kohl stick," made of ivory, bone, or wood, which had a small, spatula-shaped end.

A typical palette was round, about 4 inches in diameter, with a flat base and a round concavity in the center for mixing the ingredients, about 2 inches in diameter. The wide, flat rim around this hole was often attractively decorated with various geometric figures and patterns.

The three biblical verses that mention eye paint (2 Kings 9:30; Jer. 4:30; and Ezek. 23:40) associate it with women of bad reputation. The first two of these verses in the KJV incorrectly read "face" for "eyes."

Rouge. The use of rouge on the cheeks and lips goes back to the beginning of history and no doubt much earlier. In the lands of the Bible, rouge was made from various vegetable extracts obtained from such common but seemingly unlikely sources as seaweeds, snails, lichens, and the juice of the fruit of the mulberry tree. Rouge was bought in a pot and probably most effectively applied with the little finger of a servant girl.

The Toilet Kit. A full kit of the woman economically able to indulge in cosmetics would have included a metal, polished bronze, mirror; the makings of eye paint; cosmetic spoons, tweezers, and a knife; a stone mill for grinding eye paint; a curling rod and an ivory comb; and assorted ivory, bone, and metal hairpins. The cosmetics themselves, including henna juice (see below), had their own appropriate containers, usually small, lidded jars. The various utensils for make-up and grooming were kept in a toilet box, normally of wood, the better ones with a hinged top. Some toilet boxes were exquisitely made, with decorations of gold, or inlaid with semiprecious stones.

Henna. The fingernail and toenail paint and the hair dye of biblical people was henna. More precisely, the cosmetic dye used was red ocher, essentially a hydrated iron oxide, which, in its mixture with other natural, earthy materials, provided pigments ranging in color from an orange-yellow to deep, coppery red. In biblical times, red ocher was most often obtained from the leaves of an oriental shrub or small tree, *Lawsonia inermis*, the henna plant. It was also used, especially by Mesopotamians, to color the palms of their hands and the soles of their feet.

Miscellaneous Beauty Treatments

A mixture of ladanum and myrrh applied to the scalp was regarded as the best preventive of loss of hair.

Superfluous hair was removed by tweezers. In Mesopotamia a pumice stone was used to remove unwanted hair from arms and legs. Bear grease was supposed to prevent hair from graying, and cosmetics and magic combined to provide vain brunettes with recipes to get them naturally blonde locks.

Aristocratic Greek and Roman women tried overnight facial masks (mud packs) comprised mostly of meal or of kaolin, a clay. After removing it in the morning, the ladies put on facial powder (containing white lead powder, a toxic substance), rouge, eye-shadow, and eyelid paint.

FAMILY EVENTS

It is strange that the Hebrew language has no word specifically signifying "family" as we understand it today. Instead, it uses most often terms meaning "house" or "dwelling" or "household" for the social group that lived together under the leadership of a father, a head of a family. (The Old Testament speaks not of "establishing a family" but of "building a house," e.g., Deut., 25:9; Exod. 1:21, though this lack is now glossed over in translation.) Nor has Hebrew any specific word for "marriage," regarding the event as simply the outcome of a contract between two families for the purpose of the begetting of children (Gen. 1:28; 9:1) for the further enlargement of families.

The strangeness stands out more clearly because the Israelite society was built upon the family, and the family as the basic social unit was dependent on a negotiated agreement between the heads of two families regarding their offspring and a publicly celebrated feast cementing the relationship of the bride and groom—virtually a "marriage" by standards prevailing in the West until modern times. Most noticeably in patriarchal days and in the period of the judges, the family formed a unit for worship, with its head (male) as the priest, and a civil unit, with the father as the military leader, the judge, and the disciplinarian. But while the father is the authority figure as well as the actual authority, his family—enlarged by slaves, sojourners, concubines, less fortunate relatives, and children of all of these—functioned as a true community, not only for personal security, but also for preserving the traditions of family, clan, and tribe and for passing them on to the newer members through instruction and ritual. (On the functioning of the family in the early days, see THE LIFE OF THE NOMAD, "The Family.")

Over the early centuries of Israelite history this socio-religious-economic entity, this small world of the family, within whose circle most of life was lived by its members, developed ways and means of celebrating those major milestones that mark the road between birth and death. Chief of these were the birth of a child, the child's arrival at maturity, marriage, and death, and these will be discussed in order.

It was characteristic of the ancient Hebrews to have seen all aspects of life within a religious context or, perhaps better, through religious glasses. It is a Greek and Western notion—not at all a Jewish one—that life can be compartmentalized into distinct and definable areas marked Religious, Secular, Personal, and the like, and that these various realms have some kind of autonomy of their own. The point here is that the division of this book between Family Events and Religious Events (q.v.) is, or would have been for both Old and New Testament Jews, a totally artificial distinction.

Another warning seems in order: A succinct setting forth of these celebrations and customs has to pick a point in Jewish history as the basis for the description, for most of them changed during the two millennia of the biblical period. The 8th century seems most useful, for the traumatic experience of the Fall of Jerusalem and the Exile had not yet had their effect on normal Hebrew family life, while some of the cruder elements and non-Israelite (e.g., Canaanitish) customs the Hebrews had adopted along the way had been at least partly spiritualized and made their own. It should, however, be kept in mind that a celebration or custom known to Amos or Hosea might have had a quite different form and religious content in the time of Moses, or even Deborah and Gideon. In some cases the difference in practices will be described as they appear within the two millennia under survey.

THE BIRTH OF A CHILD

When the time came for a woman to be delivered of a child, she was usually assisted by a midwife (Gen. 35:17, Rachel; 38:28, Tamar) and by one or more older, experienced, married women of the family. Just what a birthstool was (Exod. 1:16) is not known certainly. Some scholars believe it was designed as a support for the crouching mother. Others believe it was so designed to hold a woman in travail in a half-sitting, half-lying position that expedited the birth process.

The midwives of Exod. 1:15–21 reported to Pharaoh that the sons of Hebrew mothers were eluding his death edict "because the Hebrew women are not like the Egyptian women; for they are vigorous and are delivered before the midwife comes to them." This has often been used as evidence that Israelite women were built for easy childbearing and were delivered quickly. But it is probably better regarded as the quick-witted and evasive answer of the midwives to a Pharaoh who wanted to know why his orders were not being carried out. The Old Testament has numerous references, especially in the prophetic books, to the "travail," the painful work, of parturition. Isaiah, for example (26:17), probably reflected the actuality when he wrote: "Like a woman with child, who writhes and cries out in her pangs, when she is near her time." Rachel (Gen. 35:16) "travailed, and she had hard labor." The pain of delivery was probably regarded by the Israelite mother as a curse from God, as it is explained in Gen. 3:16.

As soon as the baby was born its umbilical cord was cut and tied, and it was then washed. Next the infant was rubbed with salt, perhaps because salt was recognized in folk wisdom as a disinfectant and skin conditioner or (as others believe) because of a primitive pagan belief, picked up from others by the Israelites, that salt was a safeguard against demons and the evil eye. The child was then wrapped from navel to feet in swaddling clothes which prevented it from moving its legs about during its first days, an activity that was regarded as harmful to soft bones. (The verb "to swaddle" means to wrap or bind an infant with cloths or long bandages.)

The work performed by the midwife and relatives in assisting the mother and cleaning and swaddling the infant was never regarded as breaking the law of the Sabbath if performed on that day. Whether the labor had been relatively easy or hard, afterwards the mother was proudly happy—doubly so if her child was a son—because she had performed her basic function of producing offspring. A child was regarded as a gift from the Lord (1 Sam. 1:19-20); a large family with several sons was the greatest blessing (Ps. 127:3); and barrenness was the worst of all conditions, regarded with contempt by more fortunate women (Gen. 16:4; 1 Sam. 1:6-10).

So at the end of a successful delivery the women present congratulated the new mother (Ruth 4:14-17; Luke 1:58) and all were happily excited, while the mother could look back upon her pain in a joyful realization of her accomplishment (John 16:21). The father, who apparently was never present during the delivery, was notified (see Jer. 20:15). If the baby was not a son, the father at least could be happy his wife was capable of childbearing (sterility on the husband's part was never considered a possibility); and if the child was a son, the event was doubly blessed. However, unlike the days when a son was circumcised and a child of either sex weaned, there was no feast held on the day when a child was born.

To the Israelites there was no life after death; the concept of a resurrection or of an immortality of the soul were postexilic in origin. Therefore in the Old Testament children were cherished as the only means by which a father could enjoy an extension of himself beyond the grave, for children perpetuated a man's name and kept the memory of him alive through at least another generation or two. Children were desirable also because they supported their parents in their old age, and sturdy sons, the more the better, guarded their parents from harm and most especially backed up their father with words and deeds when disputes arose affecting family property. Daughters left the family upon marriage, but sons remained, bringing to their parents a higher standard of living, a larger measure of security, and an easier acceptance in old age of infirmities and of death itself. Devotion to the Lord was seen (Ps. 128) as the way to achieve this reward of a large, flourishing family.

Naming a Child

In Old Testament times a child of either sex was apparently named the day he was born; in New Testament times a son was probably named at the time of his circumcision (see below).

Seth (a father) named Enoch (Gen. 4:26). Abraham named Isaac (Gen. 21:3). Joseph named his sons (Gen. 41:51–52). So did Moses (Exod. 2:22) and Hosea (1:4, 6, 9), among others. On the other hand Eve (mother) named Seth (Gen. 4:25), Leah and Rachel named Jacob's sons, and Hannah, not Elkanah, named Samuel. To complete the mixed situation, "the women of the neighborhood" named Obed, son of Ruth and Boaz.

The Israelites took naming persons (and places, too) much more seriously than we do today. To them a name was not just a label provided for convenience in distinguishing one person from another. A name was an essential part of the person so named. Names should be appropriate, for the person's name was regarded as a sort of duplicate or counterpart of its bearer; there was a mystical relationship between name and thing named. The name was conceived as influencing its bearer, and the name revealed something to a person who was told it. This was not a unique approach to naming, but one that prevailed among many ancient Near Eastern peoples.

Though they probably did not understand why they did so, fathers and mothers and neighbors tried to find appropriateness of name in such things as a national event (1 Sam. 4:21), some aspect of the birth (Gen. 25:25–26), the mother's hope aroused by her delivery of a son (Gen. 30:24), or the father's feeling of delight, as Abraham's naming of Isaac ("He laughs," Gen. 21:4) in the context of Sarah's laugh at the notion that she would bear a son in her old age.

Pious Israelites often gave sons names expressing their devotion by incorporating in them the general name for God, El (e.g., *El*hanan, Ezeki*el*), or the personal name of Israel's God, Jah, derived from Yahweh, and used in a suffix form, -iah, (e.g., Hezek*iah*, Jerem*iah*). These religious names, which can usually be translated into complete sentences or meaningful phrases in English, proclaimed the name-giver's faith and trust in the Lord, or expressed the parental hopes for the child at God's hands. Isaiah, for example, means "Yahweh is salvation." Elkanah means "God has produced (this son)." Eliakim means "God will set up."

Girls were more apt to be named after plants or animals. Jacob's two wives were called Wild Cow (Leah) and Ewe (Rachel), presumably regarded as appropriate by their parents in rural Paddan-aram. We cannot determine whether Deborah's parents loved bees and honey, or wanted her to have beelike qualities, or whether a bee sting interrupted her delivery, but there was some such reason for naming her Bee. Zibiah (Gazelle), Tamar (Palm Tree), Hadassah (Myrtle), and Susanna (Lily) are other names in this category. But boys, too, found their names in animals and plants, as Caleb (Dog), Jonah (Dove) and Elon (Oak) attest.

Prior to the exile children were apparently never named after a father or grandfather: there is no evidence of it in any of the genealogies, as (e.g.) of David's ancestors and descendants (Matt. 1:1–16).

By the time the Persian King Cyrus allowed the Jews in Babylon to return to Jerusalem, the names given to Jewish children were quite different from those described above. The naming of a son after a grandfather, living or dead, a dead uncle, and even a living father became acceptable and even common in the case of grandfathers. The most prominent Jewish families had lived fifty or sixty years in captivity in Babylon, and not surprisingly these families began using names of Babylonian origin. So in the postexilic Old Testament books we find such names as Zerubbabel, Shenazzar, Mordecai, Esther, Sheshbazzar, and Belteshazzar—all Babylonian. Conversely, names compounded with El and Jah now became less frequently given.

In the next stage Greek names began to appear. After Alexander had conquered the East as far as the Indus River and Greek culture had been imposed on Palestine, we find in the literature of the intertestamental period early teachers of the Pharisees named Antigonus, Tryphon, and Symachus, and pro-Hellenistic aspirants for the high priesthood named Jason and Onias-Menelaus. When Rome in turn became master of the Near East, some Jews began naming sons Marcus, Rufus, and Paulus, among others.

The Jews, who had the greater part of their numbers dispersed in foreign lands by force or by emigration, had lost their language as well. Even at the time of the Fall of Jerusalem (587 B.C.) Hebrew was losing out to Aramaic as the language of ordinary communication. The Babylonians adopted it as their official language throughout their empire in place of Akkadian. In the next (6th) century, under Persian rule, Aramaic became the common language of the Bible world. The next conquerors of Palestine were the Greeks. Though the Greek culture was strongly pushed as a policy of the Seleucid kings, Aramaic remained the language of the Palestinian people until the Mohammedans conquered the region in the 7th century A.D. and introduced Arabic. Parts of the books of Ezra and Daniel were written in Aramaic. Jesus spoke Aramaic, and from the cross quoted Ps. 22:1 in that tongue (Matt. 27:46).

A good indication of what had happened to the language and personal names by the time of the New Testament is given in the cases of the two dominant individuals, Jesus and Paul. To take Paul first: he was born in Tarsus, a trade center with an illustrious history, its rights as a free city respected by the Romans, and whose inhabitants thereby enjoyed the full rights of Roman citizenship. A Jew, the Apostle-to-be used two names, Saul and Paul (Paulus). Saul was his Jewish name; Paul his patrician-sounding Roman name, which he undoubtedly found preferable to use in his social relations in the non-Jewish world before his conversion, and which he ultimately came to use entirely because he wished to be known as a missionary to the Gentiles. In this use of two names Paul was by no means unique among Jews living in Jewish communities in non-Jewish cities.

Jesus' name a few hundred years earlier would have been Joshua. In Aramaic the name became Yeshua, which is what his family would have called him. "Jesus" comes to us from the Greek *Iesus*, a representation of Yeshua, which was a very common name in New Testament times.

A Mother's Ritual Uncleanness

In giving birth a mother incurred ritual uncleanness—that is, she became contaminated by what was regarded as an impurity. Her "unclean" state derived from her bodily discharges accompanying childbirth. Furthermore, the uncleanness was regarded as contagious, making unclean any person or object with which she or her discharges came in contact. This state of uncleanness, spent in virtual isolation, lasted seven days for a male child and fourteen for a girl. An additional thirty-three or sixty-six-day period followed in which the mother might not touch any holy object. (No satisfactory reason for the double period for a girl is known.)

When her prescribed period of purification was finished, the mother first bathed herself carefully and then went to a sanctuary and offered a pigeon or a dove for a "sin offering" and a year-old lamb for a "burnt offering" (poor people might substitute a second bird for the burnt offering sacrifice). These ritual rules for the purification of a mother were laid down in Lev. 12:2–8. Mary carried out this law after the birth of Jesus as recorded in Luke 2:22–24.

Secondary uncleanness, for example, impurity acquired by contact with the birthing mother, ended during the evening of the same day (Lev. 11:24–25) or, perhaps more exactly, at sundown (Lev. 22:7), provided the infected person's clothing had been washed and the body bathed (Lev. 15:5–8, 10–11).

CIRCUMCISION

Circumcision is the removal of the male foreskin by cutting. In the rite of circumcision, as practiced in Israel sometime after the settlement of the tribes in Canaan, the father followed the law laid down in Lev. 12:3 and circumcised his son on his eighth day. He used a stone (flint) knife, as did Joshua at the time of his mass circumcision of the people of Israel at Gibeath-haaraloth (Josh. 5:2–3). Some scholars feel that the instruction to use a *stone* knife in an age when metal knives (esp. bronze) were available, is a proof of the ancient origin of circumcision.

Circumcision, clearly enough, came to be regarded by Israelites as the outward sign of the covenant between God and Israel, as told in Gen. 17:10–14. But why circumcision came to be practiced by many peoples in the first place is another and more obscure matter. The situation is marked by paradoxes. For example, circumcision was not commanded in the Ten Commandments; yet when Israel developed a distinct national awareness, circumcision became the prerequisite for inclusion in the community. Again, Israel was by no means the only nation to practice circumcision (see Jer. 9:25–26), and it took a long time for circumcision to attain its ultimate significance as a Jewish rite; yet the Israelites early came to despise their constant enemies in the period of the judges and United Kingdom, the Philistines, as uncircumcised and unclean, to the point where a reference to the uncircumcised was a contemptuous epithet almost synonymous with Philistines (Judg. 15:18; 1 Sam. 14:6; 17:26, 36, etc.) Furthermore, the law of Lev. 12:3 is blurred by other passages which tend to confuse the picture: for example, Exod. 4:24–26, where Zipporah hurriedly circumcises Moses' son, Moses seeming not only to be uncircumcised himself but to know nothing of the rite, and Gen. 17:25, where Abraham circumcises a son at age thirteen, suggesting that circumcision was once a rite of initiation into puberty. Finally, the references to circumcision in Deuteronomy (10:16; 30:6) and Jeremiah (9:25–26) are concerned with figurative circumcision, "of the heart," rather than with the simpler meaning of the physical operation.

Despite these obscurities in the origins and first meanings of circumcision, by the time of the Exile and after the Return the concept of Israel as a covenant people became much stronger as the community, Israel, fought to preserve itself and its traditions within a succession of alien cultures imposed on it—Babylonian, Persian, Greek, and Roman. Now the concept of the covenant with Abraham developed as the meaning of circumcision flowered. To be circumcised meant reception into the community of the people which separated itself from its heathen neighbors and consecrated itself to the one true God preached by the great prophets of the Exile and the Return. To bring about this initiation into such a community a father could and did with pride circumcise his son, as he felt sure Jewish fathers had initiated their sons from time immemorial (see Gen. 34:14-16; Exod. 12:47-48). In this sense the day of a son's circumcision was a happy day, a day of pride for father, mother, relatives, and immediate friends. While there is no record in the Bible of a celebration of the circumcision of a son, it was clearly a day to be remembered soberly and with satisfaction.

Heads of families circumcised not only their sons but also their servants, both native and foreign, in accordance with Gen. 17:12-13. No uncircumcised foreigner could share in the Passover (Exod. 12:43-49). All proselytes who wished to become full-fledged Jews were obliged to undergo circumcision, an operation which for adults is painful for several days (Gen. 34:25; Josh. 5:8). In New Testament times the requirement of circumcision caused many controversies (Acts 15:5-11; 16:3; Gal. 2:10).

The Redemption of the Firstborn

When a mother's firstborn son was thirty days old or shortly thereafter, he was taken to the local sanctuary by his father, or by both parents once the mother had completed her period of purification, and there he was "redeemed" by the payment to the priest of five shekels of silver (Num. 3:47-48). The notion that the firstborn of man as well as of beast "belonged to the Lord" (still found in Exod. 13:2; 22:29b-31) was very ancient and probably was reinterpreted by the Israelites in steps, now hard to trace, from a pagan belief common to Semitic peoples—that the firstborn of all creatures should be sacrificed to the divinity in his role as giver of fertility. By sacrificing the firstborn, which "opened the womb," the channel through which life flowed—so scholars theorize—the ancestors of the Israelites thought to guarantee the ongoing fertility of mothers, animal and human. But the Israelites were an ethical and spiritual people in contrast to their neighbors, and in their Exodus experience they found a more satisfying motivation for the dedication of their firstborn *sons* (not as earlier the firstborn of either sex) in the fact that the Lord had spared theirs while He was killing those of the Egyptians (Exod. 13:14-16; Num. 3:13; 8:17). This process of reinterpretation was further supported by teachings that showed that their God abhorred the sacrifice of children (Gen. 22:1–14; Lev. 20:2–5). Such spiritualization of primitive beliefs opened the way for the redemption of firstborn sons through service to the Lord at His various sanctuaries, that is, by dedication to Him.

Possibly as late as Samuel (1 Sam. 1:19–28) this dedication of the first-born son to service at a sanctuary could still be practiced by the truly devout. That the Levites were preceded in such service by firstborn sons is shown in Num 3:41 and 8:16–18. But the Levites gradually grew in number and influence and took over entirely the religious functions apparently first assigned to the firstborn. So by the time of the United Kingdom at least, in the ceremony of redemption the father in effect paid five shekels of silver at the sanctuary to pay for a Levite to provide the service due by the firstborn son (Num. 3:46–51; 8:18; 18:16; Exod. 34:20). Ultimately the five-shekel redemption fee became nothing more than a religious tax. Meanwhile the sacrifice of the firstborn of the flocks and the domestic animals was continued unchanged. In the case of an unclean animal, like an ass, a lamb was substituted (Exod. 34:20).

Luke, a Greek, has somewhat confused two Jewish customs in his account of the presentation of Jesus at the Temple by Joseph and Mary (Luke 2:22–24). Only Mary needed to complete her purification (earliest Greek manuscripts and RSV read: "their purification"), and the sacrifices were to that end (see *A Mother's Ritual Uncleanness*, above). She and Joseph apparently combined two family events in connection with the birth of a son—purification of the mother and redemption of the firstborn son—but the rites were separate and distinct. In the case of the "redemption" of Jesus, Luke makes no mention of the redemption fee, suggesting instead that the presentation of Jesus was similar to the presentation of Samuel by Hannah and Elkanah, that is, to the service of God (1 Sam. 1:24–28).

To the Israelite and Jewish fathers and mothers of the Bible the rite we now call the redemption of the firstborn was simply a customary act that had always been done, as far as they knew, just as they were doing it. Their parental act of devotion and the small ritual that took place at the sanctuary constituted another family event that bound parents and children more closely together and made, for a while at least, their God more real in their lives.

Weaning the Child

Normally a child was breast-fed by the mother, though sometimes a wet-nurse was employed (e.g., Num. 11:12; 2 Sam. 4:4; 2 Kings 11:2). This custom was common also in Egypt (see Exod. 2:7–9) and Mesopotamia.

What evidence we have from the Bible and the study of folk customs in the Near East today indicates that weaning did not take place until after the child's second birthday and up to the third. In the highly melodramatic Apocryphal book, 2 Maccabees 7:27, the mother-martyr tells her last remaining son that she nursed him for three years.

A few scholars believe that a wife and husband lived entirely separately until the child was weaned, that there was therefore a three-year period at least between children, and that about seven children were the most one mother was likely to bear. But there is little beyond a reference in 1 Sam. 2:5 to seven children, as though it was the normal full allotment, to support this notion; and human sexuality and the close proximity of husband and wife in the everyday life in tent, cave, or home in biblical times are against it.

When Sarah weaned Isaac, Abraham "made a great feast" (Gen. 21:8). Very probably other fathers and mothers through the biblical era celebrated a weaning in their families whenever circumstances permitted, but there was no law about it. Still, to have brought a child through infancy (whose perils were almost beyond the imaginings of medically advantaged parents in the West today) was clearly an occasion for rejoicing and a release, temporarily anyway, of the mother.

MARRIAGE

The Negotiations

Our modern concepts of marriage and of dating practices connected with "falling in love" make it difficult to comprehend the quite different approach that prevailed among the Israelites. For one thing, the prime mover in marriages in Palestine, whether in 1200 B.C. or 30 A.D., was not a young man freely choosing a girl (and being accepted equally freely by her), without much reference, if any, to parents on either side. The prime mover was the father of a son of marrying age. Next most important was the father of the young woman. It was the duty of these fathers, and to a lesser exent their wives, to arrange the best possible marriage for their children after they had passed the time of puberty. Marriage was an agreement between two heads of families, not between two individuals who were "in love."

The typical Israelite family had a restricted social circle, consisting of relatives, neighbors in the town or village, and a few clansmen living at a distance with whom contacts had been kept up. From this small world the father and mother of the prospective bridegroom surveyed their prospects for a fitting wife for their son. Once a likely wife had been identified—only occasionally one actually longed for by the son (e.g., Gen. 34:4; Judg. 14:2) —a question would be asked of the girl's father or guardian, and if no rebuff was encountered, negotiations were begun. Once the two fathers had agreed to the match, the young woman could do nothing but accept; after all, her father had authority to sell her into concubinage if he wished.

The negotiations between the two fathers were primarily with regard to the size of the *mohar*, the Hebrew word (found in Gen. 34:12; Exod. 22:16; 1 Sam. 18:25) meaning a sort of dowry in reverse. The original idea of the *mohar*, apparently, was that of a purchase price paid by the father of the groom to the father of the bride. It may also be thought of as a sum paid to the father of the young woman for the loss of her services as a helper to his wife in the running of his household, for a bride left her home forever to join her husband in his father's household. The groom's father was the gainer; the bride's the loser in economic terms.

Still further qualifications have to be made in the notion that marriage involved a payment to the bride's father for the loss of his daughter, because even in the Old Testament instances can be found which do not fit the generalization. Rachel and Leah, for example, charge Laban with "using up the money given for us" (Gen. 31:14–16). Now Jacob's *mohar* for his wives had been paid in labor to Laban, not in cash (Gen. 29:18–21, 27–28); so the charge was irrelevant unless the practice, in Paddan-aram at least, was to return ultimately the whole or a significant part of the *mohar* to the daughters, presumably as a kind of insurance fund for them in case of the death of their husbands. In two cases, at least, the girl's father gave her, as a true dowry, a field (Caleb, Judg. 1:12–15; and Job, 42:15). In later centuries a girl's father apparently often kept the *mohar* intact, as a kind of trust fund for her use in a time of trouble.

Other young men who performed a *mohar* of service to the father of the girl were Othniel to Caleb (Judg. 1:12–13) and David to Saul (1 Sam. 18:25).

Fifty shekels of silver is regarded by authorities as an average *mohar*. This figure is put forward, however, not on the basis of any plain biblical statement on the subject but because fifty shekels appears as a penalty to be paid to the father by the man who rapes a virgin, who must then marry her (Deut. 22:28–29). Also, Pharoah is known to have bought girls at Gezer for his harem at fifty shekels apiece. The amount of the *mohar* could of course vary widely with a family's circumstances.

There is little evidence to determine the ages at which boys and girls were betrothed. It seems likely to most scholars that the young men worked with their fathers several years after puberty partly to become experienced in the family's mode of earning a living, and partly to assist in the saving of enough money to pay the *mohar* and make a gift of jewelry to the bride to deck her out for her wedding and give her permanent enjoyment, the jewelry becoming hers for ultimate disposal. So, except for royal princes and sons of wealthy families, twenty is regarded as a likely age for a man to be married, and fifteen for an attractive girl. For a man, marriage was the only conceivable state; bachelorhood is never mentioned as a viable alternative.

Though not common, it was entirely possible that the young people whose marriage was in the hands of their respective fathers knew each other beforehand and even had come to enjoy each other's company. While girls were kept busy at practical household tasks and enjoyed no social life as we understand it, they were not kept in seclusion, nor did they wear veils when outside the home, as have Moslem women traditionally. The few leisure hours they knew were spent with their mothers in tent or house, and only on special occasions, as when celebrating a military victory, would they appear in the squares of a town or city. Then the older girls would play timbrels and perhaps dance in the parade. In their work in the fields (Ruth 2:2–3), with their flocks (Gen. 29:6), or in fetching water from the neighborhood well (Gen. 24:13, 1 Sam. 9:11), girls might meet boys assigned similar tasks by their families, in a normal, healthy way. At harvest festival times, too, there would be more boy-girl encounters, with singing and dancing participated in by the whole community.

The Betrothal

Once the negotiations of the fathers were concluded, the acquiring of a wife involved a further two-step process: the betrothal and the wedding. Of these, the betrothal was legally the more significant. The Bible tells us little about the biblical equivalent of our "engagement," but the business part of a betrothal may be likened to the modern-day closing of a sale of real estate from one party to another, the difference being the presence of invited guests, mostly relatives. It was a private agreement, not a religious or civil contract. Father and groom on their part appeared and made payment of the agreed-upon *mohar*. The father of the bride presumably made some statement according to formula, such as Saul is said to have made to David (1 Sam. 18:21): "You shall now be my son-in-law."

After the Exile, in some Jewish communities the groom spoke or read a declaration in response to the girl's father, if we may generalize at all from evidence found in the Jewish colony at Elephantine in Egypt, where a groom stated: "I came to thy house for thee to give me thy daughter . . . to wife; she is my wife and I am her husband from this day and forever." He thus took legal possession of her, though not yet physical. One oft-used Hebrew word for "husband" is more accurately translated "owner." Nevertheless, that marriage was (or became) more than a purchase, that it was essentially a covenant honorable among God-fearing men, is constantly proclaimed in the Bible, from Gen. 2:24 to Ezek. 16:8 to Eph. 5:21–33.

In a betrothal ceremony after the Exile, once the groom had made his pronouncement it appears that the assembled guests added their blessing upon the couple. The act of betrothal was undoubtedly followed by a feast, after which the groom and his parents returned to their home, the bride remaining in her father's house until the wedding, an interval which varied in length. The betrothal behind them, it was extremely difficult for groom, bride, or bride's father to withdraw. The laws of Israel recognized the change in status of man and woman by excusing him from military service until after his marriage (Deut. 20:7). The groom's vested interest in his bride's virginity was supported by stringent laws against her rape in the interval between her betrothal and marriage (Deut. 22:23–27). In the presence of men outside her home, the bride-to-be wore a veil, even when encountering her betrothed (Rebekah, Gen. 24:65).

The Wedding

The agreement between two families, begun with the negotiations (see above) was fulfilled on the first day of the wedding celebration when the betrothed woman was taken from her father's house to the house of the bridegroom.

The best description we have of the bridal procession in biblical times is found in the second-century Apocryphal book, the First Book of Maccabees. In 9:37–39 is narrated the conducting of the bride, with "a large escort" of friends, to a predetermined point of meeting with her bridegroom, who "came out with his friends and his brothers to meet them with tambourines and musicians and many weapons." To read S. of S. 3:6–8 immediately afterwards is to recognize, beneath the poetry, the same scene of a procession carrying the bride, as seen by the bridegroom and his party, who have already arrived at the meeting place. This procedure may be regarded as normal or typical, but not necessarily demanded. The bridegroom may often have fetched his bride at her father's house.

Probable also is that the meeting place of the two parties immediately became the scene of much traditional singing, dancing, and reciting of love poems accompanied by musical instruments (see Ps. 78:63; Ezek. 33:32; Jer. 7:34)—poems such as those found in the Song of Solomon, which is now commonly regarded as a collection of lyrics for use at weddings. Amid all the music and chatter, happiest of all the voices, Jeremiah suggests (16:9) were those of the bridegroom and the bride.

The bride was heavily veiled (S. of S. 4:1, 3; 6:7) and remained so until the marriage was consummated on the first night (see Gen. 24:65). This explains how Laban was able to substitute Leah for Rachel as Jacob's bride (Gen. 29:23–25). The bride was adorned with all the jewels she possessed

(Isa. 61:10; Jer. 2:32), some of which were usually given to her by her husband-to-be. She was dressed in bright colors (Ps. 45:14), and did not stint in her use of perfumes. Ezekiel's description of Israel, the maiden-queen, 16:8–14, may be drawn from a true-life bride. The bridegroom wore a diadem (Isa. 61:10), a simple type of metal crown in the form of a headband, or a garland of flowers twisted and bound into the form of a wreath and placed on his head. The bride, too, wore an ornamental headdress wound about her head, bound with a narrow gold or silver headband, suggesting the apparel of a queen, sometimes with a garland of flowers added (Ezek. 23:42).

From the evidence cited above it appears that the relatives and close friends of both bride and bridegroom, during the procession and at the feast at the bridegroom's house, treated the couple as if they were indeed the queen and the king implied by the diadems and the garlands. Each is carried to the meeting place on a litter. Their every wish is obeyed by bridesmaids (Ps. 45:14) and friends of the groom, including his "best man" (Judg. 14:20; John 3:29). Some of the male relatives forming the escort carry swords, as if they were royal bodyguards. At the point where the parties meet, the bride is lifted onto the litter of her bridegroom, which has been adorned for the occasion and is likened by the author of S. of S. to a palanquin of Solomon's (3:9–11). Now the procession, doubled in size, moves in the twilight towards the home of the bridegroom, a merry procession, lighted by torchbearers, accompanied by "tambourines and musicians." What bride in all Israel would not thrill to be honored as a queen on "Solomon's litter"? What bridegroom would not stand a little taller to be referred to as the "king," or fail to thrill at hearing his friends singing praises to the beauty of his bride?

Beneath the outward gaiety and ecstasy, however, lay a deeper significance to the journey together to the bridegroom's house. Now the bride has passed from the authority of the father to that of her husband. Now the process begun with the negotiations and carried on through the betrothal has been completed. He is now her owner, her lord, her master.

The procession perhaps stops along the route to rest the litter-bearers and to provide occasions for another song, another poem, a dance in honor of the bride, another blessing from well-wishers. Especially to be remembered by the couple are the blessings of relatives, such as that given to Rebekah as she set out for Isaac's home (Gen. 24:60).

The true wedding feast (e.g., "the marriage feast" of Matt. 22:2) followed the arrival of the bride and bridegroom at the latter's home (which might be but a room in his father's house, if the family was not well-to-do). At the feast the wine flowed (see John 2:1–10) and conviviality reigned. There was more music-making, dancing, singing, asking of riddles (Judg. 14:10–

18), and other simple forms of enjoying a mixed company of persons fond of one or both of the married couple. Eventually the couple retired to the wedding chamber or tent reserved for them and their act of physical union, and the guests withdrew.

The celebration, however, lasted for a week, if we may generalize from Gen. 29:27 and Judg. 14:17. Jacob wished to break off his marriage with Leah on discovering the deceit played on him, but Laban persuaded him to continue to enjoy the marriage chamber with her throughout the week's festivity. (As both biblical references above show, when the bridegroom was in a foreign country or far from his paternal home, the feast was given in the home of the bride's father or head of her family.) Not everybody stayed the whole week or returned for more celebrating every late afternoon, for the demands of ordinary life were heavy on ordinary folk in Palestine. But each evening for the week brought some renewal of the festivities and those who had been invited in the first place were warmly received until the week had expired, when all reverted to their normal routine.

If marriages in the Bible were celebrated generally across a seven-day period, rather than for five or ten or two days, it is probably due to an underlying belief that the number "seven" was the sacred, holy number. This attitude toward "seven" prevailed from ancient times to the book of Revelation, and from Mesopotamia to Egypt. The number "seven" is used symbolically throughout the Bible, so much so that it is sometimes difficult to determine when "seven" is simply numerical. The ideal number of sons was "seven" (Ruth 4:15; Job 1:2; Acts 19:14). Ritual defilements lasted "seven" days. The festivals of Passover and Tabernacles lasted "seven" days. Dozens of other instances could be used of reverence towards "seven," which obviously was considered the right, the perfect number for important things.

The most popular times of the year for weddings were spring, after the rainy season had ended (see S. of S. 2:10–14) and before the harvesting of grain crops began, and autumn, after the harvesting of fruit crops and the work of the year was over for farming families.

DEATH

A considerable degree of uncertainty pervades the significance or meaning of the rites and customs associated with death as delineated in the Bible. The various theories put forward to explain them are beyond the scope of this book. The discussion here, therefore, will be limited almost exclusively to a description of the activities that followed upon the death of a member of a family. For a discussion of the biblical views about death, the article "Death" in the *Interpreter's Bible Dictionary* is recommended.

Mourning

When death came to a member of the family, all the surviving members, including slaves, became mourners immediately and expressed their grief aloud, with much moaning, smiting of breasts, and ejaculations referring to the deceased person or to the Lord. Then—just as Joseph closed the eyes of his dead father, Jacob (Gen. 46:4), and then kissed him—it is probable that the bestowal of the last tokens of affection fell upon the oldest son present, or the most composed person at hand. Neighbors would be attracted and the circle of mourners would extend to the nearby housetops and streets. Someone would be the first of many to rend his outer garment and wrap his waist with coarse sackcloth. Others would lay aside their head ornaments and tear at their hair, while increasing their moanings and wailings. Others would retire momentarily and return with part of their beards shaved off, or a bald spot (tonsure) on their heads (Job 1:20). Still others would strew dust over their heads (Ezek. 27:30), remove their shoes, or sit on the ground in ashes (Esth. 4:3), and in real anguish cut their flesh with a knife (Jer. 48:37) until blood appeared. Such were the gestures of grief.

That the laws prohibiting cuttings, shavings, and tonsures (Lev. 19:28; 21:5; Deut. 14:1) had no apparent effect on these ancient forms, common to all Semites, is clear, for they are mentioned many times in the Old Testament (e.g., Jer. 48:37; Mic. 1:16). These ways of showing grief are most clearly delineated in the writings of the prophets in their descriptions of the grief-stricken state to which Israel will be reduced because of her sins. Of these grief-induced activities the most frequently mentioned in the historical narratives are rending one's clothes on hearing the news, donning sackcloth, and fasting. David, for example, "rent his clothes, so did all the men who were with him; and they mourned and wept until evening for Saul and Jonathan" (2 Sam. 1:11–12). He ordered Joab and all the men present to "rend your clothes, and gird on sackcloth, and mourn before Abner" (2 Sam. 3:31).

If they had the means to do so, families employed professional mourners, usually women. The function of these professionals was to assure an orderly and ritually proper ceremony. They were both soloists and orchestral conductors of the expressions of grief and tears that were most appropriately rendered at the high points of the ritual of death, burial, and mourning. They also added, on their own part, lyrical and consoling thoughts to elevate the occasion and assuage the grief of the bereaved. For a fuller discussion of the professionals, see "Mourners" in THE PROFESSIONAL LIFE.

Burial

The next responsibility of the mourning family was to prepare the body promptly for burial, for the notion of the uncleanness of a corpse ran deeply in the Law and the prophets (e.g., Lev. 21:1–4; 22:4; Num. 19:11–16; Hag. 2:13). Furthermore, to be left unburied, so that dogs or jackals or vultures might prey on the flesh, was the worst of all possible fates and dreaded accordingly (1 Kings 14:11; Jer. 16:4; Ezek. 29:5). As to exactly how the preparation for burial was done, we know nothing more than is told in the Gospels (Matt. 27:59; John 11:44; 19:39–40).

The Israelites, known after the Exile as Jews, did not cremate or embalm corpses. True, Joseph ordered the corpse of his father, Jacob, embalmed (Gen. 50:2–3) and he himself was embalmed (Gen. 50:26), but in both cases the death happened in Egypt, where the practice was general, and the body had to be transported a long way to its burial place in Palestine.

The corpse was buried in the clothes worn in life, a fact known by the presence of surviving pins and ornaments found amid the dusty remains of human bones in opened-up tombs. No coffin was used (see 2 Kings 13:21). The body was carried on a bier, both in Old Testament times (2 Sam. 3:31) and New (Luke 7:14). Very probably, because of the uncleanness taboo, the body was put into a grave or tomb on the day of the death; this was certainly true of the corpse of a criminal hung on a tree (Deut. 21:22–23).

For poor people the grave was simply a ditch laid open, into which the uncoffined body was set down and covered over with dirt. In the Kidron Valley, just east of Jerusalem, was a trench where the corpses of friendless foreigners and condemned criminals could be dumped (see Jer. 26:23; 2 Kings 23:6). For the reasonably well-off there were caves that could be purchased or dug out on the family property where the bodies could be laid to rest. For the wealthy and royalty there were tombs cut into the relatively soft but fairly waterproof limestone rock (Fig. 33), found throughout most of the inhabited parts of Palestine, in which ledges were fashioned around the walls to lay bodies on, or niches cut into the face of the walls (Fig. 34). Such tombs had room for many corpses, so the euphemistic biblical phrases employed for "he died" and "he was buried"—"he was gathered unto his people" (Abraham, Gen. 25:8) and "he slept with his fathers" (David 1 Kings 2:10)—are quite appropriate.

When a new corpse was laid to rest in a tomb of a family of substance, incense was burned. The "very great fire" made in honor of King Asa (2 Chron. 16:14) is understood by scholars as a reference to the burning of much incense in his tomb.

If a privately owned cave or tomb became full of dried bones of ancestors, some of the remains would be placed in a stone box or coffer, also called an ossuary, thereby making room for additional corpses (Fig. 35).

Tombs dating to the earlier centuries of the biblical epoch have been

33. The entry into a tomb complex north of Jerusalem (the so-called Tombs of the Sanhedren).

found to contain objects such as a weapon or a pot or a favorite personal possession, as if it had been thought that these objects would prove useful to the dead person in a later existence. However, in tombs dating to later centuries very little such material has been found among the remains. Since the Hebrews had no highly developed view of an afterlife, either of the body or of the soul, until about the second century B.C., the significance of these objects remains mysterious. Throughout the Old Testament, life is adjudged to be its own reward if a man attained a fullness of years, had sons, and was gathered to his own.

A proper cave or tomb had some means of being closed tight to prevent hungry, roaming dogs or jackals from entering (Fig. 36).

The traditional period of strict mourning lasted seven days (Gen. 50:10) and included fasting (1 Sam. 31:13). Some biblical instances indicate that public or private fastings lasted across the seven-day period, but the majority suggest that the fast was broken after sundown on each day. In any case, mourners for an immediate relative would refrain throughout the period from washing and using perfumes (2 Sam. 12:20; 14:2). Since the house of the dead person had been made unclean by the corpse, neighbors brought

34. A tomb from the first century A.D. with a niche for the body carved out of the limestone walls (in the so-called Tomb of the Kings, Jerusalem).

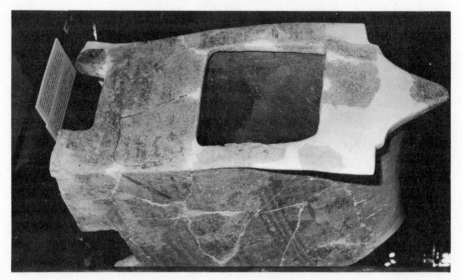

35. An ossuary from the Chalcolithic Period (Rockefeller Museum, Jerusalem).

36. The opening to a tomb of the first century A.D. Note the stone which rolls over the door (from the so-called Tomb of the Kings, Jerusalem).

food to the mourning family (Jer. 16:7) at the end of the day of the burial, during which all mourners had fasted (2 Sam. 1:12), and each day thereafter. The Jeremiah reference also mentions "the cup of consolation," which is thought to be a cup of wine also brought by consoling neighbors.

The period of mourning in the time of the Maccabees (2nd century B.C.) seems to have been concluded with a prayer and a sacrifice of atonement for the sins of the dead (see 2 Macc. 12:39-46). But the notion of atoning for the sins of the dead was connected closely with the new concept of resurrection (vvs. 43-44) and would not have been meaningful earlier in Old Testament times.

RELIGIOUS EVENTS

In discussing the religious practices of the people of the Bible, we must not think that those people shared our modern assumptions about the sharp distinction between what was religious and what was secular. No such division existed in the minds of the people of the Bible. Their everyday life was so intermingled with religious thinking that to divide it into "religious" and "secular" categories would have been an impossible task for them to attempt. However, we may take a closer look at those practices which we would classify as specifically "religious" in order to see what their customs were and what light these customs can throw upon our understanding of them as "the people of God."

THE SABBATH

The institution that stands out above all the rest merely because of its frequency and regularity is the sabbath. Every seventh day the practicing Israelite would refrain from work as a religious observance. In contrast to the less frequently celebrated yearly festivals, this observance took place every week, and, as a consequence, the existence of this observance was never out of the consciousness of the people of Israel for any great amount of time.

The word "sabbath" comes from a Hebrew word which means "to cease, to stop, to rest," so its use as a name for the day upon which all work ceased was quite apt. It is mentioned in all of the major strata of the Pentateuch. In Exod. 34:31 (J) and in Exod. 23:12 (E) we find "Six days you shall work, but on the seventh day you shall rest." It also appears in Deut. 5:12-14 (D) and in the Priestly Code in Exod. 31:12-17 (P). Since it can be found in all of these major strata, its observance must be seen as an integral part of the practice of the worship of Israel from the earliest times. However, just how early this practice began is not clear. Certainly most of the references in the Bible to the Sabbath in this early period are found in the context of the Covenant itself, and it seems to have been a part of the original Covenant agreement. The main emphasis on the observance of this day in this early period seems to have been that work ceases in order that people may dedicate the day to Yahweh. It is seen as a kind of offering of time to the deity.

During the period when Solomon's Temple was standing, the sabbath was regarded as a time to visit a "man of God" (2 Kings 4:23) or a day to celebrate with joy and mirth (Hos. 2:11; Isa. 1:13). Since physical work and business transactions were suspended for the day, people were able to frequent the nearby sanctuary in order to worship. If their homes were near enough to the city, many went to Jerusalem. It became necessary, because of the great influx of people on the Sabbath, to have two-thirds of the royal bodyguard on duty at the Temple in Jerusalem on that day to preserve order, compared with only one-third during the week (2 Kings 11). During the time of the divided kingdom people evidently felt free to make trips on the sabbath (2 Kings 4:23), and the prohibition of such travel came only as a later development (Isa. 58:13).

The significance of the sabbath changed, however, during the time of the Exile. The Temple had been destroyed, and without the Temple and its altar it was impossible to celebrate fully the sacrificial feasts of the Jewish liturgical year. Because of this difficulty, the sabbath took on a greater importance than it had previously held. It had been one observance among a number of observances when the Jews had lived in their homeland, but now that they were in Babylon without the Temple, this celebration became something that was distinctively Jewish in a pagan environment. When the Jews were forced to leave their homeland where the observance of the sabbath was taken for granted and to be exiled in Babylon where it was not observed at all, they had to undergo a serious emotional readjustment.

In some ways it must have been similar to the readjustment required of a Christian who has been raised in a so-called "Christian" country but who has moved to modern Jerusalem. The Christian from the predominantly Christian country grows so accustomed to the traditional observance of Sunday as a day when all regular work ceases that he finds it unsettling to be in a country which ignores this day entirely. What actually happens is that Saturday "feels" like Sunday all day, and Sunday "feels" like Monday. On Sunday the non-Christian shops are open and the traffic is heavy and people act as if it were a weekday. To wear "Sunday clothes" and to attend church on such a day is to emphasize one's difference as a member of a Christian minority group. It must have been a somewhat similar situation in Babylon for the Jew. The Jew was surrounded by nonobservers and his own observance must have made him all the more conscious of his uniqueness. Consequently, if he were to keep this uniqueness, it would be important to emphasize it more strongly than ever had been appropriate before.

Therefore, during the Exile the sabbath, like circumcision, became a distinguishing mark which separated the Jew from his environment in a way that was not possible when the Jew lived in his homeland. In fact, circumcision and the observance of the sabbath became the most important symbols of the Jewish religion.

The increased restrictions which were introduced in this period can be seen to have their origin as early as the time of Jeremiah. "Take heed for the sake of your lives, and do not bear a burden on the sabbath day or bring it in by the gates of Jerusalem. And do not carry a burden out of your houses on the sabbath or do any work, but keep the sabbath day holy, as I commanded your fathers" (Jer. 17:21-22). No doubt this stricter observance of the sabbath was followed by the exiles. During the Exilic period, the practices were incorporated into the Priestly Code with provisions for punishment if they were not carried out: "You shall keep the sabbath, because it is holy for you; every one who profanes it shall be put to death; whoever does any work on it, that soul shall be cut off from among his people" (Exod. 31:14-15).

When Nehemiah returned from the Exile to Jerusalem he was shocked to find that the people were largely ignoring the sabbath. "In those days I saw in Judah men treading wine presses on the sabbath, and bringing in heaps of grain and loading them on asses; and also wine, grapes, figs, and all kinds of burdens, which they brought into Jerusalem on the sabbath day" (Neh. 13:15). When he discovered that Gentiles were coming into Jerusalem and selling wares to the Jews on the sabbath, he solved the problem by locking the gates before the sabbath began and unlocking them only after it was over (Neh. 13:19). Nehemiah believed that the observance of the sabbath was no light matter!

By and large there was no external pressure to keep the Jews from observing the sabbath until the 2nd century B.C. Up until that time the Jews were free to carry out whatever religious observances seemed appropriate to them. However, during the reign of the Syrian king Antiochus Epiphanes a concerted effort was made to Hellenize all peoples under his control. This meant that the Jews were required to give up their religious observances, including the observance of the sabbath. The penalty for disobedience was death. In the battles which followed the Jews had to decide if they were to be allowed to defend themselves on the sabbath day. If they could not, they could be killed by the enemy on any sabbath without being able to offer any resistance. At last Mattathias decided that it was permissible to fight back in self-defense, but it must have been a very difficult decision to make in the light of the tradition.

From this period on, the various groups in Judaism, such as the Essenes, the Samaritans, perhaps the Sadducees, and certainly the Pharisees increased the restrictions for this day. We know that the Pharisees, for example, in the period of the New Testament, did not allow the picking of a few stalks of grain (Matt. 12:2), healing a sick person (Mark 3:2; Luke 13:14), or carrying such a small object as a pallet on which to lie (John 5:10). They did, however, permit walks to be taken away from home provided that they were no longer than a "sabbath day's journey" (about 2,000 cubits, roughly 2,000 steps). A legalistic interpretation was also allowed which stated that if food had been placed the night before at the 2,000 cubit limit, this stopping place could be counted as "home" and 2,000 cubits more could be walked from that spot.

Such restrictive and legalistic interpretations were rejected by Jesus, though he in no way rejected the institution of the sabbath itself. Instead, he taught that there were higher laws than the sabbath laws, and that the loving concern for one's fellow man had precedence over such restrictions. "The sabbath was made for man, not man for the sabbath" (Mark 2:27).

In the time of the New Testament the custom had grown up that families would eat the Friday evening meal together just before the setting of the sun. (The sabbath was reckoned from sundown on Friday evening to sundown on Saturday evening.) However, in many instances, the men formed religious brotherhoods which would gather together for this observance on Friday evenings. After the meal was finished a prayer of blessing, the Kiddush, was recited over the wine. The intention of the prayer was to usher in the sabbath and to sanctify it.

THE PILGRIMAGE FESTIVALS

The Passover

In contrast to the weekly recurrence of the sabbath, the Jewish liturgical calendar also had a number of yearly festivals. The foremost among these annual celebrations was the Passover. This spring festival occurred on the 14th day of the month Nisan (or Aviv) which is roughly equivalent to March-April in our calendar (*see* Fig. 4). A close look at the customs which constitute the celebration of this festival shows a curious mixture of what seems to be two different backgrounds: pastoral and agricultural. Most scholars believe that what we now call "Passover" was originally two feasts, the Feast of the Passover and the Feast of Unleavened Bread, which were combined at a later period into one feast. The original background of the Feast of the Passover must have been pastoral, since the ceremonies of slaying a lamb and smearing the blood on the doorposts is basically a rite which presumes a nomadic community of shepherds rather than a settled community of farmers. On the other hand, the Feast of Unleavened Bread is basically a rite which presumes a settled community of farmers which has finished one phase of the agricultural cycle and is celebrating the beginning of the next phase of that cycle—the harvest. Both of these feasts happened to have been celebrated at approximately the same time in the spring of the year, but they were celebrated by different groups. The pastoral feast may have been celebrated by the original nomadic elements which made up the people of Israel, while the agricultural feast may have been celebrated by the settled elements located in Canaan. At any rate, when we first meet the description of this feast in the Bible itself (Exod. 12:1–28), the original motives for celebrating the festival have been reinterpreted, and the primary emphasis has been shifted to the commemoration of the historical event of the Exodus. The pastoral and agricultural themes have been relegated to the background, and the redemption of Israel by Yahweh has been made the main theme.

The manner of celebrating each of the two original festivals was quite different in nature. The Passover was originally a celebration intended primarily for the family, and it was observed in the place where the family lived. On the other hand, the Feast of the Unleavened Bread was originally a celebration intended for the entire community, and its observance took place at a local sanctuary and required the participation of the whole community. When the two feasts were combined into one in order to provide a commemoration of the Exodus, they retained both of these communal and family elements by having the people celebrate part of the feast at the local sanctuary and part of it in their homes. However, during the time of King Josiah in the 7th century B.C. there was a reform movement which made every effort to eliminate all local sanctuaries and to concentrate all worship in Jerusalem at the Temple of Solomon. The intention was to centralize the worship of the Jewish people and to create a national character to their religious observances. This reform changed the basic character of Passover from a celebration which took place both in the local sanctuary and in the home to a celebration which entailed a long pilgrimage to Jerusalem for the centralized observance. Since the people had to travel to Jerusalem, they were not able to be in their homes to celebrate the elements of the feast pertinent to the home, and they had to find accommodations in the city itself in which to celebrate these rites. The sacrificial lamb was offered in the Temple courtyard, but it was taken back to those accommodations in Jerusalem to be eaten at the Passover meal. Since sacrifice at any other sanctuary had become illegal in this period, those who were unable to make the pilgrimage had to stay at home and be satisfied with a lamb which had not been killed sacrificially. The important thing to note, however, is that from this time onward, as long as a Temple existed, the Passover was celebrated in a communal fashion in Jerusalem rather than partly in the home and partly in the local sanctuary. Solomon's Temple did not remain standing very long after Josiah's reform, however. It was destroyed in 587 B.C. by Nebuchadnezzar's forces. But it was rebuilt after the Jews returned from Exile, and the national and corporate nature of the celebration lasted up until the Temple was destroyed by the Romans in A.D. 70. After that time the Passover had to be celebrated without any pilgrimage and without any sacrifice of the lamb. But the reform of Josiah had put in motion forces that eventually made the Passover the most important national festival for the Jews.

In Jesus' day the Passover retained its essential liturgical elements, but it also had acquired some of the customs of the Greco-Roman civilization which was dominant in that period. The feast had become more luxurious and lavish; the participants no longer sat on stools and ate the meal in haste, but lay around the table on couches, drank wine as in a proper feast, and ate the meal in a leisurely fashion. Since the Temple was still standing in Jesus' day, the lambs were sacrificed there before being brought to the place where the Passover was to be eaten. But it was still necessary to find a place for the feast itself. "And on the first day of Unleavened Bread, when they sacrificed the passover lamb, his disciples said to him, 'Where will you have us go and prepare for you to eat the passover?' And he sent two of his disciples, and said to them, 'Go into the city, and a man carrying a jar of water will meet you; follow him, and wherever he enters, say to the householder, "The teacher says, Where is my guest room, where I am to eat the passover with my disciples?" And he will show you a large upper room furnished and ready; there prepare for us'" (Mark 14:12 ff.). Paul sees Christ as a fulfillment of the hope of this Passover feast: "For Christ, our paschal lamb, has been sacrificed. Let us, therefore, celebrate the festival . . ." (1 Cor. 5:7 f.).

The Feast of Weeks

Greek-speaking Jews called this feast "Pentecost" (meaning "fifty days") but it was also called the Feast of the Harvest and the Day of First Fruits in the Bible (see Fig. 4). Its character was basically agricultural, though in post-biblical days the feast was interpreted as a commemoration of God's giving the law to Moses. Pentecost was linked with the Passover because the date of the celebration of Pentecost was determined by counting the days from the offering of the first fruits of grain which took place immediately after the celebration of Passover. "And you shall count from the morrow after the sabbath, from the day that you brought the sheaf of the wave offering; seven full weeks shall they be, counting fifty days" (Lev. 23:15). The "morrow after the sabbath" would, on the surface, indicate the first day of the week, Sunday, as the day on which the counting began. Seven weeks later (49 days) plus the day itself (totaling 50, thus "Pentecost") would make the Feast of Weeks always occur on a Sunday. However, there were varying interpretations of what the word "sabbath" indicated. Some saw it as Saturday, but others understood it to mean the first day of the feast of the Passover, which was also treated as a day of rest. Consequently, there were various groups who contended with each other over the computation of the date of the Feast of Weeks.

Originally, before the Reform of Josiah, the Feast of Weeks was observed locally in the sanctuaries throughout the land. But in the 7th century B.C. all sacrifice outside of Jerusalem was prohibited by Josiah, and the Feast of Weeks became, like the Passover, a pilgrimage festival where all who observed the celebration were expected to go to Jerusalem to do so. However, this feast never became so popular as the other two pilgrimage feasts, Passover and Booths.

One of the essential elements of the feast was the offering of two loaves of leavened bread made from the grain crop which had just been harvested. In many ways this feast was a completion of the celebration that had been begun with the Feast of the Unleavened Bread. Fifty days previously the people had eaten unleavened bread (*matsah*) when they began the harvest of grain. At the end of this period they used leaven again and offered the fruits of the harvest in the form of bread as a thanksgiving to God who had made it possible.

The harvest theme is the predominant theme in this feast, and it presupposes a society of settled farmers who want to celebrate the completion of their harvest with a religious festival. The Christian celebration of Pentecost, on the other hand, has no connection with the harvest theme at all. According to Acts 2:1, the Holy Spirit was given to the new Church on the very day of Pentecost. Since the feast had been a pilgrimage feast from the time of Josiah in the 7th century B.C., people had had to come from long distances to Jerusalem to celebrate. This explains why at this particular time "there were dwelling in Jerusalem Jews, devout men from every nation under heaven" (Acts 2:5). These men had come from the Diaspora to keep the Feast of Weeks, and they were present to witness the giving of the Holy Spirit to the young Church.

The Feast of Booths

The third pilgrimage feast was called by several names: The Feast of Booths (or Tabernacles, or Tents), the Feast of Ingathering, the Feast of the Lord, or sometimes simply The Feast (*see* Fig. 4). The Hebrew name of the feast, *sukkoth*, means "huts" (referring to the huts which were built as a part of the celebration). Like the other two pilgrimage feasts, this feast was basically agricultural in nature, and it was celebrated as soon as the agricultural work of the summer and early fall had been completed. After the olives and grapes had been gathered and pressed, all the grain had been harvested and threshed, and all the crops were in, the hard work of this final part of the agricultural cycle was completed. The Feast of Booths celebrated this completion by giving an opportunity for merrymaking and thanksgiving to God. In this respect it bears some resemblance to the American feast of Thanksgiving which is observed about the same time of the year. The antecedents of the Feast of Booths go back to the period of the Canaanites, who also had a similar festival at this season.

The Feast of Booths was the most popular of the pilgrim festivals and more people attended its celebration than either of the other two. After the Babylonian Captivity the Jews who remained in other lands often had to travel great distances to celebrate this feast in Jerusalem, and many were unable to do so more than once in their lifetimes.

The Feast of Booths is listed last in the lists of pilgrimage feasts given in Exod. 23:14-17, Lev. 23, and Deut. 16, and therefore seems to be thought of as occurring at the end of the liturgical year. However, looking at it from a different perspective, it came at the beginning of a new year as well. At first there was no fixed date for its celebration since the actual observance depended upon the completion of the harvests of all of the crops. Later, however, the date was fixed to the 15th day of Tishri (September–October). It lasted seven days with an extra two days added for special observances at the end of that period.

Since the name of this celebration is the Feast of Booths, it is obvious that the customs associated with the celebration have something to do with "booths," or "huts" (a word that is nearer the meaning of the Hebrew *sukkoth*). Because of the tendency of people to steal ripe fruits from a vineyard, a field or an orchard, farmers usually constructed temporary shelters nearby in which they could spend the night on guard. They would put several poles in the ground and spread green branches upon the tops of them to make huts that would not only serve as guard posts during the night, but would also keep away the intense heat of the sun during the daytime. In many instances, especially if the fields were a long distance from their homes, farmers would literally live in these huts for days at a time. Even today in Palestine the farmers continue to construct similar huts out of branches of trees for the same purpose.

When the harvests had been thoroughly completed, the moment was psychologically right for a celebration. Originally the Feast of Booths must have been celebrated right in the fields at the huts themselves. From the beginning there was much drinking and dancing associated with this feast. Up until the time of King Josiah's reform, any sacrifices which were to be offered were obviously taken to the local sanctuary, but after Josiah made it illegal to sacrifice in any sanctuary but the Temple in Jerusalem, they had to make a pilgrimage to that city for this celebration. Of course, that meant that the actual booths which had been constructed in their own fields had to be left behind, but they began to make their own huts in Jerusalem after they arrived for the sacrifice. In many ways it was an ideal arrangement, since they were able to provide their own accommodations in the city without having to live in other people's houses. Since the winter rains would not have begun in the month of Tishri, there was little chance of getting soaked if one spent the nights in these shelters, and since the temperature is not at all uncomfortable at this time, the huts provided just enough shelter to be adequate. They constructed these booths anywhere they could find a space large enough—in the streets, in open squares and courtyards, even on the flat roofs of the houses.

Although the Bible does not describe in detail some of the customs that were observed at this feast, we know from the Mishnah that during New Testament times there were several interesting observances which took place.

The first of these observances was the water libation. Each morning a procession of priests would form in the Temple area and proceed to the Pool of Siloam in order to get a pitcher of water. The pitcher was then solemnly taken back to the Temple and the water was poured on the altar in front of the Temple. Trumpets were blown and great crowds assembled to see this procession. It is probable that the original purpose of this ceremony was connected with the encouragement of the beginning of the winter rains. All summer long the skies were devoid of rain clouds, but at this season the farmers needed the rains to begin again so that their agricultural cycle could be repeated. Thus a symbolic rain was poured upon the altar as a kind of prayer for the beginning of the "former" rains, as the earliest rains were called.

Each night the Temple courtyard was thronged with men who formed processions, carried torches, and danced joyously while they chanted psalms for almost the entire night. Every morning at dawn the priests would assemble and go to the east gate of the Temple and stand with their backs to the sun, where they would state that they were doing this action because their forefathers had apostatized and worshiped the sun at this spot long ago (Ezek. 8:16).

When the people were not actively participating in the ceremonies at the Temple, they would carry around with them an object called a *lulab* which was a collection of palm, willow, and myrtle branches woven together to make a kind of ornamental switch. These would be waved in the air as they walked around the city, giving a festive air to the occasion. They would also carry in their other hand a citron, called an *ethrog*. After the feast was over the *lulab* was taken apart and the *ethrog* was eaten. These branches and the fruit were similar to those that decorated the huts that the people had built upon their arrival in Jerusalem.

The character of these observances is obviously agricultural in nature, but as time went on, the feast, like the other two pilgrimage feasts, became more and more historicized in order to remove the temptation to worship the pagan fertility god Baal even further from the people. The huts in which the people lived were said to symbolize, not the shelters made in the open fields at harvesttime, but the tents in which the Israelites had lived when they were wandering in the wilderness after their experiences at Mount Sinai. Thus the tendency to historicize all celebrations reached even to this feast.

THE OTHER FEASTS

The New Year

The question "When was the Jewish New Year celebrated?" is simpler to ask than to answer. In many ways the same question asked of our own day would be just as complicated. We observe the beginning of several new years in any 12-month period. The beginning of our calendar year is January 1, but the beginning of the academic year is usually in September. The beginning of the fiscal year is sometimes in July but the beginning of the Christian liturgical year is Advent, which comes around the end of October. We have had several new years for a long time.

It seems likely that before the Babylonian Exile, the people of Israel counted the month Tishri (September–October) as the first month of the year, according to the Canaanite practice (*see* Fig. 4). However, after the Exile they began to adopt the Babylonian way of arranging the calendar, and that made the first month of the year Nisan (March–April) which was in the spring rather than in the fall. Originally, the only major festival that was celebrated in Tishri had been the Feast of Booths. But after the Exile, other celebrations began to be observed in this month: Rosh ha-Shanah and Yom Kippur.

The name Rosh ha-Shanah means "the head of the year." It was the name which was used to designate this feast some time after the New Testament period had begun, but there is no feast celebrated in Tishri specifically by that name which is mentioned in the Old Testament itself. The first two days of Tishri had been set apart to celebrate the sanctity of the seventh month (originally this had been the first month), but there is some question whether Rosh ha-Shanah was celebrated as the New Year's Festival during the time before the New Testament. It is not mentioned in the New Testament itself, but only in the Jewish literature which was written some time after that period. When the feast is described in any detail, its character is obviously different from the other feasts which we have discussed, simply because it is not concerned in any way with nature or with history. It is a feast that deals with beginning again a new year, and the moral commitment that such a beginning requires.

Yom Kippur

On the other hand, we know more about the observance called Yom Kippur (*see* Fig. 4). This title indicates that the day was one of "covering," "atonement," "expiation," "propitiation." In the New Testament this observance was simply called "the fast" (Acts 27:9). There is no mention of this day in passages that date from before the Exile, but we do know that it became extremely popular in the post-exilic period. This day was a day of fasting and penance. No work was done just as if it were a sabbath. It was a serious day and its somber tone was much in contrast to the tone of the agricultural festivals.

The rites connected with the day are found in Lev. 16; further descriptive

material is found in the Mishnah. There are three animals used for the observance: one bull and two goats. The bull is sacrificed by the High Priest
for his own sins and for the sins of the entire priesthood. During this ceremony he takes the blood of the bull and enters into the Holy of Holies itself.
After censing the place where the ark had stood, he sprinkles blood on the
mercy seat. Then he returns and selects one of the two goats by lot so that
it can be sacrificed for the sins of the people. After sacrificing this goat, he
returns to the Holy of Holies and repeats the ceremonies with the blood of
the goat. During this time he has uttered the name of God, "Yahweh,"
several times in the various prayers that are appointed to be said. (He is the
only person who is allowed to utter the Divine Name, and it is the only
time during the year when it is permissible even for him to do so.) Then he
returns to the second goat. The first goat had been selected "for Yahweh";
the second had been selected "for Azazel." The meaning of the term "Azazel" is obscure but it may refer to some kind of demon who lived in the
wilderness. This goat is set before the High Priest who lays his hands upon
its head in order to transfer the sins of all of the people to it. Then the goat
is driven out into the wilderness of Judea where it symbolically takes away
the sins of the people.

There are a number of references to this feast in the New Testament,
particularly in the Epistle to the Hebrews, where Jesus is seen to be the Great
High Priest himself.

Hanukkah

The Feast of Hanukkah is the only feast in the Jewish liturgical calendar
which has a precise inaugural date (*see* Fig. 4). It was first celebrated on the
25th day of Kislev (the first part of December) in the year 164 B.C. Judas
Maccabeus inaugurated the feast when he purified the sanctuary and built a
new altar of burnt sacrifice in the Temple after the Temple had been defiled
by Antiochus Epiphanes with pagan sacrifices three years earlier in 167 B.C.
The feast was a commemoration of the rededication by Maccabeus, and thus
its name, *hanukkah*, meaning "dedication." The commemoration has been
observed regularly until modern times, and the festival has even grown in
importance among Jews.

In the New Testament this feast is mentioned in John 19:22. "It was the
feast of the Dedication [*hanukkah*] at Jerusalem; it was winter [the 25th of
Kislev], and Jesus was walking in the Temple, in the portico of Solomon."

One of the most important ceremonies attached to this feast is that of
lighting candles throughout the eight days of its celebration. An additional
candle was lighted each day, though the precise meaning of this ceremony as
it was originally instituted is not known. Later, a legend grew up which

attempted to explain the practice, but the original intention remains obscure. In many ways the celebration of the feast resembled the Feast of Booths, since palms were carried and psalms were sung. The resemblance may have been intentional, since Solomon first dedicated the Temple on the Feast of Booths, and it was appropriate to rededicate it in a similar manner. However, no one constructed booths on Hanukkah, and so the feasts were not identical.

Hanukkah is the only feast in the liturgical year which has its institution and inauguration recorded in a text that was written soon after the inauguration itself (1 Maccabees 4:36–59). It is also the only feast which is directly connected with the celebration of a specifically documented historical event. Unlike the agricultural feasts which became historicized as time went on, this feast was historical from the very beginning.

Purim

In contrast to the unquestioned historical character of the Feast of Hanukkah, the Feast of Purim commemorates an event which probably is not historical (*see* Fig. 4). The feast itself seems to have been a non-Jewish (perhaps Persian) celebration which was adopted by the Jews, and then given a historical rationale by the story related in the book of Esther. The celebration takes place on the 14th and 15th day of Adar (February-March). A fast was observed on the day preceding the celebration, but the two days of the feast are observed by much merrymaking, the giving of alms and presents, and great feasting. In later centuries Purim became more of a carnival in nature and participants wore masks and disguises. The high point of the celebration is the reading of the book of Esther in the synagogue. The congregation would make disturbing noises every time the wicked Haman's name was read, and would cheer when the virtuous Mordecai's name was read. The essential point of the feast is to commemorate the deliverance of the Jews from their enemies as described in the book of Esther.

The first time this feast is mentioned in a book other than Esther itself is in 2 Maccabees 15:36, and this fact probably indicates that it did not develop until late in the Old Testament period.

Having looked at the way in which the people of the Bible *lived*, we now turn to the question, "How did the people of the Bible make their *living*? In turn we will examine the world of the nomad, the work of the farmer, the duties involved in the professions, the institutions of civil service, the life of the soldier, and the various industries that existed in the biblical world.

✺ III. How the People of the Bible Worked

THE LIFE OF THE NOMAD

KINDS OF NOMADS

When we first encounter the historical people known as Hebrews in the Bible, at the time of Abraham early in the second millennium, they were nomads. That is, they were a people without a homeland or fixed location, but were constantly wandering from place to place, seeking water and pasturage for their flocks.

Several sorts of nomads have been identified by ethnologists and cultural anthropologists. For the purposes of this book a threefold classification will serve, the first type being useful only to show the kind of nomad the Israelites were *not*.

Bedouin

These are the modern Arab nomads of the Arabian, Syrian, or North African deserts. The word "Bedouin" means "man of the desert." He was and remains a camel breeder (Fig. 37); today he also uses horses. From the time that the camel was first domesticated—a date disputed by scholars, but perhaps as late as 1200 B.C.—the Bedouin have been capable of moving across sandy wastes, oasis to oasis, at a pace far beyond the capabilities of Abraham's asses (Fig. 38). Aided by the camel, who needs to be watered but once a week (Fig. 39), and whose padded feet do not sink into the sand, Bedouin have been able to survive and even thrive in regions where the annual rainfall is less than 4 inches a year (*see* Fig. 3). These are the real nomads of the sandy deserts. King Ibn Saud, the desert chieftain who as recently as 1925 built

37. A Bedouin woman with her camels in the Negev desert.

38. Camels in the desert area near Jericho.

39. Camels eating prickly pear cactus for their moisture.

the now oil-rich Arabian kingdom known as Saudi Arabia, was a classic modern example of a Bedouin chieftain or *sheikh*.

Sheep and Goat Breeders

A fully developed way of life, a culture with distinctive social institutions, was built around the raising of flocks of sheep and goats (Fig. 40). (They live contentedly together because neither one can outeat the other.) From them the owners obtained all the necessities of their life: food and materials for clothing and fabrics for tents in which to live—all of which could be sold or bartered for needed supplies in trade centers on the fringes of the wasteland (Fig. 41). A third animal, the ass, provided the sheep and goat breeder with a needed beast of burden, enabling him to pack up and move whenever the water supply dried up or pasturage failed (Fig. 42). So important was the domesticated ass that some scholars call this type of nomad the ass-nomad, to distinguish it from the camel-nomad.

An absolute necessity to the nomadic life was water for both man and beast, obtained from wells or springs, or from cisterns dug from the rocky soil and filled by winter rains. Sheep and goats must be watered once a day. Water and pasturage were not difficult to find in the late winter and spring, but once the hot drying winds of summer arrived, followed by months without rainfall, the necessities of flock-raising forced the nomads to move along the borders of the occupied, sown land, from one watering place to another. These nomads therefore might be called shepherd-nomads. This way of life can be supported in lands receiving 4 to 12 inches of rainfall annually, twelve inches being the minimum for agriculture by settled farmers.

40. A flock of sheep and goats grazing.

41. Modern Arabs bartering at the sheep market in Hebron.

42. Wild asses roaming the Judaean Desert.

Seminomads

Once a nomad begins to plant seasonal crops that can be quickly harvested, begins to acquire a claim, however loose, on territory, to dig his own wells, or to raise cattle (oxen)—even if he remains in such a place for only a few months each year—he is no longer a true nomad. Abraham, Isaac, and Jacob were moving into the seminomadic class, as is shown by their acquisition of a burial ground at Mamre and of wells, and by their building of shrines. The ass remains the essential beast of burden, and the nomadic character of the society, so beautifully formed and bolstered by institutions designed to assure the survival of the group in the desert, had in patriarchal times been unaffected.

The Desert

The typical American concept of a desert, fostered by the motion picture industry, is of a virtual ocean of sand across which marches a camel caravan hoping to find water before darkness falls. Such deserts are located in the Sahara and in the interior parts of the Arabian peninsula, but they are not a part of the scenery of the Old Testament. The "desert" to the Hebrews was the region just beyond the horizon of most of them; it was a land unfavored by rain, "a land where no man is . . . the waste and desolate land" (Job 38:26–27).

The Hebrew word used in the overwhelming majority of cases and translated "desert" or "wilderness" is *midbar*. A better translation might be "wasteland" or "deserted land," a land without habitation. The *midbar* was that particular area surrounding Palestine on the south and east where farming could not be carried on because of insufficient rainfall (*see* Fig. 3). Generally speaking, the farther one moved south or east the more barren and desolate the *midbar* became (Figs. 43, 44). But as Joel 1:20 and 2:22 attest, the *midbar* was not normally entirely without water or pasturage, particularly at the end of the winter rains. Jeremiah called it "a land not sown" (2:2), because of God's anger at Israel's sins, "the land mourns and the pastures of the wilderness are dried up" (23:10). That the *midbar* offered green fields, at least in the spring, is further attested by Ps. 65:12, and David the boy shepherd pastured his small flock in the wilderness the year of his combat with Goliath (1 Sam. 17:28). To catch and store the winter rains, somebody dug a pit or cistern (like the one into which Joseph was placed by his brothers Gen. 37:22).

The *midbar* at its worst is described in Jer. 2:6: "a land of deserts and pits, a land of drought and deep darkness, a land that one passes through, where no man dwells." In such a land there was always the possibility of attacks on the flocks by lions, bears, and wolves. The Israelites feared this land (Deut. 8:15; Isa. 34:13–14; etc.), however much the prophets tended to decry urban life and romanticize nomadic life.

Individual portions of the *midbar* were given proper names, such as "the desert of Beersheba" (Gen. 21:14) or "the desert of Engedi" (1 Sam. 24:1). "Jeshimon" (= "Desolation") was a rough, hilly land without any green cover, west of the Dead Sea and east of the line running from Jerusalem to Bethlehem to Hebron (Fig. 45). The full extent of Jeshimon can be seen

43. Barren desert with only a few small plants (Negev desert).

44. Barren desert with a whirlwind ("dust devil") on the horizon (Negev desert).

from Tekoa, and a part of it from the hills just east of Jerusalem. It received then (and receives today) little rainfall because it lay below the level of the spinelike north-south mountain ridge lying to the west; the rain clouds from the Mediterranean Sea dropped their moisture west of Jeshimon (*see* Fig. 2).

The extent of the *midbar* moves from year to year in accordance with the amount of rainfall. In a good year grain can be planted successfully on the western or northern edges; in a bad year the same land will bring nothing

45. The desert of Jeshimon.

to fruit, however bravely the grain may rise from the earth. This is especially true of the poor steppeland, grading off into semidesert, lying on the eastern borders of Gilead and Moab. In good years, then, biblical seminomads might plant a crop such as barley in the *midbar* or find lush pasturage for their sheep and goats. On the other hand, if the people living in "the sown," the farmers, felt strong enough to defend themselves, they might send their shepherds with their flocks out into the *midbar*, into territory a nomadic tribe regarded as its own. When the rainfall was bad, the good pasturage would recede, and the nomads then tended to run their herds onto the private property of the farmers in the sown.

Hence there was constant animosity and friction between the nomads and the settled folk—the desert vs. the sown. The animosity ran deeper than disputes and fighting over grazing rights. The nomad, with his free-ranging movement, regarded the sedentary farming peasant as a kind of slave. The biblical farmer in turn regarded the nomad much as people in the Anglo-Saxon world have regarded the gypsy—as a strange, irrresponsible, shifty troublemaker.

Semitic Nomads in Pre-biblical Times

The most important peoples of the Bible, with the notable exception of the Egyptians, were once nomads. The Semitic peoples, including the Israelites, Amorites, and Aramaeans, all came originally out of the Arabian peninsula, out of the desert into the sown. For reasons which today we cannot determine, and aided by factors of climate and productivity we can only guess at, the Amorites, Hyksos, and Habiru (the last-named regarded by some as the forerunners of the Israelites) increased in numbers and vitality. For shepherd-nomads the margin between a sufficient diet and starvation has always been narrow. Possibly at the time of their respective infiltrations into the sown, the inhabitant peoples were weakly ruled or had become soft. In any case, all of these peoples did break out from the desert, and once inside the sown, settling usually in thinly populated regions between walled towns but on land better than any they had known, they thrived and multiplied, and often later became the rulers of the region. So it would be with the Israelites. And once they were settled, the Midianites and the Amalekites would try to do the same.

The early history of Israel makes very little sense to the contemporary reader unless the nomadic background of this people is recognized and its institutions appreciated. Nomadism, we have said, was a way or mode of life, predating recorded history. It still exists, in Kurdistan for example. The nomadism of the Bible was forged on the anvil of survival in the wastelands bordering on the Fertile Crescent, that green belt extending from the Nile delta to the mouth of the Tigris-Euphrates River (see Fig. 1).

BASICS OF SEMINOMADIC LIFE

The Ass

The economy of the nomadic tribe was based on its herds of sheep and goats, and on the ass as the all-purpose working animal (see Fig. 42). The ass is the beast of burden of the Bible seminomads; it had been domesticated long before Israel's patriarchal age, probably from the Nubian wild ass, by Egyptians. This willing if sometimes stubborn little fellow, standing just a bit over three feet tall, could carry an impressive load of household goods or be ridden by a man, or by a woman with a child. The ass was capable of doing plowing and other farm work. Job describes evil men as those who, among other things, "drive away the ass of the fatherless"; not to own an ass was to be without a basic necessity of life (Job 24:3). To own many asses was to be wealthy (e.g., Gen. 12:16; Job 1:3). When a nomadic family moved, all their worldly goods were packed on asses, in fabric bags, jars, water in skinbags, slung across the backs of asses in packs evenly balanced. Other asses carried the women, sitting sideways, and children, too (Exod. 4:20), carried in sacks slung to the side of the beast. A 20-mile journey was all that could be accomplished by a migrating family in a day, because of the necessity to move the herds also, and to water them, normally at noon, but at least once a day.

Asses were the mounts of men of rank (Judg. 10:4, Jair's sons) and persons of wealth and influence (1 Sam. 25:20, Nabal and Abigail). Later the mule would become the mount of kings, princes, and generals; and after the return from the Exile, the horse. The prophet Zechariah (9:9) depicted the messianic king riding upon an ass, a peaceable animal of the common people for a peace-bringing Messiah. As an "unclean animal" (the ass does not part the hoof or chew the cud) the ass was forbidden as food; however, in the desperate famine in Samaria while the city was besieged by Ben-hadad of Syria (2 Kings 6:25), the rule was set aside. The ass shared in the rest from labor on the Sabbath (Deut. 5:14). In the census of animals brought back to Jerusalem by returning exiled Jews (Ezra 2:66-67; Neh. 7:68-69), asses numbered 6,720, far outstripping horses (736), mules (245), and camels 435—another indicator of their usefulness. For centuries strings of asses were the only freight carriers in Palestine. They required less water and food than a horse, which was broken into chariots in Bible lands long before it was mounted by a rider.

The color of the biblical ass was gray. Occasionally, a white one was foaled. The ass is sure-footed, which is a great asset for a beast of burden in a hilly, rock-strewn country like Palestine and in the nearly pathless wasteland areas frequented by nomads. It does not want to move very fast— it can justifiably be called sluggish—but it is capable of fair speed when lightly loaded and in the mood or prodded. The ass has none of the stubbornness of a mule or skittishness of a horse, but it does require the frequent application of a light stick smartly on the rump if a good day's journey is to be accomplished.

The story of Balaam's ass (Num. 22) reflects the intimacy that prevailed between this beast and its owner. The ass today, the fully domesticated donkey, is still used in mountainous countries where a sure-footed mount for descending steep paths is a necessity.

Sheep

The nomad's wealth was in his herds. The greater the number of his sheep and goats and asses, the wealthier he was rated, and with wealth went prestige and influence.

It is impossible today to identify with certainty the variety or varieties of sheep raised by the Israelite seminomads. They might include the Asiatic *moufflon* we see on Sumerian vases from early Babylonia of c. 3000 B.C., or the long-tailed Egyptian sheep related to a breed grown in the Ural Moun-

46. A sheep of the kind found in Israel today.

tains. The most favored variety is a flat-tailed type bred today in Palestine and regarded by experts as probably found in patriarchal times. These are long-fleeced, caramel colored, with broad tails (Fig. 46). In Old Testament times, they were white (Isa. 1:18; Ps. 147:16) and black (Gen. 30:32). The Isaiah reference suggests that white-colored wool was highly esteemed. One of the choice parts for eating was the tail, which yielded up to 10 pounds of pure fat.

But sheep were eaten only on festal occasions, or when guests were present to be honored. The male sheep was normally the sacrificial animal; far fewer rams were needed than ewes, anyway, to keep the flock increasing.

The versatility of the sheep and its role in the nomadic economy are shown by reciting the uses of this animal. In Bible times (as today) it was sheared twice a year, in spring after lambing time, and in the fall. The sheep thus produced wool for clothing. It also produced milk, from which the seminomads made butter and cheese, as well as meat if it were killed. The ewes produced one lamb annually, occasionally twins. The skins made useful bags and coverings, though not so durable or luxurious as goatskin.

Palestinian sheep of Bible times could, and can today, live off sparse grass cover, and that was their lot among the nomadic tribes of Israel. They could find grass where the human eye failed to observe it. While Palestine offered much excellent pasture country, notably in the central highlands and the plateau land across the Jordan, much of the land available to nomads was marginal at best. But sheep could be pastured in wasteland when the winter rains brought forth a seasonal greening, and in lands of submarginal rainfall for agriculture the rest of the season. They could find the grass in such places; it was the shepherd-nomad's responsibility to find the sheep its daily supply of water.

Not to be forgotten is the ram's horn of the sacrificial or slaughtered male sheep, convertible into a musical instrument. Whether the flocks ever became as large as those of Mesha king of Moab is unlikely, but there is no reason to doubt that the flocks of Abraham, Lot, and Jacob were indeed very large, so large in the case of Abraham and Lot that they needed to be split up.

Shearing was hard and dirty work, done by the men. First the sheep were lugged into a pool for a washing of their fleece. Then after they were dried out, one man would hold a sheep and another would shear off its wool. A sheep can be totally uncooperative, frightened, and troublesome. That shearing a sheep in itself doesn't hurt doesn't mean that the sheep doesn't fear for its life. The women of the family then took over the fleece and washed it again to remove more dirt and much of the natural oil in it. Later they combed the wool and packed it in fabric-wrapped bales for taking to market, to be sold or bartered for goods needed by the family. The Festival of Shearing was a happy occasion indeed, for the nomads had harvested their main crop.

Thus the sheep was the keystone in the pastoral economy of the shepherd-nomads, and would remain one of Israel's most important products after the nation settled down to a more generally agricultural society (Hos. 2:5, 9). Throughout the Old Testament wool was the most common material of clothing, cotton being unknown, linen too expensive for most people, and camel's hair too rough. (See section, THE INDUSTRIAL LIFE, "The Textile Industry.") Wool was offered, along with grain, wine, and oil, as one of the first-fruits (Deut. 18:4). Isa. 51:8 and Matt. 6:19–20 are proof sufficient of the existence of moths that fed on wool.

Goats

Perhaps equally versatile in the economy of biblical Palestine was the goat. On the basis of the species found in Palestine and Syria today (Fig. 47), we may guess that the goats of Old Testament Hebrew nomads were black-and-white or brown-and-white, with long ears and large, curved horns. However, the goats of Jacob and Laban seem to have been of a solid color, black, with a few "speckled" ones among them. The modern broken-color goats could not properly be called "speckled."

47. A typical goat found in Israel today.

Like the sheep, the goat could live on sparse pasturage. It also required watering every day. Goats were sure-footed, could climb to dizzy heights, and were more agile than sheep—and a bit less stupid, too—but were more sensitive to cold weather. The two animals got along well, with goats normally leading the way on a trek (Jer. 50:8). Because of the goat's characteristic of leading, political leaders and kings are called goats by Ezekiel (34:17; 39:18), Daniel (8:5), and Zechariah (10:3, reading "he-goats" for "leaders").

Provided with its meager essentials, the goat provided its shepherd-nomad owner and his family with almost enough to live on. A nanny goat gave up to three quarts a day of milk. To have enough goat's milk for all was a happy state (Prov. 27:27). Vegetables were sometimes cooked in goat's milk. From sour goat's milk came *leben*, a favorite dish somewhat resembling yogurt. The goat was ritually "clean," and so might be eaten. A young roasted kid was a dish highly honored and reserved for extremely special occasions; the meat of mature goats was also eaten, but required long boiling. The goat, especially the male, was a sacrificial animal (Lev. 1:10), and the male was the victim prescribed for use in sin and guilt offerings (Lev. 4:23; 9:3, 15; Ezra 6:17; etc.).

Other goat products were hair from which were made tent and garment cloth (Exod. 36:14), tent curtains (Exod. 35:6), and pillows (1 Sam. 19:13).

And by affixing drawstrings to certain places on the scraped, dehaired, and cleaned skins, precious water "bottles" (better, "bags") could be made. This was nearly always women's work too, once the goat had been slaughtered, butchered, and skinned by the men.

The children of nomads have traditionally looked after the young kids. Easily carried in the arms, they made good pets for children in the Bible. Cleaner in their habits than sheep, pet kids could even be allowed in the tent.

Flocks could become large: 220 for Jacob (Gen. 32:14) and 1,000 for Nabal (1 Sam. 25:2).

Shepherd-Nomads Summarized

The shepherd-nomads or ass-nomads or seminomads of the Old Testament made their living by raising herds of sheep and goats. They built no houses and owned no land in the legal sense, but with the aid of asses, moved their families and possessions as the seasons dictated, always needful of water and pasture lands. They were a *pastoral* folk, in contrast to the *agricultural* folk they later became when they settled in the land of Canaan. (In Gen. 4, Abel represents the pastoral life, Cain the agricultural.) These are the external, visible characteristics of shepherd-nomads.

Next we turn to the *internal* factors, the institutions of their society—for a society it was, no matter how far away from us in time, and how unformed, unorganized, and without restraints these people may seem to us. What held them together? What was the glue that held their society together? What created the basic authority, enabled them to close ranks in times of danger, enabled them to survive—and ultimately to conquer?

THE INSTITUTIONS OF NOMADISM

In the modern study of the tribal life of the Hebrews before the conquest of the land of Canaan, the following principles are held by nearly all scholars in the field: (1) The Hebrews were not true Bedouins, who are camel breeders. (2) The Hebrews never had an experience of life in the true desert, almost totally without rain—such desert as is found in the central part of the Arabian peninsula—and they had no tribal memories of such an existence. On the contrary, the true desert was to the Hebrews an awesome, even terrifying place in which existed nothing but the most ferocious animals and frightening mythical spirits. (3) There was no Bedouin civilization at the time of the patriarchs, for the camel, on which this civilization would be based, was not domesticated until c. 1200 B.C. (and any biblical references to domesticated camels before that date are anachronisms). (4) It follows from the above that studies of true nomadic Bedouin life of centuries after the patriarchs and of Arab Bedouins today must be used with great caution in attempting to delineate the practices, customs, relationships, and organizations—i.e., the institutions—that bound together and made a viable society of the Hebrew seminomads, who were already becoming a partly settled people when we first encounter them in the stories of Abraham.

Despite the need for prudent caution in the use of Arab comparisons, certain Hebrew institutions stand out prominently in the biblical accounts and are in no way negated by what scholars have learned by studying nomadic and seminomadic societies of the past and present. The institutions are: (1) the tribe; (2) blood-vengeance; (3) hospitality and asylum ("cities of refuge"). This discussion will take them up in that order.

The Family, the Clan, the Tribe

The organization of the tribe was by families and clans. The basic unit of social organization was the family. Abraham obviously was the head of a family that could include plural wives, sons and their wives and children, unmarried daughters, and slaves of both sexes. The father as undisputed head of this extended family possessed the power of life and death over the children, as the story of Abraham's sacrifice of Isaac (Gen. 22) and Jephthah's sacrifice of his daughter (Judg. 11) attest. (Note the complete acceptance by the children of the father's power in this regard.) Exod. 21:7 makes it clear that a father had the right also to sell a daughter as a bond servant. Within his own family the father was a mini-dictator whose word was law. The other side of the coin was the protection, the security, the father of a nomadic family gave to his own.

Families related by blood ties comprise a *clan*, which was nothing more than a collection of families. For survival in the borderlands between the desert and the sown, a group had to be large enough, and to have in it enough vigorous males, to prevent its being easily pushed around, and to protect and avenge individual members as necessary. Close cohesion of families and clans was therefore essential. Aiding cohesion was the strong tie of blood kinship characteristic of all nomads.

Heads of families—all related to one another by blood—formed a kind of council at the clan level. At council meetings, called whenever necessary, were brought forward territorial disputes and interfamily altercations. Land in the semidesert was not *owned* in a modern sense, but nomad groups did exercise loose claims over territory in which they were accustomed to pasture their flocks, especially if a group had dug a well or a cistern to improve its water supply. On occasion bitter quarrels arose; Gen. 26:15-22 reports a serious one in Isaac's lifetime. The protection of the rights of the clan and of the members of the constituent families was always a foremost consideration. The clan council was both a court of appeals and an enforcer of the laws developed over years by custom. The leader of a clan council gave the decision.

Above the clans was the *tribe*. This unit was composed of clans that believed they were all descended from a common ancestor. From each clan to the tribal council came the clan leader, the most highly regarded head of a family within that clan. He held his position by virtue of his proven abilities leading to great prestige, and not by vote. He might be the son of the previous leader, but more important qualifications were physical strength, courage, leadership, wealth, fairness of judgment, and the confidence of the clan's families.

The council apparently decided matters by reliance on tribal custom. If there was no applicable custom, a discussion and consideration of all opinions led to a decision which would be remembered next time as a custom. Num. 1:4–15 preserve a list of heads of tribes chosen in the same way as heads of clans, by consensus rather than by vote.

Each tribe, it is believed, established a tribal center at a place where water was reasonably plentiful and certain, to which many might come on occasions. But until the Hebrews acquired the land of Canaan they did not own or occupy land that had enough rainfall to support agriculture and a settled life. While tribes might stay in one area for months or even years, their lands were always marginal, not wanted by the settled people of Palestine, and not good enough to entice the Hebrews to become food producers and build houses. Instead, their economy was based on flocks, and sheep and goats required water daily and pasturage, in a land where neither was plentiful. Hence there was a constant tension and preparedness to move along to greener pastures on short notice. Frequent migration, not land possession, was the condition of tribal life.

It will be observed from this that the social unit, the source of law and order, security and justice, was, for most of these seminomadic Hebrews and on most matters affecting daily life, the clan of those closely related by blood, and not the town or village, with its elders and different, settled-life institutions. That would come later, replacing the family-clan-tribe institution of the seminomadic days.

Interesting to note is that the patriarchal stories preserve names for God that stress the intimate tribal-type relationship in which the deity stood to Abraham, Isaac, and Jacob. In Gen. 15:1 God tells Abraham, "I am your shield." Isaac's God is twice (Gen. 31:42, 53) referred to as "the fear of Isaac," today thought by many to be better translated "Kinsman of Isaac," and so translated in the Jerusalem Bible. Jacob's God is called "the Rock of Israel" in RSV (Gen. 49:24), also translated by others "Strong One," "Mighty One," and "Champion." There is some justification, then, for believing that to Abraham and his family God was "the Shield of Abraham"; to Isaac and his family, "the Kinsman of Isaac"; and to Jacob (= Israel) and his family, "the Champion of Israel." This would be typical of ancient nomadism in that God is never represented as merely a god of nature (as among an agricultural people) but as a god who stood in a special though awesome relationship with the great man of the clan and hence with all clan members.

Blood-vengeance

In nomadic and seminomadic life there were of course no state or town laws, no public prosecuting attorneys and local police forces which the Western world takes for granted. A different kind of institution for personal security was necessary, one that was an extension of the logic of the family-clan-tribe social order prevailing among peoples whose normal condition involved almost constant movement. This institution is called by Old Testament scholars "blood-vengeance." It stemmed directly from the nomadic fact of life that the tribe was the permanent element, while the individual was incidental. Kinship—the relationship by blood, also called "blood brotherhood"—was what held family, clan, and tribe together. This blood brotherhood, this tribal solidarity, provided the cohesion in nomadic life.

Foreign as the ideas are to us, group consciousness, tribal personality, and a brotherhood based on blood were indeed the way of life of the Hebrews from Abraham until the anointing of Saul as king, when Israel adopted a quite different institution (but without ever totally eliminating the nomadic idea). The books of Joshua and Judges are studded with examples of tribal meetings in which it is clear that the authority invested in clan and tribal leaders did not result in dictatorship, but rather, that responsibility was laid on all members of the tribe in decision-making and in execution of tribal plans and of punishment meted out. This was equally so of clan meetings.

Given this situation, an affront by an outsider to one member of a tribe or clan was an affront to the group itself. Murder was the worst affront. On one level, the security of the group and its members was at stake; an effective deterrent, one to restrain others from attempting the same crime, was needed. On a different level from that of blood brotherhood, a mystical concept of *blood* was brought to bear. Blood possessed mystical potencies; the animating spirit, the very life of man or animal, was believed to be in the blood. Blood was a serious business: because it contained this mysterious life it could be dangerous. Gen. 4:10 (Abel's blood) and Job 16:18 stress that blood must be covered; that it must not be eaten is clear from 1 Sam. 14:32–34 and Lev. 17:12–13. Lev. 17:14 expresses the prevailing view of the mysterious potency of blood.

Above all it was held that "blood pollutes the land, and no expiation can be made for the land for the blood that is shed in it, except by the blood of him who shed it" (Num. 35:33). The land was to be kept holy, undefiled, because it is the land in which the Lord dwells (vs. 34).

Out of such elements came the law of blood-vengeance. The clan assumed the responsibility for its execution. The law did not operate *within* the clan, as is evidenced by the mere banishment of Absalom for the premeditated murder of Amnon. Though blood-vengeance was a typically nomadic institution, it persisted well into Israel's history after the settling of the Hebrews into a sedentary and partly urbanized agricultural society under a monarchy. Joab, for example, excused his murder of Abner on the basis of blood-vengeance for what he regarded as Abner's murder of Asahel, Joab's younger brother (2 Sam. 3:27-30).

Bloodletting in Hebrew capital punishment is intentionally avoided by the prescription of death by stoning (Deut. 17:5-6), which also provides a means of sharing responsibility for the execution.

Cities of Refuge

There was a danger that blood-vengeance might be pushed to extremes, thereby creating even greater injustices than those it was attempting to stop. So ultimately, after the Conquest, the institution had to be mitigated by laws about cities of refuge (Num. 35:9-34; Deut. 19:1-13). These laws provided for an inquiry into the guilt or innocence of the accused. They drew distinctions between involuntary homicide and premeditated murder. Six cities of refuge were designated by Joshua, three on either side of the Jordan (Josh. 20:1-9). To any one of these cities an involuntary killer might flee and request asylum; the city elders would then decide his case. In a judgment of involuntary homicide, the killer could live there in safety under the law of asylum, but he must not leave the city until the high priest currently in office died, an event that brought amnesty to all such refugees, freeing them to return to their own home towns or to live where they wished without fear of reprisals from the dead man's kin. But in a judgment of premeditative murder the killer was turned over to the blood avengers for execution.

Hospitality

Seminomadic life, as has been described more fully above, was a group way of life. But inevitably individuals became separated from their social unit. Perhaps a male member of the family was given an assignment requiring him to travel: he might during his journey become ill or suffer an adversity of some sort; before he could rejoin his group, it might have been forced to move on, perhaps by failure of the water supply. Since this chain of events might happen to individual members of any clan or family, the custom arose of providing so unfortunate a person with *hospitality*. Regardless of clan or tribal connections, any person in such trouble might count on a welcome and the hospitality of the group to which he temporarily joined himself. Since the host himself might be needing hospitality next, he gave it to the stranger automatically. Out of nomadic necessity came the virtue of hospitality. The story of Abraham's reception of the three strangers at Mamre (Gen. 18:1–8) is the classic example of hospitality in the Old Testament, followed closely by Laban's reception of the servant sent by Abraham to obtain a wife for Isaac (Gen. 24:28–32). There must have been innumerable unrecorded instances of less grand and unplanned appearances of strangers, bringing no messages or gifts, instances involving the life and death, however, of the nomad attempting to rejoin his group.

Hospitality ultimately took on the stature of an institution, and like most institutions it became subject to abuse or excessive reverence. Lot, for example, insists that two angels in the form of men accept his overnight hospitality in Sodom; perverted men of that city demand that Lot turn the strangers over to them for homosexual sport; he replies that he cannot for they are under his protective hospitality, but offers them instead his two virgin daughters (Gen. 19:1–8). Again, an old man of Gibeah welcomes a Levite wayfarer into his home; "base fellows beset the house round about," demanding that the Levite be handed over to them "that we may know him," a euphemistic phrase referring to sexual acts. Again the host places the protection of his guest (in effect, the institution of hospitality) above the honor and even the life of his daughter (Judg. 19:16–26). Both passages reflect also the low state of daughters in ancient Israel, as was of course true throughout the biblical world.

LIFE OF A TYPICAL NOMAD FAMILY

While nowhere in the Bible are we given a complete and perfect picture of the life of a typical nomad family, still it is possible to fit together enough pieces from biblical and nonbiblical sources to recreate with reasonable accuracy the probabilities of their life.

Let us imagine for the moment another family living in the same period as Jacob. This imaginary family consists of a father with a wife and a concubine; six grown and married sons (Jacob had twelve); three unmarried daughters (three others have been married and are now a part of the families of their husbands' fathers); six male slaves and ten female slaves; and sixteen grandchildren. There are also two widows, sisters of the father. There will soon be another generation added: the granddaughters will have marriages arranged for them by the father of the family when they reach the age of thirteen or fourteen, and the grandsons will acquire wives by the time they are nineteen or twenty. The herds consist of hundreds of sheep and goats and thirty or forty asses. The family "owns" no land, but for two or three generations it has made its home base near Beer-sheba, and the men of the family regard a well there as theirs, and also the cistern the father of the family dug with his brothers a generation ago. There is also a burial plot that is recognized as theirs. The land offers good pasturage in late winter and spring, but when the hot winds come in late May and the long dry season begins, they will need to move elsewhere to places they have used in previous summers and autumns, in areas in the mountainous central part of Palestine, in regions not much inhabited by the Canaanites because they are not suited for agriculture.

During their stay in the Beer-sheba region, they are trying to raise a little barley, and if the rains cooperate they will reap enough to carry with them for baking into flat cakes. The sons and male slaves are concerned day after day with the herds. Their whole economy is based on the health and the increase of the sheep and goats. Soon it will be sheepshearing time, when the men will work hours on end, day after day, cutting the wool from the frightened sheep, washing it once, and turning it over to the women. Wives and female slaves will have hard work too, particularly in readying the wool to sell or to weave it into useful items of clothing. Undeniably the women of this family (and all nomadic women) occupy an inferior place in relation to the male. Chastity is the great virtue. Children are in the care of the older women of the family for several years. The young goats, the kids, are their pets, and from their pets they learn the basics of animal husbandry. As the boys begin to grow sturdy they are introduced to shepherding and the arts of living in the wilderness and protecting their flock and themselves. The girls are introduced to the household arts and gradually take on their share of the drudgery.

The father will handle the sale or barter of any animals the family wants to sell, especially excess male sheep and goats. He will do the same with the wool and any goat's hair tent material, goatskins or lambskins, or leather pouches and waterbags the group may have produced. He will acquire in exchange the items most needed by the family: perhaps pots and pans, the metalsmith's products, a new weapon or two, food of the sort the family has not eaten for months.

Once the worst of the spring work is over the family and other families of the same clan will celebrate with a seasonal festival in which a sheep will be sacrificed and an offering of the fat made to the Lord. To eat meat except on a festal occasion would be to devour one's own wealth, his capital. Mutton (the meat of a full-grown lamb) will be a big change, for mostly the meager diet consists of milk and curds and cheese from the animals; bread from grains raised haphazardly or acquired by barter; roots and small fruits come upon on the marginal lands; and when the family has been very lucky, partridge and quail hunted by the young men using primitive methods such as nets and slingshots, or honey found being gathered by bees in wild areas, as by Samson (Judg. 14:8-9). If the family is prospering, it will have enough produce from the flocks to barter for dates and olives and wheat, products of the settled farmers within the sown.

Life, except for the tending of the flocks, centers in the tents, especially that of the father and his wife. Here is where guests are received and the family consultations held. Clothing is simple, often threadbare, stained by travel and work, and much repaired. Baggage as we know it is not a part of their life. The worldly goods of each married couple can easily be bundled for the next trek on short notice—just about what might be put on two or three asses: the tent itself and its ropes and pegs; a few cooking utensils, and a stone for grinding meal; dried fruits, meal, herbs, and other staples; extra clothing not being worn; blankets, floor pads, skins and water bags; a bucket with its goat's hair rope; a club and perhaps a spear and a hunting knife; a few pottery jars, a platter or tray, and a lamp or two; and simple female ornaments. But these few things placed in a tent make a home, and from such homes come vigorous, alert individuals, tested and weeded out physically—man for man and woman for woman much tougher than their counterparts in the world of sedentary living. It is a stern life, stripped to the bare essentials. No wonder that in later years it will be looked back upon with longing and idealized.

There are jobs for everyone: men, the animals always; for the vigorous women, the heavy work of wool washing, skin scraping, food preparation; for all women, wool processing, fabric making, housekeeping, child raising. All learn how to contribute to the meeting of the group's needs. They adapt themselves to their complex and highly uncertain world, occasionally a perilous world. Indeed, the nomadic family's necessity is to react successfully to climate, topography, and the ups-and-downs of encounters with other peoples.

In the period of Jacob we have been assuming for our typical ass-nomad family, before the Exodus and the desert experience, the Hebrew religion was much less organized and institutionalized than it became afterward. As mentioned above (THE INSTITUTIONS OF NOMADISM), the Lord was regarded as having a special relationship with the head of the family. We know that the observance of new moon festivals was continued down to the time of the Exile (6th century B.C.), and this was an important occasion in Israel's nomadic days. So was the week-long springtime festival in which the Lord was honored for the flocks, celebrated with especial joy in the major towns in the sheep-raising semidesert regions, such as Kadesh, Horeb, and Baal-peor. Genesis tells that Abraham, Isaac, and Jacob had religious experiences (theophanies) while in migration, and wherever this happened they created altars (places of worship) to commemorate the time and place. Marriages, deaths, tribal initiations, and the like were causes for celebration and thanksgiving. In such sacrificial feasts, during which the father of the family acted as "priest," there was a strong belief that they all entered into a kind of mystical union with the Lord. This union was brought about by *blood*. Later in the priestly system the blood drained from the sacrificial animal would be sprinkled on the altar in a formal ritual. The belief in the mystical power of blood is very early.

With the exceptions noted above, the *formal* side of Israel's religion seemed not to have flourished at all in the times described in this section. There seemed to be no place for priests and incense and lampstands and music in the lives of the tough, unreconstructed men and women, who took a living, often marginal, from the lands bordering on the settled, agricultural areas of Palestine.

THE SHEPHERD

In a sense every able-bodied person in a biblical nomadic family was a shepherd, for all participated to a degree in the tending and guarding of the herds (Fig. 48). Their watering was occasionally at least—and perhaps often —entrusted to girls, as Gen. 29:6–10 (Rachel) and Exod. 2:16–19 (Reuel's

48. A modern Arab shepherd with his sheep and goats near Tekoa.

daughters) make plain. But a shepherd is better understood as a man responsible for the care and safety of sheep and goats while grazing away from the nomadic camp or the village, and capable by himself of moving a large flock without loss from one pasture to another, often many miles apart. The expert shepherd was the key to making the pastoral life work, and to the well-being of a nomadic family.

The shepherd did not disappear when the nomadic life of the Hebrews disappeared, for the raising of sheep and goats continued throughout the biblical period. But after the conquest of Canaan, after the occupation of towns and cities and the settling down of the Hebrews into homes and an agricultural economy, shepherding became but one of many occupations and lost its corporate character. It became a way of living for an individual who did not like urban ways and did like the open ranges. He might own his own flock or work for a well-to-do farmer who owned a flock as well as cultivated fields or orchards. He might be a slave. In any case, before and after the settlement in Canaan the requirements of the shepherd were the same.

The sheep must be protected. This was the first rule for the shepherd. Each animal shepherded represented a small share of its owner's capital (wealth). Each lost sheep or goat made the owner that much poorer. Each lost animal represented lost wool or goat's hair or milk, as well as a lost lamb or kid that would have been born the next year.

The dangers from which the sheep and goats had to be protected included wild beasts, theft, and weather. If these three dangers could not be controlled by the shepherd, the operation would soon fail. All three were mentioned by Jacob in his angry retort to Laban's charge of having tricked him (Gen. 31:38–40): "By day the heat consumed me, and the cold by night," he concludes—neither of which is good for animals either—"and my sleep fled from my eyes"—because of nighttime dangers. In effect a shepherd's workday was twenty-four hours long.

The shepherd, or the head shepherd of a very large flock, had decision-making responsibility for the direction he would take the flock. He had to find pasturage, he had to bring the flocks daily to water, or they would die. The shepherd knew the area surrounding his home base as well as a modern golfer knows his own golf course. The shepherd had also made seasonal migrations before and from past experience knew where water and pasturage could probably be found. He knew how to travel by dead reckoning. He knew from training and experience where caves (of which Palestine has many) might be found to provide shelter from storm or cold; protection perhaps from a prowling wild animal; and shade in the midst of a burning summer day.

Wild animals that might be encountered included lions, bears, wolves, jackals, and hyenas. The shepherd's weapons against such beasts were only a slingshot and a stout wooden club, studded with sharp pieces of metal. When a wild animal was known to be near the flock, the shepherd's usual strategy was to use the slingshot and either wound the beast or frighten it off with a barrage of stones. The shepherd also carried a long staff with the crooked handle made familiar by its appearance on Christmas cards and in Christmas pageants. A staff was more useful in climbing rocky cliffs and in helping a sheep extricate itself from some situation it had got itself into (goats got into less trouble), or in directing the sheep into the sheepfold and counting them, than as a weapon.

The shepherd's main items of clothing were leather sandals and a cloak or mantle, often of leather but usually made of camel's hair after the camel had been domesticated. His food supply he carried with him in his girdle and in his scrip, a very early kind of knapsack. His rations might include bread, cheese, dates, olives, and raisins. He would carry a water bag. Milk from the animals was immediately available, and curdled goat's milk, not unlike yogurt, was always a shepherd's chief reliance.

If the flock was very large, requiring more than one shepherd, the normal practice was to set up an encampment near water and return to it at night, where a fire made from collected brushwood would provide warmth (the temperature drops at night in Palestine are severe), add a bit of friendliness to the scene, and keep wild animals at a distance. Here a sheepfold would be built of stones, to be used again another year. Such an encampment is probably reflected in the story of Joseph and his brethren (Gen. 37:14). An encampment would surely be used if the flocks had been led a long distance from home. Booths—simple shelters to protect one from the murderous hot sun of midday, made of four or six poles supporting a roughly thatched roof —would be constructed at strategic lookout points.

Back at the camp in the evening, the sheep and goats would be separated (Matt. 25:32), each flock would be counted, and each animal checked quickly by sharp-eyed experts for injury or indications of disease. Then the shepherds would eat their evening meal, light a fire, and trust that the night would bring no peril to flock or themselves. Perhaps for a while one of them would play a flutelike instrument and they would all sing or tell stories until drowsiness came. From then on they would take turns watching the flock and trying to sort out the night cries, howls, and roars of the beasts of the lonely, uninhabited region.

In sharp contrast to this kind of large-flock shepherding was the village shepherd whose flock might consist of the one or two sheep owned by many different villagers. These he would lead out in the morning to a pasture land beyond the plowed fields, and bring them back to their owners by nightfall.

Temperamentally, a shepherd must be able not only to withstand loneliness but must positively prefer it to the social life of the town, or he will not become a good shepherd.

Clearly, in Bible times a remarkable relationship was established between shepherd and sheep. Each shepherd had his own distinctive call. The sheep, not otherwise distinguished for their intelligence, and nowhere near so nimble as goats, quickly learn to respond to a call and come to the shepherd, unless they are somehow entrapped and befuddled by their entrapment. Even if two or more flocks are mixed, the sheep when called will respond to their own shepherd (John 10:11–16). Once with their own shepherd, the sheep will remain there docilely until he has put them in a fold, or examined them, or led them elsewhere. There is no definite indication of use of sheep dogs in the Bible, though perhaps Job 30:1 should be so regarded. If so, it was rare. Israelites (and other inhabitants of Palestine) consistently regarded dogs very much as they did jackals (1 Kings 14:11; Ps. 22:16; Jer. 15:3).

Shepherd Metaphors

From the relationship of shepherd and sheep have come some of the most effective metaphors and touching expressions of the Bible. In Israel the title "Shepherd" was applied to all persons in authority—kings, government officers and officials, elders (e.g., Isa. 56:11; Jer. 23:1–4; Zech. 10:3). Elsewhere in the ancient Near East the title was applied to kings (e.g., Hammurabi) and to gods (e.g., Shamash). And how much poorer would be our understanding of God and Jesus Christ in our lives if we did not have such apt Bible verses as "The Lord is my shepherd, I shall not want" (Ps. 23:1); "He who scattered Israel will gather him, and will keep him as a shepherd keeps his flock" (Jer. 31:10); "Then he led forth his people like sheep, and guided them in the wilderness like a flock" (Ps. 78:52); "Flocks shall again pass under the hands of the one who counts them, says the Lord" (Jer. 33:13); "What man of you, having a hundred sheep, if he has lost one of them, does not leave the ninety-nine in the wilderness, and go after the one which is lost, until he finds it?" (Luke 15:3–4); "The sheep hear his voice, and he calls out his own sheep by name and leads them out. When he has brought out all his own, he goes before them, and the sheep follow him, for they know his voice" (John 10:4) (Fig. 49).

THE LIFE OF THE FARMER

Farming may be defined as the intentional cultivation of the soil for the purpose of producing a crop. Farming played a major role in the economic,

49. The separation of sheep from goats, carved on the sides of an early Christian sarcophagus (from the Metropolitan Museum of Art, New York).

social, and religious life of ancient Palestine, as it did throughout the ancient Near East. The importance of farming during the biblical period is attested by the numerous references in both the Old and New Testaments to working the soil, planting and harvesting crops, buying and selling farm goods, manufacturing wine and oil, and other matters pertaining to farm life. Most of the population of Palestine was engaged in some type of agricultural work, and those that were not so engaged were dependent upon the farming communities for their subsistence.

The importance of farming in ancient Palestine is evident in the religious structure and civil laws of its people. Canaanite religion, for example, displayed a marked interest in fertility. In the mythological texts from Ras Shamra (ancient Ugarit) on the North Syrian coast, dated around the 14th century B.C., the Canaanite god Baal is clearly represented as a fertility god. He is given the epithet "he who rides on the clouds" and is characterized as a storm and rain god:

> Now, too, the *seasons* of his rains will Baal *observe*,
> The *seasons* of . . . with *snow*;
> And ⟨he will⟩ peal his thunder in the clouds,
> Flashing his lightnings to the earth.

Elijah's encounter with the "prophets of Baal" on Mount Carmel centered about the end of a long drought and severe famine in Samaria during the time of Ahab (1 Kings 19).

Many of the religious and civil laws of the ancient Israelites also reflect an agrarian society. The Israelite religious calendar conformed to the agricultural year, and the three major religious festivals were associated primarily with the cultivation of crops (see section, RELIGIOUS EVENTS and Fig. 4). The Feast of Ingathering (Booths or Tabernacles; cf. Deut. 16:13-15) was associated with the olive harvest, and represented the final completion of the year's agricultural work in late summer and early fall, prior to the onset of the winter rains which began the new year. Although there was no fixed date for its celebration in the earlier period of Israel's history, it was eventually assigned to the latter part of the month of Tishri (September-October). Passover was in part a festival associated with the beginning of the grain harvest in April (the Feast of Unleavened Bread), and in part associated with the spring festival of the original nomadic elements of the people of Israel. Both observances were later combined to commemorate the Exodus (Exod. 12:1-28; cf. Deut. 16:1-8). Finally, the Feast of Weeks (First Fruits, or "Pentecost") was associated with the wheat harvest, which occurred in the month of Sivan (May-June), some fifty days after the celebration of Passover: "And you shall observe the feast of weeks [at] the first fruits of wheat harvest, and the feast of ingathering at the year's end" (Exod. 34:22; cf. Deut. 16:9-12).

Many Israelites believed that the farmer had been instructed in his methods by God (Isa. 28:23-26), and the third and fourth chapters of the book of Genesis witness to the struggle between the farmer and the pastoralist and the difficulties attending the farmer's life. Moreover, many of the civil and religious laws of ancient Israel were based on an agricultural mode of life. A tithe of all produce had to be dedicated to the Lord (Deut. 14:22-29). No one was permitted to encroach on the fields of another (Deut. 19:14). Only vines could be planted in the vineyard, and it was not permitted to plow with an ox and an ass together (Deut. 22:9-10). A person was allowed to partake of his neighbor's crop, but could not harvest or store it (Deut. 23:24-25). A mill or upper millstone could not be taken as security on a loan (Deut. 24:6). These, and many other examples, serve to illustrate the fact that the civil and religious life of ancient Israel was determined to a considerable degree by agricultural pursuits.

THE BEGINNINGS OF AGRICULTURE IN ANCIENT PALESTINE

Agriculture had a long history in ancient Palestine prior to the settlement of the Israelites. This phase of human existence was preceded by an even longer period during which man lived by hunting and gathering. The exact date of transition from a food-gathering to a food-producing culture cannot be documented, nor the processes by which this shift occurred precisely defined. However, present evidence indicates that man began to achieve a more or less settled form of life and to raise his own food sometime during the Mesolithic ("Middle Stone") Age some 10,000–12,000 years ago. Man's adherence to the soil began in this period, although the process was both gradual and variable. The Natufian (c. 10,000–8,000 B.C.) was a rich and distinct manifestation of Mesolithic culture in ancient Palestine. The people who belonged to this culture lived both in caves and open settlements, and were excellent hunters and fishermen. Their tools included not only barbed spearpoints and well-developed fishhooks, but also mortars and pestles and sickle handles of wood and bone slotted to receive flint blades, examples of which display a characteristic luster resulting from the harvest of cereals. The archaeological evidence for Natufian culture indicates a certain stability of settlement as well as an economy based in part on cereals. It is not known, however, whether the grain harvested was wild or domestic and the Natufian culture may best be interpreted as a people in transition from food-collecting (hunting and gathering) to food-producing (farming and breeding).

By the Neolithic, or "New Stone," Age (c. 8,000–4,000 B.C.), the earliest farm communities were established and the cultivation of the soil formed an important part of daily life. The site of Jericho, situated in the lower Jordan Valley, provides evidence for the systematic cultivation of cereals during this period. From this time on, except for the nomadic and seminomadic elements of the desert and steppe, farming occupied the central role in the economy and daily life of the peoples of ancient Palestine.

Canaanite civilization, the origins of which preceded the arrival of the Israelites into Palestine, was to a large extent based on agriculture. A portion of the land of Canaan is described in the Egyptian "Story of Si-nuhe" (c. 1991–1786 B.C.): "It was a good land, named Yaa. Figs were in it, and grapes. It had more wine than water. Plentiful was its honey, abundant its olives. Every [kind of] fruit was on its trees. Barley was there, and emmer. There was no limit to any [kind of] cattle." Following the settlement in Palestine, farmers comprised most of the population of ancient Israel. Not only villagers, but also many who dwelt in the fortified cities gained their livelihood from agriculture during the biblical period. The land of ancient Palestine is still dotted with the small villages and farm communities which have characterized the land for at least six millennia.

TYPES OF AGRICULTURE IN THE ANCIENT NEAR EAST

Two main types of agriculture were practiced in the ancient Near Eastern world. Irrigation farming was practiced by the great riverine civilizations of southern Mesopotamia and Egypt. Rain-fed ("dry") farming was practiced in most other cultivable areas of the ancient Near East, and was particularly characteristic of Palestine. The major differences between the two types of agriculture and the types of civilization they produced were the result of various geographic and climatic factors.

Irrigation Farming in Mesopotamia and Egypt

Both southern Mesopotamia and Egypt were areas of reduced rainfall, and agriculture was dependent upon irrigation. The ancient civilizations of southern Mesopotamia were dependent upon the floodwaters of the Tigris and Euphrates Rivers, and that of Egypt was dependent upon the inundations of the Nile. The regular rise of the three rivers, the annual renewal of the soil by the deposition of silt, and the warm climate were favorable to the growth of a rich plant life and an economy based on agriculture. In addition, the high degree of cohesiveness and technological skill necessary to control and utilize the floodwaters determined to a great extent the character of ancient Babylonian and Egyptian civilization. At an early age both lands developed a characteristic unity and a highly organized civil, social, and religious order. This was in sharp contrast to the land of ancient Palestine, where natural conditions interfered with the development of social and political unity, and small city-states were the characteristic form of civilization.

Although similarities existed between ancient Mesopotamia and Egypt, geographical conditions in both areas were not equal and different approaches to irrigation farming were necessary.

Ancient Southern Mesopotamia

Both the Tigris and Euphrates Rivers have their origin in the Armenian highlands of Asia Minor and are fed primarily by the melting of winter snowfall. Although there are certain distinct differences in the nature of the two rivers, both are turbulent, rapidly flowing streams and are highly erosive. Both rivers are at their lowest in September and October, and rise considerably from December on. The maximum flood stage of the Tigris occurs in April, while that of the Euphrates occurs in May.

Control of the waters of these two rivers raised specific problems for the ancient civilizations of the Tigris-Euphrates lowlands. Because the floodwaters came in the spring, cultivated areas could not be inundated as in

Egypt, and the water had to be impounded within the banks of the rivers themselves. In addition, a method had to be devised to drain off stagnant floodwater in order to reduce salinization. A system of canals was constructed by which arid areas could be watered, and waterlogged fields drained, using the variation in the relative level between the Tigris and the Euphrates. The system was not without its difficulties, however. The complex system of canals needed frequent dredging, salinization could not be entirely prevented, and the rivers often cut new channels, occasionally leaving fields and cities completely isolated. These disturbing effects created discontinuity in ancient southern Mesopotamian civilization.

Ancient Egypt

The Nile River flows northward through Egypt, creating a narrow ribbon of fertile land, limited on the east by barren highlands, and on the west by a vast desert. North of Cairo, the river fans out into a broad delta before emptying into the Mediterranean Sea. The "land of Goshen," located in the northeastern part of the Delta, was the home of the descendants of Jacob from the time of Joseph to the Exodus (see Gen. 46-47).

The annual flooding of the Nile is the result of heavy rain which falls during spring and summer in the highlands of east Africa, far to the south of Egypt. The Egyptian Nile is the combination of three streams which bring this rainfall to Egypt: the more regular White Nile; the more turbulent and periodic Blue Nile; and the equally turbulent Atbara. Minimum flood stage occurs in Egypt during May and early June, with the beginning of the inundation occurring a short time thereafter, toward the end of June. The maximum water level is reached in the area of Cairo around the latter part of September or the beginning of October. The regularity of this pattern gave rise to three agricultural seasons in ancient Egypt: "Inundation," when the floodwaters began; "Winter," or the time of cultivation, which occurred as soon as the floodwaters began to recede (sometime in October); and "Summer," which marked the harvest season and brought renewed activity. The harvest was stored in brick-built granaries until required for use (see Gen. 41:35-36, 47-49, 55-57; Exod. 1:11). Intense agricultural activity occurred throughout most of the year in ancient Egypt, except when the inundation of the late summer brought a temporary halt to this activity and the farmers turned to building and the making of handicrafts.

The Nile floods were steadier and more predictable than those of the Tigris-Euphrates lowlands, and control of the water was less complex. Moreover, the timing of the inundation in late summer was more favorable for the growing of cereals than in southern Mesopotamia, where the flood level reached its maximum in the spring. Not only did the Nile provide life-giving water, but also deposited annual layers of rich, fertile mud over the cultivable land. The Egyptian farmers practiced "basin" irrigation, which consisted of dividing the fields into shallow basins by means of earthen embankments. With the inundation, the floodwaters filled the basins, deposited their fertile silt, and remained for several weeks. The water was then drained and the fields plowed and planted.

Despite the regularity of the inundation of the Nile, the quantity of water varied from year to year, depending upon the amount of rainfall in the tropical highlands to the south. Periods of decreased rainfall would occasion drought and famine, and the ancient Egyptians attached great importance to the yearly recording of the maximum level of the Nile. The story of Joseph attests to the possibility of drought in ancient Egypt (Gen. 41). However, the agricultural wealth of Egypt was considerable in all but the poorest years.

Rain-fed Farming in Ancient Palestine

A different type of agriculture from that practiced in southern Mesopotamia and Egypt was necessary in ancient Palestine. Here the gradations between the desert and the sown are less rigid and the dominant agricultural factor is not the river but the rainfall (see Fig. 3). Throughout the land of Palestine farmland gradually gives way to the steppe and the desert. Farmers practiced rain-fed ("natural") rather than irrigation agriculture. The sharp contrast between the agricultural environment of Palestine and that of Egypt is vividly portrayed in Deut. 11:10–11:

> For the land which you are entering to take possession of it is not like the land of Egypt, from which you have come, where you sowed your seed and watered it with your feet, like a garden of vegetables; but the land which you are going over to possess is a land of hills and valleys, which drinks water by the rain from heaven. . . .

Farming in Palestine was more precarious than in either Egypt or Mesopotamia. The crop yield was entirely dependent upon the amount of rainfall, which was limited to the winter season and was insufficient in many parts of the country. The quantity of precipitation varied from year to year and decreased rapidly toward the south and inland from the coast. Drought was not infrequent and brought considerable anxiety to the ancient farmers. Extended periods of drought frequently resulted in the collapse of the entire agricultural system.

This insecurity was a particular factor along the frontiers between the desert and the sown. Drought would lead the settled population—farmers and villagers—to seek refuge elsewhere, opening the way for nomads and seminomadic bands to advance from the desert into the vacuum created by the retreating farmers. In turn, sufficient rainfall would prompt the farmers of ancient Palestine to expand into the fringe areas of cultivation, while the nomadic elements would retreat further into the desert. As a result, the frontier between the desert and the sown in ancient Palestine was never clearly defined and always fluid.

Although natural farming provided the basis for most of the agriculture of Palestine, irrigation was used within specific areas at various times. However, irrigation was not used on the same scale as in Mesopotamia and Egypt, and it was of a different kind. For example, irrigation agriculture was practiced in the northern Negev during the time of the Judean kingdom and in the Roman period. Dams were constructed in wadis (dry stream beds) in order to catch, store, and utilize the torrents of water which would fill the wadis during an occasional storm. Irrigation was also practiced within oases, such as that at Jericho in the southern Jordan Valley (Fig. 50). This gravitational type of irrigation, however, was small in scale and isolated, frequently occurring at stopping places along important trade routes.

THE GEOGRAPHY AND CLIMATE OF ANCIENT PALESTINE

The biblical farmer cannot be understood apart from the two main factors which affected his life and determined to a great extent his seasonal activities

50. The green oasis of Jericho which is watered by irrigation from the Spring of Elisha ('Ein es-Sultan).

—the nature of the land itself and its climate, especially the rainfall. As an introduction to the life of a typical Israelite farmer (see below), it is essential to describe briefly the geography and climate of ancient Palestine and to note the major crops which characterized the land.

It is necessary to remember that the land of Palestine has undergone certain changes since biblical times. Natural forces such as erosion have altered the landscape to some extent. Of even greater significance has been the activity of man. The remains of ancient cities dot the countryside in the form of small, hill-like ruins. Forests which once covered most of the hill country have largely disappeared, being replaced by fields, vineyards, barren outcrops of rock, and smaller trees and shrubs. Hill farming necessitated the construction of man-made terraces in order to provide a more level surface for planting and to retard the erosion of the soil. Terraces such as those used in biblical times cover many areas of the modern countryside (Fig. 51). Moreover, new crops have been introduced into the area which were unknown to the Israelites—crops such as squash, tomatoes, apricots, and oranges.

Despite these ongoing changes, the climate and overall geography of the land of Palestine is basically the same as it was during the biblical period. With the exception of the changes noted above, the modern visitor to the

51. Hill farming requires terracing to retain the soil on the slopes of the hills.

Holy Land can easily visualize the environment and lifestyles of the ancient Israelites, Jews, and early Christians.

The Land

Ancient Palestine was a land of great diversity, with a considerable range of environmental zones. To a large extent the result of the marginal character of the rainfall, this diversity was also a result of the natural topography of the land itself. Palestine is divided into four major north-south zones: the Coastal Plain, the Central Highlands, the Jordan Rift, and the Eastern (Transjordanian) Plateau. Within these four major zones are additional geographical units, such as the Shephelah (or "Lowlands") along the western slopes of the Central Highlands. Subdividing these north-south features are various east-west lines, such as the Plain of Esdraelon in the north, which separates the highlands of Galilee from the hill country of Samaria. Other natural divisions include the hill country of Judah, the plain of Sharon, the Philistine plain, the dome of Gilead, and the steppe and desert of the Negev.

These geographical factors tend to separate the land of Palestine into small provinces and served in ancient times as barriers to unification. Because it was a natural mosaic, Palestine was a cultural mosaic as well. The various geographical and topographical divisions, together with the somewhat related variations in climate and rainfall, greatly influenced the lifestyles of the people who resided in each district, and gave rise to various types of agriculture and crops. Moreover, much of the cultivable land in Palestine is stony and hilly. As a result, farms were quite often small, required constant attention, and were frequently terraced.

The animosity between the northern kingdom of Israel and the southern kingdom of Judah provides an example of the differences which existed between various parts of the land. Only through strong central leadership could the two areas be held together, as they were during the reigns of David and Solomon. This unity was short-lived, however, and the two areas were quickly divided into separate kingdoms (c. 922 B.C.; see 1 Kings 12:1–20). From the time of Baasha, king of Israel (c. 900–877 B.C.), and Asa, king of Judah (c. 913–873 B.C.), the ancient city of Bethel marked the southern frontier of Israel and the fortified cities of Geba and Mizpah (Tell en-Naṣbeh) the northern frontier of Judah (see 1 Kings 15:22; 2 Kings 23:8). A transverse route across the Central Highlands in the area between these frontiers represented a division between two agricultural zones: the highlands of Judah to the south, where vines predominated, and the richer hill country of Ephraim to the north, where olives flourished.

Climate and Rainfall

The Mediterranean climate of Palestine is divided into two major seasons: a dry, hot summer season from mid-June to mid-September, and a rainy winter season in the cooler part of the year, roughly from mid-October to mid-April (*see* Fig. 4). There are no true spring or autumn seasons, but only brief transitional periods of short length and overlapping character. This climate is to a large extent determined not only by the movement of the major climate belts, but also by the location of Palestine between sea and desert. Moreover, the main lines of relief run in a north-south direction, parallel to the coast, opposite the movement of the winter storms which bring life-giving rain.

The rainfall, which is marginal in character, was the primary determining factor in the life of the ancient farmer. The rainy season commenced with the "early rain" (Deut. 11:14; Joel 2:23; cf. Jer. 5:24) of October and November. The arrival of rain softened the ground for plowing and marked the beginning of cultivation. The "latter rains" of April and May brought an end to the rainy season and indicated the beginning of the harvest. This was accompanied by hot winds (the "khamsin" or "sirocco") which blew in from the arid desert. Within time, all natural vegetation dried up rapidly, turning the land into a yellow and almost desolate panorama. The heat and dryness of the summer are referred to in the Bible (Ps. 32:4; Isa. 18:4). Sunstroke was a danger in the heat of the fields at harvesttime (see 2 Kings 4:18–20).

The winter rainfall in Palestine exhibits great diversity, with variations in its amount, distribution, and reliability. Precipitation varies within the land according to geographical location, and is intensified by differences in altitude (*see* Fig. 2). As a general rule, the rainfall decreases from west to east, and from north to south (*see* Fig. 3). The Central Highlands form a barrier which prevents the rain from penetrating inland. Areas which receive the greatest amount of rainfall are the northern coastal strip and the northern highlands. The rainfall diminishes according to the degree a region is further removed from the sea, more southerly, or lower in altitude. South of Joppa (Jaffa) and on the eastern side of the Central Highlands, marked decreases in rainfall occur. As a result, vegetation is thickest on the northern and western slopes, where precipitation is greater and evaporation less.

There are, however, a few exceptions to this general pattern. For example, there is an area of sufficient rainfall which extends southward along the western edge of the Edomite (Transjordanian) Plateau, allowing a narrow southward expansion of the farming zone. This is in sharp contrast to a long finger of drought which extends northward into the Jordan Valley from the Dead Sea. Located in the rain-shadow of the Central Highlands, agriculture is impossible in this area without the use of some form of irrigation.

Besides the differences in precipitation due to seasonal and geographical factors, there is also a variation in the concentration of rainfall. A high percentage of the rain which falls in Palestine is concentrated in a limited number of days. Torrents of rain fall in brief intervals, with extended dry periods in between. Jerusalem, for example, has nearly the same average annual precipitation as London, but only within about one-third the number of days. As a result of the high concentration of rainfall in a limited period of time, flash floods are frequent. Most of the streams in Palestine are intermittent and carry water only on rainy days. Flash floods are particularly characteristic of the drier regions of Palestine, such as the Judean desert and the Negev. Deeply cut wadis (dry stream beds) line the countryside and are filled with torrents of water only after an occasional rain (Fig. 52). The water, however, is quickly absorbed or evaporates.

There are also variations in the amount of rainfall from year to year. As a result, cultivation was not as predictable or controllable as it was in Egypt and Mesopotamia. Yearly variations of rainfall in ancient Palestine created a constantly shifting pattern of agricultural zones and a fluid frontier between the desert and the sown. Drought was not infrequent, and

52. A wadi, or dry stream bed, which is filled with water only after a hard rain.

would bring cries of anguish, hunger and thirst, frustration, sickness and other maladies (see Deut. 28:15–24; Jer. 14:1–6; Hag. 1:10–11). Prolonged periods of drought would cause the land of ancient Palestine to be imperiled and nearly uninhabitable. A period of drought of more than three years occurred in the time of Ahab, king of Israel (c. 869–850 b.c.), and the prophet Elijah (1 Kings 17–18; see Luke 4:25; Jas. 5:17).

Rainfall was the primary source of water on which the ancient farmer relied. However, additional moisture was obtained for cultivation from the heavy dew which collected on the seaward slopes of the western hills, the Plain of Esdraelon, and certain other areas of Palestine (see Gen. 27:28; Judg. 6:36–40; Ps. 133:3). The heavy dew of the coastal plain west of Beersheba was of particular importance for cultivation. Dew was regarded with much favor, and its absence a curse, since it was the only source of moisture during the dry, rainless months of summer (see Deut. 33:28; 2 Sam. 1:21; Isa. 18:4; Zech. 8:12). On clear, calm summer nights the cooling ground surface would react with the high humidity to condense the moisture. The dew evaporated quickly with the renewed heat of the day (Hos. 6:4; 13:3; Mic. 5:7).

Israelite farmers during the period of the monarchy frequently tried to store auxiliary water in cisterns hewn into bedrock (Fig. 53). Cisterns were used to water crops, to provide drinking water, and to store water in times

53. A cistern cut from bedrock.

of siege (see 2 Kings 18:31; Jer. 41:9). Uzziah, king of Judah (c. 783–742 B.C.), had cisterns cut in order to store water for his herds, vineyards, and fields (2 Chron. 26:10). The typical cistern of the Israelite period, as indicated by archaeological evidence, had a bottle-shaped reservoir with a narrow opening at the top, and was lined with a lime plaster. Stone-lined shafts connected the rock-hewn cistern with the ground surface when necessary. Frequently, the opening to the cistern was capped by a large flat stone. Slime and debris would collect in the cisterns. The prophet Jeremiah was imprisoned in a slime-filled cistern, but was later rescued (Jer. 38:6–13).

LAND USE AND CROPS

The land, climate, and rainfall pattern determined to a high degree the use to which the land was put and the crops that could be grown. Farming was the dominant mode of life in ancient Palestine, and was practiced primarily in three major cultivation zones. These zones consisted of the northern coastal plain, the hill regions of the interior (especially the Shephelah), and the upper portions of the Jordan Valley. Crops were grown in certain other areas of ancient Palestine as well. However, these regions—particularly those to the east and south—were marginal and less productive. These marginal zones were primarily the domain of the pastoralist, although flocks were also tended on the slopes and crest of the Central Highlands.

At the time of the Israelite settlement in the hill country, forests and woodlands spread over the Central Highlands, making large-scale farming difficult. The land was also hilly and rocky, limiting the size and intensity of true farming. As the lowlands and plains were absorbed or taken over under Israelite control, and as areas of alluvial soil and forests were cleared, larger areas could be farmed. Wheat was grown on the better-drained areas of the Sharon and Esdraelon Plains, and in the downfaulted basins of Manasseh. Olive trees were at home on the well-watered slopes of Ephraim, and in the somewhat drier climate of Judah the vine predominated, although wheat and olives were grown as well.

Grain crops, such as wheat and barley, could also be cultivated in the southern coastal zone. This area, however, consisted of a broad transition zone which was subject to drastic fluctuations in rainfall. Drought was a constant threat and crop failure frequent. Subterranean storage pits dating to the Persian period (5th–4th century B.C.) have been discovered on several archaeological sites in this area and in the adjacent southern foothills of the Judean highlands. It appears that these storage pits were dug to provide long-term storage of surplus grain to be used in times of drought.

No stable agricultural settlements were located in the northern and central Negev. This land could not be farmed except in limited areas around springs, or in relation to irrigation projects and dams which were constructed to collect and retain the water from broad wadis which would fill up during an occasional winter storm. Such use was mainly limited to the time of the kingdom of Judah, and more extensively during Nabatean and Roman times. The southern Negev and the Arabah were desert wastelands.

In summarizing the general features of land use in ancient Palestine, the following pattern can be noted. The southern and southeastern part of the land was mainly pastoral in character. The Transjordanian Plateau was also to a considerable extent pastoral in character, but with the addition of some agricultural use, particularly to the north. The coastal area and the highlands formed the primary agricultural zones, basically favorable to the olive, but also to grain (wheat and barley) and vine cultivation.

The description of the land which the Israelite people were to settle outlines the basic agricultural products of ancient Palestine (Deut. 8:7-8):

> For the Lord your God is bringing you into a good land, a land of brooks of water, of fountains and springs, flowing forth in valleys and hills, a land of wheat and barley, of vines and fig trees and pomegranates, a land of olive trees and honey. . . .

These basic crops are mentioned time and again throughout the Old Testament. The three basic products—grain, wine, and oil—appear together frequently in all periods (e.g., Deut. 7:13; 11:14; 2 Kings 18:32; 2 Chron. 32:28; Neh. 5:11; 13:12; Hos. 2:8, 22; Joel 1:10; Hag. 1:11; Ps. 104:15). Grain, wine, and oil retain their importance in the New Testament, and form the basis for numerous parables (e.g., Matt. 25:4; Mark 2:22; Luke 6:1; 1 Cor. 15:37).

Wheat and barley ("bread") were the most widespread crops cultivated in Palestine, and the basic form of sustenance. These cereals were grown on the coastal plain, in the valleys, in clearings within the forests on the hills, and on the plateau. Wheat was the most preferable of the grains (see Ps. 147:14), and the best wheatfields were located in Galilee. Barley can grow on poorer soils and can withstand a drier climate. It was therefore of greater importance in marginal areas of cultivation, particularly to the south and east. Barley, rather than wheat, was predominant in the Philistine Plain.

The olive ("oil") ripens slowly, and is confined to areas with a true Mediterranean climate (Fig. 54). Severe frost is harmful to the olive, but the fruit can withstand long periods of drought and can be picked anytime during the early rainy season. Olive cultivation was concentrated on the coastal plain and on the western slopes of the Central Highlands (see Judg. 15:5). Olives could also be grown along the edge of the eastern plateau of

54. A grove of olive trees in Galilee.

Gilead, even as far south as the Dead Sea. They were grown here during the Roman period.

Vineyards ("wine") are found primarily on the sides of hills (Isa. 5:1; Amos 9:13). They were grown "upon the mountains of Samaria" (Jer. 31:5), as well as in the highlands of Judah (Fig. 55). The vine, with its long roots, is able to resist both severe cold and prolonged drought. The heavy summer dew of the mountains aids the swelling of the grapes, which ripen during the late summer when there is little water and it appears that the land is desolate. The vine, however, requires the greatest care. It must be carefully pruned and hoed (see Isa. 5:6), and protected from wild animals during the late summer heat (see S. of S. 2:15).

Among other crops cultivated were various fruits, such as the fig (Fig. 56), whose tree provided shade and was a symbol of security (1 Kings 4:25; Mic. 4:4; Zech. 3:10). The early ("first-ripe") fruit of the fig tree was highly valued (Jer. 24:2; Hos. 9:10; Mic. 7:1; Nah. 3:12), and the blossoming of the fig tree marked the nearness of summer (Mark 13:28). Sycamore figs were also grown (Amos 7:14), and covered the Shephelah (1 Kings 10:27). Stands of these trees formed part of the royal estate of King David (1 Chron. 27:28). Other fruits which were grown in Palestine included: pomegranates (Deut. 8:8; S. of S. 4:13), such as those found in the area of Gibeah (1 Sam. 14:2), and which might be squeezed for juice (S. of S. 8:2) (Fig. 57); pistachio nuts and almonds (Gen. 43:11; Eccl. 12:5), the latter of which

55. Unripened grapes on the vine.

56. A fig tree with its broad leaves.

57. Pomegranates on the bush.

was the first fruit to blossom (see Jer. 1:11–12) (Fig. 58); and dates, which grew around Jericho in the Jordan Valley and around Elath near the Red Sea. Grapes, figs, pomegranates, and dates (*see* Fig. 23) were valuable sources of sugar. The only other source of sugar, until the Hellenistic period, was wild honey (1 Sam. 14:26–27). Besides the fruits, there were vegetables, such as cucumbers (Isa. 1:8), beans and lentils (2 Sam. 17:28; Ezek. 4:9), and spices, such as mint, dill, and cummin (Isa. 28:25, 27; Matt. 23:23).

HISTORY OF FARMING IN THE BIBLICAL PERIOD

A brief summary of the history of farming during the period of the Old and New Testaments is presented below. Not every detail is recorded, since the main purpose is to provide a general summary of the historical changes in the development of farming. Many factors affected both the relationship of the farmer to his land, and the position he held in his community. Nevertheless, his lifestyle remained essentially unchanged throughout the biblical period.

Patriarchal Period

From the time of the Patriarchs (early 2nd millennium B.C.) down to the settlement in the land of Canaan (late 13th century B.C.), the Israelite

58. A branch of an almond tree in blossom.

people followed a nomadic pattern of life (see section, THE LIFE OF THE NOMAD). They moved along the fringes of the settled land, and did not establish permanent settlements (see Gen. 13). Flocks of sheep and goats, and perhaps some cattle, furnished most of their food, clothing, and shelter. They migrated with the seasons and pasturage, and quarreled with others over water rights (see Gen. 26:17–33). They occasionally occupied marginal grasslands and planted seasonal crops (see Gen. 26:12).

Period of the Judges

Settlement in the land of Canaan introduced changes in the Israelite way of life. The period of the judges (late 13th–last quarter of the 11th century B.C.) represented a time of transition and adaptation to village life, with frequent encounters with belligerent neighbors, as attested throughout the book of Judges. In the early stages of this transition, it appears that the Israelites were primarily engaged in tending flocks (e.g., Judg. 5:10–11, 16, 24–25), principally in the area of Gilead and Bashan in the Transjordanian Plateau (see Num. 32; Deut. 3:12–20; Josh. 1:12–15). As the process of settlement unfolded, however, the Israelites took over the fields, cisterns, vineyards, and olive trees of the Canaanites (see Deut. 6:10–11; Josh. 24:13), and settled in the highlands of Judah, Ephraim, and Galilee. Archaeological evidence has confirmed that the areas initially occupied coincided with regions watered by sufficient rainfall for cultivation.

Small fields were cleared out of the forests of the highlands in order to provide sufficient room for cultivation, and terraces were constructed on the slopes of the hills. The vast wheatfields of the plains were not available to the Israelites at this time (see Judg. 1:19, 27–36; 15:4–5). Because of the lack of security, crops and villages were frequently destroyed by invading nomadic bands (see Judg. 6:2–5). It was sometimes necessary for the Israelite farmers to conceal their activity (see Judg. 6:11).

It appears that Gideon was a farmer of moderate wealth (see Judg. 8:24–26), with cattle and servants (Judg. 6:25–27), sheep (Judg. 6:37), vineyards and wheatfields (Judg. 5:11; 8:2). Micah also appears to have had some wealth (see Judg. 17:1–5, 10–12). Most of the Israelite farmers, however, had only small fields and little wealth. The possession of land was of great importance, as indicated by the laws of redemption (see Ruth 3–4).

Period of the Monarchy

The picture of farming portrayed in the Old Testament for the period of the monarchy (c. 1020–587 B.C.) is one of large-scale cultivation, with farmers, herdsmen, and various commercial agents and government officials drawn together under centralized political and administrative organizations (see section, THE CIVIL LIFE). There was generally greater prosperity and security (see 1 Kings 4:20); there was considerably more farmland available for cultivation; and there were more advanced techniques and tools, which allowed the farmer to produce (rainfall permitting) larger crops.

Agricultural products formed the basis of the national economy, and farmers comprised the majority of the population. The typical farmer led a provincial, rustic mode of existence, and was concerned primarily with his own welfare and his own fields, orchards, and vineyards. He had little or no interest in the political structure or commercial enterprises of the nation, other than those which affected his own pattern of life (see 1 Kings 12:1–20). His small farm was confined primarily to the fields and terraces inherited from his ancestors along the slopes of the Central Highlands, and provided little more than the immediate needs of his family or local community.

However, life for the Israelite farmer was considerably more complex during the period of the monarchy than it had been before. There were new arts and crafts, new political forces, new social and religious concepts, international constraints and pressures, mass production techniques, taxes (1 Kings 4:7–28), and other nationally imposed responsibilities (1 Kings 5:13–18; 15:22).

The greatest threat to the farmer was the loss of his land, and the limitations of freedom and self-sufficiency that this implied. The institution of the monarchy threatened the agricultural system based on the independent farm (see 1 Sam. 13:11–18). Private fields and vineyards were taken over by kings and wealthy landowners, either through purchase or by force (1 Kings 16:24; 21:1-16; see Isa. 5:8; Ezek. 45:8; 46:18; Mic. 2:1-2). Large commercial farmlands, vineyards, and royal estates were established which were worked by tenants. Such an estate belonged to King David, and included fields, vineyards, olive and sycamore trees, pastures and flocks (1 Chron. 27:26-31).

During the period of the monarchy large areas of Palestine were converted into farmland and more efficient farming tools and techniques were developed. Iron plowshares and sickles gradually (but never completely until Roman times) replaced similar tools of flint, stone, and bronze. Large public and governmental storehouses—such as those excavated at Megiddo, Hazor, and Beer-sheba—were constructed to store the grain, wine, and olive oil which were collected from taxes imposed on the farmer's fields, or built up from the surplus produced by the royal estates and other large farmlands (see 1 Kings 9:19; 2 Chron. 26:10). Ostraca (documents written on broken pieces of pottery) discovered among the ruins of the Israelite royal citadel at Samaria record the taxes of wine and oil which were collected and apparently stored there sometime between the reigns of Joahaz (c. 815-801 B.C.) and Jeroboam II (c. 786-746 B.C.). Agricultural products were often traded to other nations in return for goods or services not available within Judah or Israel (see 1 Kings 5:10-11; 2 Chron. 2:7-10, 13-16; Ezek. 27:17).

Regions located on the fringe of the arable land, which were not previously farmed to any large extent, were settled and cultivated during the period of the Judean (southern) kingdom. These settlements were associated with fortresses constructed along the main roads through the northern and central Negev. Some of these fortresses, such as those excavated at Tell 'Arad and Ramat Matred, date to the time of Solomon (10th century B.C.). However, the great expansion into this semiarid region appears to date from around the time of Uzziah, king of Judah (c. 783-742 B.C.), who "built towers in the wilderness, and hewed out many cisterns, for he had large herds, both in the Shephelah and in the plain, and he had farmers and vinedressers in the hills and in the fertile lands, for he loved the soil" (2 Chron. 26:10).

Survey work and excavation along the western slopes and highlands of the central Negev have documented a series of fortresses, generally associated with small agricultural settlements, dating from the 9th to the 7th centuries B.C. In this arid climate, with hot dry summers and relatively cool winters, rain falls only in the form of scattered winter storms between October and May. Rainfall is limited and fluctuates widely, and it is possible to cultivate the area only in depressions (wadis) where runoff water collects. This "desert" agriculture requires the construction of dams, rock-

cut channels and cisterns, and other features in order to collect and distribute the available water, and to prevent the erosion of the soil. It appears
from the archaeological evidence that the farmers of Judah were the first
to settle the area to any large extent and to develop a crop system based
on floodwater irrigation. This system was later elaborated upon during the
Nabatean to Byzantine periods (c. 200 B.C.–A.D. 600) (Fig. 59). A similar
system was developed in the arid Judean Buqei'a where fortresses, dams,
and cisterns dated to around the time of Jehoshaphat (c. 873–849 B.C.; see
2 Chron. 17:12) and Uzziah (2 Chron. 26:10) have also been studied. This
evidence, as well as other biblical and archaeological evidence, attests to the
extensive agricultural use to which the land of Palestine was put during
the monarchical period.

Postexilic Period

The Babylonian Exile in 587 B.C. brought to an end the rich culture and
civilization which the Israelite people had carved out of their Palestinian
homeland. Only the poorest inhabitants of the land were left (2 Kings
25:12), and the agricultural use of the land was greatly diminished. There
were no longer any royal estates, nor any settlements in the marginal areas
such as the Negev and Judean desert. In the highlands, only small, impoverished farmsteads remained. To those that returned from Babylonia, the
land appeared desolate and forsaken (see Neh. 1:3; 2:17; 5:1–5). Although

59. A Nabataean cistern in the Negev desert.

they proceeded to repair the agricultural terraces on the hillsides, and to restore the agricultural installations, the farmers were slow to reestablish themselves (cf. Mal. 1:2–3). Conditions, however, later improved, and by the New Testament period the farmlands were even more extensive and productive than during the period of the monarchy.

New Testament Period

The life of the farmer in the period of the New Testament was not much different from that during the Old Testament period. The same basic crops (grain, the olive, the vine) formed the major portion of the agrarian economy, and the same seasonal pattern of existence was followed. A few new crops had been introduced, but in general the staple foods remained the same. Rice was now grown in wet terrains, such as in the Plain of Esdraelon, but the tomatoes, bananas, and citrus fruits grown in modern times were still unknown. Fowl and eggs, however, which were not known in Palestine in the days of the Israelite monarchy, were known in the New Testament period (Matt. 23:37).

The main differences between the Old and New Testament worlds existed in the overall social and political structure, and in the tools and technology available to the farmer. By the New Testament period, the entire Mediterranean world reflected the same basic cosmopolitan culture. Roman lifestyles were imitated, and the fashions of the day were copied from those of Greece and Rome. Large gains had been made in intellectual activity and cultural development. These changes probably had little effect on the daily life of the typical farmer.

The farmer's life, however, was affected by the structure of the Roman government and the advances made in technology. Roman rule implied heavy taxes, and it is certain that the taxes were felt to no small degree by the farmer (see Luke 19:1–8; 20:22–25). Roman administration also created greater social stratification than had been the case during the Old Testament period. Ever since the Hellenistic period (c. 330–63 B.C.) cultural influence was greater in the city and the town than it was among the large and scattered farm population. Within the urban environment Hellenistic and Roman influence was dominant. However, the native Semitic traditions persisted in the countryside. The typical farmer was still a simple, industrious laborer whose life centered about his small village and his fields. But those who lived in the city had far surpassed the farmer in social charm, intellectual status, and wealth. A greater gap developed between the two levels of culture than ever before. There were a number of wealthy landowners, such as the "rich fool," who possessed large fields and erected numerous barns and granaries (Luke 12:13–21). There were others who owned vineyards and rented the land to tenants (Matt. 21:33-41). In contrast to such wealthy landowners stood the vast majority of farmers who either owned small fields or vineyards, worked as tenants on a large estate, or hired themselves out as simple laborers for a daily wage (see Matt. 20:1-16).

During the Early Roman period (63 B.C.-A.D. 70) there was a great expansion of agriculture and trade. Roman efficiency in building roads and aqueducts, in developing new sources of water, and in clearing new areas for settlement contributed to the expansion of farmlands. Prior to the Babylonian Exile (587 B.C.) a considerable part of the Galilean highlands was a forested frontier region. By the time of the New Testament rich wheatfields were located in lower Galilee. Similarly, the Romans developed vast wheatfields in the reasonably well-watered area of Bashan on the eastern plateau. Irrigation projects and official Roman encouragement created a scattering of dense agricultural settlements over the central Negev. Moreover, the western edge of the Transjordanian Plateau was dotted with olive orchards as far south as the lower limit of the Dead Sea.

Other technological improvements were made in the grinding of grain and in the production of olive oil. A large rotating stone mill turned by donkeys replaced the saddle quern as a means of grinding grain into flour. This rotary quern consisted of a conical lower stone, over which rested an hourglass-shaped upper stone, the top of which served as a hopper for the grain (Fig. 60). The upper stone was turned on the spindle of the lower

60. Millstones from the ancient Roman city of Pompei. These stones date from the first century A.D.

stone by means of a handle or pole which projected horizontally from the waist of the upper stone. The rotary quern could be driven by horses, donkeys, or slaves. More advanced designs of olive crushers and presses were also introduced into Palestine by the Romans, producing greater quantities of oil with less effort (see "Olive Cultivation," below).

THE LIFE OF AN ISRAELITE FARMER

In order to grasp a better understanding of life on a farm during the biblical period, it would seem appropriate to postulate a hypothetical Israelite farmer and his family, and to describe their yearly activities. In so doing, not only will it be possible to present a picture of farm life, but also to summarize the events of the agricultural seasons, and to describe the various farm tools. It is to be understood that the family, its village and fields, and the events described do not represent actual historical circumstances. Nevertheless, the picture portrayed accurately reflects what is known about the farmer's mode of life, as far as it can be reconstructed on the basis of biblical and archaeological evidence.

Our hypothetical farmer, Abiram, will be placed in the northern kingdom of Israel during the time of the divided monarchy (c. 922–721 B.C.). Although there were different styles of farming (some farmers specialized only in vineyards, others in olives or grain, while others cultivated a mixture of crops), it will be assumed that Abiram cultivated all three of the basic crops of ancient Palestine, as well as subsidiary vegetables and spices for his own use. In this way it will be possible to follow the entire agricultural year from beginning to end, starting with the first rains of the winter season and ending with the final harvest of fruit in the late summer.

It will also be assumed that Abiram owned his own land and was of moderate wealth. There were others who were much poorer, with little or no land and fewer possessions. There were also those who were far wealthier, who owned rich pastures and fields, possessed numerous servants, and for whom some of the poorer farmers labored in the fields. In addition, there were large royal estates belonging to the king (see section, THE CIVIL LIFE), such as those owned by such kings as David (c. 1000–961 B.C.; see 1 Chron. 27:25–31), Ahab (c. 869–850 B.C.; see 1 Kings 21:2), or Uzziah (c. 783–742 B.C.; see 2 Chron. 26:10). These estates were overseen by various officials appointed by the king, and farmed by some of the king's servants, prisoners of war, and hired tenants. From these estates, and from the fields and vineyards of the wealthy landowners, came most of the agricultural goods on which foreign trade was based (see 1 Kings 5:10–11). Life on these estates was different from that of Abiram and his family, who owned their own house and fields, but the seasonal activities were much the same.

The Village and Fields

Abiram lived with his family and tilled the soil in the broad uplands of Manasseh (see Josh. 17:7–11), on the eastern side of the plain of Salim, which stretched to the east and south of the important city of Shechem (Tell Balâṭah, near modern Nablus). His farm consisted of a moderately sized parcel of land on the fertile valley floor, on which wheat was cultivated, and stands of vines and olive trees situated on the adjacent, well-watered hill slopes. The fields, vineyards, and olive groves of other members of his village lay nearby.

Israelite farmers did not live on their farmlands, and so Abiram and his neighbors lived not far from their fields in the village of Salem. It was a small village, consisting of little more than a few close-packed houses in which the farmers lived, the workshops of local craftsmen, a threshing floor, simple installations for pressing grapes and olives, a spring from which fresh water could be obtained, and a small open area used by the general community for meetings, festivals, and a local market. There was no fortification wall, nor any other means of protection against intruders.

Abiram's village and farmland were situated within the administrative district controlled by Shechem in the Ephraimite hill country. Shechem was located on the western side of the plain of Salim, opposite Abiram's village. It sat on the lower slope of Mount Ebal, and guarded both the pass between Mount Ebal and Mount Gerizim and the main road from Jerusalem to the north. Shechem was an important city, well fortified, and had a long and sacred history (see Gen. 12:6; 33:18–20; Josh. 24; Judg. 9; 1 Kings 12:1 ff.). It was the first capital of the northern kingdom of Israel (1 Kings 12:25), and the "center of the land" (Judg. 9:37). Shechem was later to become important to the Samaritans, who built a temple on Mount Gerizim in the 4th century B.C. (see John 4:20).

Shechem provided security and protection for Abiram and his fellow farmers, as well as a center for worship and a market for the purchase and exchange of goods and produce. The city also functioned as the seat of local judicial authority and as a collection point for the taxes which Abiram was required to pay each year. The taxes imposed upon Abiram consisted of a portion of the grain crop, olive oil, and wine from each year's harvest (see section, THE CIVIL LIFE). These taxes were recorded and sent to the royal storehouse at the capital city of Samaria, located northwest of Shechem on the other side of the Ebal-Gerizim pass. Wine from the Shechem area is recorded on one of the Samaria ostraca (documents written on broken pieces of pottery—in this case, tax receipts) dating to sometime between the reigns of Joahaz (c. 815–801 B.C.) and Jeroboam II (c. 786–746 B.C.).

The Household

Abiram's family consisted of himself, his wife, and his five children—three boys and two girls. Abiram did not have private servants, although he would occasionally hire laborers to work in his fields or to take care of occasional chores. Neither did he possess any flocks, since it was all that he could handle to cultivate and harvest his fields. However, Abiram did possess a pair of oxen, with which he plowed his fields and threshed his grain.

Abiram's house was of the so-called "four-room" variety typical of the period of the Israelite monarchy. It was somewhat smaller and less pretentious than houses of similar form located within the walls of such cities as Shechem, Tirzah (Tell el-Far'ah, N.), Mizpah (Tell en-Naṣbeh), Hazor, and Megiddo—the sites of which have all yielded examples to the archaeologist's spade. However, the house was much better constructed than the two- or three-room structures huddled together in the poorer villages of Israel and Judah.

The house was not perfectly symmetrical in plan, since it had to fit into the available space among the other close-packed houses of Abiram's village (Fig. 61). A narrow street ran in front of the house, and an even narrower alley along one side. The remaining two sides abutted the walls of houses be-

61. A modern refugee village near Jericho. The houses are made of mud brick and must be similar to houses made of the same material in biblical times.

longing to Abiram's immediate neighbors. The foundations of the house were constructed of stone, while the superstructure was of mud-brick, coated with a lime plaster (*see* Fig. 15). The flat roof consisted of beams of wood overlaid by smaller branches and sticks. A surface composed of layers of straw, and hard-packed lime and mud sealed the roof (*see* Fig. 20). A low parapet ran around its outer edges (see Deut. 22:8). Because of deterioration caused by winter rains, the roof had to be resurfaced and packed down by means of a cylindrical-shaped limestone roller each year.

A large central courtyard—open to the sky—formed the main room of the house, and was entered from the street through a doorway in the front wall. The other three rooms—some subdivided by partition walls—were arranged lengthwise along each of the remaining three sides of the court-yard. The central courtyard provided space in which the women could cook, grind grain, weave, and perform other household chores (Fig. 62). It also served as a place for eating meals and entertaining guests, as a play area for the younger children, and as a space in which Abiram and his sons could sharpen and repair the various farm implements. In the center of the court-yard was a baking oven and cooking hearth constructed of small stones and clay (*see* Fig. 18). A rectangular storage bin occupied one corner, and along the adjacent wall was a heavy saddle quern used for grinding grain.

62. The courtyard of a reconstructed house from the period of the Israelite monarchy. Note the roof supports and the loom set up for weaving (from the Ha-Aretz Museum, Tel Aviv, Israel).

63. The sleeping room in a reconstructed house from the period of the Israelite monarchy (from the Ha-Aretz Museum, Tel Aviv, Israel).

The room along the east side of the house was paved with a cobblestone floor, and open to the courtyard except for the wooden columns which supported its roof. It was here that Abiram sheltered the pair of oxen and kept his plow and other tools. The room on the opposite side of the house—somewhat larger and fully enclosed except for two entranceways off the courtyard and a few open windows—provided quarters for sleeping and relaxation (Fig. 63). Here were found the personal items of family life—the clothes, inexpensive but well-made jewelry, various toilet and cosmetic articles, and the children's toys. Along the entire back of the house was a narrow, rectangular room, with an underground grain silo at one end and rows of storage jars along the walls (Fig. 64). In this room were stored the household provisions. The roof of the house could be reached by a narrow stairway of stone and wood, and provided a refuge from the heat during the hot summer nights.

Much of the food consumed by Abiram and his family was grown on their farm. The daily fare consisted primarily of parched or cooked wheat or barley, garnished with lentils, beans, and other vegetables. Onions, leeks, and garlic provided additional flavoring. Moreover, some of the grain was ground into coarse flour, mixed with olive oil, and baked into flat cakes of bread. Sweets were provided by fresh or dried fruit and wild honey, some of which were purchased in the market. Meat, generally lamb, was only occasionally used, particularly at festive and other important occasions. It was

64. Storage jars in a reconstructed house from the period of the Israelite monarchy (from the Ha-Aretz Museum, Tel Aviv, Israel).

acquired, along with wool, from the herders who sold these commodities in the market at Shechem. Wine and goat's milk were used for drinking.

The Agricultural Seasons

The work of farmers such as Abiram was determined by the pattern of the seasons in regular, calendrical fashion. This pattern is recorded in a copy of an agricultural calendar inscribed in good classical Hebrew on a small plaque of soft limestone, discovered by R. A. S. Macalister in 1908 at the biblical site of Gezer. The calendar dates from the second half of the 10th century b.c., and summarizes the yearly activities of the ancient Israelite farmer:

> His two months are (olive) harvest,
>   His two months are planting (grain),
>   His two months are late planting;
> His month is hoeing up of flax,
>   His month is harvest of barley,
>   His month is harvest and *feasting*;
> His two months are vine-tending,
>   His month is summer fruit.

It can be assumed that Abiram followed a schedule roughly equivalent to the one described above. However, the Gezer calendar is organized according to the beginning of the civil year, while the true agricultural calendar began with the planting season (autumn). The later Jewish calendar, which was taken over from the Babylonians toward the end of the Judean monarchy, began in the spring.

The ancient agricultural year may be divided into three general seasons: planting ("sowing"), harvesting ("threshing"), and vintage (vine and olive). This division appears in the Book of Leviticus according to the order of the later Jewish calendar: "And your threshing shall last to the time of vintage, and the vintage shall last to the time of sowing. . . . " (Lev. 26:5; see Amos 9:13). For the purpose of describing the various agricultural duties of Abiram and his family, the following outline may be formulated: grain cultivation (plowing, planting, hoeing, harvesting, threshing, and winnowing); vine cultivation (including the production of wine); and olive cultivation (including crushing and pressing). This outline accounts for the majority of the seasonal activities of our hypothetical farmer. Other responsibilities would have included the tending of various vegetables and auxiliary fruits, and the repair and upkeep of his tools and home.

Grain Cultivation

The cultivation of grain occupied most of Abiram's time. Over half of his yearly work was spent in planting and harvesting barley and wheat. Other crops were sown during the planting season, but these were of minor importance in relation to the cereals. Plowing and sowing went on simultaneously with the beginning of the winter rains, and the harvest season came toward the beginning of summer. Throughout the winter Abiram was concerned about the rainfall. Sufficient rain was necessary to assure a good crop —a drought could mean economic disaster and famine. Also of concern were the hot, dry winds from the eastern desert (Hos. 13:15), the periodic plagues of locusts (Joel 1:4; Ps. 105:34-35), and various plant diseases such as mold and mildew (1 Kings 8:37; Amos 4:9).

Plowing

Abiram and his family were thrust into their busy schedule each year by the commencement of the winter rains toward the latter part of October and the beginning of November. These "early rains" (Deut. 11:14; Joel 2:23) softened the soil for cultivation, and indicated that it was time to plow the ground and sow seed. This season lasted from about mid-November to mid-January, varying in its beginning and end according to the geographical location of the farmland and the kinds of seed sown.

Abiram's efforts at plowing were crucial. If done properly and the soil penetrated sufficiently, not only would the crop grow well, but also the

65. A yoke of oxen plowing.

fertility of the land would be preserved. All but the youngest children in Abiram's family worked in the fields during the planting season—no one was exempt from the farm chores (see Prov. 20:4). All of the villagers would be in the fields during the day, toiling without rest to prepare the ground for planting and sowing seed.

The ground would first be cleared of any rocks and stones. Abiram, or one of his sons, would guide the plow across the field behind the two oxen to break up the ground and scratch shallow furrows in its surface (see Isa. 28:24-25; Hos. 10:11-12). Long, straight furrows were required (see Ps. 129:3), and it was necessary to look ahead continually so that the oxen and plow would not stray (see Luke 9:62). Plowing was a slow and tiring process, and only a limited area could be prepared each day (Fig. 65).

The plow used in the fields by Abiram and the other Israelite farmers was a simple device, similar to those still used in modern times by a few Arab farmers, and not unlike those used by early settlers in America. Unlike the latter, however, Abiram's plow did not have a curved, flattened plowshare and could not turn a true furrow. Instead, the blade of the plow consisted of a conical-shaped metal tip (Figs. 66, 67) fastened over a tapered wooden tailpiece. Several examples of conical-shaped plowshares dating to the Israelite period—mainly of iron but occasionally bronze—have been recovered in archaeological excavations at Beer-sheba, Megiddo, Gibeah, Tell Jemmeh, Tell Beit Mirsim (Debir?), and elsewhere. The tailpiece of the plow curved upward and was attached to a handle. A horizontal shaft was tied at one end to the "knee" of the plow, where handle and tailpiece joined, and braced by additional struts. The opposite end of the shaft was attached to a double yoke —a straight cross member made from the limb of a tree—to which the oxen

66. Pottery and iron tools from the Iron Age I period in the time of the Israelite monarchy. Notice the pointed metal plow share and the metal hoe in the lower right corner (from the Rockefeller Museum, Jerusalem, Israel).

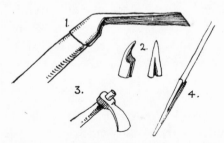

67. Iron tools from the Iron Age I period of the Old Testament: (1) mattock; (2) plough-points; (3) adze; (4) ox-goad.

would be hitched. This early plow could only scratch the upper surface of the ground, opening it to a depth of some three to five inches.

Abiram, or one of his sons, would walk behind the plow, holding the handle in one hand to depress the blade. A staff or goad was carried in the other hand to spur and direct the oxen (see 1 Sam. 13:21; Acts 26:14). While Abiram's plow was pulled by a pair of oxen (see 1 Kings 19:19), other farmers used a pair of donkeys (see Isa. 30:24). It was not unusual,

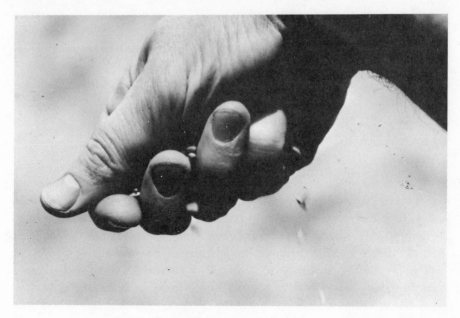

68. Seed being sown by hand.

however, for only a single animal to be used. The law code forbade the yoking of an ox and an ass together (Deut. 22:10).

Planting

The sowing of the seed would immediately follow plowing, as the shallow furrows did not remain open very long in the soft ground The main crops consisted of wheat and barley, along with a few vegetables, spices, and possibly some flax. The best practice was to rotate the crops from one field to another, alternately sowing the land and leaving it fertile. This was not always practiced, however, resulting at times in decreased production and eventually destroying the fertility of the soil.

The seed was generally scattered over the ground by hand (Fig. 68). As a result, some seed never matured—it might be eaten by birds, choked out by other growth, or fall on an area of insufficient soil for mature growth (see Matt. 13:3-8 and parallels). Generally, however, farmers such as Abiram and his family were careful enough to scatter the seeds only within the plowed field so that very little would be lost (see Isa. 28:25). In Assyria and Babylonia a hollow vertical tube with a receptacle at the top was attached to the plow. Seeds would drop from this "seeder" to the ground behind the plowshare. This device does not appear to have been used in ancient Palestine.

Abiram's wife and daughters were usually the ones to sow the seed after the plowing. During the first two months of planting (mid-November to mid-January), the grain seeds—flax, barley, and wheat—were sown. During the time of late planting (mid-January to mid-March), summer crops—such as sesame, millet, lentils, cucumbers, and other summer vegetables—were seeded. After the seeds were sown, Abiram would drive his oxen and plow back over the cultivated ground in order to trample the seeds into the ground and cover them with earth.

Hoeing

Between the time the grain was planted and the harvest season, Abiram and his family would watch over the new crop, protecting it from birds and wild animals, and occasionally cutting weeds with a hoe and loosening the ground around the wheat and barley. The occasional hot, arid winds from the desert and the threat of drought posed constant concern.

The hoe which Abiram used consisted of two sticks, one much shorter than the other, bound together by a cord to form an acute angle. A thin metal blade, with either a narrow or wide span, was attached to the end of the shorter arm to provide a digging edge (*see* Figs. 66, 67). Such hoes are frequently depicted on Egyptian reliefs and wall paintings, and several examples of both narrow and wide blades are known from archaeological excavations in Palestine. In the more rugged hilly regions and in vineyards where plows could not be used, the hoe was used for loosening and breaking up the soil (see Isa. 7:25). Because of constant use the blade of the hoe had to be sharpened frequently (see 1 Sam. 13:20–21).

Harvesting

"Do you not say, 'There are yet four months, then comes the harvest'?" (John 4:35). These words spoken by Jesus accurately portray the timing of the seasons, for the grain harvest in ancient Palestine began some four months after the first furrow was scratched in the earth's crust. The process of growth from planting to harvest is summarized in the parable of growing grain (Mark 4:26–29):

> And he said, "The kingdom of God is as if a man should scatter seed upon the ground, and should sleep and rise night and day, and the seed should sprout and grow, he knows not how. The earth produces of itself, first the blade, then the ear, then the full grain in the ear. But when the grain is ripe, at once he puts in the sickle, because the harvest has come."

Flax, if sown, was harvested from mid-March to mid-April, prior to the barley harvest. The flax was either pulled out or cut close to the ground with a hoe so as not to waste any of the stalk. The stalks were then dried (see Josh. 2:6), the seeds removed, and the stalks soaked in order to loosen the outer fibers. After another drying, the fibers were separated from the core, combed, and spun into thread for the manufacture of linen (see Ezek. 44:17-18), or made into cord (see Ezek. 40:3).

Abiram, however, did not grow flax and was concerned primarily with the two main harvests: the barley harvest in April and early May, and the wheat harvest from mid-May to mid-June. The harvest season was a time of renewed activity for Abiram and his family. To avoid loss, the harvest had to be completed as quickly as possible. Everyone in the family was put to work in the fields. Additional hands might be hired to assist in the harvest when necessary (see Matt. 9:37-38). The fields belonging to the royal estates of the king were harvested by hired laborers, servants, and slaves (see 1 Sam. 8:14-17; 1 Chron. 27:26). What was left in the field after reaping could be gathered ("gleaned") by widows, orphans, the poor, or alien residents (see Ruth 2). Hebrew religious law provided for the practice of gleaning by prohibiting the owner of a field from clearing it completely (Lev. 19:9-10; 23:22; Deut. 24:19-21).

The climate during the harvest season was hot and humid. In order to take advantage of the cooler morning hours, Abiram and his family would rise early to work in the fields. Even then the work was difficult and tiring. Sunstroke was not uncommon, especially among the women and children (see 2 Kings 4:18-20). Nevertheless, the harvest was a time of rejoicing and was accompanied by singing and chanting (see Ps. 126:5-6; Isa. 9:3). Joy would be absent, however, when drought or pestilence resulted in a poor or meager harvest.

In harvesting the barley and wheat, Abiram made use of sickles with curved iron blades set with rivets in a wooden haft. Earlier farmers had depended on blades of flint, copper, or bronze. Bronze was still used for sickle blades and other tools and implements in the time of Abiram, but iron had been in general use since the time of King David (10th century B.C.; see 2 Sam. 12:31; 1 Chron. 22:3).

Abiram and the other reapers would each hold a stalk of grain in his left hand, and cut it off close to the ear with a sweeping motion of the iron sickle held in his right hand (see Isa. 17:5; Ps. 129:7) (Fig. 69). The grain was laid on the ground in small bundles or tied together with a straw (see Ruth 2:16). One member of the family would collect the small bundles and tie them into larger bundles, or sheaves (see Gen. 37:7). When the grain was bound and dry, it was collected and placed on a small cart to be taken to the village threshing floor (see Job 5:26).

69. Reaping the wheat harvest with a sickle.

Threshing

Once the harvested grain was thoroughly dry, Abiram would take it to the threshing floor located near the edge of his village (see 1 Kings 22:10). The threshing floor consisted of a specially prepared flat surface, either of rock or beaten earth, located in an open space exposed to the wind. The grain was spread out on the hard surface, and was beaten or threshed to separate the kernels of grain from the straw. The threshing floor used by Abiram belonged to the village, although those in other areas were privately owned (2 Sam. 24:16, 18).

Small quantities of wheat or barley, as well as the more delicate crops such as dill or cummin, were threshed by beating the stalks with a stick or rod cut from a branch of a tree (Judg. 6:11; Ruth 2:17; Isa. 28:27). Larger quantities of grain might be trampled under the feet of animals (see Deut. 25:4). It was common, however, to thresh large yields, such as Abiram's, with a threshing sledge pulled by an ox or donkey (see 2 Sam. 24:22) (Fig. 70). The sledge consisted of a flat wooden board or frame, which had a curved leading edge, and was set with sharp stones or pieces of metal on the underside (see Isa. 41:15). To add weight, the driver would stand on the sledge or place stones on it. The small children of Abiram's village would enjoy riding on the sledge as it was pulled over the grain by the ox. A cart with rollers might also be used to thresh grain (see Isa. 28:27–28). The animal pulling the sledge could not be muzzled, and was allowed to eat his fill of the grain (Deut. 25:4; see Hos. 10:11).

Winnowing

Winnowing followed threshing, and consisted of tossing the threshed grain into the air so that the wind could separate the lighter elements (chaff) from the heavier kernels, which would fall in piles to the ground (Isa. 41:15–16). Threshing was done in the late afternoon or evening, when

70. An Arab boy standing on a threshing-sledge which is being pulled by a horse.

the wind was blowing (see Ruth 3:2). Two types of implements were used by Abiram and other Israelite farmers in winnowing. The one tool resembled a modern pitchfork, with long, broad wooden prongs (Isa. 30:24; Jer. 15:7; Luke 3:17). The other tool was a shovel-like instrument with a broad, shallow scoop (Isa. 30:24). Winnowing of small quantities of grain might also be accomplished by sifting the chaff through a woven sifter (Fig. 71).

Miscellaneous Aspects

The threshing and winnowing of the wheat completed the harvest season. It was a time for great joy and festivity (see Deut. 16:9-11). Two religious feasts were associated with the harvest: the Feast of Unleavened Bread and the Feast of Weeks (*see* Fig. 4).

The Feast of Unleavened Bread, later associated with the Exodus and celebrated as Passover (see Exod. 12:8; Num. 9:2-14), began with the offering of a new sheaf of grain and unleavened bread at the beginning of the barley harvest (see Lev. 23:10-11; 2 Kings 4:42). It was permissible to eat only unleavened bread at this time (see Josh. 5:11).

The Feast of Weeks (later "Pentecost"; Acts 2:1; 20:16) was celebrated in observance of the wheat harvest (see Exod. 34:22), seven weeks after the beginning of the barley harvest (see Lev. 23:15-17; Deut 16:9-10). This

71. An Arab woman sifting the chaff from the wheat through a woven sieve.

feast marked the end of the grain harvest season, and probably was originally known simply as the "Feast of Harvest" (see Exod. 23:16). New grain would be offered, along with two loaves of leavened bread (Lev. 23:16–17). The harvest feasts were two of the three annual pilgrimage feasts of the Israelite people (2 Chron. 8:13; see section, RELIGIOUS EVENTS).

Besides the celebration of the feasts, the harvest season meant the annual payment of the taxes on grain for Abiram and the other farmers of Israel (see section, THE CIVIL LIFE). This grain would eventually be stored in the great storehouses of the king for use as a trade item, as food for the king's table (see 1 Kings 4:7, 22), or as feed for the king's horses (see 1 Kings 4:28).

The rest of the grain was either sold by Abiram in the market at Shechem, or stored for household use. Chopped straw was retained to feed his oxen, or to use as a filler in making mud bricks or pottery. The kernels of grain were stored either in widemouthed storage jars (*see* Fig. 64) or in the underground silo in the back room of the house. Throughout the year the grain would be used for food, or ground into coarse flour on the saddle quern which sat in the open courtyard. This quern consisted of a heavy basalt stone with a saddle-shaped upper surface, worn through constant use (Fig. 72). A smaller oblong stone, worn smooth on its flattened lower surface, was held in both hands and rubbed back and forth over the kernels of

72. A saddle-quern used for
grinding grain.

grain on the saddle. The grinding, which was done by Abiram's wife or
daughters, was tedious work. In the New Testament period commercial
mills with donkey-driven, rotary querns produced larger quantities of flour
with less effort.

Vine Cultivation

Abiram's vineyards were located on the lower slopes of the hillside, just
above his fields (see Isa. 5:1; Jer. 31:5). Viticulture had a long history in
the land of ancient Palestine, and Hebrew tradition ascribed its origins to
Noah (Gen. 9:20). When Abiram's ancestors settled in the plain of Salim,
they had cleared the lower slopes of the hill of stones and planted the vines
(see Ps. 80:9; Isa. 5:2). The vines had taken root and were now some of
the choicest in the highlands of Ephraim (see Isa. 28:1). The vines stood
along the hillside in rows about 8 to 10 feet apart, and trailed along the
ground over a wide area (see Ps. 80:9–11). Artificial trellises apparently
were not used until the Roman period, but by growing close to the ground
the vines were able to soak up the moisture of the dew which covered the
slopes of the hill during the hot, humid, rainless summer. Enclosing the
vineyards was a low wall or "hedge" constructed of small stones or thorny
bushes to keep predators from trampling the vines or devouring their fruit
(see Isa. 5:5; Matt. 21:33; Ps. 80:12–13).

The vineyards were tended, following the grain harvest, during the two-
month period from mid-June to mid-August. It was at this time, during the
heat of the summer, that the vines would blossom (see S. of S. 2:13; Hos.
14:7) and begin the slow process of developing into fully ripened grapes (*see*
Fig. 55). After the blossoms had developed into ripening grapes, Abiram
and his family would hoe the ground, cut off the nonbearing branches, and
prune the vines. The process is described by Isaiah (Isa. 18:5; see also John
15:1–2):

> For before the harvest, when the blossom is over,
>   and the flower becomes a ripening grape,
> he will cut off the shoots with pruning hooks,
>   and the spreading branches he will hew away.

The pruning hook may have consisted of a small, sharp, knifelike instrument with a hooked blade. However, references to beating spears into pruning hooks (Isa. 2:4; Mic. 4:3) may be interpreted to imply that these tools had a long handle. A curved iron blade, with rivet holes at the haft end, was found at Tell Jemmeh, and may have been a pruning hook.

The grapes on the vine ripened toward the end of July, and the harvest occurred in August and September. During the vintage season vinedressers such as Abiram would erect crude watchtowers (see Isa. 5:2) and temporary huts made out of branches in the vineyards. They would live in these structures while the grapes were being gathered to guard the fruit from thirsty animals, which sought the grapes as a source of moisture during the late, hot summer. The practice has continued up to the present day.

Most vineyards, such as Abiram's, were harvested by the owners themselves, or by hired hands (see Matt. 20:1 ff.). Large vineyards might be rented to tenants, the owner receiving a share of the harvest as payment (see S. of S. 8:11; Matt. 21:33 ff.). At harvest the bunches of grapes were cut from the vine by the members of Abiram's family with a sickle-shaped knife. The grapes were carried from the vineyard in baskets covered with vine leaves. Gleanings would be left for widows, orphans, and sojourners (Lev. 19:10; Deut. 24:21). Some of the grapes would be eaten fresh, while others would be soaked in oil and water, and set in the sun to dry into raisins (see 1 Sam. 30:12; 2 Sam. 16:1).

Wine Production

Most of the fully ripened grapes would be squeezed for their juice and made into wine. The pressing season was a time of joy and singing (see Isa. 16:10; Jer. 48:33). The grapes would be dumped into a large shallow basin, generally hollowed out of bedrock, but occasionally cut out of a rectangular or round piece of stone. The juice would be squeezed from the grapes by treading over them with the feet (see Job 24:11; Amos 9:13), and the garments of the treaders would be dyed red from the juice (see Isa. 63:3).

After treading, as much of the pulp and seeds as possible were removed, and the grape juice transferred into a nearby vat. This vat also was generally hollowed out of bedrock, but was deeper than the pressing basin and lined with plaster. The initial fermentation process took place in this vat. When the fermentation was complete, the wine was either dipped out of the vat and filtered through a linen cloth, or decanted through a rock-cut channel, into a filtering basin. Further refinement would take place in the filtering basin.

When the process was complete, the finished wine was dipped from the filtering basin and funneled into large storage jars, which were sealed with a layer of olive oil. The jars were then placed into bottle-shaped chambers which were chiseled out of bedrock. These "wine cellars" kept the wine at a cool temperature for aging and later use. Royal wine cellars are mentioned in a list of David's officials (1 Chron. 27:27).

Facilities for manufacturing, bottling, and storing wine were discovered at the site of ancient Gibeon (el-Jib) during archaeological excavations directed by James B. Pritchard in 1959 and 1960. Included among the remains were wine presses, fermenting tanks, settling basins, storage jars, funnels, stoppers, and 63 subterranean wine cellars. This ancient "winery" was last used toward the end of the 7th century B.C.

Olive Cultivation

Abiram's olive orchard stood on terraces on the higher slopes of the hill, immediately above his vineyards. The olive tree has a considerable life span, and will produce heavily for hundreds of years (see Fig. 54). Abiram did not know how old the trees in his orchard were, for they had been there long before his ancestors had occupied the land at the time of the Israelite settlement. They still produced a large crop, and the oil derived from the olives was excellent.

The gnarled trees required little attention throughout the year, except at harvesttime. They grew easily on the rocky soil of the terraces, required little water, and it was necessary for Abiram simply to loosen the soil around the trees with a hoe at periodic intervals. The only major enemy of the trees was the swarms of locusts which would occasionally plague the land (see Amos 4:9).

The olive harvest and the manufacture of oil, occurring between mid-September to mid-November, completed Abiram's agricultural year. During this time the ripened olives were picked off the branches and then crushed and pressed in order to obtain their valuable oil. A good tree could produce from 10 to 15 gallons of olive oil a year.

The olives were picked before they were quite ripe. It was preferable to pick the olives by hand if possible, so as not to spoil them. When the olives were too far off the ground to be picked, Abiram and his family would gently shake the branches, or beat the branches with long twigs or wooden sticks (see Deut. 24:20; Isa. 17:6; 24:13). As with grain and grapes, some olives were to be left for gleaners (Deut. 24:20).

Oil Production in the Old Testament Period

During the biblical period, as in later times, the production of olive oil was a major industry. The production of the oil involved two main stages:

the crushing of the fruit, and the pressing of the crushed pulp. Although olives might be stored for a time after harvest, it was better to crush and press them immediately after picking.

The first stage in the production of olive oil was to bruise, or partially crush, the olives without crushing the kernels. The earliest means of bruising the olives, still used in the time of the Israelite monarchy, was accomplished by treading or pounding. Treading was done with the feet in a shallow rock-cut basin in much the same manner as treading grapes (see Mic. 6:15). The best oil, however, was obtained by beating or pounding the olives with a pestle in a stone or rock-cut mortar (see Exod. 27:20; Lev. 24:2; 1 Kings 5:11). A small circular basin, cut into bedrock and equipped with a mortar on one side, was discovered in one of the industrial areas at the site of ancient Gibeon (el-Jib). The excavator suggests that olives were crushed in the mortar, with the oil collecting in the basin. There is no trace in the Old Testament period of the more efficient roller mill, which was apparently introduced into Palestine during the Persian-Hellenistic periods (5th–1st century B.C.).

To obtain the oil after bruising, the kernels were separated from the pulp, and the pulp transferred to an open wicker basket and gently shaken. The basket acted as a strainer, with the top layer of oil being skimmed off. This produced first quality or "pure," oil. Another method possibly used was to store the oil and juice in a settling basin, after separation from the kernel and pulp. By this method the water of the juice could be drawn off through a spout in the bottom of the basin, and the pure oil poured out afterward. Several moderate-sized pottery basins with spouts on one lower side are known from archaeological excavations in the land of ancient Palestine, and it is possible that these basins functioned in the above manner in the production of olive oil.

Oil of a lower quality could be obtained by soaking the pulp in hot water, and then applying pressure on the soaked pulp by means of stone weights. The collected oil would again be allowed to settle in a basin in the same manner as before. A third, and much poorer, quality of oil could be obtained by repeating the operation. Beam-presses (see below) do not appear to have been introduced until the Hellenistic period (late 4th century B.C.).

Olive Production in the New Testament Period

Major technological improvements in the production of olive oil had been introduced by the New Testament period. The remains of roller mills or "crushers," and beam presses of Roman date, are known in a number of places throughout the Holy Land. The same two stages followed in the

73. A pair of millstones.

production of olive oil in the Old Testament period were used in the New Testament period, but with different technology.

The olive "crusher" of the Roman period consisted of a large stone-cut basin with a circular trough. A solid vertical column stood in the center. Over this central column was attached a horizontal wooden beam, which could be pivoted about the column. Two wheel-shaped millstones were placed on the arms of the wooden beam (Fig. 73). The millstones rotated around the central column of the basin, crushing the olives in the trough. A system of wedges and washers kept the millstone from coming into direct contact with the sides and bottom of the trough so as not to crush the kernels of the olives, but simply to bruise the skin. The millstone of an olive crusher may have been the source of the imagery used by Jesus in a discourse on humility (Matt. 18:6 and parallels).

The Roman beam press was used to squeeze the oil from the pulp of the crushed olives. The crushed pulp would be placed in nets or baskets on a shallow circular basin or platform, and covered by wooden blocks or pads. A long wooden beam, set in a wall or support behind the press, extended over the pressing platform. One or more heavy stone weights were attached to the free end of the beam, applying considerable pressure on the olive pulp and pressing out the oil. The olive oil would collect in a vat connected to the pressing basin by means of a channel or trough. Additional pressings would produce lesser grades of oil. Some presses were operated by means of a screw attached to the beam and a stone weight.

Conclusion

The olive harvest and the production of oil completed the cycle of the ancient agricultural year. It was at this time that farmers, such as our hypothetical Abiram, would celebrate the Feast of Ingathering (see Exod. 23:16; 34:22). This festival probably was celebrated outdoors originally (see Judg. 21:19–21), and did not have a specific date. It was a feast celebrated by the farmers at the moment when all the produce of the fields (Exod. 23:16), and all the produce from the presses (Deut. 16:13), had been gathered. The time of its celebration depended on the variations of the seasons. It marked the end of the year for the farmer, prior to the coming of the first ("early") rains of winter, which indicated the beginning of a new agricultural year and the activity of a new planting season.

The calendar of events sketched in relation to Abiram represents the seasonal activities and the lifestyle of a farmer during the biblical period— both Old and New Testaments. Although certain social and cultural, as well as technological, changes occurred during the time between the two testaments, the general character of the farmer remained the same. The farmer was tied to the land—to the seasons, the crops, the soil, the rain— and to his own handiwork in his fields, vineyards, and olive orchards.

THE PROFESSIONAL LIFE

The term "professional" is not strictly appropriate to the occupations of the Bible because ancient Near Eastern society was structured differently from ours in many respects. Care must be taken, therefore, not to apply modern terminology or patterns of thought to the professions of the Bible without being aware of the possible modifications thus introduced. In terms of the biblical data, a "profession" may be defined as a regular occupation (something other than a skill used primarily within the household), sufficiently distinct to require special capability, training, or knowledge.

The life of the Hebrews as portrayed in the Bible was one centered about the family, the clan, or the small community. Most households grew their own food and provided many of their own necessities. As a result, a number of professional services were originally performed by the various members of the household. Some of these household duties (e.g., the making of pottery, singing and chanting, offering sacrifices) only later became specialized skills or professions (e.g., the potter, the musician, the priest) with the growth of a more complex and diverse Israelite and Judaic society.

Within the structure of the household or clan various skills developed into hereditary crafts handed down from father to son in a family workshop. Specialists appeared who devoted all their time to making specific items, such as wooden furniture, pottery vessels, or musical instruments; providing certain luxury items, such as perfumed oil and spices, gold and silver jewelry, or richly dyed cloth; or performing particular tasks, such as recording deeds and other documents, reading and interpreting the law code, or offering sacrifices in the temple. In time, professional guilds were established for common social and economic benefits by craftsmen who manufactured a similar product and experts who provided a particular service. Members of a guild frequently would reside in a specific sector or quarter of a city or found a community around a village workshop devoted to one occupation, one type of product.

The professions of ancient Israel cut through every strand of biblical society—the religious, the civil, the military, the industrial, the private—and included such specialists as the predecessors of our clergy, accountants, physicians, engineers, teachers, miners, smiths, diplomats, musicians, and secretaries. There were also professional classes of women who worked as midwives, weavers, mourners, singers, and even prostitutes. The heads of the various guilds and professions in some cases achieved considerable power and social status.

Within each profession there were specific requirements for membership and long periods of training or apprenticeship to acquire the necessary skills. The degree of achievement represented by some of these professions is apparent from the ascription of "wisdom" (hokmah) to men of specific skills: to builders (Prov. 24:3), to craftsmen (Exod. 31:3 f.; 35:35; 1 Kings 7:14; Isa. 40:20; Jer. 10:9), to sailors (Ps. 107:27), to professional mourners (Jer. 9:16), and to snake charmers (Ps. 58:6). This use of the term "wisdom" designates a type of professional expertise and attests to the reality that certain craftsmen and artisans were indeed regarded as professionals by their contemporaries.

In the following pages a survey will be made of some of the professions mentioned or inferred in the Bible. Attention will be given to the origin and development of professions within Israelite society, to the office or specialization defined by each profession, and to the lifestyle of its members. The evidence is taken primarily from the Old and New Testaments. Added details and relevant illustrations are drawn from extrabiblical sources and archaeology where appropriate. Some of the occupations of the Bible which may be considered part of the professional life of ancient Israel are dealt with more fully elsewhere (e.g., individual craftsmen under THE INDUSTRIAL

LIFE, public and state officials under THE CIVIL LIFE, the professional soldier under THE MILITARY LIFE, and the physician under MEDICINE).

PRIESTS AND LEVITES

Because of its significance and the prerogatives it arrogated to itself, the priesthood stands out as the most obvious class of professionals in the Bible. The priesthood was a basic concept in Israelite religion, as it was in other religions of the ancient Near East. The essential duties of the Israelite priest as an attendant of a deity were sacrificial and ritualistic. His main function was to represent the people before God (see Heb. 4:14 ff.). This responsibility often led to excessive concern with ritual purity and sacrifice (Isa. 1:11–15; Amos 5:21–24), reliance on the exactness of the Law (Matt. 26:59–68), and political and social privilege (Matt. 21:23; John 18:19–24; Acts 5:17–18).

The term "priest" (Hebrew *kohen*) occurs more than 700 times in the Old Testament, and was used to designate any priest, whether he be Israelite (2 Chron. 15:3; Jer. 18:18; Ezek. 44:15), Philistine (1 Sam. 5:5; 6:2), Midianite (Exod. 2:16), Egyptian (Gen. 41:45; 47:22), or Canaanite (2 Kings 10:19; Jer 48:7). The common Greek term for priest occurs over 80 times in the New Testament, again in relation to any priest (Luke 1:8; Acts 6:7; 14:13; Heb. 10:21; Rev. 5:10).

Related to the term "priest," and at various periods in the history of Israel either associated or identified with it (Deut. 17:9; 18:1; 27:9; 2 Chron. 11:13–14; 13:9–10), was the name "Levite." A Levite was not directly equivalent to a priest. The name referred initially to a clan (Exod. 32:25–29; Judg. 17:7–13; 19:1, cf. Deut. 14:29; 18:1; 26:11–13) and later became the designation for a certain group of priests (Deut. 33:8–11; 2 Chron. 13:9–10). During the time of the Second Temple the Levites were ministers rather than priests (Ezra 8:15–20; Ezra 2:36–40 = Neh. 7:39–43).

The establishment of the priesthood in Hebrew society is traditionally associated with Moses, who consecrated his brother Aaron and his descendants as priests (Exod. 28:1; 29:35–36; Lev. 8). The ordination of the Levites is also represented as being of Mosaic origin (Exod. 32:25–29; Deut. 33:8–11). Based on this and the threefold division of the priesthood in postexilic times—high priest, priests, and Levites—tradition has assumed that the priesthood was a constant throughout Israel's history. Modern scholarship, however, has been able to recognize that this view is late in origin and that the priesthood went through a number of phases in its historical development. This development and its related theological problems are the concern of biblical scholars and are not of immediate concern here; however, these factors cannot be ignored in the description of the professional life of the Hebrew priest.

The Priesthood before the Period of the Monarchy

At the time of the biblical Patriarchs (c. 1800 B.C.) there was no official priesthood. The various acts of worship, such as prayer, the giving and receiving of blessings, and in particular the offering of sacrifices, were the responsibility of the head of the family or clan (Gen. 22; 31:54; 46:1). Priests are not mentioned in the Bible during the early, formative period of Israel's history except in reference to the priesthood of established nations or city-states which had an urban culture and with it a developed priesthood (Gen. 14:18; 41:45; 47:22). A true priesthood did not arise in Israel until the period of the monarchy, when Israel too became an urban culture and had to appoint a professional priesthood to oversee the Temple and take charge of the ever more complicated ritual associated with Israel's worship.

Premonarchical priests in Israel were connected with a particular sanctuary, each sanctuary being attended by a hereditary family of priests. The Elides were situated at Shiloh (1 Sam. 1–4), the Aaronides at Bethel (Judg. 20:27–28), a family of priests at Nob (1 Sam. 21–22), and Levitical priests at Dan (Judg. 17–18). During this period the term "Levite" still retained its tribal connotation and did not designate a particular office as in later post-exilic Judaism. Levites may have been preferred as priests (Judg. 17–18), but "priest" and not "Levite" stood for the name of a profession and the two were not synonymous.

Also, the priesthood was for a long time not an ordained or appointed office, but rather a craft or profession. A person was a priest solely because he, or his hereditary family, exercised priestly functions. Priests functioned as attendants of a sanctuary and custodians of sacred objects (Judg. 17:7–13; 18:3–6, 14–20, 30–31; 20:27–28; 1 Sam. 4:3–4). Their duties included the offering of sacrifices and the burning of incense (Fig. 74). However, the rite of sacrifice still was not the privilege of the priesthood. Gideon (Judg. 6:25–27), Manoah (Judg. 13:15–23), and Elkanah, Samuel's father (1 Sam. 1:3, 21), were not priests and yet they sacrificed as did the Patriarchs before them.

The only activity specifically assigned to the early Hebrew priests in the Bible is the consultation of oracles by means of the Urim and Thummim, or sacred lots (Exod. 28:30 and Num. 27:21). Scant information exists as to what these objects looked like, what they were made from, or how they were used. In all probability they were some sort of marked stone, clay, or wooden object—perhaps a form of dice. They were stored in the breastplate worn

74. An incense altar from Megiddo dating from the Iron Age I
period of the Old Testament (from the Rockefeller Museum,
Jerusalem, Israel).

by the priest (called "the breastplate of decision," Exod. 28:15, 30), described
as a small, square pouch or bag of gold and fine cloth inset with twelve
precious stones, one for each of the twelve tribes of Israel (Exod. 28:15-30;
39:8-21) (Fig. 75). The breastplate in turn was attached to the ephod or
outer priestly garment (Exod. 28:28). The Urim and Thummim were cast, or
consulted, by the priest to determine God's response to a question. This
technique of consultation was limited to a simple yes–no answer. Consultation could take place either at the sanctuary (Judg. 18:5-6; 1 Sam. 22:9-10,
13, 15) or away from it (1 Sam. 14:36-42; 23:6-12; 30:7-8). Priests in the
more developed periods of Israel's religious heritage had the duty of giving
practical instruction ("torah"), an extention and refinement of their earlier
function as consultors of the Urim and Thummim. The priesthood at Shiloh
—at one time the most important sanctuary in Israel (1 Sam. 4:1-7:1)—stood
on the line between the Israel of the Judges and the new Israel of the
monarchy. Oracular consultation was developing into judicial "torah" (see
Jer. 2:8; 18:18). By the time of the divided monarchy priests were relinquish-
ing the primitive form of consultation (see 2 Kings 22:11-20).

75. The priestly breastplate was a pocket which contained the Urim and Thummim. It was suspended from the shoulders where it was attached by shoulder-pieces. The lower part was tied with bands which went around the waist (see Exod. 28:15–30).

The priests of the premonarchical era generally did not receive a direct wage for their work—there was as yet no state which could provide this. Periodic gifts and the right to withhold a part of the sacrifice appear to have been their only subsistence. This practice occurred at Shiloh (1 Sam. 2:13–14), and seems to have been standardized (see Lev. 7:28–36). The Levite hired as a personal priest by Micah presents a special case. He received wages of "ten pieces of silver a year" along with his clothing and "living" (Judg. 17:10).

The Priesthood during the Period of the Monarchy

The establishment of the monarchy in Jerusalem under David ushered in a new development in the lifestyle of the Hebrew priest. While Levite-priests and others apparently continued to function in the outlying sanctuaries of Israel in much the same way as those before them, the priesthood established by David in Jerusalem (2 Sam. 8:15–18) became a part of the royal court. The chief priest (not *high* priest, as in later, postexilic Judaism) was an official in charge of the private sanctuary of the king and the head of a complex hierarchy of temple functionaries, as was true in other states in the ancient Near East (Egypt, Mesopotamia, Phoenicia).

Priestly duties during the monarchy included the consultation of oracles and the pronouncement of blessings and curses. At the beginning, the priest played only a minor role in the sacrificial ritual, pouring out the blood, offering incense, and placing upon the altar the portion of the sacrificed animal meant for God. King Solomon, for example, offered the sacrifices at the dedication of the Jerusalem Temple himself (1 Kings 8:62–64), while the priests performed lesser duties (2 Chron. 7:6). Later, sometime in the 8th–7th centuries B.C., the former consultative duties diminished in importance and the sacrificial ritual became increasingly reserved to the priesthood. Consultation with God passed from the responsibility of the priest to that of the prophet (1 Kings 14:1 ff.; 22:5 ff.; 2 Kings 3:11; 8:7–13; 22:11–20). The manipulation of the Urim and Thummim gave way to the teaching of customary laws and "torah," or instruction (Deut. 31:9–13; 33:10; see Hos. 4:6; Mic. 3:11; Jer. 18:18; Ezek. 7:26). As early as the judicial reform under King Jehoshaphat in the 9th century B.C. tribunals were established in Jerusalem made up of priests and elders (2 Chron. 19:8–11). This new priestly duty—as a judge in controversies involving the Law and matters of religion—is reflected in the book of Deuteronomy (12—26), dated traditionally to the reform of Josiah around 622 B.C. (2 Kings 22:3—23:25). Worship was centralized in Jerusalem, and the priesthood was given responsibility for all matters relating to Hebrew religion. The sacrificial ritual became a monopoly, associated with priestly concepts of ritual purity and holiness (Deut. 33:10).

Ritual and Sacrifice at the Jerusalem Temple

Worship at the Temple in Jerusalem, accompanied by its symbolic acts and manifold sacrifices, must have been an impressive sight. It is not known for certain how regularly the act of worship and sacrifice was performed, but apparently it was fairly frequent. Major ceremonies would be celebrated at the yearly festivals (see section, RELIGIOUS EVENTS). In addition, there were weekly services on the Sabbath. Moreover, it was possible to make a sacrifice any day of the week—worshipers could approach God as they saw fit or felt the need. One priestly regulation required the maintenance of a continuous burnt offering as a sign of God's presence before His people and of the sanctification of His Temple (Exod. 29:39–43; 2 Kings 16:15).

There must have been a considerable number of priests in Jerusalem around the time of King Josiah (c. 640–609 B.C.). The effect on the visitor's mind made by the Temple of Jerusalem itself would have been overwhelming (Fig. 76): magnificent walls; thick, gold-plated double gates; an enormous outer court with its shiny bronze laver filled with clear spring water for ritual acts of cleansing; a towering altar of smooth, well-cut stone on which the sacrifices were made (Fig. 77); and a sanctuary constructed in magnificent style in Phoenician workmanship standing in the courtyard as impressive to the Israelites then as is the Parthenon on the Acropolis in Athens to us today.

To a worshiper bringing a lamb to sacrifice, the Temple was a busy place. Many others would be waiting for their turn—some with grain or cereal,

76. The Temple of Solomon viewed from the East entrance.

others with lambs or doves, maybe even a few with cattle. There would also be the minor offices of the Temple: the singers and musicians, chanting and playing their music in a ritual procession; the guardians of the Temple, standing at attention in full dress at the many entrances to the courtyard; the Levites, dressed in their plain white linen garments, preparing to cut the throats of the sacrificial animals (Ezek. 44:11); and other Temple officers, all busy in their prescribed daily tasks. Finally, there would be the priests themselves—some standing in a group off to one side, discussing with the king's retainers the cost of replacing a bronze washstand smashed by a sacrificial bull; some preparing themselves to offer sacrifices by cleansing their hands in the holy water, dressed in clean, white linen garments; others returning to their private quarters, tired, hot, and splattered with blood from

77. The altar of burnt offering at Solomon's Temple (see Ezek. 43:13-17).

offering forty sacrifices for a group of shepherds from Hebron; and others, not visible to those in the outer court, who were in the sanctuary waving incense censers, dressed in their ritually pure priestly garments, accompanied by the chief priest in his crown, robe, ephod, and breastplate.

If a whole burnt offering was to be given in the courtyard of the Temple (see Lev. 1:3–17), the sacrificial animal would be brought before the priest for inspection as to quality. If acceptable, the worshiper presenting the sacrifice would then place his hand on the animal's head, and the animal would be slain—in early times by the worshiper himself; in later times by a special class of Levites (Ezek. 44:11). The priest would then take the blood of the animal, step up on the raised platform on which stood the altar, and, after presenting the blood before God, throw it against the altar. Next he would cut the carcass into pieces and place them on the altar after washing off the legs and entrails with water. The sacrifice would then be burnt in its entirety. Perhaps after chanting a prayer or repreating a brief formula, the priest would descend the altar steps, purify himself again by washing off the blood of the sacrifice in a laver, and turn to attend to the next sacrifice. Besides the offerings presented by worshipers, there were daily burnt offerings by the priests, and perhaps for the king as well (Exod. 29:38–42; 2 Kings 16:15).

For solemn acts of worship there were special priestly vestments. Generally, these were not to be worn outside the Temple sanctuary (Ezek. 42:14; 44:17–19). The lesser priests were dressed in simple fashion: four garments consisting of a coat or robe (Exod. 28:39–40; 39:27); a girdle or belt (Exod. 28:39); a headdress or "turban" (Exod. 28:39–40; 39:28); and breeches or undergarments (Exod. 28:42; 39:28; Ezek. 44:18). The chief priest had the same garments, but of much finer quality (Exod. 28:4; 39) (Fig. 78). In addition, he wore the symbols of his high office—four additional pieces of equipment made by "skillful workmanship": a blue woven robe with a border edged in bells of gold and pomegranates of cloth (Exod. 28:31; 39:22–26); the ephod, or outer garment, made of fine materials and decorated with gold and onyx stones (Exod. 28:6–14; 39:2–7); the breastplate, attached to the ephod and looking perhaps like a cloth pendant, decorated in gold and inlaid with twelve precious stones (Exod. 28:15–30; 39:8–21); and a plate or crown of pure gold inscribed with the words "Holy to the Lord" and fastened to the priest's turban or headdress (Exod. 28:36–38; 39:30–31). Shoes are not mentioned, and it is not known whether they were used, or whether the priests administered barefoot (see Exod. 3:5; Josh. 5:15). Another set of garments—of ordinary linen and unadorned—was worn by the chief priest when he entered the Holy of Holies on the Day of Atonement (Lev. 16:4).

78. The vestments of the Chief
Priest (see Exod. 28).

The Priesthood after the Period of the Monarchy

The capture of Jerusalem by Nebuchadnezzar, the king of Babylon, in
587 B.C. (2 Kings 25:1–4; Jer. 39:1–3) and the subsequent destruction of
the Temple along with the rest of Jerusalem (2 Kings 25:8 ff. = Jer. 52:12 ff.)
brought a temporary end to the priesthood. Some priests were apparently
slain in the battle (Lam. 2:20), and the leaders of the Temple were taken
to Riblah, in Syria, and slain alongside other leaders of the city (2 Kings
25:18–21 = Jer. 52:24–27). Other priests had already been taken into captivity
in 597 B.C. (Jer. 29:1), including perhaps Ezekiel (see Ezek. 1:3 and 33:21).

With the Return, the priesthood quickly reasserted itself, and its most
prominent members became the leaders of the Jewish community. A threefold hierarchy characterized postexilic Judaism, consisting of high priest,
priests, and Levites. The distinction between priests and Levites now firmly
established (Ezra 2:36–40; Neh. 7:39–43), the Levite became a minor officer
of the cult (see Ezek. 44:4–31). Moreover, the priest—especially the high
priest—now enjoyed a more commanding position, both as mediator and as
sole religious and civil leader. Jerusalem had become not a civil capital, but
a spiritual capital; the high priest was no longer subordinate to the king,
and the only sacral institution of Judaism remaining was that of the priesthood. The holiness of the priest was accentuated in relationship to the re-

duced holiness of the people. This is the concept of the priesthood that appears in the New Testament (Matt. 26:57–68; John 11:49–53; 18:13–24; Luke 6:4; Acts 5:17–18). With the destruction of the Second Temple in A.D. 70, the priesthood became obsolete and the preservation of the Judaic tradition devolved upon both Jewish rabbis and Christian apostles.

PROPHETS

In contrast to the priest and the Levite, whose essential functions were sacrificial and ritualistic in character, stood the Hebrew prophet, who acted as a spokesman for God and performed a more heuristic function within Israelite society. In discussing the manner of life and the role of the prophet in ancient Israel, a distinction must be made between two types of prophets. Within the one category belong the classical prophets of the 8th century B.C. and later (Amos, Hosea, Jeremiah, and others) whose prophecies were canonized in the prophetic books of the Old Testament. Within the other category belong the visionaries and seers who appeared early in Israel's religious history and continued to function down through the time of the classical prophets.

The Early Prophets

The early Hebrew prophets—mainly visionaries and seers—were frequently members of a professional guild, referred to in the Old Testament as "sons of the prophets" (1 Kings 20:35; 2 Kings 2:3–7). These prophets lived and prophesied as a group, learned their profession from a master or prophetic leader, and could be attached to a local shrine (1 Sam. 10:5; 2 Kings 2:3) or to the royal court (1 Kings 22:5 ff.). The seer, or professional prophet, was the person approached by both the Israelite people (see the story of Saul's asses, 1 Sam. 9:5 ff.) and the king (1 Kings 22:5 ff.) for advice.

It is not entirely clear just how early in the history of ancient Israel associations of cult prophets appeared. However, they are attested throughout the period of the monarchy, from the time of Saul in the 11th century B.C. down to the fall of Jerusalem in the early 6th century B.C. Samuel is depicted as the head of a band of prophets (1 Sam. 19:18–24), a "man of God" (1 Sam. 9:6), or as a "seer" (1 Sam. 9:9) who headed a company of prophets (1 Sam. 19:20) associated with a sanctuary or high place (1 Sam. 9:11 ff.) located either at Ramah (1 Sam. 8:4; 19:18) or Gilgal (1 Sam. 10:8). The 9th-century prophets Elijah and Elisha are also represented as heads of a prophetic guild (this seems to be the force of 1 Kings 19:16). Prophetic guilds are attested as late as the time of Amos (Amos 7:12–14) and Jeremiah (Jer. 27:16).

The seer employed a variety of methods to ascertain the will of God. One of the most frequent methods was through some type of ecstatic experience, brought on by group participation in dancing, the playing of music, and in the case of "the prophets of Baal," divination and self-inflicted wounds (see 1 Kings 18:17 ff., especially vss. 26–29). Among David's court officials were "certain of the sons of Asaph, and of Heman, and of Jeduthun, who should prophesy with lyres, with harps, and with cymbals" (1 Chron. 25:1; cf. vss. 2–6; also 2 Chron. 29:30). Similarly, 1 Sam. 10:5 mentions "a band of prophets coming down from the high place with harp, tambourine, flute, and lyre before them, prophesying." Other references simply relate that the prophets "were prophesying" (1 Kings 22:10), without describing the means by which their ecstatic state was achieved. In many respects the early prophets of Israel were akin to the diviners, visionaries, and prophets of other areas of the ancient Near East as known from literary texts discovered at Mari, from the biblical story of the non-Israelite diviner, Balaam (Num. 22–24), and other sources.

Functions of the Prophets

Within the general role of the prophet as messenger of God, the Hebrew prophet performed a number of particular tasks at various times in the history of ancient Israel. One of the functions of the prophet during the period of the monarchy was to anoint the king and to ensure the accession of God's rightful choice. The prophet Samuel, for example, anointed both Saul (1 Sam. 10:1) and David (1 Sam. 16:13). Similarly, Nathan pledged God's support for the house of David (2 Sam. 7:4–17) and played a role in the anointing of Solomon as king over Israel (1 Kings 1:32–40). With the breakup of the united monarchy at the close of the Solomonic era, "the prophet Ahijah the Shilonite" symbolically professed Jeroboam's right to the throne of Israel (1 Kings 11:29–39). Somewhat later, Jehu was anointed king over Israel by a disciple of Elisha (2 Kings 9:1–13). That this was a specific function of the early prophets of Israel is attested by God's command to Elijah to anoint Hazael king over Syria, Jehu king over Israel, and Elisha prophet in place of himself (1 Kings 19:15–16).

Another function of the Hebrew prophet during the period of the monarchy was to act as an adviser to the king and to assist in interpreting the political affairs of the Hebrew nation, especially in wartime. The prophet Nathan is specifically designated as a member of David's court (1 Kings 1:8, 22 ff.), and before him, Gad is called "David's seer" (2 Sam. 24:11). An unnamed prophet of the 9th century B.C. predicted Ahab's initial victories over Ben-Hadad, king of Syria (1 Kings 20:13 ff.), while yet another from a prophetic guild prophesied his eventual defeat and death at the hands of the Syrians (1 Kings 20:35 ff.).

The picture is even more distinct in relation to the events preceding Ahab's third campaign against Syria, in association with Jehoshaphat, king of Judah (1 Kings 22). The scene may be visualized as follows: with two successive victories over the Syrians to his credit (1 Kings 20:16-21 and 29-34), Ahab, the king of Israel, was anxious to extend his success and sought the support of Jehoshaphat in his venture (1 Kings 22:1-4). "Arrayed in their robes," sitting in regal splendor on their thrones (perhaps inlaid with ivory, such as found in the ruins of Ahab's palace at Samaria), the two monarchs awaited the judgment of the prophets of Israel who were prophesying before them at the threshing floor at the entrance to the city gate of Samaria (1 Kings 22:5-10). This band of prophets (presumably supported by Ahab) did not disappoint the king and gave him a favorable response to his request for the "word of the Lord" (1 Kings 22:6, 11-12). Ahab must have been elated at the prophets' enthusiastic prediction of victory, and it is not difficult to imagine his relief on the one hand and his zeal to begin his campaign on the other. His ecstasy was short-lived, for there appeared on the scene one Micaiah-ben-Imlah, a prophet whom Ahab despised, "for he never prophesies good concerning me, but evil" (1 Kings 22:8). Somewhat reluctantly, Ahab had sent for Micaiah at the request of Jehoshaphat (1 Kings 22:7-9) and appealed for a reassuring response (1 Kings 22:13). The prophet's word was even more damaging than Ahab could imagine. Not only did Micaiah predict Israel's defeat, in sober opposition to the king's prophets, but he also prophesied Ahab's death on the battlefield, and threw salt on the wound to Ahab's pride and expectation by ridiculing his group of royal prophets as well (1 Kings 22:17-23). The prophet was struck on the cheek (1 Kings 22:24) and imprisoned (1 Kings 22:26-27), but the result was as Micaiah prophesied, and Ahab was slain in battle (1 Kings 22:34-35).

This story illustrates not only the role of the prophet and prophetic guild in the administration of the royal kingdom, but also the tension between prophets who might be tempted to provide only the desired answer, and individuals—such as Micaiah-ben-Imlah—whose main concern was the pronouncement of God's word and the interpretation of history in terms of divine intervention.

The Classical Prophets

The classical prophets of ancient Israel, in contrast to the early Hebrew prophets and seers, do not appear to have belonged to professional guilds of prophets (see Amos' emphatic assertion that he was *not* a member of a prophetic guild: Amos 7:12-15). Instead, the classical prophets were charismatic individuals who "professed" the word of God at a particular moment in history. These members of Israel's prophetic heritage who introduced a universal view of history into Israel's faith are considered by many scholars to be representative of the highest ideals in Israelite religion.

The fundamental role of each of the men whom we have come to call collectively the classical prophets of ancient Israel (8th–5th centuries B.C.) was to be a messenger and interpreter, specifically a messenger who announced God's word, pronounced God's judgment on his people, and interpreted the events surrounding Israel's history as seen in the light of God's covenant. In formulating the message the prophet borrowed from various traditions and employed various symbolic actions. The basic form of the prophet's message was not original, but typical of the royal messenger in the ancient Near East and borrowed from that source, probably by way of the prophets of the royal court as known from Byblos and Mari. The close relationship is apparent in the manner of the early prophets of Israel, such as those mentioned in the books of Samuel and Kings, and is visible in the form of the message in the canonical prophets.

However, unlike the prophetic circles of the rest of the ancient Near East, the classical Hebrew prophet considered himself to be an interpreter of history, announcing God's message to his own present age and pointing to the past and future only as they were relevant to the present. The individuals who prophesied in ancient Israel performed a specific task within Israelite society, acting as the means by which divine significance was imparted to history. They were not merely diviners who predicted the future, but men who envisioned the results of contemporary social, economic, political, and religious life and who proclaimed through word and deed that which they saw and comprehended. Lesser, pseudo-prophets may have been tempted to provide a false but favorable interpretation of events in order to achieve personal favor or to hold on to their position; but in Israel's prophetic heritage, the truthfulness of such messages was based on God's judgment of history (1 Kings 22; see also Deut. 18:15–22).

Classical and Early Prophets Contrasted

The essential element which separated the classical prophets, such as Isaiah, from the earlier prophets of Israel was the religious and moral content of their message. In their prophetic pronouncements the classical prophets condemned the "high places" (Jer. 7:30–34; 19:5; 32:35; Hos. 10:8; Amos 7:9) and directed violent attacks against sacrifices (Isa. 1:11–15; Jer. 6:20; 7:21–22; Amos 5:21–23; Mic. 6:6–7). They contrasted this with the call to do justice and obey God (Isa. 1:16–17; Jer. 6:16; 7:23; Amos 5:24; Mic. 6:8). They looked back to the past, to a return to Israel's youth (Jer. 2:2), a memory of the time when God made a covenant with Israel, and when Israel was faithful (Hos. 2:14–23). This was a message taken up in a later era by the Essenes of Qumran, and later still by Christian monasticism.

Besides the prophetic word, the classical prophets drew upon symbolic actions to impress God's message upon the minds of their audiences. Hosea's marital experiences functioned as an illustration of the relationship of Israel to God. Ezekiel dug through a wall with his hands and disappeared into the night with his baggage as a symbol of the exile (Ezek. 12:1–16). Jeremiah emphasized his prophetic words by smashing a potter's earthen flask on the ground before the elders of Jerusalem (Jer. 19). Funeral laments were also used by the prophets to depict the misfortunes of Israel, her king, and her enemies (Jer. 9:9–11; Ezek. 19:1–14; 26:17–18; 28:12–19; 32:2–8; Amos 5:1–2).

Each prophet delivered his message in relationship to his environment, his own religious experience (Amos 7:15; Isa. 6; Jer. 1:4–10), and his individuality. It was not an easy task to perform. There was no salary or fee, no promised easy life. The prophet had to face his own inner doubts, as was the case with Jeremiah (Jer. 1:6) and the reluctant Jonah. Also to be confronted were the fears of an unbelieving populace, the taunts of disagreeing colleagues, and the political troubles and inherent social injustices of the times. Who could possibly want to stand up at a time when the armies of Nebuchadnezzar were investing Jerusalem; when merchants were selling cheap merchandise and unbearable food at exorbitant prices; when man, woman, and child alike were reveling in the streets and in the sanctuaries; and when the poor were being deprived by unscrupulous priests and royal officials of even the little which they owned? Let a prophet tell an important personage that he was wrong, and the prophet might be spat upon or stoned. Inform the priests and the royal officials that they were taking advantage of their positions and oppressing the people, and one might be imprisoned or even put to death. These and many other such perils were experienced by the classical Hebrew prophets. Nevertheless, each believed in his message, in what he was proclaiming, and each believed in God without reservation. Taken together, these men represent a high point in the history of Israelite and Judaic religion.

The Manner of Life of the Prophets

There is almost no information in the Bible as to how the Hebrew prophets sustained themselves, or how they dressed. They came from a variety of backgrounds. Elisha seems to have been a farmer (1 Kings 19:19–21). Amos clearly was a herdsman and cultivator of sycamore trees from Tekoa (Amos 1:1; 7:14). Jeremiah belonged to a priestly family in Jerusalem (Jer. 1:1), and Ezekiel was a priest (Ezek. 1:3). It seems reasonable to assume that prophets who were associated with the royal court such as Gad

(2 Sam. 24:11) and Nathan (1 Kings 1:8, 32) under David, the prophets of Ahab (1 Kings 22:6, 10), and "the king's seers" under David (1 Chron. 25:1-6) and Josiah (2 Chron. 35:15), were supported by the royal administration. Samuel was able to feed himself with a portion of the sacrifice (1 Sam. 9:12-13, 19, 22-24). A number of prophets received various contributions for their services: Samuel (1 Sam. 9:7-8), Ahijah (1 Kings 14:2-3), and Elisha (2 Kings 4:42; 8:7-9; cf. Elisha's refusal in 2 Kings 5:15-16). It also appears that prophets sustained themselves by living off the land, such as on soup made from wild foodstuffs (2 Kings 4:38 ff.). In still other cases, a wandering prophet would be offered the hospitality of food and lodging by local residents, as was the case for Elijah at Zarephath in Phoenicia (1 Kings 17:9 ff.) and for Elisha in Shunem (2 Kings 4:8-10). The prophet Jeremiah apparently had private means of support (see Jer. 32:6 ff.), although the source of his money is not identified.

The dress of a prophet is so rarely mentioned that in most respects it may be presumed to have been like that of other men of the period. Certain prophets, however—notably Elijah and Elisha—were distinguished by a garment of haircloth, held by a leather girdle about the waist (2 Kings 1:8; cf. Zech. 13:4 and Matt. 3:4). This garment was apparently an outer mantle which at that time symbolized the wearer's prophetic office (cf. 2 Kings 2:8 and 2:12-15). Occasionally, clothing was used by the prophet in a symbolic gesture, as when Ahijah "clad himself with a new garment" and proceeded to tear it up into twelve pieces, giving ten of the remnants to Jeroboam as a symbol of the ten tribes which were to make up the kingdom of Israel (1 Kings 11:29 ff). In another era, Isaiah was directed to remove his shoes and "sackcloth" (itself a symbol of mourning) and walk naked and barefoot as a prophetic action (Isa. 20:2-6; cf. Mic. 1:8). It appears that stripping oneself of clothes and going naked was, at one time at least, a sign of prophesying (Saul in 1 Sam. 19:24).

Female Prophets

It does not seem to have been unusual to have women called to the prophetic office in ancient Israel. Indeed, the prominence of prophetesses attached to the sanctuary of Ishtar at Mari in the early 2nd millennium B.C. suggests that the appointment of female spokesmen for gods had a long history in the ancient Near East. In the Old Testament Miriam (Exod. 15:20) and Deborah (Judg. 4:4) are designated as prophetesses, although this may stem from a later desire to honor these women as such, just as Abraham (Gen. 20:7), Moses (Deut. 34:10; 18:15-22), and Aaron (Exod. 7:1) are spoken of as prophets. However, at least two women are known unmistakably to have belonged to prophetic circles. The first is Huldah, who was consulted by the priest at the command of Josiah, king of Judah, in regard to the Book of the Law (2 Kings 22:12–20). The second is the prophetess Noadiah, who is mentioned as an accomplice in the attempt on Nehemiah's life in the Temple at Jerusalem (Neh. 6:14). The unnamed prophetess who was the mother of Isaiah's child, Maher-shalal-hash-baz (Isa. 8:3), may be a third, although many scholars believe that "prophetess" here means only Isaiah's wife. In the New Testament a prophetess, Anna, of the tribe of Asher is mentioned (Luke 2:36), and it is recorded that the four unmarried daughters of Philip the evangelist prophesied (Acts 21:9).

Prophecy after the Fall of Jerusalem

With the destruction of Jerusalem followed by the Exile, prophecy in Israel ceased and its function was replaced in part by apocalyptic. A revival of prophecy, however, was fully expected (see Joel 2:28–29) and communities arose, such as the Essenes at Qumran, in which the hope of prophetic renewal was retained. In the New Testament John the Baptist, "the prophet of the Most High" (Luke 1:76), clad in a "garment of camel's hair, and a leather girdle around his waist" (Matt. 3:4)—a reflection back to the haircloth worn by Elijah, and perhaps Elisha, as a symbol of their prophetic office (2 Kings 1:8; 2:8, 12–15)—marks the renewal of prophecy as understood by the Christian Church (Luke 7:24–28; Matt. 11:7 ff.). Jesus was acclaimed as a prophet (Matt. 21:11 and elsewhere) and regarded himself as one (Mark 6:4 and elsewhere). From its beginnings, the Church viewed prophecy as a characteristic of its existence (see Acts 2:14 ff.). Agabus was the name of a prophet from Jersualem (Acts 11:27–28), and there were "prophets and teachers" in the Christian community at Antioch (Acts 13:1). For Paul, prophets were an essential part of the Christian ministry (1 Cor. 12:28) and important for the edification of the Church (1 Cor. 14:1 ff.). From their beginnings in ancient Israel to their incorporation into the Christian community, prophets played an influential role and represented a significant lifestyle in the Israelite, Jewish, and Christian communities.

MAGICIANS AND DIVINERS

Throughout history man has been strongly attracted to the occult, including the use of magic and various methods of divination. Biblical texts associate the arts of the diviner and the use of magic with the Egyptians (Exod. 7:11) and the Babylonians (Isa. 47:9–15). A special class of priests in ancient Egypt practiced sorcery and were trained to predict future events (Gen. 41:8). One method of divination consisted of interpreting the patterns formed by oil poured on top of water in a bowl or cup, a skill attributed to Joseph (Gen. 44:5, 15). This procedure may be compared with the modern practice of reading tea leaves or coffee grounds in the bottom of a cup.

The arts of the occult were even more highly refined in Assyria and Babylonia, where practitioners spent considerable time learning incantations and perfecting ritual exercises. The priests and sorcerers of Assyria and Babylonia, like their Egyptian counterparts, were respected as highly trained professionals and accorded distinctive titles. Two well-known practices associated with ancient Mesopotamia were astrology (see Isa. 47:13) and the interpretation of dreams (Dan. 2:2, 4:7). One of the most developed arts of divination was hepatoscopy, or the art of predicting the future by studying the color and shape of the livers of sacrificial animals. Ezekiel refers to this practice (Ezek. 22:21). Detailed instructions for the interpretation of the livers were inscribed on clay models, several examples of which have been uncovered by archaeologists. A number of such models are known from Mari on the Middle Euphrates and Ras Shamra (ancient Ugarit), along the Mediterranean coast of Syria. One was found in a Canaanite temple at Hazor in northern Israel dated to around 1500 B.C.

Numerous passages in the Old Testament refer to diverse forms of the occult and their practitioners, including "diviners," "sorcerers," "enchanters," "dreamers," and "magicians." Most of these practices were forbidden by Israelite Law (Deut. 18:9–14; Lev. 19:26, 31; 20:6) and denounced by the classical prophets (Isa. 3:2–3). Death was prescribed for mediums (Exod. 22:18; Lev. 20:27), and the use of magic was frequently linked with adultery (2 Kings 9:22; Mal. 3:5). The prophet Ezekiel condemned the practice of necromancy, understood by him and Near Eastern peoples as being communication with the spirits of the dead (Ezek. 13:17–20); and Jeremiah appealed to the Israelites not to trust in diviners, dreamers, soothsayers, and sorcerers (Jer. 27:9–10; cf. Zech. 10:2). Isaiah proclaimed that God controlled all things and was the one

> who frustrates the omens of liars;
> and makes fools of diviners;
> who turns wise men back,
> and makes their knowledge foolish.
> —Isa. 44:25

Worship of the heavenly bodies and the related phenomenon of astrology, a fine art in Babylonia from at least the 8th century B.C., were not a regular part of Israelite society. Both were considered idolatrous. Many scholars judge the introduction of star worship into Israel to be due to Manasseh, who "built altars for all the host of heaven in the house of the Lord" (2 Kings 21:5). The altars were removed by Josiah (2 Kings 23:5). Jeremiah informed the people not to be dismayed at the signs of the heavens

(Jer. 10:2). The New Testament projects the same critical view toward magic and divination. Paul called the magician Bar-Jesus (Elymas): "You son of the devil, you enemy of righteousness, full of deceit and villainy" (Acts 13:6–11).

Despite all the pronouncements against the occult, professional diviners and magicians did play a role in the development of Israelite society and religion. Both Joseph (Gen. 40:12; 41:15) and Daniel (Dan. 2) were honored as interpreters of dreams. Many decisions are represented in the Bible as having been made in relation to the "casting of lots," a form of divination (e.g., Lev. 16:8–10; Josh. 18:10). Related to this method was the use of the Urim and Thummim in making decisions (see Fig. 75), an important privilege and duty of the early Hebrew priests (Exod. 28:30; Num. 27:21; 1 Sam. 14:37–42; 28:6). Israelite kings resorted to the divination of the prophets of Baal and Asherah (1 Kings 18:17 ff.) and of magicians (2 Chron. 33:6). Furthermore, the miracles performed by the prophets Elijah (1 Kings 17:21; 18:30–39, etc.) and Elisha (2 Kings 2:14, 19–22, 24; 4:3–6, 38–41, etc.) suggest the employment of magic. It is only in the classical prophets that there arose a strong condemnation of anything related to the occult. Their condemnation does not seem to be directed primarily against the practices themselves, but against their idolatrous use and Canaanite setting. Throughout the biblical period, a continual tension existed between the desire to trust in God and the wish to relieve one's anxiety about the future. This tension was present when Saul consulted the witch of Endor (1 Sam. 28:6–25) after having banned her profession (1 Sam. 28:3, 9).

PHARISEES AND SADDUCEES

The Pharisees and the Sadducees were Jewish sects in existence during the time of Jesus and the early years of Christianity. Jesus criticized both sects as failing to interpret "the signs of the times" (Matt. 16:1–4) and warned his disciples of their teachings (Matt. 16:6–12).

The Pharisees

The Pharisees appear as a distinct, well-established religious and political party shortly after the Maccabean revolt (167 B.C.). Their precise origins, however, cannot be determined. They have been traced back to the Hasidim, or "pious ones," who themselves arose sometime in the 4th or 3rd century B.C. and who stressed the observance of Jewish ritual and the study of the Law (Torah). The seeds of Pharisaism were sown during the Exile, when the Jewish community was deprived of the Temple and its ritual. The Pharisees considered themselves as the successors of Ezra and Moses (see Matt. 23:2), and by the beginning of the Christian era they formed an influential association of zealous students and teachers of the Law.

The Pharisees, in opposition to the Sadducees, believed that the law given to Moses consisted of both the written Law (the Pentateuch, or first five books of the Old Testament, also called Torah), and the oral law (unwritten religious tradition). By New Testament times Pharisaism represented the religious beliefs and practices of a large part of the Jewish community. The chief concern of the Pharisees was holiness based on the observation of the Law, a concern which the New Testament suggests was sometimes carried to extremes (Matt. 23).

One of the major functions of the Pharisees was the teaching and preaching of the Law. Since they believed that God could be worshipped outside the Temple and, like the prophets, held that God was not to be satisfied by bloody sacrifices, the Pharisees fostered the synagogue as a place of worship and instruction. In this respect Pharisaism represented the immediate predecessor of rabbinic Judaism (see "Teachers and Rabbis" below).

The apostle Paul was originally a Pharisee (Acts 23:6; 26:5), educated in Jerusalem "at the feet of Gamaliel" (Acts 22:3), one of Pharisaism's most respected scholars (Acts 5:34). The opposition of Jesus and his apostles to the Pharisees was not directed against their doctrine, but against their abuse of it (Matt. 23; Mark 12:38-40; Luke 11:37-54). In fact, Pharisaic doctrine had much in common with that of Christianity and prepared the ground for such concepts as a belief in a Messiah, angels and spirits, resurrection and immortality.

The Sadducees

The Sadducees were a variant Jewish religious sect during the period of the Second Temple who formed a party of priests and aristocratic families. The sect apparently arose sometime following the Maccabean revolt (2nd century B.C.), and it opposed the beliefs and practices of the Pharisees down to the Roman destruction of the Second Temple in A.D. 70. The Sadducees traced their origin to Zadok, the priest appointed by Solomon to be in charge of the Temple in Jerusalem (1 Kings 2:35). It is most probable, however, that the direct forerunners of the Sadducees are to be placed in the period following the Return, when members of the priesthood were established as leaders of the Jewish community.

Representing the conservative, priestly tradition in Judaism, the Sadducees denied the validity of oral tradition espoused by the Pharisees and retained only the Mosaic Law as normative. They rejected the Pharisaic beliefs in resurrection (Acts 4:1-2), immortality, and angels—a factor which frequently gave rise to disputes betwen the two sects (Acts 23:8–10). Along with the Pharisees, the Sadducees were berated by both John the Baptist (Matt. 3:7–10) and Jesus (Matt. 16:1–12). Since the Sadducees consisted of the wealthier and more aristocratic elements of Jewish society, including influential priests and merchants, they wielded a considerable power over the political and economic life of the Jews in Palestine. For example, they could command the arrest of the apostles (Acts 5:17–18). Their very existence being dependent on the Temple and its sacrificial ritual, the Sadducees ceased to exert any major influence after the destruction of the Jerusalem Temple in A.D. 70, leaving the moral and religious leadership of the Jewish people solely in the hands of the Pharisees.

THE ESSENES

The Essenes formed a third sect, or school of religious thought, in Judaism during the last two centuries B.C. and the first century A.D. Although not mentioned in the New Testament, the Essenes are referred to in several ancient documents as a separatist party who divorced themselves from official Judaism. Along with the Pharisees with whom they shared some common traits, Essene origins are probably to be sought in the Hasidic movement (see "The Pharisees"). However, the Essenes were opposed to the Pharisees as well as the Sadducees, Jerusalem priesthood, and Hasmonean dynasty. Sometime during the second half of the second century B.C., the Essenes removed themselves from the mainstream of religious and social life of Jerusalem and set up their headquarters along the western side of the Dead Sea in the area of Qumran and 'Ain Feshkha. Here they lived as an ascetic community in a state of eschatological expectation. In many ways, their style of life can be compared with that of present-day communes.

Interest in the Essenes has been heightened in recent years by the discovery of the Dead Sea scrolls from 1947 onwards and the excavation of the communal ruins of Khirbet Qumran between 1951 and 1956. Here, on a plateau overlooking the Dead Sea, the late Father Roland de Vaux uncovered the ruins of a group of buildings occupied by a closely-knit community which bore many similarities to what is known about the Essenes from ancient historical documents. The complex was inhabited as early as the latter half of the second century B.C. and was destroyed by the Roman army in A.D. 68. Together with fragments of contemporary manuscripts recovered from eleven caves in the vicinity, which probably represent a portion of the community's library, the buildings provide an insight into the customs, religious beliefs, and social structure of its occupants.

The excavated remains included a laundry, pottery kilns, a kitchen, a refectory or common dining hall, an assembly room, several cisterns for the collection of rain water or for daily ritual ablutions, and a scriptorium for the writing and copying of religious and sectarian manuscripts. The members of the community ate, prayed, studied, and worked in the communal buildings, but apparently slept in nearby caves and in huts and tents set up in the surrounding area. Individuals worked as agriculturists, shepherds, and craftsmen. They took frequent baths for purposes of ritual purification, followed special rules of authority and conduct, and adhered to communal ownership of property. Special attention was given to the copying and studying of religious documents, which included Biblical manuscripts also revered by the early Christian church, such as the Psalms and writings of the Prophets. Although the evidence is not conclusive, the prevailing opinion is that the Qumran community was related to the Essenes.

TEACHERS AND RABBIS

Education in Israelite Society

The character of ancient Israelite education was far different from today's well-defined system of public and private schools. General education in Hebrew society was the responsibility of the father, who provided his children with the knowledge required for daily living, the skill necessary to pursue the hereditary occupation of the family, as well as basic social, moral, and religious principles (e.g., Exod. 12:24–27; Deut. 4:9–10; 6:7, 20–25; 32:46; Prov. 4:1). The mother also took part in this teaching process (Prov. 1:8; 6:20; 31:1), a role for the mother which is unique in the literature of the ancient Near East. Much instruction by the parents may have taken the form of the admonitions to young men preserved in the book of Proverbs.

Training in the special skills of certain crafts was provided within professional guilds. Such instruction had a long and developed history in the ancient Near East. Scribal schools, or "Tablet Houses," are known to have existed in Egypt, Syria, and Mesopotamia at an early date (Fig. 79). School tablets in Akkadian cuneiform display on one side a sign, word, or brief sentence in the teacher's hand and on the other side the pupil's efforts to copy the teacher's example. Other tablets, written in Sumerian and dated to the early 2nd millennium B.C., outline the education of a scribe. One text describes a student's inefficiency:

> He inscribes a tablet—he doesn't bring it off effectively;
> He writes a letter—he gets the wrong address (?);
> (If) he goes to divide an estate, he won't (be able to)
> divide the estate.
> H. W. F. Saggs, *The Greatness That Was Babylon*
> (New York: Hawthorn Books, Inc., 1962), p. 437.

79. Ancient clay tablets with cuneiform writing on them.

There are no direct references in the Bible to schools or to professional teachers as a distinct occupation. It is possible, however, that the professional scribes of the Israelite monarchy ("secretaries" in 2 Sam. 20:25; 1 Kings 4:3; 2 Kings 22:8, and elsewhere) were trained in much the same manner as the Assyrian and Babylonian scribes. It is also possible that the scribal techniques were handed down from father to son in ancient Israel, or from "master" to "pupil" in the sense of apprenticeship. Such appears to be the case in other professions, for example the temple musicians (1 Chron. 25:8).

Prophets and priests provided instruction in ancient Israel, but again not in the sense of a professional teacher. In the case of Elisha, the younger prophet seems to have followed his "master," Elijah, for some time—learning by daily instruction and example—before replacing Elijah upon the latter's death (see 1 Kings 19:16, 19–21; 2 Kings 2). Similarly, the child Samuel was given to the priests at Shiloh not merely to be educated, but to be trained as a resident member of the staff (1 Sam. 1–3). The sons of David (1 Chron. 27:32) and Ahab (2 Kings 10:1, 6) may have received formal education, but apparently not from professional teachers. Jehoash, the king of Judah (c. 837–800 B.C.), was instructed by the priest Jehoiada (2 Kings 12:2). Elsewhere priests and Levites are represented as teaching the Law (Torah), as for example during the reign of Jehoshaphat (2 Chron. 17:8–9) and after the Return (Neh. 8:7–9).

The Rabbi

Related to the concept of teacher is the title "Rabbi" ("my master"), which is used in the New Testament as a designation for teachers of the Law in general (Matt. 23:7–8) and as a title of respect for either John the Baptist (John 3:26) or, more frequently, Jesus, particularly in the Fourth Gospel (John 1:49; 4:31; etc.). The title first appeared toward the beginning of the Christian era and designated a person well-schooled in Jewish Law, and hence a teacher of the Law (John 3:2 and Luke 2:46). There is no specific mention in the New Testament as to the teaching method provided by the Rabbi, but it cannot have been too different from that of the Talmudic period (3rd–6th centuries A.D.). Instruction was given in association with synagogues, such as those found in the Galilee region where the Rabbis reorganized themselves following the Jewish wars with Rome (67–72 and 135 A.D.). A number of the synagogues have been partially restored, as at Beth Alpha (Fig. 80), Capernaum (Fig. 81), Chorazin (Fig. 82), and Meiron.

The Law formed the basic text from which the Rabbi taught. This text was supplemented by various explanations and interpretations derived from oral law codified in the Mishna (c. A.D. 200), and by additional discussions on the Law recorded in the Talmud (3rd–6th centuries A.D.). The teacher (Rabbi) would sit on a raised platform surrounded by his students, who sat on the ground before him in a semicircle. Most instruction was oral. The goal was to memorize the Law and all the instruction that applied to it.

The Rabbi was not paid for his teaching; he earned his livelihood from more secular pursuits, such as farming or carpentry. He was, however, exempt from taxes and could be compensated for loss of income suffered while engaged in voluntary work of a religious nature. In addition to lecturing at the rabbinic school, the Rabbi provided instruction to the general public at certain religious festivals, and he might preach following the reading of the Scripture in the synagogue.

While the above sketch is incomplete, it provides some indication as to the character and responsibilities of the Rabbi as he appears in the New Testament. Jesus taught and preached in the synagogue (Matt. 4:23; 9:35), as did the apostles after him (e.g., Acts 14:1; 17:3). Jesus also instructed his followers in the rabbinic manner (see Matt. 5–8). The tradition of the teacher as an instructor of religious and moral principles was continued in the Christian Church (Eph. 4:11; 2 Tim. 1:11; Jas. 3:1). Paul ranked teachers third in importance after apostles and prophets (1 Cor. 12:28–31).

80. The partially restored synagogue at Beit Alpha has a mosaic floor which contains symbols from the Bible as well as a zodiac with Hebrew titles on the seasons and months.

81. The synagogue at Capernaum has been partially restored. This building was probably built on the site of the synagogue of the first century A.D. mentioned in Mark 1:21.

82. The top of the ark which contained the Torah scrolls in the synagogue at Chorazin. This site is mentioned in Matt. 11:21.

SCRIBES

The scribal profession was directly related to the origins of writing and to the beginnings of record-keeping in the ancient Near East. The scribe in Mesopotamia was an important member of society, responsible for the supervision of archives, the recording of deeds and business transactions, and the composition of various historical annals and literary texts. Scribes in Egypt were responsible for recording the Nile flood levels, maintaining accounts of the royal granaries, and copying numerous religious texts such as the *Book of the Dead*. Assyrian scribes at the time of Abraham had their own schools, or "Tablet Houses," where they were formally instructed in the art of writing (see TEACHERS AND RABBIS, above). Practice tablets recovered from these schools range from the almost unrecognizable scratches of the beginner to the polished style and penmanship of the well-trained professional. Many scribal tutors obtained their remuneration through student tuitions, while others were attached to palaces and especially to temples.

Scribes in Ancient Israel

The scribal profession entered Israelite society with the establishment of the administrative organization of the Hebrew monarchy. The king's scribes (or secretaries) were government officials attached to the royal court

83. An Israelite scribe with his scribal kit.

84. An ancient writing board. The sunken surface of the "page" was covered with beeswax and a stylus was used to make impressions on the wax (from the Metropolitan Museum of Art, New York).

(2 Sam. 8:17; 1 Kings 4:3). Scribes generally performed a number of duties, all associated in some way with writing. A scribe was one of the king's counselors (1 Chron. 27:32), and he might act much as an American secretary of state (2 Kings 18:18). He collected and recorded tax money for the palace and the Temple (2 Kings 12:10; 22:3–4). He transcribed documents, signed and filed deeds and legal contracts (Jer. 32:10–14), and wrote from dictation (Jer. 36:4).

Scribes were members of professional guilds, possibly hereditary (1 Chron. 2:55). Senior scribes were assigned their own chambers in the royal palace (Jer. 36:12) or Temple (Jer. 36:10), a practice common to much of the ancient Near East. A scribe might also be attached to the commander of the army (2 Kings 25:19). A writing case attached to his girdle or waistband was a means of identifying a scribe (see Ezek. 9:2–3). This case contained the scribe's tools, which probably did not differ much from those used by the scribes of other nations depicted on various reliefs and paintings and which are known from preserved specimens of the actual objects themselves: reed pens or brushes, an ink palette on which the ink could be mixed, several cakes of ink, a water jar, and perhaps a sharp knife (Fig. 83).

The Israelite scribe wrote primarily with pen and ink on parchment and papyrus. He may also have made use of writing boards of wood or even ivory (Fig. 84), such as are known from contemporary Assyrian reliefs and from actual examples discovered in the palace of Sargon II at Nimrud. Documents (known as "ostraca") were also written on broken pieces of pottery. Two major collections of ostraca written in Hebrew script are known. One of them was discovered in the ruins of the royal palace at Samaria and consists of tax receipts for oil and wine dating to the first half of the 8th century B.C. The other collection is composed of twenty-one ostraca found in a destroyed guardroom of the last Israelite city at Lachish. Included among the documents were letters of correspondence between the military commander of Lachish and a northern outpost during the last years of Judah (c. 589–588 B.C.).

Scribes after the Exile

The scribal profession in Judaism changed with the Exile. By the time of the Second Temple, the scribe had become a recorder and interpreter of the Law (Ezra 7:6, 10). Scribal decisions in regard to the Law developed into a corpus of oral tradition which the Pharisees considered as equal in authority to the written law (see "Pharisees and Sadducees," above).

The Jewish scribe took great care in transcribing the Law. He wrote on parchment produced from an animal designated as clean. He would trace and square lines on the parchment with a ruler so that the results would be straight and uniform. The writing was now done with a quill pen dipped in black ink. Erasures were forbidden, and careful attention was given to the spacing, formation, and spelling of the words. The task may have been performed in a room similar to one interpreted as a *scriptorium* discovered among the ruins of the Essene community at Khirbet Qumran on the western shore of the Dead Sea. Fragments of writing desks covered with plaster and of two inkwells, one of which still retained dried ink, were found in the room. A low, plastered platform with cup-shaped cavities was reconstructed from fragments; it may have been a table used for ritual purification in the copying and handling of the sacred manuscripts. Scribes sat at the desks in the *scriptorium* and copied the treasured manuscripts. A reader might dictate as others copied. Some might copy directly from scrolls propped open with sticks.

In the New Testament scribes are presented as judges, teachers, and keepers of the Law. Associated with the Pharisees, the scribes opposed Jesus for violating their traditions (Luke 23:10), and were criticized in turn by Jesus as hypocrites (Matt. 23:2–12).

ENGINEERS AND ARCHITECTS

There is little in the biblical data itself to suggest that ancient Israel had a class of professional architects. The construction of buildings and monuments appears to have been the responsibility of craftsmen or master masons. Even these seem to be of non-Israelite origin, such as Hiram, the Phoenician master craftsman from Tyre who was in charge of the details of Solomon's Temple in Jerusalem (1 Kings 7:13 ff.; 2 Chron. 2:13–14). On the other hand, the extent and overall organization of Solomon's building activities, not only in Jerusalem (1 Kings 5–7) but also throughout the rest of his kingdom (1 Kings 9:15, 17–19), must have required some type of architectural planning and supervision. Such planning may be indicated in the epilogue to the building of the Temple: "The house was finished in all its parts, and according to all its specifications" (1 Kings 6:38; see also 2 Chron. 3). Uzziah's invention in respect to the defenses of Jerusalem may provide a second example: "He made engines, invented by skilful men, to be on the towers and the corners, to shoot arrows and great stones" (2 Chron. 26:15). It is not known whether the statement refers to actual catapults, or to a new type of battlement along the city walls as suggested by the Israeli archaeologist, Yigael Yadin.

Engineers during the Old Testament Period

The biblical evidence for "engineers" is similarly deficient. However, some technical expertise must have been available to the Israelites who cut the water systems (10th–8th centuries B.C.) known from archaeological excavations at Hazor, Gibeon, Megiddo, and Jerusalem (Figs. 85, 86, 87). These water systems are remarkable tributes to the men who designed and built them. The shaft and tunnel of the water system at Hazor, for example, were constructed in relation to the prevailing water table.

Even more remarkable was the achievement of the engineers who constructed the Siloam tunnel in Jerusalem. In ancient times a city had to be located near a constant supply of water, such as a perennial spring. Even with a good water source, there remained the problem of assuring the supply during a siege. In David's reign Jerusalem was supplied with water from the spring Gihon, located in the Kidron Valley at the foot of the eastern hill on which the ancient city stood. A 130-foot-long tunnel, cut into the rock, ensured access to the spring from inside the city wall in time of siege (Fig. 88).

An even more remarkable water system utilizing the Gihon spring was constructed by Hezekiah (late 8th century B.C.) in the face of the growing threat of Assyrian conquest (2 Chron. 32:1–3). The water shaft in use when David captured Jerusalem (2 Sam. 5:8) had long since been abandoned as inadequate, and the water of Gihon flowed down the Kidron in a rock-cut channel along the "king's garden" (Neh. 3:15; Isa. 8:6). The city's water supply was therefore unprotected and approach to it could be easily prevented by a besieging army, thus making a long siege unendurable to the inhabitants. To prevent such a disaster, Hezekiah blocked access to the spring from outside, and dug a tunnel which brought the water into the city itself (2 Kings 20:20; 2 Chron. 32:3–4; cf. Neh. 3:16 and Sirach 48:17) (Fig. 89).

The construction of this tunnel is remarkable. It is 1,749 feet long, leading from the spring to a pool at the southwest end of the eastern hill, and carries water to this day. An inscription commemorating the completion of the tunnel was discovered by a schoolboy exploring it in 1880, and provides the information that it was dug from both ends simultaneously. Only the latter part of the text is preserved:

> [. . . when] (the tunnel) was driven through. And this was the way in which it was cut through:—While [. . .] (were) still [. . .] axe(s), each man toward his fellow, and while there were still three cubits to be cut through, [there was heard] the voice of a man calling to his fellow, for there was *an overlap* in the rock on the right [and on the left]. And when the tunnel was driven through, the quarrymen hewed (the rock), each man toward his fellow, axe against axe; and the water flowed from the spring toward the reservoir for 1,200 cubits, and the height of the rock above the head(s) of the quarrymen was 100 cubits.

J. B. Pritchard (ed.), *Ancient Near Eastern Texts*[3]
(Princeton: Princeton University Press, 1969), p. 321.

85. The subterranean water system at Hazor.

The path of the tunnel meanders, rather than running in a straight line, but the error at the point where the two excavation parties met is minimal—only about a foot in elevation. Some 850 cubic yards of rock were removed during the construction of the tunnel, and it has been estimated that it would have required nearly 200 days to complete it. This was no ordinary achievement, and the Siloam tunnel stands as a monument to the skill of ancient Hebrew engineering.

Engineers during the New Testament Period

Following the Hellenistic occupation of Palestine in the late 4th century B.C., and especially during the time of the Roman Republic, architectural and engineering achievements became even more standardized and professional. The Temple built by Herod the Great and destroyed in A.D. 70 required sound architectural planning and skillful engineering, as indicated by still-standing portions of the outer walls (Fig. 90) and by recent archaeological excavation around the Temple Mount (Fig. 91). Achievements in engineering of the Greeks and Romans, such as harbors and aqueducts, were readily

86. The subterranean water system at Gibeon.

87. The subterranean water system at Megiddo.

88. The water from the Spring Gihon runs into this cave. On the left is the entrance to the tunnel which was constructed to give the inhabitants of Jerusalem secret access to the water supply (which lay outside the city wall) when the city was under siege by an enemy.

89. Hezekiah's Tunnel was constructed to bring the water supply of Jerusalem inside the city itself.

90. Part of the temple platform built by Herod the Great still stands. The larger stones at the left of the figure date from the time of Herod.

apparent to the Jews and early Christians. The apostle Paul was familiar with many Greek temples and theaters, as well as with the Acropolis in Athens. Many Jews and Chrstians alike traveled on the well-designed, stone-paved roads laid down by Roman engineers throughout the Holy Land.

Further word should be given about one of the outstanding achievements of the Hellenistic-Roman world—the construction of aqueducts. Stretches of the aqueducts, such as that which fed Caesarea on the Mediterranean coast of Israel, are still visible (Fig. 92). According to Josephus, riots occurred when Pontius Pilate used Temple funds to construct an aqueduct for Jerusalem (Josephus, *Antiq.* XVIII. iii. 2 and *Wars* II. ix. 4). Portions of the aqueducts which supplied Jerusalem were identified by various archaeologists during the 19th century (Fig. 93).

91. Recent excavations south of the temple platform have uncovered part of the grand staircase which led up from the lower city to the Temple of Herod.

92. Part of the aqueduct which led water into Caesarea during the Roman period is still visible above ground.

93. A portion of the aqueduct south of Jerusalem constructed by Pontius Pilate.

Since the flow of water in all Roman aqueducts was controlled by gravity, the source of the water had to be situated at a higher elevation than the city which it supplied. Recent survey work (1969) has identified three sources of water which fulfill this requirement south of Jerusalem and has traced the remains of several aqueducts. The preserved portions of the aqueducts range in date from the time of the Second Temple to the period of the Mameluke Sultans of Egypt (began A.D. 1250). One aqueduct traverses some 13 miles from its source southwest of Bethlehem to a large cistern system on the Temple Mount. Various installations were constructed to capture and transport the maximum amount of water: hewn ducts, barrel-vaulted chambers, and subterranean aqueducts. Numerous topographical obstructions necessitated a long, meandering path from the springs to Jerusalem. Some sections were built on high foundation walls, while other sections consisted of mere channels hewn out of rock. Sections of the aqueducts tunneled through ridges (one tunnel passes beneath Bethlehem) and spanned wadis by means of bridges. One aqueduct—repaired throughout antiquity—remains in use today.

MERCHANTS

A merchant was a professional who sold or exchanged goods and products. On a local scale, a merchant could be the owner of a small retail

94. Part of the bazaar, or *suq*, in Jerusalem.

business, a craftsman displaying his wares, or a villager offering his fresh produce. The Bible mentions the sale of such products as oil (2 Kings 4:7), pottery (Jer. 19:1), clothing (Jer. 13:1–2), wine, fish, and other foodstuffs (Neh. 13:15–16). Trade would frequently be carried on in a marketplace, located around an open square or along narrow, perhaps colonnaded, streets onto which opened row after row of small, awning-covered shops. The tradition of these markets, or "bazaars" (1 Kings 20:34), is retained in the Middle East today in the *suqs* of such cities as Beirut, Damascus, and Jerusalem (Figs. 94, 95). While the persons trading in these markets were in one sense merchants, they were primarily farmers, sheepherders, and craftsmen.

On an international and more professional level, a merchant organized and directed large-scale trade. Such trade has a long history in the ancient Near East, where it was necessary for nations to trade—sometimes at quite a distance—for the raw materials of existence. Old Assyrian "merchant colonies" were already established in various parts of the Near East by the late 3rd millennium B.C. One of these colonies has been discovered at Kultepe (southern Turkey), and has produced cuneiform documents recording the sale and shipment by caravan of various commodities, as well as international trade laws regulating market prices.

The biblical Patriarchs may have been involved in a similar type of trade.

95. Seeds and nuts for sale in the bazaar, or *suq*, in Jerusalem.

The late W. F. Albright has argued that Abraham and his clansmen were active in transporting goods across Syria and Palestine by means of donkey caravans. Later, during the time of the Israelite monarchy, camel caravans plied between Arabia and Israel. The transporting of goods by camel caravans is reflected in the biblical story of Solomon and Sheba (1 Kings 10:2). Extrabiblical sources have shown that the merchant in charge of the caravan was given an allowance and required to keep daily records of all expenses encountered along the way.

Compared with their neighbors, the Hebrews were not a merchant people. Most commerce was controlled by others, in particular by the Canaanites ("Canaanite" was often used as an appellative with the meaning "merchant") and their successors, the Phoenicians, whose merchant activities were legend during the period of the First Temple (c. 950–587 B.C.; see Isa. 23; Ezek. 27). Only after their loss of independence in 587 B.C. did the Jewish people generally turn toward more extensive commercial pursuits.

Israelite participation in international trade is most obvious in the reign of Solomon. Commercial ties were developed especially with Tyre, and were controlled by the state. For his building activities in Jerusalem, Solomon exchanged grain, oil, and wine with Hiram, the king of Tyre, for the necessary timber (1 Kings 5:6–11; 2 Chron. 2:15). Solomon also relied on Tyrian skill in order to build a fleet of ships at the port of Ezion-geber on the Gulf of Aqabah (1 Kings 9:26–27; 10:11; 2 Chron. 8:17–18). Moreover, Solomon obtained horses from the north and chariots from Egypt and sold them to the kings of Syria (1 Kings 10:28–29). The evidence for foreign trade during the period of the divided monarchy is less extensive. It appears that there were Syrian merchants in Samaria and Israelite merchants in Damascus during the reign of Ahab (1 Kings 20:34).

The merchant was an international, cosmopolitan figure. He could afford to dress well and had access to luxuries not available to others. He was required to be able to speak, read, and write several languages besides his own. Familiarity with trade regulations, tax systems and basic monetary units, weights and measures was a necessity. The merchant understood the value of marketable goods and what they were worth on the open market. He would also know his way about many of the major cities, probably having visited a number of them often, and would feel at ease in presenting his goods in any royal court. The merchant was, in short, an international figure, an entrepreneur.

SAILORS

Mariners, or sailors, are mentioned only occasionally in the Bible. Israel was not a seaward nation and depended primarily on the Phoenicians in this respect. References to sailors in the Bible are to Phoenicians or other non-Israelite peoples (see Isa. 23; Ezek. 27; and Jon. 1:3–5, where the reference is to a Phoenician merchantman). That the Israelites were not at home with the sea is apparent from the statement that Hiram, king of Tyre (Phoenicia), sent "seamen who were familiar with the sea" to Solomon at Ezion-geber (1 Kings 9:27).

The sailor, however, would have been a familiar person in Israel, especially in such ports as Ezion-geber on the Gulf of Aqaba, or Joppa (2 Chron. 2:16) (Fig. 96), and in Acco and Achzib (Phoenician ports) on the Mediterranean coast. The sailor would have been bronzed and toughened by the wind, sea, and sun. His hands would have been calloused from furling sails, tying down cargo, and raising and lowering the ship's anchors. His muscles would have been well developed from manning the oars (Ezek. 27:26) or fighting the tiller. Sailors lived in simple style, perhaps near the port in houses typical of other coastal city dwellers. Most of the sailor's time, however, would have been spent at sea—for periods of up to three years,

96. The ancient port of Joppa, or Jaffa, on the coast of Israel.

which was the length of time for the voyage to "Tarshish" (Spain?) and back (2 Chron. 9:21). Occasionally, the sailor might become lost or wrecked at sea (Ezek. 27:34). An excellent account of a sailing venture—the route, the length of time at sea, the work, and the dangers encountered—is preserved in the description of Paul's voyage from Caesarea to Rome (Acts 27:1—28:16).

CRAFTSMEN

Craftsmen are professional people engaged in manual skills. Unlike the merchant, the craftsman is primarily concerned with the manufacture of wares and products, and only secondarily with the distribution and trade of the merchandise itself. Craftsmen are designated by a variety of terms in the Bible: skilled workers, artisans, masters, craftsmen. A number of specific crafts are mentioned, including carpentry, tentmaking, basket weaving, pottery, ivory and wood carving, jewelry making and metalworking (see further under THE INDUSTRIAL LIFE for more information on particular types of craftsmen).

In ancient Hebrew society many of the crafts were executed in the home or in small shops adjacent to the home. The biblical craftsman was part of a long tradition handed down from father to son, generation after generation. He was familiar with his raw materials, and could work them with

97. A reconstructed potter's wheel (Ha-Aretz Museum, Tel Aviv, Israel).

great skill. Quite often—as do artisans today—he kept secret some special feature of his work, revealing it only to members of his own family. He was industrious and worked long and hard at his specialty in a small, often poorly lit room. He was proud of his work, and gained much satisfaction in completing each piece produced by his hands. He was also a free citizen (slaves were not generally trained in the crafts in ancient Near Eastern society) and was limited only by his ingenuity, the extent of his skill, and the prevailing styles of his society.

Workers in a particular craft often joined together in a guild, or professional association, similar to those of the early prophets and temple musicians. The organization of the guild was patterned after that of the family (1 Chron. 4:14, 21); there were even groups of craftsmen who worked specifically for the king (1 Chron. 4:23). Other guilds are known from post-exilic times (Neh. 3:8, 31–32).

Shops were often called by the name of the craftsman's specialty, such as "the potter's house" (Jer. 18:2) or "the house of linen workers" (1 Chron. 4:21). Frequently, the people of a single craft together would occupy a certain quarter or area of a city. There was a "Fuller's Field" in Jerusalem at the time of Isaiah (Isa. 7:3) and a "Bakers' Street" during the days of Jeremiah (Jer. 37:21).

Archaeological evidence has helped to illustrate and contemporize the

98. Loom weights affixed to a reconstructed loom from the period of the Israelite monarchy (Ha-Aretz Museum, Tel Aviv, Israel).

lifestyle and the skills of ancient biblical craftsmen. Because of the impermanent nature of archaeological remains and the fact that many craftsmen operated in their own homes, not many details have been preserved in the archaeological record. However, the few objects that have survived provide valuable information as to the technical skill of certain craftsmen. In some cases entire workshops have been identified: the potter's kilns, clay bins, potter's wheels (Fig. 97), scrapers; the weaver's needles and loom weights (Fig. 98); the jeweler's uncut stone, bronze borers, and molds.

The biblical craftsman was a simple, unsophisticated person. Many have thought that most craftsmen were illiterate until after the Exile, but this cannot be proven. On the whole he made little profit from his efforts, but it is not unreasonable to surmise that he was like most craftsmen today—proud of his work and content with his place in society and manner of living.

MUSICIANS

Music played an important role in ancient Israelite society, as is evident from the collection of hymns preserved in the book of Psalms. A significant number of the Psalms are attributed to David, and others to musicians. Brief notes provide such instructions as "with stringed instruments," and "for the flute," "to the choirmaster," and "for the memorial offering." Psalms bearing such notes suggest the presence of professional musicians in Israelite society.

By tradition the inception of music among the Hebrews was attributed to Jubal, "the father of all those who play the lyre and pipe" (Gen. 4:21). Musicians were noted throughout the ancient Near East. There are Egyptian and Mesopotamian references to Canaanite musicians, as well as numerous representations of musicians on reliefs, cylinder seals, carved ivories, and metal bowls. A scene from a Theban tomb dated to the reign of Thutmose IV (c. 1425–1417 B.C.) depicts an Egyptian harpist, lutist, dancer, player of the double pipe, and a lyrist.

It is generally accepted that David was responsible for the appearance of professional musicians in Israelite society (see 1 Chron. 6:31–48; 15:16–16:6; 25:1–31). Associated with this attribution is the tradition that David himself was an accomplished musician, "skillful in playing the lyre" (1 Sam. 16:16–23). The professional musicians introduced by David were primarily associated with the Temple and the royal court. They were organized into guilds (1 Chron. 15:16 ff. and elsewhere) similar to those of the early prophets and craftsmen. The guilds were apparently headed by the "chief of musicians," who was in charge of all singing and playing of instruments (Neh. 12:46). It is not indicated how the musicians were paid, but most likely they received compensation from either the royal court or the Temple treasury. In postexilic times the musicians were apparently exempt from taxes and conscription services along with other Temple professionals (Ezra 7:24) and were supported by Temple revenues (Neh. 12:47). A musician could also be a seer or a prophet (1 Chron. 25:1–6).

The professional musicians of the Hebrew monarchy performed a variety of tasks and played at a variety of functions. They performed "with great joy" at the king's enthronement festival (1 Kings 1:39–40; 2 Kings 11:14). They blew trumpets before battles (1 Chron. 13:14) and celebrated victories (2 Chron. 20:28). The court and temple musicians played at the procession of the Ark into Jerusalem, "making merry before the Lord with all their might, with songs and lyres and harps and tambourines and castanets and cymbals" (1 Sam. 6:5); at the dedication of Solomon's Temple, "arrayed in fine linen, with cymbals, harps and lyres . . ." (2 Chron. 5:12–14); and at the offering of the burnt sacrifice by Hezekiah (2 Chron. 29:25–30). Musicians were sometimes engaged to play at private festivals and banquets (Isa. 5:12; 24:8–9).

A number of musical instruments are mentioned in the Bible (Fig. 99). Some of these are: a wind instrument with a double pipe (1 Sam. 10:5; 1 Kings 1:40); a trumpet (2 Sam. 2:28); a type of lyre, played by David (1 Sam. 16:16, 23); another type of lyre, larger and with a deeper tone (2 Sam. 6:5; 1 Kings 10:12); and cymbals (2 Sam. 6:5; Ezra 3:10). Examples of instruments such as pipes, cymbals, and clay rattles, have been unearthed at several biblical sites, including Hazor and Megiddo. A pottery incense stand dating from the 10th century B.C. from Ashdod is decorated with figures playing cymbals, double pipe, lyre, and tambourine [see *Archaeology* 23 (1970), pp. 310–311].

The musician's contribution embraced the entire register of Hebrew society. He brought joy, gladness, relaxation, and even sorrow. The essence of the professional musician is summed up in a verse from a Psalm (42:4):

> These things I remember
> as I pour out my soul:
> how I went with the throng,
>   and led them in procession to the house of God,
> with glad shouts and songs of thanksgiving,
>   a multitude keeping festival.

MOURNERS

Mourning was a traditional ritual attached to the death and burial of a person. The mourners included all those who were affected by the death (1 Sam. 25:1; 2 Sam. 1:11–12; 1 Kings 14:13). A stock phrase would be used for these events, such as "Alas, my brother" (1 Kings 13:30; Jer. 22:18) or "Alas, lord" (Jer. 34:5). In other cases the mourner would compose a personal lament honoring the deceased, such as David's laments over Saul and Jonathan (2 Sam. 1:17–27) and Abner (2 Sam. 3:33–34).

The ritual of mourning led to the development of professional mourners, mainly women, who would bewail and lament a death, generally for a fee. They were called "singing women" (2 Chron. 35:25), "mourning women" (Jer. 9:17), or "skilful women" (Jer. 9:17). On one end of the sarcophagus of King Ahiram of Byblos (c. 12th–10th centuries B.C.) is depicted a group of four Canaanite professional mourners. The women are shown standing with bared breasts: the two on the left are beating their breasts (see Isa. 32:11–12); the two on the right have their arms raised, perhaps tearing their hair (see Isa. 22:12; Jer. 7:29).

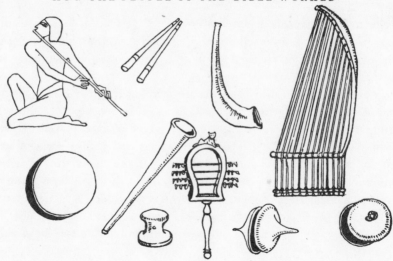

99. Musical instruments in the Bible. *From top left*: flute, double oboe, ram's horn (shofar), Assyrian harp. *From bottom left*: hand drum, metal trumpet, rattle, sistrum, loud cymbals, high-sounding cymbals.

Beating the breasts and cutting or pulling out the hair were two of the many techniques used by the mourner. Other known techniques were wearing sackcloth (a mourning garment of dark goat or camel hair, Jer. 6:26; Isa. 32:11), tearing one's garments (2 Sam. 1:11; 3:31), scattering dirt on the head or lying in the dust (Jer. 6:26; Ezek. 27:30), wailing and weeping (Ezek. 27:30–32), and lacerating the body (Jer. 16:6; 41:4). In the New Testament the flute is associated with mourning (Matt. 9:33). The classical prophets made use of the lament to symbolize the destruction of a nation, such as Tyre (Ezek. 27:2–9, 32–36), Egypt (Ezek. 32:2–8), and even Israel itself (Jer. 14:1–10).

PROSTITUTES

Prostitution had a long history in the ancient Near East. Prostitutes, who received rations from temple storehouses, were an integral part of the Sumerian ritual associated with the goddess Inanna. The cultic staff of the Assyrian goddess Ishtar also included female prostitutes. Canaanite religion, like Mesopotamian religion basically a fertility cult, had both male and female prostitutes attached to its sanctuaries. Prostitution—both sacred and secular—was a fact of life throughout the ancient Near East at least two millennia before the arrival of the Israelites into Canaan.

Sacred prostitution was not native to the religion of Israel, but was adopted at various points in time from Canaanite society. Because of this tendency toward syncretism, Deuteronomic Law (c. 7th century B.C.) expressly forbade both male and female prostitution—sacred and secular (Deut. 23:17–18). However, other biblical passages appear to withhold condemnation of the practice, if not condone it. The Canaanite prostitute Rahab, who assisted the Israelites in the capture of Jericho (Josh. 2:1 ff.), was not condemned, but was accepted into Israelite society (Josh. 6:22–25). The final sentence "and she dwelt in Israel to this day" suggests that the tradition is an etiological legend explaining the origins of prostitution in Israelite society (prostitution became a factor in Israelite life only after the settlement in Canaan). Moreover, the Levitical laws expressly forbade the association of the priests with prostitutes (Lev. 21:7, 9), but said nothing about it in relationship to the rest of Israelite society. On the whole, however, prostitution was forbidden as an idolatrous Canaanite practice.

Nevertheless, prostitution did exist and it fluctuated in and out of Israel's religious heritage during the period of the monarchy. Very conceivably there were sacred prostitutes connected with the sanctuary at Shiloh in the premonarchical period (1 Sam. 2:22; cf. Exod. 38:8). The book of Kings relates that Asa did away with male prostitution (1 Kings 15:12). Later, Josiah destroyed "the houses of the male cult prostitutes" (2 Kings 23:7), which had apparently been reintroduced earlier by Manasseh. This verse provides explicit information that a specific area of the Temple precinct had been assigned to prostitutes.

The most emphatic condemnation of prostitution came from the classical prophets, who associated harlotry with infidelity to God (Jer. 2:20; Ezek. 16:28; 23:5). Hosea represents the culmination of this condemnation, using his marriage to a prostitute (Hos. 1:2–9) as a figure for Israel's unfaithfulness (Hos. 4:1–19).

THE CIVIL LIFE

The term "civil life" refers to the structure of a society, the form of government under which the society is organized, and the interactions of its constituent elements. Social and political institutions and processes are of primary importance in defining the civil life of a society. The civil life of the Israelites, Jews, and early Christians includes both the sociopolitical institutions of biblical society and the interrelations of various peoples in light of these institutions. Factors which must be considered are the rights of individuals, the responsibilities of people to each other as a community or a nation, and the functions performed by government officials. In the following discussion attention will be focused on the structure of biblical society, the historical development of its civil institutions, and the officials who administered the Israelite monarchy.

THE STRUCTURE OF BIBLICAL SOCIETY

The early history of the Israelite people was defined by a nomadic or seminomadic way of life. The social organization of the nomadic society was centered in the family, was governed by family and tribal tradition, and was ruled by the patriarch. Each family, or its larger structural units the clan and tribe, formed a complete social element in itself. The family consisted of the patriarch, his wives, unmarried daughters, sons and their wives and children, and various slaves. The clan consisted of a collection of families related by blood; the tribe was composed of clans who traced their ancestry to a common source.

The basis of social cohesion, of law and order, of security and justice within the Israelite nomadic way of life was the institution of the family, clan, and tribe. Nomadic society was defined by common descent, rather than by common residence. Even when the Israelites settled in Canaan and eventually became a nation, they retained the essentially unstructured character of their earlier nomadic ways. As a result there existed throughout Israel's history a tension between the desert (the nomadic way of life) and the sown (the sedentary, agrarian way of life). Portions of Israel continued to remember her nomadic past nostalgically; this is particularly visible in the writings of the classical prophets during the period of the monarchy. Israelite society was basically simple, family oriented, and unstratified.

Settlement in the land of Canaan brought about a change in Israelite society. The center of social and political life shifted away from the family and the tribe and toward the village and small town. Territorially defined communities were substituted for ethnically defined ones. Municipal laws, rules, and regulations arose to replace or expand tribal laws and traditions. Life was demarked by common residence rather than by common descent, although recollection of the latter never completely died and lingered on to some extent through the period of the monarchy. Society became more complex; interrelations more varied; and Canaanite influences (city life, agriculture, etc.) were absorbed. From time to time a need was felt for some sort of central political or military authority (e.g., the "Judge"), an idea which prepared the way for the development of the monarchy in ancient Israel.

Further changes occurred with the centralization of power and authority in the hands of a king and the resulting monarchical form of government. Israelite society became still more complex, tending to become cosmopolitan and urban in structure, if not in actual fact. While most of the people still maintained close ties with the land, and many remembered their nomadic past, the economic and political life of the country was now determined by those who dwelt in the city. Foreign alliances were formed and foreign commodities, goods, and influences spread throughout Israel. A surplus of agricultural goods was produced, the standard of living rose, and a type of class-oriented society developed. The city-dwelling aristocracy (court personnel, military chiefs, wealthy merchants and successful craftsmen) stood in contrast with the majority of the people of Israel, the peasant agriculturists of the north and the shepherds and small farmers of the south.

In addition to the sharp contrast between city-dwellers and farmers, Israelite society throughout the nation became much more diversified after the monarchy was established. The range now included the king; elders; civic governors; king's officials and other men of rank and influence; the "people of the land," the whole body of citizens composed primarily of agriculturists, shepherds, and other simple folk; resident aliens, who were foreign in origin but lived more or less permanently in the midst of Israel; traveling foreigners, who were not protected by law but could count on customs of hospitality; wage earners, or free men who hired themselves for a certain period at a definite job; independent craftsmen and professionals, who were organized into guilds and who made their living from a particular skill; merchants, who directed trade and business, either in their own local communities or on an international scale; and slaves and household servants of various types and ethnic background. All of these elements made the structure of Israelite society during the period of the monarchy diverse and cosmopolitan.

After the destruction of Jerusalem by the Babylonians (587 B.C.), urban life collapsed in Palestine and the structure of Israelite society reverted for a short time back to the agricultural and seminomadic society of the period before the monarchy. However, following the Return and the eventual Hellenization of the entire ancient Near East, urban life was reestablished on a much grander scale. Greek and Roman society and political institutions were imposed upon the basically simple, family-oriented structure of Jewish society, and social institutions became even more intricate than during the period of the monarchy.

Tensions within Israelite Society

Several additional factors contributed to the character of biblical society. First of all, Israelite society was never wholly integrated. Each of the "twelve tribes" of Israel had its own history and traditions prior to the settlement in the land of Canaan. The differences among the tribes are clearly evident in the book of Judges. In fact, that book gives the reader the impression that the narrative was put together in a piecemeal fashion from a store of individual tribal traditions, each complete in itself. Thus, despite a common heritage and a common faith which fostered some sense of unity and interdependence, the Israelites never formed a single, homogeneous community. The condition was most apparent in the division into a northern kingdom (Israel) and a southern kingdom (Judah) after the death of Solomon (1 Kings 12:1–20).

Geographical dissimilarities and barriers within the land of Palestine also worked against complete social, economic, and political cohesion. Palestine is a composite land, easily divided into smaller units by various geographical features. The presence of unconquered Canaanite city-states at the important junctures between the geographical units deterred communication among the tribes of Israel. These geographical factors contributed greatly to the fluctuations in Israel's size and her sense of national unity throughout her long history.

Palestine's variations of climate also tended to support regional cultural separateness. For example, the amount of precipitation decreases from north to south and from west to east (see Fig. 3). Areas receiving the largest amounts of rainfall are the coastal strip and the northern highlands. In these areas agriculture was the primary occupation. To the south and east much of the area is poorly watered, and in certain places, such as the Judean desert and the Negev, the land is sterile and barren. There the ability to grow crops has always been difficult, if not impossible, and the economy in Bible times was always dominated by sheep raising.

Furthermore, the increasing heterogeneity of Israelite society, accompanied by various transformations in her way of life, her social organization and even her culture, tended to foster differences and disunity. This was particularly the case with Israel's urban population during the period of the monarchy. These transformations were slower in developing, and at times were either ignored or opposed by the rural population of Israel. Antagonism and cultural differences grew and intensified between the city dwellers and the rural population throughout Israel's history.

While oversimplified, the above sketch of biblical society provides a background for understanding the historical development of the civil institutions of ancient Israel and the administrative officials associated with the institutions.

THE CIVIL INSTITUTIONS OF BIBLICAL SOCIETY

Civil institutions underwent repeated changes throughout the biblical period, from the early beginnings of the people of Israel in the days of the Patriarchs (early second millennium B.C.), down through the formation of the Christian Church during the Roman period (1st century A.D.). The civil institutions of ancient Israel, therefore, must be approached from a historical perspective. Particular attention, however, must be given to the institutions and government officials for which the documentation is most complete and the institutions most fully developed—the period of the monarchy (c. 1020–587 B.C.).

For convenience, four historical periods may be distinguished (*see* Fig. 5). The first is the patriarchal period, from the time of Israel's beginnings (early second millennium B.C.) down to the time of the settlement in Canaan (late 13th century B.C.). The second is the period of the judges, from the time of the settlement down to the establishment of the Israelite monarchy under Saul (last quarter of the 11th century B.C.). The third is the period of kingship, including both the united monarchy under David and Solomon (c. 1000–922 B.C.) and the divided monarchy (concluding with the fall of Samaria in 721 B.C. for the Israelite kingdom, and with the fall of Jerusalem in 587 B.C. for the Judean kingdom). The fourth and final period is that of foreign rule, including Neo-Babylonian hegemony (c. 587–539 B.C.), Persian domination (c. 539–330 B.C.), Hellenistic civilization (c. 330–63 B.C.), and Early Roman rule (63 B.C.–A.D. 70).

Civil Institutions During the Patriarchal Period

Patriarchal society can best be described as seminomadic and pastoral. It was essentially a tribal society, based not on territorial principles (the period of the judges) or sociopolitical classes (the period of the monarchy), but rather on family units. Blood relationship was the determining factor, with genealogical principles the underlying framework for all social and legal regulations. These principles are evident in Abraham's instructions that Isaac be wed to a woman from his ancestral territory and a member of his own family (Gen. 24:2 ff.). The framework is also apparent in Jacob's request to be buried "with my fathers" (Gen. 47:29–31). The civil life of this tribal society was directed and controlled by the head of the family. Members were not subject to written rules or chosen officials, but rather to tribal traditions and the honest and just rule of the patriarch. On increasingly complex levels of organization, the decisions of the patriarch, the clan council, and the tribal council were binding. Law and order, security, justice, and matters of daily life were based on rules of common descent and family ties rather than on regulations and institutions deriving from common residence. Primary institutions included: that known as blood-vengeance, which provided personal security and preserved the integrity of the tribe; the custom of hospitality, which was an extension of the manner of tribal life; levirate ("brother-in-law") marriage, the essential purpose of which was to preserve and perpetuate the male-family line and prevent the alienation of family property (Deut. 25:5–10); and the rule of family solidarity, which established the obligation to aid and to protect one another (Lev. 25:25, 47–49; Jer. 32:6–7). These institutions helped to sustain the security of family ties, and were a direct expression of tribal organization (see section, THE LIFE OF THE NOMAD).

Civil Institutions During the Period of the Judges

Settlement in the land of Canaan brought about the gradual disintegration of the tribal regime. To be sure, the individual family unit was still bound to the institutions characteristic of patriarchal society, and these institutions continued to exert some influence throughout Israel's history. However, following the settlement in Canaan, a shift occurred away from the primary sociopolitical unit of the desert, the tribe, toward that of the sown, the town and village. Communities were defined primarily by territorial ties rather than by family ties. Tribes no longer functioned and moved as a unit, but scattered and dissolved into smaller elements which settled in homes and villages within the boundaries of a specified "tribal" territory (see the list of "inheritances" in Josh. 13: 1—19:51). Sons no longer remained within the household of their father, the patriarch, but established their own households when they married.

During the period of the judges, the tribal organization of the desert ceased to be self-sufficient and was replaced by the growth of craft specialization and a more complex division of labor. The typical Israelite lived in a village and farmed his few acres. The territory in which he lived consisted of a number of small agricultural and pastoral villages, centered about either an unfortified town or a fortified city (see Judg. 11:26). Towns and cities functioned as places of refuge, markets, administrative centers, and as places where specialties not found in the village could be obtained.

Moreover, Israel dwelt among Canaanite city-states during the period of the judges. The new settlers found themselves resistant to certain aspects of Canaanite culture, and drawn by others. The influence of Canaanite civilization undermined some traditional Israelite values and institutions, such as marriage to one's own kin (see Judg. 4:5–6).

In the village-oriented society which characterized the period, the tribal patriarch no longer held the position of authority that he exercised under the seminomadic regime. Basic traditions were kept alive within families, and freedom to act rested in the hands of individuals. There was no centralized authority: "In those days there was no king in Israel; every man did what was right in his own eyes" (Judg. 21:25). Communal decisions rested with the elders or heads of families (see "The Elders," below). However, the elders could not impose decisions against the popular will, at least in the early period. Each (male) member of the community was considered to have as much right to voice his opinion as another. The tribal chieftains of the desert were superseded by an assembly of adult freemen, headed by a council of elders.

The period of the judges was one of transition and adaptation in Israel's history, climaxing in a movement toward a centralized monarchy in the days of Samuel and Saul (last quarter of the 11th century B.C.). Israelite society during this period lacked any real political cohesion. There was no standing army, no royal tax, no monumental architecture, and no extensive international trade—factors which marked the Israelite monarchy. From what can be gathered from the biblical data, Israel in the days of the judges was a loosely organized federation of twelve tribes. The basis of the federation was a religious covenant periodically renewed at a central shrine. While the Greek term "amphictyony" (meaning "to live in the neighborhood" of a shrine) has been used to characterize this phenomenon in Israel's history, the actual nature and internal structure of the "Twelve Tribes of Israel" is still one of the primary subjects debated by biblical scholars. Whatever the precise nature of the league's organization, it appears to have stood as a symbol of religious unity, and represented the initial phase in the establishment of a national unity (see Josh. 24).

An Israelite Family in the Days of the Judges

The typical Israelite in the period of the judges lived with his wife and unmarried children in a small, poorly constructed house with few conveniences other than those necessary for a simple existence. The family may have belonged to the tribe of Issachar and lived on the border of its territory in the area of Jezreel, at the foot of Mount Gilboa (see Josh. 19:17–18) (Fig. 100), in the days of Gideon (Judg. 6:1—8:32). In fact, they may have witnessed Gideon's rout of the Midianites in the Jezreel Valley (Judg. 7:1–23).

Together with his wife and children, the Israelite would have worked all year round tilling his fields and providing the daily necessities of life for himself and his family. Little was left to sell or trade, and existence would have been eked out from day to day. The typical Israelite stood midway between the nomad of the desert and the city dweller, and would have had contact with both. He could look out over the Jezreel Valley and catch a glimpse of the caravans moving along the great east-west route from the Mediterranean coast to the Jordan Valley, and the route which carried traffic from southern Palestine to the Galilean highlands and beyond to the north. Marauding bands of nomads from the Syrian desert to the east occasionally appeared. In addition, his home was not far from the Canaanite cities of Megiddo and Beth-shan.

100. The Jezreel Valley near Mount Gilboa.

This householder lived during a period of change and international stability. The security and authority which he knew under the patriarchal system was no longer absolute and was being replaced by the decisions of the elders of his community. On the other hand, since there was no absolute authority, he was free—within the limitations of traditional and convenantal law—to decide his own destiny, so to speak.

For each household, as well as for the entire community, it was a time of adaptation and adjustment. Some had been associated previously with village life and had tilled the soil, but for many who came from the desert it was a time of transition to an agrarian manner of life. For these people the urge to return to the seminomadic past must have been particularly strong. Settling down in a permanent home and adjusting to the pattern of planting and harvesting crops on a yearly basis must have created anxieties.

The general poverty of the family and their lack of technical skill created further anxieties. Archaeological excavations suggest that Israelite towns of the 12th century B.C. were rather crude and devoid of many aspects of material culture. This stands in contrast to the well-constructed Canaanite cities which were contemporary with or preceded the Israelite communities.

The typical Israelite who lived during the period of the judges would have been concerned also with the precariousness of his position, as well as that of his neighbors. Raids by desert bedouin, attacks from neighboring states, and confrontation with Canaanite enclaves within Israel's midst constituted a continuous threat (Judg. 3:1–6). There was always the danger of invasion and oppression (Judg. 3:8, 12–14; 10:7–9; etc.). The typical Israelite household had to be ready to defend itself at any time (Judg. 4:10; 5:14–15; etc.).

Life was not altogether difficult during this formative period of Israel's existence. There was peace among the tribes of Israel, and internal disputes were adjudicated by the elders in accordance with traditional procedures. Yearly pilgrimages to the official shrine of the tribal league would have provided a festive occasion for all to enjoy. There were no taxes to pay; there was no absolute authority; and each household was permitted to maintain its own existence, to enjoy its own produce, and to benefit from close personal ties with its community.

The council of elders and the emergence of a unique type of leader, the charismatic "judge," were two institutions characteristic of the period of the judges. These subjects are discussed more fully below.

Elders in the Period of the Judges

One of the few institutions of Israel during the period of the judges was that of the elders. The elders of Israel were the heads of families within a town who formed a kind of borough council (see 1 Sam. 30:26–31). In the period of the judges, the leaders of communities are variously referred to as "elders," "officials," "chiefs," "princes," or "heads of the families" (e.g., Judg. 5:15; 8:14; 1 Sam. 2:8). Elders were, properly speaking, men with full beards —in other words, full-grown males of responsible conduct who were accorded high respect: "wise, understanding, and experienced men, according to your tribes" (Deut. 1:13; cf. Exod. 18:21–22). The number of elders for each town probably varied with the size of the community—the number at Succoth is given as 77 (Judg. 8:14; this number may represent the entire population of males in the assembly).

The elders were responsible for making decisions relevant to the welfare of the community (see Deut. 21:18–21). They provided arbitration in disputes, acted as judges in questions of a legal nature (Deut. 19:11–12), gave advice and wise council, and acted for the community in certain religious matters (Lev. 4:13–21, especially vs. 15). In effect, the elders took over the authority and responsibility of the seminomadic patriarchal father. They were local dignitaries who maintained and upheld the community, and formed its governing body.

Representatives from the elders of each community or tribal territory within "Israel" would meet periodically in a council, generally referred to in the Bible as "the whole congregation of Israel" (Josh. 22:16) or the "chiefs, the heads of the congregation" (Josh. 22:30). This council—which might represent only a part of Israel—would meet to decide such matters as rebellion or breach of (covenant) faith (Josh. 22:10–34) or the selection of a leader in time of war (Judg. 10:18).

Elders in the Period of the Monarchy

The office of elder continued in Israelite society into the period of the monarchy. It was the elders of Israel who made a covenant with David and anointed him king (2 Sam. 5:3; cf. 2 Sam. 2:4). Jezebel, the wife of Ahab (c. 869–850 B.C.), wrote in the king's name to the elders of Jezreel (1 Kings 21:8); Jehu (c. 842–815 B.C.) corresponded with the elders of Samaria in his efforts to eradicate the house of Ahab (2 Kings 10:1–11); and Josiah called "all the elders of Judah and Jerusalem" to hear the reading of the book of the covenant (2 Kings 23:1–2). The evidence suggests the elders formed a type of municipal council during the period of the monarchy and governed the local affairs of their respective cities. It is clear, moreover, that the elders were subject to the authority of the king and had no national influence as they apparently had during the period of the judges.

The elders of a city were responsible for the welfare of their community. Responsibility included the resolution of domestic quarrels and local disputes, the ratification of deeds and contracts, and jurisdiction over the courts. In performing their duties, the elders sat at the city gate, where all community affairs were discussed and resolved (Gen. 23:10, 18; Deut. 21:19; 22:15; Prov. 31:23) (Figs. 101, 102). Anyone passing the area of the city gate would be able to witness the transactions of this municipal council. The classical prophets referred to the local courts when they demanded "justice in the gate" (Amos 5:15; Zech. 8:16). An actual case held at the city gate is described in the book of Ruth (4:1–12). Job 29:7–25 provides another description of an urban public assembly and the manner in which its business was carried out. Archaeologists have uncovered numerous city gates dating from the monarchical period which have plastered benches along the walls of the

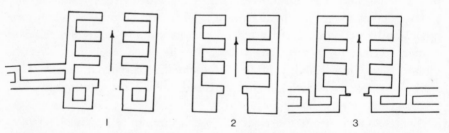

101. The design of the Solomonic Gates at (1) Hazor, (2) Megiddo, and (3) Gezer. The arrow points the entry to the inside of the city. All three gates were attached to a casement wall and had two towers, one on either side of the outside part of the structure. The three rooms on each side of arrows in the drawing had benches around the walls.

side rooms and open squares on the inner sides of the gates. It is such a setting that is depicted by Job as he recalls:

> When I went out to the gate of the city,
> when I prepared my seat in the square.
>
> (29:7)

The office of elder survived the dissolution of the monarchy (Ezek. 8:1; 14:1; 20:1).

Elders in the Period of the New Testament

During the New Testament period, a council of elders existed in each Jewish community. The most important of these councils was the Sanhedrin of Jerusalem, which traced its origin back to the council of seventy elders appointed by Moses (Num. 11:16–25). This council had both legislative and judiciary responsibilities, although its roles varied according to the type of political authority under which it functioned. Under Roman rule the Sanhedrin held general administrative authority over the Jews and represented the community in their relations with Rome. Their primary duty was judicial, interpreting religious law and handing out punishment to offenders (see Matt. 15:2; Mark 7:1–5).

102. The remains of the Solomonic gate at Gezer, looking from inside the city towards the outside.

The office of elder in the early Christian Church appears to stem from its similar institution in Judaism. Elders in the New Testament are associated with apostles and apparently functioned in an administrative role in the Christian community at Jerusalem (Acts 11:30; 15:2, 4, 6, 22–23; 16:4; 21:18). Paul and Barnabas appointed elders in churches which they established in Asia Minor (Acts 14:23). Paul met with the elders of the church at Ephesus on his final trip to Jerusalem (Acts 20:17). Elsewhere the elders appear as leaders of local churches with pastoral responsibilities (Jas. 5:14; 1 Pet. 5:1–5).

The Judge

The traditional view of the book of Judges regards this work as an account of two different classes of personalities—the so-called "major" and "minor" judges—who "judged" Israel during the unsettled "dark ages" between the death of Joshua (c. 1200 B.C.; Josh. 24:29–30) and the establishment of the Israelite monarchy under Saul (c. 1020 B.C.; 1 Sam. 10:1–26). According to this classification, the "major" judges (Othniel, Ehud, Deborah, Gideon, Jephthah, and Samson) were charismatic leaders chosen by God to deliver or "save" Israel from affliction and foreign domination (Judg. 3: 9–10, etc.). These persons were the "ideal" chiefs, divinely appointed in times of crises for immediate spontaneous leadership. If the picture portrayed in Judges is to be accepted, there was no tribal council, no organized government, no political cohesion—only charismatic military chieftains.

On the other hand, according to this dual classification system, the "minor" judges (Tola, Jair, Ibzan, Elon, and Abdon—some would also include Shamgar) were noncharismatic tribal leaders with a permanent office who served as legal experts or jurists. These individuals are considered to represent the only distinct occurrences of the office of judge in Israel prior to the monarchy, acting within the confederation to settle disputes and dispense the law.

Recent scholarship has indicated, however, that the distinction between the two classes of judges is artificial and greatly oversimplified. In the first place, the Hebrew term which is translated "judge" clearly has a much wider range of meaning. In the second place, since their role in Israelite society apparently was similar, there is no reason to differentiate between the "major" and "minor" judges.

Without becoming involved in detailed linguistic and lexical analysis, it is sufficient to point out that the labels "judge" and "charismatic judge" are too rigid. The Hebrew term (shōfēt), generally translated "judge," is broader than that and basically refers to a person who has authority to make administrative decisions. One of the aspects of this authority was to act as arbiter and administer judgment. If we accept this more exact definition, a judge was one who carried out various acts of government, that is, a "leader." The term does not imply a permanent, dynastic ruler such as a king, but indicates a more casual, unstructured authority. A judge was neither a unique charismatic "savior" nor an institutionalized magistrate, but rather an administrator and leader of a loosely organized federation.

From this new perspective it is evident that there is little technical difference between the "major" and "minor" judges. Both groups of judges governed Israel, or portions thereof. The only distinction is the manner in which the two are portrayed in the Bible. The activities of the five "minor" judges are summarized briefly (Judg. 10:1–5; 12:8–15) while those of the "major" judges are described in more detail (e.g., Jephthah, Judg. 10:6–12:7). Perhaps the lack of information about the "minor" judges reflects interludes of relative peace and successful administration.

To sum up: a judge (to retain the traditional title) was a person who was brought up within "Israel" to act as general leader, administrator, and arbiter. He functioned with limited authority over a loosely organized federation which was struggling to achieve some sort of national unity in the period preceding the establishment of the monarchy. A judge did not necessarily administer before "all Israel," for in most cases his authority was limited to a few tribes (or even to a single tribe). In fact, it is considered probable that some of the judges were contemporaries.

It appears that a judge was chosen and appointed by the elders. This is explicitly stated in the case of Jephthah (Judg. 10:18; 11:5–11). It may be implied in the theological prologue to the activities of others: "But when the people of Israel cried to the Lord, the Lord raised up for them a deliverer . . ." (Judg. 3:9, 15; etc.). Once he had defeated the enemy, the judge could act as military leader (e.g., Judg. 3:9–10), arbiter (e.g., Judg. 4:4–5), and administrator (e.g., Judg. 8:1–3). Clearly, he was not a king, as is evident in Gideon's refusal of this office (Judg. 8:22–23), but the temporary leader of a tribe or a federation of tribes. The last person to possess this authority was Samuel, who "judged" a nearly united Israel as priest, prophet, military commander, and general administrator (1 Sam. 7:5–11, 15–17; 8:1–22; 10:25; etc.).

Under the monarchy the office of "judge" designated a professional jurist (see 2 Sam. 15:2–6). Those who held this office were appointed by the king (the supreme judge) to provide legal arbitration in each city (see 2 Chron. 19:5–7).

Civil Institutions under the Monarchy

The institutional character of Israelite society underwent considerable change with the establishment of the monarchy (c. 1020 B.C.). The coronation of Saul as king (1 Sam. 10:1, 17–24) created a national state with a well-organized political structure. Tribal and clan traditions persisted, and were not entirely absorbed by the monarchical organization superimposed on them. Nevertheless, monarchical rule weakened tribal and local self-government, resulted in a society made up of divergent social and political classes, and centered authority in the hands of a single person.

The process by which authority was centralized in the person of a king was accelerated by the Philistine threat to Israel's existence. Israel during the period of the judges was a loosely organized federation of tribes which lacked any real political cohesion or national unity. In contrast, the Philistines were organized, had a well-trained professional army, and enjoyed a military superiority in weapons as a result of their monopoly of bronze and iron metallurgy (1 Sam. 13:19–22; 17:4–7). The Israelites lived primarily along the central mountain range. The Philistines controlled the coastal plain, the Shephelah, the Negev, and most of the Jezreel Valley. The concerted effort by the Philistines in the latter half of the 11th century B.C. to establish permanent control over land held by the Israelites led to a decisive struggle for the control of the Shephelah and to the institution of the monarchy in Israel. The Philistine victory near Aphek (1 Sam. 4:1–11) was a major blow to the Israelites. This defeat, coupled with the loss of the Ark of the Covenant (1 Sam 4:11) and the presence of Philistine garrisons in the central hills (1 Sam. 10:5; 13:3–4), brought about Israel's demand for a king: "that we also may be like all the nations, and that our king may govern us and go out before us and fight our battles" (1 Sam. 8:4–5, 19–20).

With the reluctant assent of Samuel, the last of the "judges," the Israelites elected their first king, Saul (1 Sam. 8:4—11:15). Saul, who is depicted according to tradition as a charismatic judge in the account of his victory over the Ammonites (1 Sam. 11:1–11), represents the transition to a primitive but organized national state. Under Saul, however, the monarchy was barely established. Continued wars with the Philistines, which eventually led to Saul's death (1 Sam. 31:1–13), limited the king's efforts solely to military matters. Apparently only a single government official was appointed, and that was Abner, the commander of the army (1 Sam. 14:50). While the beginnings of a standing army may be attributed to Saul (1 Sam. 14:52), there was no real change made in the internal structure of Israel and an administrative organization still was lacking.

The Israelite nation took more concrete shape under David. David was first anointed king over Judah (2 Sam. 2:1–4), and then acclaimed king over all Israel (2 Sam. 5:1–3). Under his leadership the Philistine threat was ended (2 Sam. 5:17–25; 1 Chron. 14:8–17) and the ground prepared for the development of the institutions of centralized government. A royal capital, the king's own city, was established at Jerusalem (2 Sam. 5:6–9; 1 Chron. 11:4–8). The transfer of the Ark to the city (2 Sam. 6:1–19; 1 Chron. 15:1—16:43) and the creation of a national priesthood made Jerusalem the religious as well as the political center of the nation. David also appointed a royal cabinet (2 Sam. 8:15–18; 20:23–26), providing Israel with a central administration. The first census was undertaken (2 Sam. 24:1–9), and a regular army, composed of Israelites who were professional career men and foreign mercenaries, was established (see section, THE MILITARY LIFE).

Israel as a nation attained her greatest complexity under Solomon (c. 961–922 B.C.). Solomon solidified the position and economy of the nation by establishing a commercial alliance with Tyre (1 Kings 5:1–12), and by entering into marriage alliances with other nations (1 Kings 11:1), the most notable of which was with Egypt (1 Kings 3:1; 7:8; 9:16, 24). Solomon exploited the commercial position Israel held along major trade routes and increased her trade (see 1 Kings 9:26–28; 10:1–29). He also strengthened the royal administration created by David (1 Kings 4:1–6) and reorganized the land into 12 administrative districts (1 Kings 4:7–19). Both taxation (1 Kings 4:20–28) and forced labor (1 Kings 5:13–18) were introduced into the state. Although the nation split in two following the death of Solomon (c. 922 B.C.), and was never again reunited, the monarchical system of government remained in existence throughout the history of Israel (c. 922–721 B.C.) and Judah (c. 922–587 B.C.) (see Fig. 5).

The political, economic, and social institutions created by the monarchy introduced new sociological factors into Israelite society. On the positive side, the monarchical form of government was conducive to stability and efficiency. Kingship created a permanent, well-organized administration and a stable economic and social environment. A king ruled the nation with absolute authority throughout his lifetime, and barring a change in dynasty, was succeeded by a logical representative of the same line. The king was assisted by a cabinet made up of professional administrative, judicial, and military officials. Stability, relative peace, and prosperity followed, and with them a national consciousness.

On the negative side, the people of Israel had to relinquish certain freedoms and accept new obligations. The greater part of the burden of maintaining the nation fell upon her citizens. Moreover, this burden was imposed on the people by a central authority, the king. As a result, the people of Israel had to surrender control over their individual destinies. They had to pay taxes to the state (the king), were liable for military service, and were at times pressed into forced labor (designated the *corvée* by scholars). The government bureaucracy was open to corruption and the weaknesses of pride, money, and power. These shortcomings were all too apparent at times, and were frequently the object of prophetic judgment (e.g., Jer. 22:13-17; Amos 6:1-8, etc.). Finally, growing internationalism made Israel vulnerable to the lifestyles and influences of her neighbors, and tore at the roots of her semi-nomadic past.

Samuel's statement concerning "the ways of the king" is an excellent description of the burdens imposed upon Israel in order to establish and maintain the monarchy (1 Sam. 8:11-17):

> These will be the ways of the king who will reign over you: He will take your sons and appoint them to his chariots and to be his horsemen, and to run before his chariots; and he will appoint for himself commanders of thousands and commanders of fifties, and some to plow his ground and to reap his harvest, and to make his implements of war and the equipment of his chariots. He will take your daughters to be perfumers and cooks and bakers. He will take the best of your fields and vineyards and olive orchards and give them to his servants. He will take the tenth of your grain and of your vineyards and give it to his officers and to his servants. He will take your menservants and maidservants, and the best of your cattle and your asses, and put them to his work. He will take the tenth of your flocks, and you shall be his slaves.

Institutions which characterized the Israelite monarchy were a regular army, royal taxes, and a professional administration. In addition, the establishment of the Israelite monarchy created a division of power and wealth in the nation which resulted in a type of class-oriented society (see Amos 5:11). There were kings, aristocrats, common people, and slaves. There were administrators, judges, royal officials, and heads of influential families. There were also small land owners, farmers, craftsmen, and laborers. The French archaeologist and biblical scholar, Father Roland de Vaux, was able to trace the growth of an upper social class in Israelite society by means of the differences in house construction at Tell el-Far'ah, the site of biblical Tirzah (see 1 Kings 14:17).

The Reaction of the Israelite People to the Monarchy

How did the various strands of public and professional life affect the average Israelite during the period of the monarchy? This is difficult to establish with certainty, since the normal life of the people of Israel, their everyday existence, and their innermost thoughts are not spelled out in the Bible, nor are they capable of reconstruction on the basis of archaeological evidence. However, for the moment, let us create a hypothetical Israelite farmer, Shaphan, residing in the northern part of Palestine in the period immediately following the death of King Solomon (c. 922 B.C.).

103. The Plain of Jezreel or Esdraelon.

Shaphan lived in the Plain of Esdraelon, not too far from the royal store city of Megiddo (Fig. 103). Megiddo was a magnificent city. It stood on a spur of the Carmel mountain range which projected into the Plain of Esdrae-lon from the southwest (Fig. 104). A person walking the ramparts of the city could view the entire width of the plain (Fig. 105). Whenever Shaphan looked up from his work in the fields at the strongly fortified city, he felt a sense of security. The city was surrounded by a strong, well-built fortifi-cation wall (Fig. 106). Entrance was gained by means of an impressive six-piered gateway with guardrooms on either side. An outer gate, along the approachway running up the steep side of the mound from the northeast, added further protection (Fig. 107).

The masonry of the city walls and gateway was dressed flat with a beautiful finish. It provided a plainly visible example of the richness of Solomon's kingdom, and of the craftsmanship of the Phoenician masons employed by the king (1 Kings 9:15; 2 Chron. 2:13–14). On the southern side of the city, opposite the main gate, stood a magnificent porticoed build-ing of two stories, surrounded by an enclosed courtyard. This was the resi-dence of both the governor of Megiddo and one of Solomon's district tax officials. The building, and others of similar construction, stood in sharp contrast to the rest of Megiddo, which consisted of small, undistinguished houses built of relatively poor rubble masonry. Shaphan's own home was of the latter type. He had built it himself, with the help of his oldest son, and although he was proud of the accomplishment, it could not compare with the fine mansions of hewn stone of the government officials of Megiddo.

104. Megiddo, seen from the plain to its northeast.

105. The plain to the north and east of Megiddo, seen from the top of the ruins of the ancient city itself.

There was a marked contrast in the furnishings of the homes as well. Shaphan's home was furnished with rough carpets which his wife and daughters had woven from wool purchased from the sheepherders of the hills. The furniture and utensils were simple, everyday articles either made by Shaphan's family or purchased for a reasonable price in the open market just inside the city gate of Megiddo (*see* Figs. 16–18, 22, 63, 64). The patricians of Megiddo, however, had fine beds inlaid with carved ivory (see Amos 3:15; 6:4), magnificent draperies of dark purple Tyrian cloth, and table vessels and utensils of bronze, silver, and gold. The contrast was remarkable.

For the moment, Shaphan was resting in front of his house, gazing up

106. A model of the reconstructed ancient city of Megiddo (in a museum located at the site).

107. Reconstruction of the ancient gate at Megiddo.

at Megiddo in the distance. His farm was cultivated for grain crops, and he and his sons had just finished threshing the wheat harvest (sometime in May). The bulk of the grain would be sold in the market at Megiddo. Shaphan had already stored what he and his family would need in the stone-lined bins sunk into the clay floor of his courtyard. Another portion was set aside for delivery to Baana, the chief officer and tax collector for the province in which Shaphan lived (see 1 Kings 4:7, 12).

The payment of this tax gave Shaphan reason to reflect on the structure of the society to which he belonged. On the one hand, the monarchy provided him and his family considerable security. There were no raids or wars as recalled in songs which his father had told him were written either during the Philistine wars of Saul and David or in the days when there was no king in Israel. Shaphan's family was safe on their farm, and they were free to live as they pleased—or at least live as they could afford to. Moreover, local authority still resided in the hands of the elders (see "The Elders" above) and the public assembly of which Shaphan, as an adult freeman, was a member. The public assembly met only occasionally, but the elders of the city met almost daily. They sat on long stone benches along the wall inside the city gate, attending to the business of the city, settling local disputes, or merely discussing the affairs of the day (see Ruth 4:1–12). The elders of Megiddo were honest and wise, and could be trusted to provide fair decisions, although other cities were not so fortunate (see Amos 5:12).

Nevertheless, despite the relative security around Megiddo, there was cause for concern. The tax imposed by the king was a hard burden to bear. Shaphan's small farm barely provided enough for his own needs. Yet he was obliged to present the best part of his crops to the officer of the province in order to support the royal administration (see 1 Kings 4:7; 22–23, 27–28).

It also was difficult for Shaphan to accept the fact that by the end of the next month he would be on the slopes of Mount Lebanon, helping to transport cedar logs from Phoenicia to Jerusalem for a new extension of the king's palace (see 1 Kings 5:13–14). Taxes were a burden that could be accepted, but forced labor was impossible to reconcile with one's own conscience. It seemed that the burden might be eased, however, for the representatives of all Israel were currently meeting with King Rehoboam to plead for a lessening of this service (see 1 Kings 12:1 ff.). Whatever the outcome, Shaphan was convinced that the monarchy had brought about definite changes within Israelite society.

THE ADMINISTRATIVE ORGANIZATION OF THE ISRAELITE MONARCHY

The administrative organization of the Israelite monarchy is known primarily from the period of the united monarchy under David (c. 1000–961

B.C.) and Solomon (c. 961–922 B.C.). Evidence from the period of the divided monarchy is less explicit, and pertains primarily to the governmental structure of the Southern (Judean) Kingdom (c. 922–587 B.C.). What textual evidence there is suggests that the civil, military, and cultic administration which evolved under the leadership of David and Solomon was retained in its basic structure throughout the monarchial period in both Israel and Judah. This information is supplemented to a degree by archaeological data.

The members of the king's cabinet are enumerated in three passages in the Old Testament. Two of the lists date from the time of David (2 Sam. 8:15–18, with its parallel in 1 Chron. 18:14–17; and 2 Sam. 20:23–26) and the third from the reign of Solomon (1 Kings 4:1–6). Noting that certain additions were made in each succeeding list, the members of the "royal cabinet" can be listed as follows: King; Minister of the Palace; Royal Secretary; Royal Herald; Commander of the Army (see section, THE MILITARY LIFE); Superintendent of the District Prefects; Superintendent of the Forced Levy; and Chief Priest (see section, THE PROFESSIONAL LIFE).

The King

Whether he ruled over a united monarchy or the individual kingdoms of Israel or Judah, the king was the most celebrated person in the nation. He was wealthy, owned considerable property, had a virtual monopoly of the international trade, regulated the economy of his kingdom, directed all military operations, and ruled the land with absolute authority in all matters of state and religion. The authority of the king was recognized as permanent and absolute. Under his control was a complex administrative organization set up to provide an efficient means of managing the kingdom and preserving its integrity and strength. All power was consolidated in the king, and he appointed officials at both the cabinet (1 Kings 4:1–6) and district levels (1 Kings 4:7–19). The king was also the supreme judge of the land, and represented the final court of appeals in judicial matters (2 Sam. 8:15; 1 Kings 3:16–28; 1 Kings 7:7).

The king was the legitimate owner of a vast royal estate. This included not only his royal capital, but also vineyards, olive groves, various livestock, and other types of property (1 Chron. 27:25–31). The estate was frequently expanded through conquest and annexation (2 Sam. 10:15–19, 12:26–31), gifts (1 Kings 9:16), or direct confiscation (1 Kings 21:1–16).

As for his monopoly of the nation's international trade, Solomon derived great wealth from his trading ventures to Ophir and possibly Tarshish with Hiram of Tyre (1 Kings 9:26–28, 10:22; 2 Chron. 9:21). He probably concluded a trade agreement with the Queen of Sheba as well (1 Kings 10:1–15). He also traded in Egyptian chariots and Cilician horses with the kings of

Syria (1 Kings 10:26–29). Jehoshaphat attempted to restore the sea-borne trade to Ophir at a later date, but was unsuccessful (1 Kings 22:48; 2 Chron. 20:35–37). Ahab, one of the early kings of the Israelite kingdom, established a trade agreement with Ben-hadad, the king of Syria (1 Kings 20:34).

Major building programs were also undertaken by the king. Solomon's achievements are well documented and consist of the Temple (*see* Fig. 76) and royal palace at Jerusalem (1 Kings 5:1—7:12), and numerous fortifications, storehouses, and chariot cities (1 Kings 9:15–19). Archaeological excavations have uncovered the remains of some of Solomon's building enterprises. Well-built fortification walls and six-pier gateways discovered in 10th century levels at Hazor, Megiddo, and Gezer (*see* Fig. 102) attest to the widespread and well-designed constructional activities directed by Solomon. Other kings also engaged in building projects, but on a lesser scale. Archaeologists have uncovered the remains of the royal citadel constructed at Samaria by Omri and his son Ahab (1 Kings 16:24, 28–33). This citadel consisted of several buildings situated in open courtyards, the whole complex surrounded by a massive enclosure wall. The walls of the buildings were constructed in an excellent masonry style in which the stones were beautifully finished and accurately fitted (Fig. 108). A deposit of ivories was discovered in debris in one sector of the royal quarter, some of which probably date from the reign of Ahab, and others to the reigns of succeeding kings down to the time of the fall of Samaria in 721 B.C. (Fig. 109). The great variety of themes depicted on the ivories attest to the wealth of the Israelite kingdom and helps to illustrate Ahab's "ivory house" (1 Kings 22:39).

The king was also the supreme military leader of the nation. Although he appointed a field commander to handle most military matters, the king was still capable of leading his army and made all top-level decisions. David directed the efforts against the Syrians and the Ammonites (2 Sam. 10:6–14) and took part in the final victory (2 Sam. 10:15–19). Ahab of Israel led his forces in battle against the Syrians (1 Kings 20:16–21, 26:34, 22:29–35), and other kings of Israel and Judah directed their war efforts as well.

The king's various endeavors and the maintenance of his kingdom required a considerable sum of money. Fortunately, there were several sources from which the king could draw. First of all, he had available the resources of his royal estate. Income could also be derived from his various commercial ventures and the taxes imposed upon imports and transit goods (1 Kings 10:14–15). There was also the tribute imposed on defeated armies and vassal states by David (2 Sam. 8:2–12), Solomon (1 Kings 4:21), and apparently Uzziah (2 Chron. 26:8). In addition to these sources, the king imposed an annual tax on the people of the land (1 Sam. 8:14–17; 1 Kings 4:7, 22–28).

The king appointed not only the administrative and military chiefs of the

108. Ninth century B.C. Israelite wall at Samaria. Note the "headers" (the stones with only their heads showing toward the outside) and the "stretchers" (the stones with their sides showing toward the outside).

nation, but also the chief priest (2 Sam. 8:17; 20:25; 1 Kings 4:2). He could dismiss the chief priest from office as well (1 Kings 2:26–27). This authority over religious matters was derived from the fact that the king was the anointed one, the "Messiah," blessed with the "Spirit of the Lord" (see 1 Sam. 16:13; Ps. 45:6-7; 89:19-21). The nation's welfare and prosperity in both secular and sacred matters were dependent on the king—he was himself, in fact, a sacred person. He was invested with the responsibility of maintaining Israel's religious heritage and empowered with the right to perform religious acts. The king could offer sacrifices, and did so on various occasions such as at the dedication of the Temple (1 Kings 8:62–64), the dedication of a new altar (2 Kings 16:10–16), or at major religious festivals (1 Kings 9:25). King David conceived the plan to build the Temple in Jerusalem (2 Sam. 7:1–3) and erected the initial altar there (2 Sam. 24:25). The Temple was built by David's son and successor, Solomon (1 Kings 5:1—6:38). Jeroboam I of the Northern Kingdom later founded the sanctuaries in Bethel and Dan to rival the Jerusalem Temple (1 Kings 12:26–33). The king also had control of the Temple treasuries (2 Kings 12:4-15, 18; 16:8; 18:15–16; 22:3–7), and the Temple service itself, as evident in the reforms initiated by Josiah (2 Kings 23:1–25). He was the religious as well as the political head of the kingdom.

109. Designs taken from the ivories found at Samaria which date from the Ninth and Eighth centuries B.C.

The king lived in his royal palace together with his many wives, children, and personal servants. His *harem* was considered a luxury and a privilege. It was a mark of wealth and power. Solomon is supposed to have had "seven hundred wives, princesses, and three hundred concubines" (1 Kings 11:3). There was no official "Queen," although one woman generally held the king's preference (see 2 Chron. 11:21). The mother of the king commanded deep respect—in effect she was the "Queen-Mother" and the symbol of the continuation of the dynasty—and had considerable influence in the royal court (1 Kings 2:19; 2 Kings 11:1-3).

The king and his *harem* produced a number of children. The male children were remanded initially into the care of a nurse (2 Kings 11:2) and when of age, entrusted to respected elders for instruction (2 Kings 10:1, 6; 1 Chron. 27:32). When grown, all but the prince selected by the king to succeed him were given money and land by their father and left to lead independent lives (2 Chron. 11:23; 21:3). Some performed duties within the court (1 Chron. 18:17).

The king and his family were surrounded by a multitude of minor officials and personal attendants. Included among the servants were soldiers, eunuchs, cupbearers, bakers, and a host of other household functionaries, including male and female singers (2 Sam. 19:35). The Queen of Sheba was amazed at the retinue which attended King Solomon (1 Kings 10:4-5):

> And when the queen of Sheba had seen all the wisdom of Solomon, the house that he had built, the food of his table, the seating of his officials, and the attendance of his servants, their clothing, his cupbearers, and his burnt offerings at the house of the Lord, there was no more spirit in her.

In addition to the household servants, the king had an "armor-bearer" who was his squire and military aide, a position held by David under Saul (1 Sam. 16:21). With the advent of the use of the chariot in Israel during the reign of David, the king's aide rode as his "shield-bearer" (2 Kings 9:25). Western Asiatic chariots were drawn by two horses and manned by a crew of two: a driver and the fighting man. The king's chariot, however, carried three: the king, his driver, and his aide, who carried a shield for the king's protection. This arrangement is depicted on numerous reliefs from Assyria and other parts of the ancient Near East. One such relief depicts the Assyrian king, Sargon II (c. 722-706 B.C.), standing in his chariot with bow fully drawn, his driver beside him, reins in hand, and his "shield-bearer" to the rear, poised to offer protection. Such is the picture presented when Jehu slays Joram and usurps the throne of Israel (2 Kings 9:21-25).

Besides his military aide, the king also had a contingent of carefully chosen bodyguards for his personal protection (2 Sam. 23:8-39; 2 Kings 11:4-12). This select group of military warriors stood guard at the entrance to the king's palace, bearing shields of gold or bronze (1 Kings 14:25-28). There was also a contingent of "runners" who served as a police force to clear a path before the king as he rode his chariot through the narrow, winding streets of a city (2 Sam. 15:1; 1 Kings 1:5).

The most significant event in the king's rule was his enthronement. This gave him the authority of the throne, granted him title to the royal properties, and established him as God's elected choice. In the Judean kingdom the act of enthronement was a renewal of the Davidic covenant and the sole right to the throne (see 1 Chron. 28:4-8). The official enthronement ceremonies included five distinct acts, the initial three of which took place in the Temple and the latter two in the throne room of the palace. Two coronation accounts are preserved in the book of Kings, that of Solomon (1

Kings 1:32–48) and that of Jehoash (2 Kings 11:12–20). The king was first invested with the emblems of royalty, which included the royal crown (2 Kings 11:12; cf. 2 Sam. 1:10) and "the testimony," which may have been the giving of a royal (throne) name as was the case in ancient Egypt. The king was next anointed by the priest, which established him as God's anointed choice (1 Kings 1:39; 2 Kings 11:12). The third ceremonial act of enthronement was the proclamation of the anointed as king, and his acclamation by the people (1 Kings 1:39; 2 Kings 9:13; 2 Kings 11:12). The proclamation "Long live the king," generally accompanied by the clapping of hands or the blowing of trumpets, was a recognition and acceptance of the king's authority by his subjects. Following this, the entourage moved amidst shouting, singing, and the playing of music from the Temple to the palace, where the king was seated on the throne (the symbol of royal power), marking his assumption of power and rule (1 Kings 1:46; 2 Kings 11:19).

Throughout the ancient Near East the statement "to sit on the throne" (1 Kings 16:11; 2 Kings 13:13) meant the same as "to begin to reign" (1 Kings 16:8, 23 etc.). The king then received all the high officials of the state, who would pay him homage, each in his turn (1 Kings 1:47). This final act may be represented on a number of reliefs, carved seals, and other ancient works of art which depict a king seated on his throne receiving a long line of various servants and dignitaries. The enthronement festival marked the beginning of the king's reign, and established him with absolute power throughout his lifetime. In due course, he had the responsibility to appoint one of his sons to be enthroned after him as the next monarch (1 Kings 1:30; 2 Chron. 21:3).

The Minister of the Palace

Many authorities believe that the Minister of the Palace or Royal Steward (literally "he who is over the house") occupied a high office similar to that of the Vizier in ancient Egypt. The Vizier was second in authority only to the Pharaoh and administered the kingdom in his name (see the Joseph story, Gen. 41:39–57). Others, however, argue that the Minister of the Palace was merely the overseer of the king's estate, an office similar to the "Chief Steward" in Egypt. The office of the Minister of the Palace is first mentioned in the reign of Solomon (1 Kings 4:6), and is known from both Israel (1 Kings 16:9; 2 Kings 10:5) and Judah (2 Kings 18:18).

In several cases the Minister of the Palace appears to have been endowed with considerable authority. Jotham, the son and heir apparent to King Uzziah of Judah, was Minister of the Palace under Uzziah and was "governing the people of the land" in his place after the latter became incapacitated by leprosy (2 Kings 15:5). A most important passage is Isaiah's account of the dismissal of Shebna from the office of Minister of the Palace (Isa. 22:15–25). Shebna held the office early in Hezekiah's reign and was demoted and replaced by Eliakim, an event which can be seen as taking place before the time of the Assyrian siege of Jerusalem (701 B.C.), since by then Eliakim was Minister of the Palace and Shebna was Royal Secretary (Isa. 36:3). Eliakim is depicted as leading a three-man delegation before the representatives of Sennacherib to discuss the terms of surrender (2 Kings 18:18 ff.). It is clear that the Minister of the Palace held the highest rank of any of the king's officials. His office was symbolized by a distinctive robe and girdle (Isa. 22:21), and he was given a specific jurisdiction (Isa. 22:22): "And I will place on his shoulder the key of the house of David; he shall open, and none shall shut; and he shall shut, and none shall open." This responsibility relates to a special function of the Egyptian Vizier, who would open the gates of the Pharaoh's house, thus marking the beginning of the official court day. An identical function is implied for the Minister of the Palace in Jerusalem.

The removal of Shebna from the office of Minister of the Palace was apparently caused when he presumed the authority to carve a tomb for himself "on the height," perhaps an area reserved for the interment of kings (Isa. 22:16). In 1870 the French archaeologist Charles Clermont-Ganneau discovered two inscriptions chiseled into the façade of a rock-cut tomb in the necropolis of Silwan (Siloam), situated on the steep east slope of the Kidron Valley opposite the site of biblical Jerusalem. One of the inscriptions begins with the words: "This is [the sepulcher of . . .] yahu who is over the house." It has been suggested that the damaged name is to be restored as "Shebna," and that the tomb is to be identified with the one cut by the minister of the Palace referred to above (Isa. 22:16). While his suggestion must remain hypothetical, it is clear that at least one Minister of the Palace of the kingdom of Judah built a monumental tomb on the steep rock face of the Kidron valley opposite Jerusalem, and this in itself attests to the importance of the official.

Of additional interest is a seal impression discovered in unstratified debris at the site of ancient Lachish. The seal impression was apparently affixed to a papyrus document in antiquity, and bears the name and title of one "Gedaliah, Minister of the Palace." It has been shown that the person referred to in the inscription is probably none other than the Gedaliah who was appointed governor over the people of Judah by Nebuchadnezzar, king of Babylon, following the destruction of Jerusalem in 587 B.C. (2 Kings 25:22–26; Jer. 39:11–41:18). If so, then the seal indicates that Gedaliah was perhaps the last Minister of the Palace of the Judean kingdom. The seal would be an illustration of his importance.

The Royal Secretary

David's royal cabinet included a secretary, Seraiah (2 Sam. 8:17; "Sheva," perhaps a title, in 2 Sam. 20:25), whose two sons held the office under Solomon (1 Kings 4:3). This official was the Royal Secretary, and one of the top officials of the king's cabinet, ranking only below the Minister of the Palace (cf. Isa. 22:15, 20–22 with Isa. 36:3). The Royal Secretary functioned primarily as the king's private secretary and was responsible for all royal correspondence, both foreign and domestic. In addition, he was the head of the royal archives and charged with the keeping of the royal annals.

The annals and all royal correspondence would be stored in the archives, which was the office of the Royal Secretary and a room or building within the king's palace. This section of the royal palace in Jerusalem is referred to as "the secretary's chamber" in Jer. 36:12. It was in this office that the scroll written by Baruch the scribe under Jeremiah's dictation was deposited and stored prior to its destruction by King Jehoiakim (Jer. 36:20–23). State annals, diplomatic correspondence, and other documents were stored in archives throughout the ancient Near East as early as the 3rd millennium B.C. A number of these archives have come to light through archaeological excavation. One of the archive rooms of the Northwest Palace at Nimrud (8th century B.C.). was equipped with burnt-brick writing benches and two rows of storage boxes which served as "file cabinets" for various documents.

Part of the foreign correspondence of the Egyptian Pharaohs Amenophis III and IV (14th century B.C.) was discovered at el-Amarna in Egypt, together with the record office and the living quarters of the scribes. The record office at el-Amarna was known as "the letter-place of the Pharaoh" and its chief scribe designated as "the royal letter-writer," a not altogether inappropriate title for the Royal Secretary of the Israelite kings. It is reasonable to assume that "the secretary's chamber" in Jerusalem was similar to other archive rooms in the ancient Near East, although perhaps on a smaller scale.

The annals which would have been kept in the Scribal House in Jerusalem were most likely written on papyrus so that any chance of their ever being recovered is slim. That these annals did exist, however, is indicated by the numerous references to such in the Bible. The earliest, the "Book of the Acts of Solomon" (1 Kings 11:41), is thought to have been compiled by one of Solomon's counselors following his death. The other two, the "Book of the Chronicles of the Kings of Judah" and the "Book of the Chronicles of the Kings of Israel," are more clearly court documents. References to these sources in the Bible cite such matters as war records (1 Kings 14:19; 2 Kings

14:28 and 22:45), building projects: the cities of Asa (1 Kings 15:23), Ahab's "ivory house" (1 Kings 22:39), the tunnel and pool of Hezekiah (2 Kings 20:20), and conspiracies against the throne (1 Kings 16:20; 2 Kings 15:15). These matters are precisely those which would be recorded in court annals, and it is not unreasonable to assume that the responsibility of such was given to the Royal Secretary and that the annals themselves were stored in "the secretary's chamber" in the royal palace.

Beyond his charge to keep the state annals and handle royal correspondence, the Royal Secretary served on at least two committees for the collection of money for repairs to the Jerusalem Temple—one under King Jehoash (2 Kings 12:10–12), the other under King Josiah (2 Kings 22:3 ff.). In the latter instance, Hilkiah, the chief priest, discovered the "book of the law" and gave it to Shaphan, the Royal Secretary, who in turn reported the discovery to the king (2 Kings 22:8–10). This event suggests that the secretary's main concern was with writing and the keeping of written records rather than the collection of money. But the Royal Secretary could also act as a "Secretary of State," as indicated in the negotiations between Hezekiah, king of Judah, and the representatives of Sennacherib, king of Assyria (2 Kings 18:17–37). Lesser scribes are mentioned elsewhere in the Old Testament, and we may assume that they would work under the direction of the Royal Secretary. (See "Scribes" under THE PROFESSIONAL LIFE).

The Royal Herald

This office was held by a man named Jehoshaphat during the reigns of both David and Solomon (2 Sam. 8:16; 20:24; 1 Kings 4:3). There is little biblical information concerning the role of this official. He was one of the three delegates sent by King Hezekiah to negotiate with Sennacherib's high officials during the siege of Jerusalem in 701 B.C. (2 Kings 18:18, 37). He was assigned by Josiah to help regulate the money collected to repair the Temple (2 Chron. 34:8). Linguistic analysis, however, indicates that the Hebrew title does not mean archivist or "recorder" as translated in both KJV and RSV, but rather "herald," or "one who calls, announces." A parallel is found in the Egyptian office of "herald," the official spokesman for the Pharaoh, and may have provided the model upon which the Israelite office was patterned.

The Royal Herald, following Egyptian practice, had the task of directing communications between the king and the nation, and of handling protocol at the royal audiences. Official ceremonies at the royal court were regulated by strict protocol (see 1 Kings 2:19). The Royal Herald would announce visitors to the king at audiences, provide the king with periodic reports on the status of the kingdom, and proclaim to the people the orders of the king. He was the intermediary between the king and the people.

Superintendent of the District Prefects

Annual taxes were first imposed upon the Israelites during the period of the United Monarchy when it became necessary to secure a regular source of income for the state. The process was initiated by David, who ordered a census (2 Sam. 24:1–9), the initial step in establishing both a tax base and a military draft. A true system of taxation was completed under Solomon, who divided the kingdom into 12 tax districts each one of which was governed by an appointed prefect ("officer," 1 Kings 4:7–19). The Superintendent of the District Prefects was the appointed cabinet member "over the officers" of the administrative districts (1 Kings 4:5).

The precise function of the administrative districts was to simplify the collection of taxes. It was up to the Superintendent to oversee the entire bureaucratic system, making sure that it operated properly. The Superintendent had to maintain accurate written records. His was a role that required a certain familiarity with both the land and its people, a technical knowledge of weights, measures, and other business tools, as well as political acumen and a high degree of literacy.

Although the evidence is scattered, the administration of both Israel and Judah during the period of the Divided Monarchy appears to have followed a system similar to that used by Solomon. "Governors of the districts" are known in Israel at the time of Ahab (1 Kings 20:14–21), and a reference to the "store-cities" of Jehoshaphat, king of Judah, likewise implies organized administrative districts (2 Chron. 17:5, 12). Moreover, there is almost universal agreement among scholars that a list of the provinces of Judah is preserved in the book of Joshua (Josh. 15:21–62). The only difficulty yet to be resolved concerns the date of the list, although a date in the reign of Jehoshaphat (c. 873–849 B.C.) is perhaps to be preferred (see 2 Chron. 17:2).

Annual taxes from each of the 12 Solomonic districts furnished the royal court with supplies for one month each year and stocked grain for the horses in each district (1 Kings 4:27–28, cf. vs. 22–23, 26; I Kings 9:19). Additional taxes were imposed when necessary. Menahem exacted 50 shekels from each of the wealthy citizens of Israel in order to appease Tiglathpileser III ("Pul"), king of Assyria (2 Kings 15:19–20). Likewise, Jehoiakim was forced to impose a special tax on all of Judah in order to raise the tribute money demanded by Pharaoh Necho of Egypt (2 Kings 23:33–35).

In general, the wealthy and the city dwellers paid their taxes in money, whereas the rural members of society paid their taxes in produce. The latter taxes would be collected by the district governor (see 1 Chron. 27:25–31) and stored in royal granaries or storehouses (see 1 Kings 9:19; 2 Chron. 32:-

110. The "storehouse" found at Hazor.

28). A number of "storehouses" dating from the monarchical period have been excavated in Israel (e.g., Megiddo, Hazor [Fig. 110], Beer-sheba). These buildings—functionally close to modern warehouses—are laid out on a similar plan which consists of a large rectangular space divided into three long, narrow rooms by two rows of stone pillars. Evidence indicates that the two side rooms were storage areas for various agricultural products, while the center room served as a passageway.

A collection of ostraca (documents written on broken pieces of pottery) discovered in the royal citadel at Samaria provides archaeological evidence for the administration of the Northern Kingdom of Israel sometime within the reign of King Joahaz (c. 815–801 B.C.) and Jeroboam II (c. 786–746 B.C.). The ostraca in question are tax receipts for wine and oil collected from the district of Samaria. Included on each receipt is a personal name, which is perhaps that of the tax official or governor to whom the tax was delivered. The receipts were found among the remains of a building in the courtyard of the citadel which may have been a government storehouse.

Also of importance are a number of "royal seal impressions" stamped on the handles of storage jars found on various Judean tells and dating to around 700 B.C. These seal impressions bear the insignia and title of a king of Judah along with the name of one of four cities. It is thought that the four cities represent the administrative districts or "store-cities" of King Hezekiah (c.

715–687 B.C.) and that the jars were containers for taxes paid in oil and wine (see 2 Chron. 32:27–29).

Superintendent of the Forced Levy

In addition to annual taxes, the citizens of Israel and Judah were subject to the military draft and periodically to the *corvée*, or compulsory labor. Both Jehoshaphat (2 Chron. 17:14–19) and Amaziah (2 Chron. 25:5) called up men to arms. The military draft was the basis for a standing army necessary for the security and preservation of the nation—a method much in evidence in modern times as well. However, it was forced labor which many Israelites objected to. It was this aspect of the Solomonic administration which became the primary reason for the division of the United Kingdom (1 Kings 12:1–20).

The Superintendent of the Forced Levy was the officer in charge of all compulsory labor, first Canaanites (1 Kings 9:20–21) and then, during Solomon's reign, Israelites also (1 Kings 5:13–14). This administrator appears initially in the second list of David's cabinet members (2 Sam. 20:24). The same person, Adoram or Adoniram, continued to hold the office through the reign of Solomon (1 Kings 4:6; 5:14), and was ultimately stoned in a "labor dispute" at Shechem (I Kings 12:18). The office does not appear again in the Old Testament, although there are further references to forced labor.

There is no doubt that David created the office, probably on the pattern of a similar Canaanite institution. A letter (writen in cuneiform on a clay tablet) from the Canaanite prince of Megiddo to the Egyptian Pharaoh Akhenaten in the 14th century B.C. indicates the use of forced labor for cultivation in the Jezreel Valley. The practice is also known from 18th-century B.C. documents from Mari on the Middle Euphrates and at Alalakh overlooking the Orontes River in northwest Syria. Political control over former Canaanite territories provided David with the manpower necessary for the introduction of the *corvée* into Israel (cf. Judg. 1:28, 30, 33, 35 with the accounts of David's conquests in 2 Sam. 8, 10, etc.).

Forced labor was a universal phenomenon in the ancient Near East, but in general was limited to slaves or foreigners. The Israelites in Egypt were enrolled in forced labor when "there arose a new king over Egypt, who did not know Joseph" (Exod. 1:8–14). After the settlement in Canaan, Joshua imposed compulsory labor on the Gibeonites (Josh. 9:21–27). David imposed it on the defeated Ammonites (2 Sam. 12:31), and it appears that all defeated enemies were liable to this service (1 Kings 9:20–22; see also Isa. 31:8). Indeed, the building projects and general administration of a nation necessitated a large labor force. This was especially so under Solomon, who undertook not only to build himself a Temple and a palace in Jerusalem (1 Kings 5:1–7:12), but also a number of other projects (1 Kings 9:15–19).

Solomon, however, went beyond the universal practice of imposing compulsory labor on citizens of occupied territories. In addition to some seventy thousand "burden bearers" (literally "basket carriers") and eighty thousand "hewers of stone" (1 Kings 5:15) who were non-Israelites ("aliens," 2 Chron. 2:17–18), Solomon "raised a levy of forced labor out of all Israel; and the levy numbered thirty thousand men. And he sent them to Lebanon, ten thousand a month in relays; they would be a month in Lebanon, and two months at home" (1 Kings 5:13–14). The Israelites eventually revolted against this practice (1 Kings 12:18) and the Superintendent of the Forced Levy is not found elsewhere in the Bible. These facts suggest that the *corvée* was not regularly applied to the Israelites themselves and was limited mostly to the reign of Solomon. It reappears for a brief moment during the reign of Asa, king of Judah (1 Kings 15:22), but at a time when immediate military action had to be taken against Baasha, king of Israel (1 Kings 15:16–22). The walls of Jerusalem were rebuilt under the direction of Nehemiah with volunteer rather than with forced labor (Neh. 2:17 ff.).

CIVIL INSTITUTIONS DURING THE PERIOD OF FOREIGN RULE

With the destruction of Jerusalem by Nebuchadnezzar in 587 B.C. the national existence of ancient Israel came to an end. The entire Holy Land became a satellite of succeeding empires—Neo-Babylonian, Persian, Hellenistic, and Roman. Some of the local, village-oriented institutions survived and even took on a new prestige. The elders, for example, survived the collapse of the monarchy and appeared during the Exile (Ezek. 8:1; 20:1). They administered civil and religious affairs following the Return (Ezra 10:8), and even into the New Testament period (Matt. 21:23; 26:3). However, there was no longer an indigenous civil government, and the Jews and Jewish-Christians after them became theocratic communities centered about priestly law and religious ethics.

Civil life in Palestine during the days of foreign domination can be visualized as a hierarchy of small villages, larger cities, districts, and provinces. Although the names and titles might change, political administration was controlled by various dignitaries, court officials, and governors. The structure of society was also interwoven with the presence of foreign military contingents necessary to preserve order and retain control.

Although most of the population consisted of subjects, at least during the period of Roman domination some individuals were citizens of the Empire. A number of pro-Roman provincials were given citizenship in the last years of the republic, and the process was accelerated under empirical rule until citizenship was extended to all free inhabitants of the Empire in A.D. 212. Citizenship was even sold by the wife of Emperor Claudius (A.D. 41–54; see Acts 22:28). The same verse states that Paul was born with the status of a Roman citizen.

Roman citizenship carried certain rights. A citizen could not be punished without a trial (see Acts 16:35–39); neither could one be examined by scourging or even bound (Acts 22:22–29). An important right was the right to "appeal to Caesar" and be tried in Rome (Acts 25:10–12). This right could not be revoked once it was exercised (see Acts 26:32). Those officials who appeared during the time of foreign domination and are mentioned in the Bible include the governor, the prefect (procurator), the proconsul, and the tax collector.

The Governor

The governors mentioned in the Bible were officers who administered over a definite territory or province. Gedaliah was the governor of the province of Judah appointed by Nebuchadnezzar following the Babylonian destruction of Jerusalem (Jer. 40:5) and was subsequently murdered by the Ammonites (Jer. 41:1–3). A seal believed to have belonged to Gedaliah while he was apparently Minister of the Palace under the last king of Judah was found at Lachish.

Under Persian administration Palestine and Syria were included within the boundaries of the Fifth Satrapy, one of the large administrative areas of the Persian Empire. This area included all the land "Beyond the River" (i.e., west of the Euphrates) and was administered by a satrap, or "governor," who resided in Damascus (Ezra 4:10–11, 16–17; 5:3, 6; 6:6; Neh. 2:7, 9; etc.). The satrapy was subdivided into smaller provinces (see Esth. 1:1) similar in size and concept to the provinces established earlier by the Assyrians and the Babylonians. These units were administered by "governors" responsible to the satrap in Damascus. Two of these provinces were Samaria (the former Israelite kingdom) and Judah (the former Judean kingdom). Sheshbazzar (Ezra 5:14), Zerubbabel (Hag. 1:1), and Nehemiah (Neh. 5:14, 18, etc.) were governors of the province of Judah who are mentioned in the Bible. Two additional governors are known from seal impressions recovered among the archaeological remains of Ramat Raḥel, south of Jerusalem.

The Prefect (Procurator)

Persons who filled the office of prefect in the early Christian period are referred to in the New Testament as "governors" (e.g., Luke 3:1). Roman provinces, such as Judea, which were rugged, undeveloped, and close to the boundaries of the Roman Empire, were under the control of the emperor, and governed by an official of high rank. The Roman governor (prefect) was responsible for both financial administration and military control of the province. An imperial governor differed from the proconsul of senatorial provinces in the higher military authority which he exercised and in the indefinite term of office he enjoyed (subject to the decision of the emperor). The governor of Judea was under the direct supervision of the legate of Syria.

Some question exists as to whether Pilate and other early Roman military governors should be referred to as procurators or as prefects. An inscription found at Caesarea in the summer of 1961 by a team of Italian archaeologists bears the name of Pontius Pilate and, although damaged, attests to the title "prefect" (Fig. 111). The difficulty over the correct terminology is that changes occurred in the title of this official during the history of the Roman occupation of Judea. Each change (from "prefect" to "procurator" to a title of consular rank) was brought about by the necessity to strengthen the military administration of Judea, and the step-up in title was accompanied by a further augmentation of the Roman garrison. It appears that the title "prefect" should be applied to Pilate, at least during the early part of his administration. The title "prefect" may have been succeeded by that of "procurator" during his governorship (he is called "procurator" by Josephus and other early historians), but this is uncertain. The change in title may not have occurred until the time of the first Jewish revolt (A.D. 70), when it became necessary to increase the military forces occupying Judea.

111. An inscription found at Caesarea with the name of Pontius Pilate upon it.

Three Roman governors of Judea are mentioned in the New Testament. Pontius Pilate (A.D. 26–36) was prefect at the time of Jesus (Luke 3:1; 13:1; Matt. 27:1–26), and hence judge at his trial (Mark 15:1–5 and parallels). Antonius Felix (c. A.D. 52–58) and Porcius Festus (c. A.D. 58–62) held the office at the time of Paul's trial. According to Acts, Festus succeeded Felix while Paul was imprisoned at Caesarea (24:27). The prefect had supreme authority over the province and, except in the case of Roman citizens who could appeal to the Roman Emperor, his judgment was final (see Acts 23:12–26:32). The governors of Judea generally resided in the palace built by Herod the Great at Caesarea ("Herod's praetorium," Acts 23:25), although they frequently spent the winter in Jerusalem.

The Proconsul

The proconsul was a governor of a province which was administered by the Roman senate. He was appointed by the senate for a period of only one year, but this appointment could be renewed. The proconsul's main responsibilities were to maintain peace and to supervise the collection of taxes. Senatorial governors were supplied with small garrisons of auxiliary troops, and sometimes lacked the military authority of the imperial governor (prefect or procurator). During Paul's journeys, Sergius Paulus was proconsul of Cyprus (Acts 13:7) and Gallio of Achaia (Acts 18:12–17). Gallio was appointed by Claudius (A.D. 41–54) in either A.D. 51 or 52, as indicated by an inscription bearing his name discovered at Delphi, Greece.

The Tax Collector

Under Persian rule a system of taxation was administered in each province by a satrap ("governor"). This money was paid into the royal treasury, and was exacted from the people in the form of "tribute, custom, or toll" (Ezra 4:13). Priests, Levites, and other Temple personnel were exempt from the tax, at least during the reign of Artaxerxes (I, 465–425 B.C.; see Ezra 7:24). In addition to the tax paid to the royal treasury, there was a tax imposed for the upkeep of the governor, a tax which Nehemiah said he did not exact (Neh. 5:14–15).

Four main kinds of heavy taxes were placed on the people of Judea during the period of Roman rule: a tax on land, payable either in kind or in money; a poll tax; a tax on personal property; and customs duties on exports and imports. Residents of Jerusalem bore an additional house tax. Moreover, the Jewish people also were subject to an annual payment of a half shekel to the Temple in Jerusalem (Matt. 17:24).

A census, or enrollment, was ordered by Augustus (27 B.C.–A.D. 14) for the purpose of taxation. It was probably a delayed response to his census of

8 b.c. which brought Joseph and Mary to Bethlehem, where Jesus was born (Luke 2:1–7). The New Testament mentions another enrollment which evoked a strong reaction from the Jews (Acts 5:37). Among those who appear in the Gospels, Matthew was a tax collector, or better, a customs official (Matt. 9:9). When Jesus first encountered Zacchaeus, at Jericho, "he was a chief tax collector, and rich" (Luke 19:1–10).

Tax collectors were held in low esteem (Matt. 9:10–11; Luke 5:27–30), not only because the Jews detested the taxes (see Matt. 22:17–21), but also because of tax collection procedures. Regular taxes, such as that on land, were the direct responsibility of the Roman governor. The collection of other taxes, such as that imposed on movable property, was sold out to private individuals. These individuals (tax collectors; or "publicans") paid a fee in advance for the right to collect the tax, hoping to achieve a profit in the transaction.

THE MILITARY LIFE

It has been truly said by others that the most constant activity of people living in the world of the Bible in Old Testament times, next to sustaining life by labor, was warfare. Indeed, there are few years in the thousand-year period covered by Old Testament history in which there was not a campaign being waged by one of the nations or peoples of the Near Eastern world against another.

On a smaller scale there were almost constant skirmishes, raids, and ongoing vendettas between groups smaller than tribes, over such matters as grazing rights to pasture lands and ownership of wells and cisterns. Sometimes, too, food had to be obtained by seizure from those not related by blood, to prevent starvation. If the head of an aggrieved clan or family made the decision to settle an issue by force, every adult male picked up his weapon and responded to the call. The response was ingrained and automatic, rather than required under fear of penalty for refusal. (The clans of Scotland provide an almost modern example of such blood-group behavior.) This common spirit, this unquestioning readiness to respond to a call to defend the honor and interests of a small group, was an important factor in the creation of Israel the nation.

WARFARE DURING ISRAEL'S TRIBAL PERIOD

A useful place to begin a discussion of biblical warfare and the military life is with the ideas that governed the practice of it, as seen in the literature of Israel. Basically, secular historians would say, wars in Old Testament times were what wars have almost always been: attempts by one power to seize by force territory—more of it, and more fertile—and booty, including often slaves and an annual tribute from those defeated.

"Holy Wars"

Clearly the Israelites, until the time of David's United Kingdom, waged war under a "holy war" concept. This concept, in Israel's case, was dependent on the Hebrew understanding of their God, Yahweh. The liberated Tribes, under Moses, met Yahweh at Sinai (Exod. 19:16–19). Yahweh's first attribute was that of a mountain god associated with storms (see also Exod. 20:18; Judg. 5:4; 1 Sam. 2:10; 7:10). Another of Yahweh's attributes was that he was a god of war: "The LORD is a man of war" (Exod. 15:3; cf. Ps. 24:8). He will do battle for them (Josh. 10:13–14; 1 Sam. 17:45) and lead them to victory. Yahweh graciously chooses Israel as His people, and they freely covenant with Him to serve Him. He becomes their god, a tribal god, theirs alone. Yahweh on His part declares: "But if you . . . do all that I say, then I will be an enemy to your enemies, and an adversary to your adversaries" (Exod. 23:22; see also Exod. 17:16; Num. 31:3). On the basis of this understanding of their God, the Israelites developed an ideology that made war a totally religious affair.

Preparation for War

Since Israel's God was invested with the qualities of a warrior-god, and was the principal agent in the waging of a war, His support was essential for victory. So it was all-important that divine approval and backing be sought before a campaign or battle was begun. Some of the methods used to obtain a positive oracle that assured the effective intervention of God on Israel's side were: dreams (Judg. 7:9–14; Gideon); consultation with the Urim (1 Sam. 28:6, Saul) or the chief priest's ephod (1 Sam. 30:7, David); and the word of prophets (1 Kings 22:5–8, Ahab). When Saul, before the battle of Gilboa, could get no reply at all by using various approved methods, he turned to the witch of Endor (1 Sam. 28:19).

By reason of the covenant between Israel and her God, the land of Canaan was a sacred land (see, e.g., Exod. 3:17; 32:13; Deut. 6:3–23; 9:3–5). Therefore, after the Conquest, any invasion of it by a foreign army necessarily involved the Lord and brought forth His wrath against the invader. Still, that support had first to be sought, and then further steps taken to "sanctify" the war. To this end sacrifices were offered by the priests, and the support of religion was thrown behind the military (Num. 10:8–9; Deut. 20:2). The citizen-soldiers, since they were offering service to the Lord, sanctified themselves (Josh. 3:5) with the prescribed purification rites and refrained from sexual intercourse (1 Sam. 21:4–5; 2 Sam. 11:11). Israelite soldiers, from

Moses to David, are portrayed as playing, in effect, a priestly role, that of "holy persons" in the Lord's service for the duration of the war. To this end they must also purify the camp itself and keep it free of excrement (Deut. 23:9–14).

But Yahweh does more than merely sanctify a war and provide moral support: he actually fights for Israel and helps her army by terrorizing or panicking enemies (Exod. 23:27–28; Josh. 10:10; 24:12). In turn, Israel must carry out His fierce wrath (1 Sam. 28:18). Israel's wars are Yahweh's wars (e.g., Exod. 17:16; 1 Sam. 25:28). Israel's enemies are His enemies (e.g., Judg. 5:23, 31). Yahweh is called Israel's "banner" (Exod. 17:16), "shield" and "sword" (Deut. 33:29).

The whole nation of Israel was regarded as an army (e.g., Exod. 6:26; 12:17, "hosts"), and a name for Yahweh becomes "God of hosts," that is, the God of Israel in His war-god character (Exod. 15:3; 1 Sam. 1:3; 15:2, etc.). The booty taken in a battle belonged to Yahweh and came under the ban (i.e., became "taboo") as being "devoted to the Lord" because of a vow made before the battle in hope of victory (Num. 21:2–3; Josh. 7:1–2).

The battle standard of Israel in her tribal period was the Ark, which was also regarded as the sanctuary, the residence, of the Lord God of hosts. To lose it, as the Israelites did to the Philistines (1 Sam. 4), was a national disaster; yet even in the hands of the enemy at Ashdod, this symbol of the Lord retained its potency (1 Sam. 5).

Military Leadership

Under such a concept of war a professional and experienced military leadership was outside the concern of the tribes. Primary trust was placed in a calm confidence in the Lord (Exod. 14:13; Deut. 20:3; Josh. 10:8, 25) and the historical readiness of every able-bodied male member of a family or clan, including slaves, to turn himself into a soldier under the command of his leader. In times of great danger a clan or tribal head would issue a rallying cry that would be quickly carried to the entire group and followed by a prompt and almost automatic response from his blood-related herdsmen-members. The account of Abraham's rescue of Lot (Gen. 14:14–16) is the classic example from patriarchal days of this sort of tribal military engagement.

As has been shown earlier (see section, THE LIFE OF THE NOMAD), tribal life changed sharply and tribal institutions deteriorated when the seminomadic Israelites became settled agriculturalists after the Conquest. Allegiance gradually shifted from clan and tribal chiefs to the spread-out towns in which the Israelite farmers lived and near which they planted their fields and vineyards. Israelite culture slowly but surely slipped into syncretism with

Canaanite ways. This was the situation that is described in Judg. 2:8–23.

"Then the Lord raised up judges," charismatic leaders—people with special God-given gifts which they used for the good of tribe and nation—who rallied one or more of the tribes to take up arms against neighboring peoples oppressing them. These leaders are commonly introduced in the book of Judges with these words: "The Spirit of the Lord came upon him" (e.g., Othniel, Judg. 3:10). It was the possession of this gift that prepared them for leadership. They were "judges" not primarily in the sense that they held court, but in the sense of "deliverers" or "liberators," people who in moments of crisis restored order and put Israel back on the right track of loyalty to God. As we read the accounts of their triumphs over Israel's enemies, we today may regard Deborah, Gideon, and Jephthah as military experts; but biblical writers indicate that they, and the other nine judges, held their command not by reason of their own capabilities but by virtue of their special gift of the Spirit. Likewise with Othniel: "The Lord raised up a deliverer . . . Othniel. . . . The spirit of the Lord came upon him . . . ; he went out to war, and the Lord gave Cushan-rishathaim . . . into his hand."

Included among these raised-up leaders was one untypical judge, Samson, who was essentially a strong-man hero whose exploits along the borders of Philistia with Israel's enemy to the west became part of the nation's folklore. The Spirit was withdrawn from Samson for cause (Judg. 16:20), as it would later be withdrawn from Saul (1 Sam. 16:14); with its departure went also the authority to lead. Leadership was thus conferred and withdrawn by the Lord.

Calling Out an Army

The people were called out to battle by various methods: by sounding a trumpet (Judg. 3:27, Ehud; 6:34, Gideon; 1 Sam. 13:3, Saul) (see Fig. 99, Shofar); by sending messengers (Judg. 6:35; 7:24, Gideon); and by sending messengers who dramatized the recourse to war by performing a symbolic action (Judg. 19:29–30; 1 Sam. 11:7). It was a tribal right to refuse to join another tribe in a campaign, but a town within a tribe that refused was cursed (Judg. 5:23, Meroz). Once a tribal decision was made no individual member could shirk his duty (Judg. 21:1–5); this principle was applied to the entire population of the city of Jabesh-Gilead (21:8–15). Saul reminded the people of Israel of their individual duty in a dramatic manner in 1 Sam. 11:7. (In a later era laws were drawn to provide exemptions from military service under certain conditions [Deut. 20:5–9].)

The Army of Deborah and Barak

In the book of Judges we find many illuminating evidences of how wars were fought in Palestine c. 1200-1050 B.C. The ideology of a holy war and its conduct flourished, but the details that survive underneath the stylized account enable today's readers to piece together and recreate the opposing strategies and tactics, the battle scenes, and the terror and bloodshed of the hand-to-hand combat.

An example is the story of the triumph of Deborah, a prophetess and judge of the tribe of Ephraim, and the trustworthy Barak of the tribe of Naphtali, over Sisera, a general in the army of Jabin, king of the Canaanite city-state of Hazor. The account is found in Judges 4, supplemented by a roughly parallel poetic version in ch. 5, known as the Song of Deborah, an epic composition that is one of the few contemporary source materials we have for the period of the Judges.

Jabin, king of Hazor, a city on the main road to Damascus north of the Sea of Galilee, had been oppressing the tribes of Naphtali and Zebulon, whose lands lay west and southwest of Hazor, between the Jordan Valley rift and the Phoenician coastal lands. Deborah ordered Barak to call up an army of militiamen from the two affected tribes, and to assemble them at Mount Tabor, in the hill country north of the Valley of Jezreel, safely out of reach of Sisera and his dreaded Canaanite chariots that controlled the level trade routes and the valleys. Deborah undertook to "draw out Sisera, to meet you by the river Kishon with his chariots and his troops" (Judg. 4:7). Word brought to General Sisera that Barak had assembled an army at Mount Tabor was perhaps enough to induce him to lead out "all his chariots of iron, and all the [infantry] men who were with him" (4:13) at Harosheth, one of Jabin's military outposts, generally thought to be at the foot of Mount Carmel, between Megiddo and the Mediterranean. The sorry state of the arms of the citizen-soldiers is caught in Judg. 5:8: "Was shield or spear to be seen among forty thousand in Israel?"

The strategy of Deborah was to keep Barak's militiamen up above the valley, in rough country where Sisera could not attack them with his chariots. What the exact Israelite tactics were is unclear, but as both Judges 4 and 5 suggest, Sisera in due course allowed his chariot force to get between Barak's men and the Kishon River ("the waters of Megiddo") which runs in a northwesterly direction toward the Mediterranean Sea. The Kishon can only be described as "a torrent" (5:21) after a heavy rain. So what apparently happened was that Deborah and Barak, seeing the rain and perceiving the exposed position of Sisera's chariots as the river became swollen, charged down from a hillside (5:15) and with their axes and swords and by the sheer force of numbers drove the Canaanites back toward the river, where some of their heavy, iron-clad chariots (including Sisera's own) became mired in the mud. Panic ensued; all who could fled for their

112. The so-called sickle sword. In contrast to a real sickle, the cutting edge of this sword is on the outside of the curve of the blade. It was used in a slicing rather than thrusting fashion.

lives, with the Israelites in hot pursuit. Once a rout was on, there was little hope that the routed forces could escape the sharp edge of the sword.

Swords in the Era before the Philistines

It was the Philistines who introduced the straight, two-edged sword into Palestine, about 1100 B.C. Previously, in the Israelite tribal period being discussed here, the standard sword had only one cutting edge, and was slightly curved, the sharp edge being the outer one. The inner edge was blunt and thicker, to provide heft and give force to a blow (Fig. 112). Normally the blade was of metal, the hilt of wood. This type of sword had developed from a less effective, ax-like cutting tool with a long hilt and short blade to one in which hilt and blade were about equal in length. It was a smiting weapon, not a piercing one, and was in common use among all Near Eastern nations in the period c. 1500–1100 B.C., as depicted in rock carvings in Anatolia, ivory carvings from Megiddo, and sword specimens found in excavations at Gezer and Ugarit, and in the tombs of the Egyptian Tutankhamun and the Assyaian Adad-Nirari.

The phrase so frequently encountered in Joshua and Judges, "and he smote them with the edge of the sword," is most appropriately applied to this one-edged, curved sword in use at the time of the Conquest.

The two-edged straight sword used by Ehud (Judg. 3:16) is better thought of as a kind of dagger, or as the beginning of the development of the long, straight-bladed, two-edged sword. A curved sword of typical size for the time of the Judges could never be made unnoticeable by a person bent on assassination, nor could it be thrust into the victim's abdomen before he knew what was happening.

The Ax and the Mace

The function of both ax and mace was to smash in the head of an opponent in hand-to-hand fighting (Fig. 113). Only the head of either of these weapons was not made of wood. The wooden handles were fitted into the heads in a socket-type union. The mace was probably the earlier

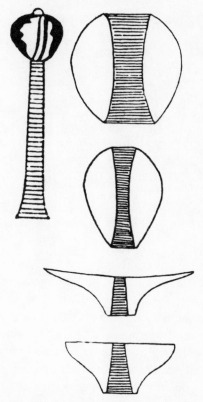

113. The mace consisted of a heavy, round object affixed to a handle. The ax (the lower two objects) was similarly constructed. Both mace and ax were intended for hand-to-hand combat.

in development, for its head was normally made of stone. The ax was designed to pierce a metal helmet and penetrate the skull. Hence metal was required, and a more functional design of the head. The different ax-head shapes shown in Figure 113 were developed to work efficiently against enemies differently armored. Essentially each type was designed to *cut* or to *pierce*, and the stronger the defensive armor of the enemy, the longer the blade and the shorter the piercing edge. Sometimes the wooden handle was fitted into a socket in the metal blade, and sometimes the rear of the blade was fitted into slits in the handle, and bound into position.

The Sling

The sling changed but minimally through the centuries and, in fact, remained in military use until A.D. 1700. (See description of this weapon and its use below, "The Weapons of David's Army").

114. Spears and shields used in the Egyptian army. (Reliefs from Queen Hatshepsut's temple, located at Deir el-Bahri, which date to 1489–1469 B.C.)

The Spear

As with the shield, the spear found little or no use among the Israelites until Saul's time. Among the massed infantrymen of the armies of the greater nations surrounding them, the spear was a basic weapon (Fig. 114). It was not thrown, as was the lighter javelin, but was used in a two-handed thrusting motion. Only the tip and the butt were of metal, the shaft being of wood. Chariots of all nations except the Egyptians were fitted with a spear-holding socket at the rear of the vehicle; it was the weapon of the chariot driver, to be used when the chariot became caught in the midst of hand-to-hand fighting. The Egyptian chariots were equipped with the lighter, shorter javelins, which were thrown. (See "The Javelin," below.)

The Bow

The composite bow (Fig. 115) was perhaps the most powerful weapon in the armies of the great empires while Israel was still a loosely-knit confederation of tribes. But specialized workshops were needed for the production of good bows and arrows in the quantities needed to supply an army. Not until David's empire would the bow figure in the Israelite weaponry (see "The Bow," below, in THE WEAPONS OF DAVID'S ARMY).

The Shield

Shields were not used by the Israelites in their tribal days until after they settled in Canaan.

Some shapes used by Egyptian soldiers of the period are shown in Figure 114. Normally, shields were made of wood covered with leather, stiffened with strips of metal or with studded nails. No actual shields have been found in Palestinian excavations. (See "The Shield," below.)

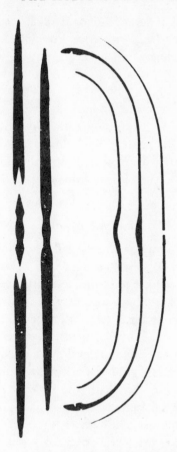

115. The individual pieces of a composite bow. *From left to right*: first the two pieces of thin wood are glued together onto a smaller center piece, as in the second drawing, shown face forward. The same is seen in the side view in the third drawing. Then a strip of sinew was glued to the back (*left*) side of the wood as seen in the fourth drawing. Finally, sections of horn were glued to the front (*right*) side of the wood, as seen in the fifth drawing.

Armor

Armor, notably the coat of mail, appeared in response to the piercing capabilities of an arrow shot from a composite bow. The chariot driver especially required defensive protection of his upper body. Archers, too, required protective armor, for they also used both hands in performing their specialized military task. The answer developed against the arrow was the coat of mail, comprised of several hundred small metal scales attached to a leather or cloth garment (see "Protective Equipment," below). Armor was not worn by Israelite soldiers prior to David's rule.

The Helmet

That Hittite charioteers and infantrymen wore metal helmets is well known from reliefs and wall paintings dating from the period between the Exodus and the United Kingdom. Since Egyptian soldiers are not depicted wearing helmets until after the Exodus, it is doubtful if any Israelites owned them; however, lack of archaeological evidence prevents any generalization. See "Helmets," below.

The Chariots of the Pharaoh of the Exodus

The first organized army encountered in the Bible is the army of the Egyptian Pharaoh (very possibly Rameses II, who ruled c. 1290–1229 B.C.).

The Egyptians, if they were to control territory along the Fertile Crescent toward Mesopotamia, had to have mobility of military movement—i.e., had to be able to deliver a strike force with far greater speed than the normal 15 miles per day of an army of infantrymen. Egypt's eastern borders and the main routes to the northeast were on level ground. So for the Egyptians an effective chariot force was a logical major military reliance.

The Egyptians brought the chariot to a level of performance never attained by the Canaanites, from whom they first got it, about three centuries before the Exodus. By mid-14th century B.C. Egyptian design had moved from 4 to 6 spokes per wheel (page 289); the body was lightened so that the axle could be moved back to the very rear of the body, without increasing the burden on the horses; and the axle was lengthened. As a result of these design improvements, the wheels were virtually free of the body and sharper turns had been made possible without any loss of speed or stability.

Two men manned the Egyptian chariot: a driver and an archer equipped not only with bow case and quiver, composite bow and arrows, but with javelins, the quivers for the arrows and javelins being fixed to the side of the chariot's body. As with those of the Canaanites and Hittites, Egyptian chariots were drawn by two horses.

When the Israelites fled from Egypt, the Pharaoh "made ready his chariot and took his army with him, and took six hundred picked chariots and all the other chariots of Egypt with officers over all of them . . . and he pursued the people of Israel as they went forth defiantly . . . and overtook them encamped at the sea" (Exod. 14:6–9).

Egyptian Infantrymen

The Egyptian infantrymen of the Exodus account (who perhaps were stationed at the border forts mentioned in Exod. 14:2) were equipped with axes (See Fig. 114). The blades were long and narrow, the outer, piercing edge much the narrowest part. The sword of the Egyptian infantryman of c. 1280 B.C. was of the curved or "sickle" type, a smiting weapon, with a blade longer than the hilt. In a very short time the Egyptians would adopt from the Sea Peoples the two-edged straight sword, a weapon capable of piercing as well as smiting.

For defensive protection the Egyptian infantryman of the army of Rameses II was equipped with a comparatively small shield made of wood covered with leather, rounded at the top and somewhat wider at its shoulders than at its base. A strap was fitted to his shield in such a way that it could be slung across the soldier's back when he was marching, or protect his head and back when he was scaling a city wall. Probably only charioteers and the archers who rode beside them were fitted with coats of mail, which were expensive to make and therefore provided only to those who were unable to carry a shield in battle. It is doubtful whether Egyptians wore battle helmets as early as 1280 B.C., but the wall reliefs of Rameses III, about 100 years later, depict his infantrymen as wearing head-fitting helmets, almost surely of leather, that covered their ears.

In addition to archers in chariots, the Egyptians attached units of archers to their infantry formations, and assigned them to their crescent-shaped single-masted naval ships powered by sails and oars.

Now, as the Israelites made good their escape into the desert, began the period in which the wars of Israel were a sacred activity, "holy wars," the wars of Yahweh (see Exod. 17:16; Num. 21:14; 1 Sam. 25:28)—a concept of war that would not be changed to an organized and secular (profane) activity of the state until the election of a king over the nation.

The Tribal Armies at Their Best

The opening chapter of the Book of Judges (esp. vv. 19, 21, 27–35) seems to reflect accurately the inability of the Israelites to win a pitched battle or to capture a fortified city by a head-on assault. Both types of action were avoided as much as possible. More typical was their use of spies and psychological warfare, as at Jericho (Josh. 2:1-6); ruses to lure defenders out of their walled cities (e.g., Ai, Josh. 8); and spies to search for a traitor who would open a city gate for an Israelite task force, as at Bethel (Judg. 1:23-25).

When pitched battles were fought, the results were disastrous (1 Sam. 4:1–11; 31:1–7).

One method of engaging the enemy showed the Israelites at their best. It was used as early as the battle of Rephidim between Amalek and Israel under Moses and Joshua (Exod. 17:9)—fighting a true holy war with a small and select body of warriors (the size of the corps ruling out a pitched battle). This strategy was employed against Midian (Num. 31:1–12). Saul, too, had his best successes after Jabesh-gilead with a select army of 3,000 men (1 Sam. 13:2) and later with but 600 (1 Sam. 14:2). In these instances Saul was defending the highlands of Ephraim by means of guerrilla actions —hit-and-run attacks, ambushes, and other tactics in which number mattered but little, mobility and knowledge of the terrain a great deal.

The Israelite military capabilities throughout the period from the Exodus to the monarchy under David were not of the textbook sort, but their tactics at times were well chosen to solve their military problems. The most vivid example is found in the account of Gideon's victory over the invading Midianites, told in Judges 6:1–8:12. Again a select group of fighting men (only 300) with a high morale is employed. They are trained for a specific task. The coordinated attack upon the nomadic horde, including wives and children, is made in the middle of the night. Surprise is a major element, reinforced by the creation of confusion through the use of night-shattering trumpet blasts and the battle-crazed war-cries of Israelites carrying torches and setting fire to tents, terrifying the sleeping Midianites, the women and children and camels alike, creating total panic. The chase of the unnerved Midianites and their steady slaughter as they tried to make their way back to their desert homelands to the East were relentless and irreversible.

By such tactics the Israelites were able to offset to a large degree the superior weaponry and numbers of the enemies among whom they lived. But with the increasing numbers and power of the Philistines along the sea coast and in the region of the Plain of Esdraelon, the freedom of action of the Israelites was limited mostly to the hill country of central Palestine. And when Saul attempted to meet Philistine encroachment head-on at Gilboa, he lost his life and made necessary for Israel an entirely new approach to warfare and military life, under King David.

SOLDIERING UNDER DAVID

A working understanding and appreciation of the army created by David is reached by distinguishing first between the professional army and the militia or "army of Israel." Once this distinction is clearly drawn, many uncertainties and confusions arising from an uninformed reading of the books of Samuel and of Kings disappear.

The Professional Army

The first step toward forming a professional army was made by David's predecessor, Saul. As Israel's military leader, Saul was at a tremendous disadvantage in his nearly constant wars with the Philistines by reason of the fact that the Philistine army was comprised of professional soldiers, both infantrymen and charioteers, who stood by, ready for action. Saul's (Israel's) army had to be called from their fields or their occupations, hastily organized and equipped, and sent into battle with little preparation. (Israel's disadvantage in weaponry will be discussed below; see "The Sword" in THE WEAPONS OF DAVID'S ARMY.)

Saul set about to change this state of affairs by initiating the recruiting of a standing army, mainly of Israelites. This is clearly reflected in 1 Sam. 14:52: "There was hard fighting against the Philistines all the days of Saul; and when Saul saw any strong man, or any valiant man, he attached him to himself." But Saul's kingdom was poor. He himself lived in a modest-sized stone "palace" in the town of Gibeah (Tell el-Ful), north of Jerusalem, where he kept a small retinue of close friends and warriors. Most of these, 1 Sam. 22:7 suggests, were Benjaminites, and so perhaps were preferred as companions-in-arms by this Benjaminite king. Doeg, however (1 Sam. 21:7; 22:18), was an Edomite, and David (1 Sam. 16:18–21) came from Judah. Personal valor was the all-important criterion for military recognition. Though Saul made a start at building a cadre of professionals, his inability to support many from private income or national revenues prevented him from going far with his idea. In fact, at the end of his life he and Jonathan were the leaders in battle, and though Abner is later called Saul's commander-in-chief, he seems never to have held a top battle command.

During Saul's rule the people of Israel were not ready for an army other than a people's army. A standing professional army was not in keeping with the tribal traditions and the prevailing belief in the decentralization of government and of military power. To many Israelites it may have reflected the adoption of a Canaanite element of society, as it did when Ahimelech recruited mercenaries some generations earlier (Judg. 9:4).

The Start of David's Professional Army

David's professional army grew out of his flight from Saul and his settling down temporarily as a brigade leader with headquarters in a cave at Adullam, a town in the no-man's-land strip between the Israelites and the Philistines along the western border of Judah. To Adullam came—no doubt in response to a word-of-mouth invitation from David—some 400 men (1

Sam. 22:1-2) disgruntled younger sons, debtors, men in flight from authority, men seeking new careers, excitement and perhaps even violence, under the charismatic national hero-in-exile.

So large a body of men, living in a region notably infertile because of its limestone subsoil, needed employment. David found it for all of them by selling their services to Achish, "king of Gath," one of the 5 cities of the Philistine pentapolis. (Gath was located somewhere in or near the southern Shephelah; the identification of its *tell* is uncertain, perhaps Tell es-Safi.) Gath's outlying regions included extensive and important grain fields that ran out as far as the lands were fertile. These had to be protected from nomadic desert tribes to the south. David in effect offered "protection" from food-stealing raids by hungry nomads; he and his men would be "enforcers" of peace and stability on the southern borders (1 Sam. 27). He would also, he said, make raids on the border towns of Judah to the east, and bring booty back to Achish. Since Saul's hatred of David was known throughout Philistia as well as Israel, Achish naturally assumed that David was eager to harass Saul by brigandage along the borders of his small kingdom. Thus Achish would be getting double service from David. (Hiring mercenaries of other nationalities was a common practice among Canaanite and Philistine city-states.)

David solved his own dilemma by raiding "Geshurites, Girzites, and Amalekites" (1 Sam. 27:8-12), desert tribes of the region south of Gath, while reporting to Achish that the booty he brought to him came from raids on towns of Judah. This deception could be maintained only by preventing any of the suddenly attacked nomads from escaping to tell the truth.

In this fashion David built a small striking force made up of men of courage, physical toughness, and lack of squeamishness over violence that would later provide his army with the professional competence and experience required to train and lead militiamen. He was also sorting out the top leaders from those who would play supporting roles. He was building a tightly knit group. He was giving commands involving life and death for all, and seeing that they were being carried out. He was generating loyalty and devotion toward himself. He was fitting himself for ruling.

Meanwhile, the group grew to 600. From later lists of David's officers and outstanding individual fighting men we know that his men came from various places (2 Sam. 23:8-39; 1 Chron. 11:10-41). While the majority came from Judah, there were several foreigners, including an Aramaean from Sobeh, an Ephraimite, a man from Manasseh, one from Gad, and a Hittite (Uriah) among others. Furthermore, David made friends and a reputation in Gath, so that when later he conquered the Philistines, 600 men from Gath came over as mercenaries (2 Sam. 15:18) to him as to the one king around with a future, and they remained loyal to him throughout his life.

Mercenaries

The basic meaning of "mercenary" is a person who serves merely for wages. Here the more specialized meaning is used: a soldier hired for service in an army other than that of his own country. Thus Ittai the Gittite (= from Gath) was a mercenary, while Joab and Benaiah, for example, were Israelite "professional soldiers." In Israel a mercenary had no standing and no "rights" as a member of an Israelite family, clan, or tribe. A mercenary was not free. In effect he belonged to the king. He had no loyalty to anyone but the king. So totally did the mercenaries belong to a king that when he died they, like concubines, passed to his heir. On his side the king housed and fed them, and rewarded them in various ways.

As the ties of the mercenaries were directly to the king, so was their loyalty. They became his most trustworthy bodyguards; indeed this function soon became their chief one. David stationed them near him in Jerusalem (2 Sam. 11:9, 13; 15:14, etc.). They were organized under a separate command, with Benaiah as their commander (2 Sam. 8:18; 20:23). (David had been commander of Saul's much smaller royal corps, 1 Sam. 22:14.) Later in David's career these royal troops would accompany him on his flight from Jerusalem at the time of Absalom's rebellion (2 Sam. 15:18), and they would form the escort for Solomon at his anointing as successor to David (1 Kings 1:38, 44).

Cherethites and Pelethites

The Hebrew words here, transliterated into English, are *karethi* and *palethi*. *Karethi* almost certainly means Cretans. *Palethi* is widely thought by scholars to be a corrupted form of *palishti* ("Philistine"), corrupted perhaps by its constant use with the similarly formed word *karethi* (*palethi* nowhere appears without its partner).

The Philistines were but one of several "peoples of the sea," closely related, who about 1200 B.C. made their appearance at the eastern end of the Mediterranean, and after land and sea battles with the Egyptians, settled on the strip of coastline lying between Mount Carmel on the north and the desert beyond habitable Palestine on the south. In addition to the Philistines these "sea peoples" included the Cherethites, the Tjekker, the Danuns, the Sherden, and the Tursha. The Tjekker are known to have occupied the coastal city of Dor, just south of Mount Carmel. The Philistines, who seem to have been the most numerous and prominent of these new arrivals in Palestine, settled down in a five-city league west of Judah: Ashkelon, Ashdod, and Gaza on or near the sea, and Ekron and Gath inland. The Cherethites, a relatively small group, settled to the south and southwest of Gath, on the edge of the Negeb. Some or all of these people had come to Palestine from Crete or from that region of the Mediterranean, or had some past history of residence on that island. Hence *karethi*, "Cretans," which becomes in English "Cherethites." To most Old Testament writers, all these people were included under the term "Philistines." "Cherethites and Pelethites" may be regarded as a nice-sounding synonym for Philistine mercenaries who formed the largest part of David's royal troops or bodyguards, with the possibility that many of them were truly Cherethites, who joined him after his defeat of the Philistines. In fact, the term throughout David's lifetime is roughly the equivalent of the royal guards. Some scholars believe that the Cherethites and Palethites composed the entire bodyguard in David's time.

The "Carites" of 2 Kings 11:4, 19, the guards at the time of the overthrowing of Athalia, are commonly regarded as the Cherethites under a corrupted name.

Parallel to the body of mercenary bodyguards, a small army of professional soldiers was recruited by inducements to young and courageous Israelites—Saul out of desperation, David wittingly. Saul, David was advised, would "enrich with great riches, and will give [the man who defeats Goliath] his daughter, and will make his father's house free [of taxes] in Israel." An offer like Saul's was rare, but he was in a desperate spot, in great need of a champion to defend Israel in a man-to-man combat. A more common method of rewarding a unit or outstanding individual warriors may be described in 1 Sam. 8:14–15: "He [the king] will take the best of your fields and give them to his servants" (vs. 14) or give them a claim on the tithes (vs. 15). Frequently there was booty from defeated enemies, and always the carousing society of fellow soldiers who at least knew where the next meal was coming from. Steady wages would follow when David had had time to organize his kingdom and the revenues needed to support professional troops as well as his royal household.

Specialized Royal Troops

The Hebrew text of 1 and 2 Samuel employs words which seem to suggest differentiated functions among the mercenary royal guards, but any precise differences are hard to pin down. For example, some of the royal guards seem to have been employed as "runners," the running being done before the chariot of the king as he moved about the capital, as a ceremonial show, or for security purposes, or both. Prince Absalom used runners (2 Sam. 15:1) and so did Prince Adonijah (1 Kings 1:5). Some think that the runners were also used as royal messengers and to carry out various missions for the king, such as bringing an individual before the king.

Another term used for royal troops means only "those who obey, who answer the call," that is, servants, in the limited sense of those responsible to the king. A third term seemingly identifying a different group of royal troops means "youngsters," but in a military sense, as reflected in our word "cadet," or perhaps in the medieval sense of a young man of high class, a "squire" or young knight. RSV rather consistently translates this term as "young men" (1 Sam. 21:4; 25:5, 6). "Cadets" of David and Ishbaal fought each other at Gibeon (2 Sam. 2:14) but in vss. 12 and 13 they have just been called "servants." Jonathan (1 Sam. 20:21–22) had a "young man" or "cadet," and Joab had ten (2 Sam. 18:15), and in the context of these passages clearly a young man is meant. Yet the "young men" of 2 Sam. 16:2 seem to be merely the men of the royal bodyguard who accompanied David on his flight, the veteran mercenaries of 2 Sam. 15:18.

It is known that the royal troops were a considerable force with a regular "watch" system or roster for guarding the palace and later, under Solomon, the Temple. Some must have been fleeter than others, some better at hand-to-hand fighting, some especially suited for guarding the physical person of the king. But it seems not possible to assign specialized roles to this or that group. What does emerge most clearly is that these royal troops and most especially his foreign mercenaries were David's in every respect; that he gave them rewards of both material and intangible nature that assured him of their loyalty and affection; and that they played a very great part in insulating him from any enemy, external or internal, in war or peace, who might wish to kill him.

Professional Israelite Soldiers

In the section above, headed "The Start of David's Professional Army," the gathering of the first recruits at Adullam was described. Here we will use Joab, Abishai, and Benaiah as examples of professional soldiers and through them demonstrate the uses of the standing army. In the sections following, to the end of "The Army of the People of Israel," the theories of Professor Yigael Yadin, Israeli archaeologist (Hazor, Megiddo, etc.) and former major-general and chief of the general staff of the Israeli Defense Forces in the 1957 war with the Arabs, have been adopted.

"David departed . . . and escaped to the cave of Adullam; and when his brothers and all his father's house heard it, they went down there to him" (1 Sam. 22:1). Among those who joined his first group were undoubtedly Joab, Abishai, and Benaiah. Joab and Abishai, and a younger brother, Asahel, who would later be killed in self-defense by Abner, were called "the sons of Zeruiah" (2 Sam. 3:39, etc.). Zeruiah was an older sister, perhaps half-sister, of David, who was the youngest of Jesse's children. So Joab and Abishai were David's nephews, but probably very little younger than he, for Israelite wives often bore their first child at age fifteen.

Along with such relatives as Joab and Abishai came Benaiah, whose background is unknown except that he came from Kabzeel in southern Judah and was the son of a priest named Jehoiada. So too came many other young men, probably discontented with their lot back home (1 Sam. 22:2), willing to risk their lives and their futures by throwing in their lot with that of the charismatic young outlaw-hero.

The Thirty

The names of some of these first recruits are undoubtedly preserved in the lists of "The Thirty" found in 2 Sam. 23:18–39 and 1 Chron. 11:20–47. These lists do not at all agree, containing discrepancies due probably to corruptions of the text across the years, and cannot be made to conform. It is conjectured that these lists originally were consistent in giving the name of the warrior, the name of his father, and the name of the town, country, or clan he came from. The list in 2 Sam. 23 has the curious error of listing 34 names, then concluding "thirty-seven in all." The 1 Chron. list is also of 34, not 30, and it then adds 16 additional names, making a total of 50.

The best way to understand "The Thirty" is to regard the period of David's rise to full power as a heroic age, an age of heroes, an epic age with an epic account of the bravery and triumphs of its heroes that has been compared not unreasonably with Homer's epic account of the Trojan War, *The Iliad*. These Israelite men, at the start of their careers, had to live by their wits and their physical prowess. They must have become tougher and more proficient fighters with each new raid and adventure. Fighting men of all nations in all centuries when resting in their own camp, have held wrestling matches, mock or semi-serious bouts of hand-to-hand fighting, and tests of physical prowess of various kinds. As time went by, some of David's men emerged as heroes worthy of song and legend. Of Benaiah, for example, it is recorded that "he slew two lionlike men of Moab; and he went down also and slew a lion in the midst of the pit in time of snow" (2 Sam. 23:20; 1 Chron. 11:22). Benaiah is also said to have been suddenly confronted by an armed Egyptian soldier when he himself had only a staff. Undaunted, Benaiah closed with the Egyptian and tore his spear from his grasp, whereupon he dispatched the man with the latter's own weapon (2 Sam. 23:21; 1 Chron. 11:23). "David set him over his bodyguard."

Joab, by contrast, probably early showed capabilities as a military tactician, one who could figure a way to achieve a goal, to win a battle, by finding the right method to overcome an enemy's strategy or advantage of position. If not earlier, at least after the time of the capture of Jerusalem, managed by Joab's entry with men via the city's water shaft (1 Chron. 11:4–7) (*see* Fig. 88), Joab had emerged as the man to serve as commander-in-chief of David's military establishment. His brother Abishai seems to have been Joab's immediate second in the line of command of military operations. When the Israelite army had to be split in two to fight a two-front engagement, Joab kept command of a task force and placed Abishai in command of the rest (2 Sam. 10:9–14). Later Abishai led David's forces, composed of militiamen from Judah and the professional troops, against Sheba (2 Sam. 20). If "The Thirty" was, as Professor Yadin believes, a kind of supreme army council, then Abishai, as its head (2 Sam. 23:18), may be thought of as a chief of staff of the military establishment.

"The Thirty," then, were first heroes and then military commanders, ultimately being formed into some kind of organization, given responsibility, Yadin says, for setting up the rules of military discipline, for training and advancement of middle-level officers, and for providing leadership to the militiamen. Their number fluctuated, and some of the original members were in course of time replaced because of death or disability. (David reigned about 40 years.) "The Thirty" were the cream of David's professional, full-time military men, with special responsibilities as commanders and trainers of the army of the people as distinct from the smaller professional army and from the royal bodyguard troops which Benaiah commanded.

The Three

In the "golden age" of David's rising empire the folk heroes were the outstanding warriors in hand-to-hand combat. An army which had a relatively small number of hard-bitten infantrymen each of whom was able quickly to dispatch two or three enemies who attacked him simultaneously would soon create panic among Israel's foes, while lending courage to their fellow soldiers of lesser prowess. "The Three" apparently were the most famous of David's combat troops, just as earlier David had become the most famous of Saul's warriors: "Saul has slain his thousands, and David his ten thousands" (1 Sam. 18:7).

The names of the men who comprised "The Three" are given in 2 Sam. 23:8–11, and two of the three are named in 1 Chron. 11:11–14. A comparison of the lists shows that confusion exists somewhere in the name of "the chief of the three," said in 2 Sam. 23:8 to be "Josheb-basshebeth, a Tah-chemonite," and in 1 Chron. 11:11 "Jashobe-am, a Hachmonite." (Many scholars regard "Josheb-basshebeth" in 2 Sam. 23:8 as an error of a copyist.) The two lists agree on Eleazar, the son of Dodo, but some editor or copyist of Chronicles dropped out the name of the third man, which the reader expects to be given at 1 Chron. 11:15.

Peacetime Uses of the Professional Army

The first duty of the king's professional soldiers was to protect his body. The next was to quell any rebellion, real or incipient, by dissident factions within the twelve-tribe empire.

But once David had pushed back the Philistines and enlarged his territory eastward and northward at the expense of Edomites, Ammonites, and Syrians, he had a whole new set of military problems, even in peacetime. For one thing, he had to create military and supply bases nearer to scenes of possible action than Jerusalem. Though not mentioned in connection with David's reign, the following cities, at a minimum, by reason of their strategic location, were almost certainly used to house an experienced commander-administrator and enough professional troops to form a regional military commission: Megiddo, Hazor, Bethshan, Succoth (as a forward base for campaigns against Syria), and Lachish (at the southwest corner of Judah). From such strategic centers very possibly border patrols and "intelligence officers" operated to keep an eye on defeated nations outside Israel's expanded borders. Occupation forces may have been required inside these foreign countries. Evidences of regional military commands under later kings is found in 2 Chron. 11:11–12 (Rehoboam) and 1 Kings 20:15–20 (Ahab).

These regional commanders probably had an ongoing line-of-command relationship with the tribal leaders of their region and the tribal commanders of militiamen units of 1,000 (possibly there were larger units also), so that David's scheme for providing the country with an organized militia, called up in rotation, would be carried out efficiently (see "The Army of the People of Israel," below). Conceivably training of tribal units was organized and directed by professional officers posted at such regional military centers.

Chariots under David

Under David's leadership, with its resulting territorial gains, Israel came out of the hill country into possession and military control of flat country, notably along the borders of Philistia, the Plain of Esdraelon, and along the routes from the Jordan fords northwards to Phoenicia, Damascus, and Mesopotamia. The use of infantrymen and slingers, perhaps with some archers, was not the most effective way to control such easily traveled routes. Chariots were. It is difficult to believe that David could have ranged far into Syria on level trade routes without any chariot force whatever. The well-known passage, 2 Sam. 8:3–4 (paralleled by 1 Chron. 18:3–4), in which

116. A chariot of the XVIIIth Dynasty in Egypt.

David hamstrung (KJV, "houghed"; modern "hocked") the horses captured from Hadarezer, except for 100, should not be regarded as evidence that David had no chariots at all, but either that his chariot contingent was up to its full strength, or that it needed only 100 horses to restore it to its full complement. Horses were an expense, in food, care, and stables.

In any case, since David and Joab were both military experts and totally practical men, we may be sure that in peacetime their troops were practicing chariot driving in simulated military actions, perhaps comparing Egyptian and Mesopotamian chariot models, and becoming well acquainted with their repair (*see* Fig. 116). It is reasonably certain that the use of chariots by Israel began with David. It was then greatly expanded by Solomon as almost a complete substitute for reliance on drafted foot soldiers, and chariots achieved their peak numbers in Israelite history during the reign of Ahab, king of Israel, who contributed 2,000 chariots—more than any of his allies—to the combined forces of Syrian and Palestinian kings in the battle of Qarqar in 853 B.C., in which the Assyrian king, Shalmaneser III, was turned back.

If David had a cavalry corps—fighting men riding an animal—they were mounted on mules, not horses. Mules were more suited than horses to ride to battle in the hill country because they were much more sure-footed and less fractious. It appears that not for well over another hundred years would any nation develop the stirrup and the spur that would give a man on horseback control over his mount's actions. (Horses were first ridden with a bridle as the only control.) Absalom rode a mule into battle (2 Sam. 18:9).

Recruits for the Professional Army During the United Kingdom

As long as David's fortunes prospered, there was no problem over recruits to fill manpower needs within his professional army. It was essential only that he pay them regularly and house them decently. Some recruits no doubt came from members of the royal family and its many collateral branches; from sons of officers already in the army; and from outstanding individuals in the Israelite militia, perhaps spotted by one of "The Thirty." Furthermore, good fighting men might come over from a defeated enemy, provided that their prowess and bravery impressed David's own mighty men. The other chief source was probably strong and brave young Israelites without wealth or property or prospects through inheritance, who found country life dull and were attracted to the military life.

Under Solomon there were no more victories in the field, in fact Solomon never fought a battle. With this lull in the military activity in the Near East, along with a burgeoning commerce along the international trade routes that crossed his empire on the land bridge between the historically great powers (*see* Fig. 1), Solomon built up the chariot force to patrol the highways and provide a highly mobile show of force at key points and wherever trouble might arise. We may therefore infer that recruiting in Solomon's reign leaned heavily toward men with experience with horses and chariots, or strong motivation to undergo training for the chariot corps. The opportunity for booty and glory became a lesser motivating force. Under Solomon, to be a soldier was to have a rather routine job in the military.

After the united monarchy split into two nations it became more difficult for the kings of Judah and Israel, especially the former, which was the poorer and less populous nation, to pay their own professional troops, and so recruiting fell off. Hezekiah's troops deserted during Sennacherib's siege of Jerusalem in 701 B.C.

Distinct Biblical References to the Professional Army

The following battles of David's reigns were fought by his regular or standing army (i.e., his professional soldiers) only: the capture of Jerusalem from the Jebusites (2 Sam. 5:6-10 and 1 Chron. 11:4-9); the battles against the Philistines in the Valley of Rephaim (2 Sam. 5:17-25), just west of Jerusalem; and the first campaign against the Ammonites (2 Sam. 10:6-14). In all these cases the combat area was limited, or thought to be, and the military requirements called for a relatively small striking force capable of carrying out orders with speed and of delivering a devastating knockout blow. The professional army also had to do most of the work in putting down Sheba's rebellion (2 Sam. 20:1-22).

In wars of movement, fought in a wider arena of action, the professional army was joined by the militia, as in the second campaign against the Ammonites (see below). In such cases Joab is portrayed as commander-in-chief of the military, Abishai as second in command; and some of the professional soldiers, notably "The Thirty," assumed command of the militia units. David clearly was in command during the campaign in Syria at the start of the second campaign against the Ammonites, and he resumed command again during the revolt of Absalom. In the battle that ensued, David divided his small combined forces into three units, one commanded by Joab, one by Abishai, and the third by Ittai the Gittite (= man of Gath, a mercenary).

The Army of the People of Israel (the Militia)

Professor Yadin regards the passage 1 Chron. 27:1–15 as a most important document for understanding the organization of the militia, the "drafted" army of male citizens twenty years and over. He views it as relating most decidedly to the organization of David's citizen-army and not as a theoretical blueprint never put into practice, nor a table of organization dating from the time of King Josiah over 300 years later, as others have suggested.

In a united kingdom, no longer a tribal league, David recognized (Professor Yadin suggests) that the old method of rallying several or all of the Twelve Tribes of Israel to provide fighting men was obsolete. This method had failed Israel in battles with the Philistines in the time of Eli, and the Ark had been lost. The Philistine troops were better trained, better armed. Calling up the tribes took too long; those troops that did appear were mostly untrained and badly led; tribal rivalries and bickerings over which tribe was being given the dirty work to do were endless. Their weapons were homemade and substandard. Besides, some tribes were larger than others, a fact that now had to be compensated for in any call-up system. The problem remained: David needed an army of militiamen to wage wars and defend territories in his enlarged kingdom, where the battles were no longer fought in the hills and valleys of Judah and Ephraim.

The answer to his problem may well be found in 1 Chron. 27:1–15, taken in conjunction with the list of tribal leaders that follows in vss. 16–22. Professor Yadin's interpretation of these passages is that each tribe organized as many units (say of 1,000 men each) of men of military age as the tribal population would permit. These tribal "home guard" units were commanded back home by officers tribally selected. Every month 24,000 men were called up, in a rotating system, not as individuals, but as (in our example), 24 units of 1,000 men apiece. Perhaps Dan (a small tribe) had only 5,000 men of military age. When the turn of these came for active duty, their contingent of 5 units would be joined by a contingent of 19 units from a much larger tribe. Thus differences in tribal population were taken account of, and tribal responsibility divided fairly.

When these 24,000 men reported for duty (probably at one of the several army base cities), their tribal commanders played a lesser role, for they became subordinate to a commanding officer, probably either one of "The Thirty" or a professional officer assigned by that military group. Other professional soldiers—infantrymen, slingers, archers, supply corpsmen, etc.—would be assigned to the regional corps for training the men throughout their 30-day tour of duty in peacetime. In wartime the units would be moved rapidly into the people's army, or army of Israel.

This system provided professional and cohesive leadership, disciplined training, and morale. It enabled David to build up a reservoir of trained citizen militiamen by taking them from their work and homes one month a year. It left a lot of authority with the tribes—for recruitment, for handling unusual hardship cases, for appointing unit commanders, and for organizing what we might call home-guard duties. And perhaps the tribes, without reference to the king, organized the rotating system so that no unit would be called up an unfair number of times, for example, right at the season of the grain harvest. The system had flexibility. In times of peace in all quarters of the empire the monthly call-up could be modified in some manner, such as having the units whose turn it was stay at home but in a state of alert, or perhaps engage in purely local drills. The call-up could be tempered to the actual military needs of the moment.

That there was some such system—one depending at root on an efficiently carried out census of all males—is strongly indicated by the account of the census David initiated and by his assignment of responsibility for it to "Joab and the commanders of the army" (2 Sam. 24:2). Most scholars regard the census as having a military purpose, and some go further and regard David as having knowingly or unknowingly transformed the Israelite idea of war from a holy war to an instrument of foreign policy. To accomplish this transformation David had to run counter to the tradition that wars were fought when necessary by a mass response to the call of a charismatic leader, i.e., one inspired by God to do so. David elected instead to institute a register for purposes of conscription as his method of building military manpower. Because this step meant abandonment of the traditions of a holy war, it was protested probably by some vocal elements among the people, maybe by Joab, and clearly by the historian (2 Sam. 24:1-9).

The Law taught (Exod. 32:32-33) that God kept a book, a register, of the members of the Israelite community; this belief is reflected in such diverse later Old Testament writings as Ps. 69:28, Isa. 4:3, Mal. 3:16, and Dan. 12:1. For David to put names on a register was to arrogate to himself one of the prerogatives of the God of Israel. Hence its sinful nature.

From the time of David's systematizing of the militia army by some form of conscription, the idea of a holy war in which Yahweh led His people lost all influence.

Units Within the Army

No table of organization showing the size and relationships of the units in either the professional army or the militia is given in the Bible. However, there are a few references to units composed of 10 men and of 50 (Exod. 18:21; Deut. 1:15; 1 Sam. 8:12; 2 Kings 1:11 ff.). There are many more references to units of 100 and 1,000 (e.g., 1 Sam. 17:18; 18:13; 22:7; 2 Sam. 18:1; 1 Chron. 13:1; 2 Chron. 1:2). In ascending order of size, these units are comparable to modern military units called the squad, platoon, company, and regiment.

By types of soldiers, infantrymen were the greatest in number, but slingers and archers were important components of the professional army and of the militia. They very probably were formed and trained by companies, which were then attached to the command of a larger unit. Later the drivers and fighting men of chariots comprised chariot units whose commanders in wartime would serve directly under the commander-in-chief.

If there was any use of cavalry during the period of the united kingdom, the cavalry consisted of princes, aristocrats, and officers riding *mules*, not horses. 2 Sam. 13:29, 18:9, and 1 Kings 1:33 support the use of mules as mounts. Horses ridden by men do not appear in ancient reliefs until military actions of a later period are represented.

The Professional Army Against the Ammonites

The Egyptians, the Assyrians, and the Babylonians have bequeathed to us many realistic representations of their military actions aganst different enemies—reliefs and friezes, sculptured and painted pictorial bands around the walls of buildings built to display them. An Egyptian relief at Medinet Habu glorifying Rameses III, for example, shows Egyptian troops engaging the Philistines, and in so doing gives us invaluable authentic, contemporary data on the weapons and uniforms of Israel's rival for control of western Palestine.

By contrast, archaeologists have unfortunately come upon no drawing or representation of the Israelites in action. The Israelite prejudice against representational art is probably a major reason for this (see ISRAEL AND THE DECORATIVE ARTS), and kings of enemy nations never, of course, showed Israel in any other guise than that of a vassal, suppliant king and as captives paraded before their conqueror. It is possible, however, to recreate the movement of the military forces in David's war against the Ammonites, as told in 2 Sam. 10 and 1 Chron. 19:6—20:3. A close reading of these nearly parallel accounts enables deductions to be drawn. First, both accounts read:

"He [David] sent Joab and all the host [or "army"] of the mighty men." (The term "the mighty men" is a code word signifying that David used his professional army. Contrast with 2 Sam. 10:17 and 1 Chron. 19:17, "He gathered all Israel together," "all Israel" being the code word for the militia, the people's army.)

The one notable contradiction in the accounts occurs in 2 Sam. 10:6 and 1 Chron. 19:7, where the former reads "foot soldiers," the latter "chariots." The former reading is surely the correct one, for no such numbers of chariots as 32,000 is ever even suggested in the boastings of the great king-warriors of the great empires in Near Eastern history. The Chronicles account in the same verse, however, supplies the enlightening words "encamped before Medeba" as the location of the Syrian troops. This is another key evidence as to what happened: Joab found himself caught between two enemy armies. How did this happen?

That David sent the small professional army suggests that he believed them capable of teaching the Ammonites a lesson for their humiliation of the members of his peaceful mission to them. David seems not to have known that the Ammonites had brought in Syrian allies. Professor Yadin proposes this understanding of what transpired, on the basis of the mention of Medeba as the campsite of the Syrian forces. He points out that there are three ford-crossings of the Jordan that may be taken for entering the region in which lay the Ammonite capital, Rabbah (Rabbath-ammon), located near the headwaters of the Jabbok River in Transjordan. The shortest route to Rabbah was via the ford at the north end of the Dead Sea. The ford next farther north was near Jericho, but the route eastward thereafter passed over rough terrain most of the way. The third ford was at Adamah, crossing into the Valley of Succoth, the route thereafter approaching Rabbah from the north, after describing a huge arc. This would have been the longest but the safest route. Joab, perhaps anxious to get the job over and done with, chose the shortest, the most southerly. This took him on a due easterly course most of the way, past the town of Medeba, and thence north to Rabbah. The Syrians let him pass by, and then followed him northward. The Ammonite army "came out of Rabbah and drew up in battle array; . . . the Syrians . . . were by themselves in the open country" (i.e., able to use their chariots, 2 Sam. 10:8) behind him. The nutcracker began to close on Joab and David's mighty men. Joab quickly split his forces, he himself leading an attack on the Syrians with a portion of the army before they closed in on him and robbed him of all freedom to maneuver or escape, while Abishai, leading the remaining troops, held off the Ammonites. Joab scattered the Syrian forces, and the Ammonites, seeing or hearing about the rout of their allies, retreated into their defensed capital. Joab, by prompt and decisive action, had saved David's professional army, whereupon he retreated to Jerusalem to plan another campaign.

The Combined Forces of David's Army in Action

David was not only a poet and king, but a highly-skilled military leader. He and Joab having been overconfident, David now devised a totally different strategy, based on a realistic assessment of the real danger to him in the foreign alliance—the Syrians. Hs intelligence agents must have reported to him that a league of Syrian city-states was readying an army to return to the aid of Rabbah. This time David called up the militiamen (2 Sam. 10:17, "all Israel") for what he foresaw as an engagement in open territory, requiring many more soldiers and supplies for a much longer campaign. He then led his combined forces across the Jordan at Adamah and into the Transjordan highlands. Thence, supplied from either Succoth or Mahanaim northwest of Rabbah, he turned not south toward the Ammonite capital, but north along the King's Highway toward Syria, anticipating the southward movement of Syrian troops. Here at a place named Helam, which biblical geographer Denis Baly believes may have been on the site of the later town of Alema, the battle was joined. The Syrians were routed. They made peace, paid tribute thereafter, and lost all interest in their old allies, the Ammonites. David was free to redirect his forces to an unhindered siege of Rabbah though he himself returned to Jerusalem, where, perhaps in his boredom, he encountered Bathsheba one afternoon.

When Joab and the professional soldiers were about to capture Rabbah, having done the hard, dangerous work of breaking down a city's outer defenses, he urged David to come and take charge of "the rest of the people" (the militiamen) and engage in the final action so that the capture of Rabbah would be a triumph of Israel's king and of the people's army, and not that of General Joab and mercenaries and fulltime soldiers (2 Sam. 12:26–31).

Supplies

As a boy David had been given food by his father to take to his older brothers, who were in Saul's army, encamped in the Valley of Elah, confronted by Philistines (1 Sam. 17:12–18). He also carried with him ten cheeses for the commander of the unit in which his brothers served. This is strong evidence that an Israelite army, until David's reign, had no commissariat. Citizen-soldiers apparently brought with them a supply of bread, grain, and cheese to start them off, and were then supplied to some degree by relatives back home. For the rest, they lived on what could be obtained freely or taken by force from fellow Israelites in the neighborhood of their campsite.

"David left the things in charge of the keeper of the baggage" (1 Sam. 17:22)—a kind of ancient quartermaster or supply sergeant, perhaps a trusted, overage soldier whose honesty was known to the commanding officer of the unit. These two evidences of a very primitive supply system probably reflect the actual situation in any Israelite army in the period between the settlement in Canaan and the establishment of an administrative system for military and civil purposes under David.

THE WEAPONS OF DAVID'S ARMY

After the breakup of the Hittite kingdom (toward the close of the 13th century B.C.) and the decline of the Egyptian empire, hastened by the arrival of the Sea Peoples on the southeast corner of the Mediterranean Sea, there followed a period of about 250 years in which evidences of how wars were fought in Bible lands are slim. Rameses III (c. 1198–1166 B.C.) created detailed portrayals of his land and sea battles with these newcomers—engagements which were inconclusive but which drained Egyptian resources. Thereafter, further sculptured and painted reliefs of comparable scope and exactness of detail would have to await the rise of the Assyrian empire about 900 B.C., whose kings wished to record their military exploits for posterity by means of monumental buildings.

The reliefs of Rameses III (at Medinet Habu) show us the weaponry of the Philistines, the chief of the Sea Peoples, who would soon become the mortal enemies of the Twelve Tribes of Israel. The Israelites had entered Palestine from the east at approximately the same time as the Philistines arrived on Palestine's Mediterranean coastline. It is from these Medinet Habu reliefs that we know that the Philistine soldiers wore feather-topped helmets and a coat of armor that covered the upper body, and that they carried a small round shield (Fig. 117). Unlike the Egyptians, they relied little on the bow and arrow, but were normally armed with a spear and a long, straight, two-edged sword.

The Iron Age was just beginning. The Philistines, though they did not introduce iron into Palestine (see e.g., Josh. 6:24 and 22:8; Judg. 1:19), knew how to work it and where to get it. Furthermore, their policy toward the hill-dwelling Israelites was to hold for themselves control of all metalworking in Palestine, thus making it difficult and expensive for their enemies to obtain weapons. This Philistine monopoly of metallurgy is recorded in 1 Sam. 13:19–22. It was broken by David's victory over the Philistines, aided by Philistine mercenaries wielding Philistine weapons. David knew well the value of metals suitable for military use (2 Sam. 8:8; 1 Chron. 22:3). Even iron tools were soon in use throughout his little empire (2 Sam. 12:31).

In describing the weaponry and the protective equipment of soldiers in

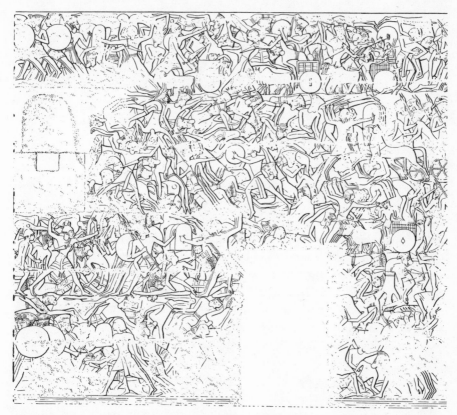

117. The battle between Ramesés III and the Philistines as seen on the relief at Medinet Habu, XXth Dynasty (1192–1160 B.C.). The Philistines wear feather-topped helmets with chin-straps and hold straight swords. The Pharaoh's army is composed of Egyptian soldiers and Sherden mercenaries (who are shown with disk-and-horn topped helmets and carry a round shield with straight sword).

David's army, scholars have first of all extrapolated from the Philistine usage as shown in the above-mentioned Egyptian reliefs. They then have combined such deductions with information given in the battles described in the books of Samuel, with archaeological investigations of the period known as Iron Age I (1200–920 B.C.), and finally with what illustrated monuments of the Aramaean city-states and Neo-Hittite kingdoms offer to our understanding of the subject. These reliefs date to about the last quarter of the 10th century.

The Offensive Equipment of David's Army

After David's reign was well established, the Israelite soldier in his army was equipped for battle with one or more of the following weapons: sword,

118. The round shield and straight sword of a
Sherden, one of the "Sea Peoples."

spear, javelin (also called a lance), bow and arrows, and sling. Before the
end of his reign David had almost certainly introduced the chariot.

The Sword. The sword used by David's infantrymen was a two-edged
straight sword, tapering toward a point (Fig. 118). The blade was thicker
along the midrib and tapered toward the sharp edges. It was carried in a
sheath attached to a belt around the soldier's waist. Some reliefs show the
sheath also supported by a strap slung over the left shoulder. This weapon
was for hand-to-hand combat, and was carried by archers and slingers, as
well as by spearmen.

The Spear. The spear of David's infantrymen was larger and heavier
than the javelin (see below). It was not thrown, as was the javelin, but was
used in a thrusting motion designed to pierce the armor and the body of an
enemy. The shaft was of wood. The spear's head, its piercing part, was
made of metal, shaped to receive the shaft in a socket-type union (Fig. 119).
Sometimes the other end was fitted into a metal butt, so designed as to enable the infantryman to thrust the weapon into the earth, to stand upright.

The Javelin. This weapon was smaller and lighter than the spear. A
javelin was thrown, not thrust, and thus may be thought of as a large
thrown arrow, with a sharp metal tip for penetrating (Fig. 120). The trail-
ing end or butt was weighted with metal to give the weapon better control,
balance, and striking power on impact. A well-known Greek representation
of an Aegean soldier preparing to hurl a javelin shows a cord wound around
a portion of the shaft, and a loop of the cord over the fingers of the warrior.
As the javelin was released, the unwinding cord would impart a spin to the
javelin that would increase its range and keep it on a steady flight toward its
target, just as a football spiraled by a passer's hand achieves its distance and
accuracy. A barrage of javelins hurled from some distance away into approaching enemy troops might rout them quickly. Men trained for javelin

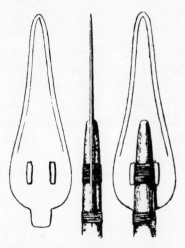

119. Spears sometimes had two holes pierced into the metal. These holes were probably used for fixing the wooden haft of the spear to the metal point.

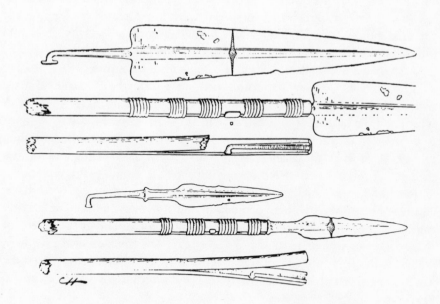

120. Javelin heads were affixed to the haft by inserting the tang into the split wood, and then by tying cords around the haft.

throwing would be equipped with several, which they carried in a large quiver.

The Bow. This weapon by David's time had developed into a relatively complex, tough, and elastic weapon known as the composite bow. Figure 115 shows how pieces of thin wood, animal tendons and sinews, and sections of animal horn were laminated and glued together to form an integrated "body" that would assume a double convex shape when put under tension by the taut string attached to both ends of the body. The archer increases this tension in the body of the bow by drawing back the string with his right hand, which must also control the base of the arrow in a shooting position. It is the sudden release of the tautened string that sends the arrow on its way to an aimed-at target.

The bow and arrow was a long-range weapon in Bible times, with considerable accuracy and power of penetration at a range of 300 yards, and of diminished accuracy and smiting power for another 300 yards. It was the development of the double-convex, composite bow that hastened the development of the coat of mail as a protective armor against the arrow.

Bows and arrows were a chief reliance of the defenders of the ramparts of besieged cities. A composite bow was an expensive item to produce, and so was treated with great care and kept in a bow case when not in actual use. Bows were manufactured in special workshops created by kings solely for their production. Undoubtedly, David had such a specialty shop into which he caused to be brought the various materials required.

Archers were specialists, but every army had to have them.

The Arrow. Arrows had three parts: the arrowhead, made of hard material, such as flint, bronze, iron, or bone; the body, made of reed or wood; and the tail, made of feathers. Sometimes the arrowhead was designed to be inserted into the body (a "tang"), sometimes to receive the body into its base (a "socket"). Various shapes and sizes of arrowheads and various methods of release, as depicted on monuments, are shown in Figure 121.

Reed had an advantage for the *body* in that it was strong, easy to shape, and readily furnished with an arrowhead and feathers. The *head* in David's time was generally of bronze, thicker in the middle, and of a variety of shapes, some of which are shown in Figure 121. The function of the *feathers*, which might be arranged somewhat differently by different arrow makers, was to keep the tail of the arrow from wandering off the direct course to the target.

Large numbers of arrowheads, of many different designs, have been found in Near Eastern excavations, attesting to the importance and wide use of the bow and arrow, especially in the defense of a city. Archaeologists have recently established classifications of arrowheads by size, shape, and weight.

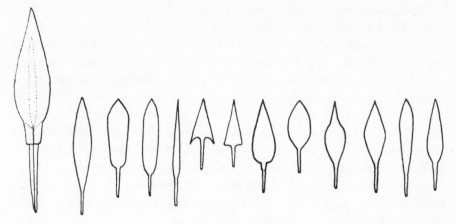

121. Various types of arrowheads.

For the layman, the point of these investigations is that ancient archers sought constantly to develop a more efficient arrowhead for the penetrations of the body armor worn by the enemy. So they tried many different designs. The *weight* of an arrowhead was important because of the relationship between the force necessary to draw the bow and the total weight of the entire arrow, including head, shaft, and feathers. For an arrow's effectiveness, *speed* was an important factor: how was the *weight* of an arrowhead and the entire arrow relevant to *speed*? Ancient archers seem to have sought an answer to this question also, and to have decided to use heavier arrowheads in the defense of cities (firing from city walls) than they would use in open-field battle, when they would be firing at longer range. (The heavier the arrowhead, the lower the velocity, affecting armor penetration negatively, and the shorter the distance of the arrow.)

Arrows were carried in a lightweight quiver designed to hold 20–30 arrows. An archer on foot carried these slung on his back or over his shoulder. An archer in a chariot had his quiver affixed to the outside of the cab.

The Sling. The sling has been known as a regular weapon of warfare from the Bronze Age to the 17th century A.D. Like the bow, it is another long-range weapon, and one requiring a highly specialized skill. It was a weapon used by herdsmen to protect animals. David, famed for his accuracy with this weapon (1 Sam. 17:50), would have had great numbers of slingers among his professional soldiers and among the militiamen. Slingmen were almost certainly trained in units and fought alongside archers. Benjaminites, at one time anyway, produced some remarkably accurate slingmen (Judg. 20:16). A good slinger was considered at times to be a match for an archer in distance, accuracy, and effectiveness.

The ancient sling consisted merely of an oval piece of leather or cloth, about 3 inches long, with leather thongs or rope cords attached to opposite edges. This patch or "hollow of the sling" (1 Sam. 25:29) cradled a round, smooth stone (Fig. 122). This the slingman held in his left hand (normally), and with his right hand he tautened the thongs. Raising both arms above his head, he released his left hand and swung the sling around his head several times to gain momentum. He then released one of the thongs or cords (the other being tied to his middle finger), allowing the stone to shoot forward toward its target. Achieving the accuracy required to become truly useful in battle demanded a great deal of training and constant practice.

Sling pellets, or "stones," could also be fashioned of clay, and could be ovoid as well as round. By postexilic times some slingstones were made of lead in molds.

The Chariot. By David's time the chariot had become a moderately sophisticated vehicle and weapon of war. In the 13th century B.C., for example, Canaanite chariots had their axles very little to the rear of the center of the chariot body. But by then the Egyptians, who learned about horses and chariots from their Hyksos invaders (c. 1700 B.C.), had developed chariot design to make it both lighter and more maneuverable. This they accomplished by moving the axle to the back of the body (*see* Fig. 116). To compensate they supported the body by a part known as the pole, made of a hard wood, which was attached to the rear crosspiece of the body frame. This pole, as it emerged from the forward underside of the body, curved upward and then forward between the two horses. A yoke for the horses was attached by nails to the forward end of this pole.

The wheels in the Egyptian chariots of c. 1200 B.C. were not only at the rear but were set at the end of axles which were about 10 inches wider than the body. Thus the wheels had a 5-inch clearance on each side.

Chariot wheels were now made with six spokes. They were about 3 feet in diameter. "Tires" were made of a wood such as pine that could be easily warped to the desired shape. This Egyptian model was a chariot of stability and considerable maneuverability. It was light enough to be carried by the crew of two when necessary. It would remain the standard of excellence for several hundred years.

The chariots of David's era can be thought of as a highly mobile platform for offensive fighting men. Quivers were affixed to the front or rear sides of the body to hold arrows for the archer. There was also a holder for javelins, should either driver or archer need a thrusting weapon or one to hurl. The wooden body frame, hitherto covered with leather, at least in front, began to be strengthened by bronze or iron armor plate to prevent

122. An Egyptian slinger from a painting in Beni-Hasan.

penetration of the chariot body by a piercing weapon, such as a javelin or arrow.

The manufacture of chariots could be carried on successfully only in workshops designed for that one purpose. Egyptian wall paintings dating from 1340 B.C. show that, even so early, the manufacture of the several component parts of a chariot was the work of specialized groups of laborers— one group making the rims of a wheel, another group the spokes, another assembling the wheels, etc., foreshadowing by many centuries the assembly line production techniques of modern automobile makers. Leather and metals and woods of various sorts had to be acquired and brought together at the place of manufacture. Chariots also required horses, and horses involved any king seeking a formidable chariot corps in additional complications and expenses. David probably knew all these costly pitfalls when he kept only 100 of the captured Syrian horses (2 Sam. 8:4).

Protective Equipment

The Shield. For protection, the sword and spear-bearing infantryman in David's army carried a small, round, convex shield, grasped in the left hand by a "handle" at the center of the reverse side (*see* Fig. 118). As the helmet and the coat of mail became more effective, the shield could be, and was, reduced in size to give the infantryman greater freedom of action. The shield had straps so that it could be slung over the back when he had no need for it or wanted freedom of his left hand or arm, as in climbing a rocky hillside or fording a river. The larger, rectangular Egyptian-type shields with round tops, like those lost by Rehoboam to Pharaoh Shishak (1 Kings 14:25–26), were used on royal ceremonial occasions only.

The typical fighting man's shield was made of wood and covered with leather. The top part that would protect his head and neck was often strengthened by nailing metal discs or plates on to the wooden frame. The small, light, round shield came to David's army from the Sea Peoples, via the Philistines and the Canaanites. It was a shield well-suited to hand-to-hand combat. Previous to the arrival of the Philistines, shields carried by Canaanite and Syrian infantrymen had been more rectangular.

Helmets. The exact design of Israelite helmets in David's time is not known. The best guess is that it was not basically very different from the helmets of other nations whose uniforms we know more about. That is, the helmet would be made of bronze, generally rounded to deflect arrows or sword blows, and perhaps pointed in a distinctive manner, or decorated, to facilitate identification of one's own troops in the midst of a battle (Fig. 123). It probably covered the ears and came down to the eyebrows. The experienced soldier, remembering how hot his head had been while he was marching and fighting in a previous campaign, would probably immediately cover the metal outside with some kind of insulating material, such as cloth.

Coat of Mail. This type of armor for the fighting man who did not carry a shield was standard in well-equipped armies of c. 1000 B.C., which David's army rapidly became. To visualize how the hundreds of small pieces of metal—often compared to fish scales—were laced together, see Figure 124.

123. A typical Assyrian helmet.

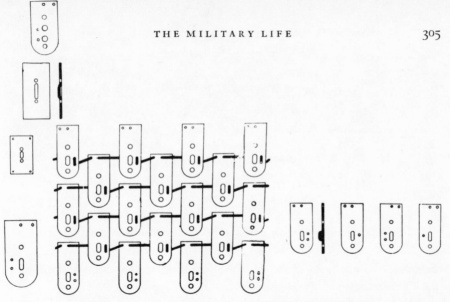

124. Scales of armor separated to show the lacing design.

This form of armor was sewed to a close-fitting cloth or leather shirtlike garment with sleeves nearly to the elbow. For fighting men in chariots, who could not use a shield and did not need to be fast of foot, coat-of-mail armor was also designed as a skirt to protect the abdomen and thighs. The vulnerable spots for the fighting man wearing coat-of-mail armor were at the crude joint of the sleeve to the chest garment (1 Kings 22:34-35) and in the gap between the upper and lower garment when the fighter was most active. A wide, close-fitting leather collar, stiffened by pieces of metal or studded with decorative nails, was normally worn to protect the throat.

The manufacture of coats of mail was complicated, and could therefore be organized only by the king.

Walled Cities. The capture of Rabbah (Rabbath Amman) is tersely described in 2 Sam. 12:26-31. In the first part of the siege Uriah the Hittite, husband of Bathsheba, met his death (2 Sam. 11) at the base of the city wall. Actually this city appears to have had two citadel-type fortifications, called "the royal city" (where the royal family and its court lived) and "the city of waters," which archaeologists believe was a heavily walled area surrounding the city's water supply. Joab with his professional soldiers destroyed and captured these strong points, and then urged David to come and take command of all the Israelite forces present at Rabbah, including the militia (being held in reserve by Joab), and "capture the city." By this phrase Joab probably meant assault those portions of the city still occupied by the Ammonite citizen-defenders. Probably this part of Rabbah was fortified also, but "the royal city" and "the city of waters" would have offered greater resistance because of their importance to the defenders and their stouter

125. The city of Lachish had two fortified walls and a double gate.

defensive design. Once these had been breached and occupied, the fate of the city was clear.

The walls of a city like Rabbah in David's time, before the development of the battering ram and the resultant wider use of massive, solid masonry walls in response to this new offensive weapon, were what is now called "casemated." Walls of the casemate type were in effect double walls, with an inner "skin" of shaped stone. Each wall was made of cut stone, and the space between them was divided into rooms by walls running at right angles to the outer wall. These rooms were used for storage, or soldiers' quarters, or filled full of rubble. An outer skin nearly 10 feet thick, dating to the 13th century B.C., has been found at Hattussas, capital of the Hittites; but walls of such massiveness were probably not encountered by Joab at Rabbah. Still, any well-constructed wall with wide ramparts for the defenders and with rectangular towers built on the outer surface of the wall to house and supply troops that could cover the walls between such towers with the fire of their archers, presented great difficulties to an attacking army.

In addition to walls and towers, a city also had to have gates (Fig. 125), and the larger the city the more convenient for citizens and tradesmen it became to have several gates and additional small entries (postern gates). Every entrance was a point of weakness, penetrable by a breaching action by infantrymen hacking at them with axes, ramming them with beams or logs (a true battering ram was a later development), or as a result of setting them afire with torches. While infantrymen would be trying such methods, the attacker's archers and slingmen would be ordered to keep the defenders on the city's walls and in its towers busy by showering them with arrows and stones.

The defenders were at an enormous advantage in a breaching action as long as the gates could be preserved intact, for they were free to drop or throw stones from the ramparts, as well as rain arrows down on anyone approaching the wall or a gate, while remaining relatively well protected themselves.

Other ways of attacking a walled city were by infantrymen scaling the walls, using scaling ladders; by breaking the wall at a weak or weakly-defended point by prying at stones with spears and swords, hammers and axes; by tunneling from a distance to the foundations of the wall and then undermining it. Several or all of these methods might ultimately be employed. Putting a city under a protracted siege, depriving it of further food or supplies, cutting off its water supply (as at Rabbah), and various ruses to lure the defenders out of the city into battle or to get a commando party inside the city to overpower guards and open a gate were the other means of solving the problem.

The Bible's account of the taking of Rabbah does not tell us just how its fall was brought about. What we may be sure of was that the final capture of the Ammonite capital was a bloody business, even more terrifying to women and children and old people than to soldiers inured to the sight of blood and the shrieks of the dying. Those who survived may well have wished themselves dead (see 2 Sam. 8:2; 12:31).

SOLOMON'S MILITARY BUILDING PROGRAM

In the absence of any significant threat along the borders of his empire, Solomon was, in a military sense, able to coast on the accomplishments of David. Solomon's orientation of the army toward the chariot has been discussed above (see "Chariots under David" and "Recruits for the Professional Army"). His military significance is as an administrator and builder of defenses. Solomon was uniquely free to direct his diplomacy toward commercial ends and his domestic policy toward the unification of his people and toward a public building program.

Solomon built "the wall of Jerusalem and Hazor and Megiddo and Gezer . . . and Lower Beth-horon and Baalath and Tamar in the wilderness, in the land of Judah" (1 Kings 9:15, 17–18). The cities mentioned by name as being rebuilt or more strongly fortified were located at strategic points in Israel and Judah. Only Baalath's site is less than certain. In addition to these, Solomonic fortifications have been found by excavation at Beth-shan, Lachish, and Ezion-geber.

"Cities for His Chariots"

Among the cities which Solomon rebuilt, the following were probably also chariot cities: Megiddo (*see* Figs. 104, 106), Gezer (*see* Fig. 102), Taanach, and Hazor. The phrases of 1 Kings 9:19, "and the cities for his chariots and the cities for his horsemen," most probably means not new cities but cities with new facilities to house the chariot contingents. No doubt, too, the capital city, Jerusalem, also had its chariots and horsemen and stables. According to 1 Kings 10:26, Solomon had 1,400 chariots and 12,000 horsemen (charioteers and stable hands), figures that are not seriously challenged by scholars, whereas "forty thousand stalls of horses for his chariots" (1 Kings 4:26) is regarded as an exaggeration. If the so-called "chariot stables" uncovered at Megiddo, a building now dated from the reign of Ahab and its function under dispute on the basis of its dimensions, was indeed a stable for chariot horses then it was capable of stalling no more than 450 horses for Ahab. Since each chariot required 3 horses, 2 for pulling it in action with 1 horse held in reserve, a complement of 150 chariots for Megiddo a truly strategic center is suggested. In which case 1,400 chariots for Solomon's army distributed among various chariot cities can be justified.

Under Solomon, with military supplies and food stores available at the cities listed above, the logistics of supplying a military force in action away from its regional center was made relatively simple by the reduction of the distances food and military matériel would have to be transported in a country only some 200 miles from top to bottom. Supply transport was by sturdy wagons pulled by oxen, pack asses, mules, and now for the first time by horses. There is no biblical record of any campaign waged by Solomon or his commanders, the greater empires being quiescent during his reign. What 1 Kings 11:14-25 records is the appearance on the Palestinian scene of an Edomite rebel with Egyptian connections and an Aramaean guerrilla leader, both operating on the outer fringes of Solomon's empire toward the end of his reign. The citizen army, the militia, was never called up, professional soldiers manning the various regional military centers and the outposts, and patrolling the trade routes.

In his building program Solomon vastly increased the dimensions of Jerusalem, largely to the north of the City of David, which occupied only the spiny promonotory at the SE. corner of the city later known to Jesus. Once his Temple and palaces were completed (or perhaps simultaneously), Solomon built defensive walls surrounding the new areas. Unfortunately, Jerusalem has been so thoroughly destroyed so many times since, and so completely rebuilt—and is today a busy modern city—that no traces of Solomon's fortification have been found except a massive buttressing with very large stones of a section of the Millo (1 Kings 9:15; 11:27), a terraced portion of the steep E. slope of David's Jerusalem.

At Ezion-geber Solomon developed a seaport on the Gulf of Aqabah for joint ventures in trade, with Hiram of Tyre as his partner, along the coastline of the Arabian Peninsula and NE. Africa. Ezion-geber seems also to have been the industrial center for the copper and iron dug from the mines of the Arabah and of Edom. Solomon controlled all N.-S. roads and the trade routes running W. from the desert lands into the Mediterranean world. From trade caravans he collected tolls (1 Kings 10:15). His mercantile agents ("the king's traders," 10:28) were everywhere. It may be said that Solomon's monopoly on international trade in his country was virtually total.

The Solomonic Gates at Megiddo, Hazor, Gezer

At Megiddo, Hazor, and Gezer, modern archaeological excavations, unlike those at Jerusalem, have found unmistakable evidences of the Solomonic fortifications built with forced labor referred to in 1 Kings 9:15. Megiddo, probably captured by the Israelites for the first time in David's reign (Josh. 17:12 and Judg. 1:27 nullifying Josh. 12:21), Solomon completely rebuilt, with a governor's residency and inner citadel, large public buildings, a protected access to water, and a surrounding casemate wall (see "Walled Cities" above) with a new and improved kind of main gate. Exact duplicates of Megiddo's gate have been found by archaeologists at Hazor and Gezer (see Figs. 101, 102).

As will be seen from the drawing of the plan of the Solomonic gate (see Fig. 101), the approach, the ramp-roadway, which was gradually inclined uphill, led a person walking or riding in a cart or chariot, or a contingent of enemy soldiers, toward the city gate at an angle that brought them under fire of bowmen on the city walls well before they came to the main gate. And an approaching party was forced first to pass through an outer gate where it could be scrutinized by sentries. Once friends or enemies passed this checkpoint they continued on to the main gate. What would be seen facing them were two square towers flanking a pair of massive wooden doors, opening outwards, the whole facade about 55 feet wide. Inside the much narrower opening (about 14 feet wide) a vehicle entered a covered area about 65 feet long, with another gate at the farther end. The sides of this vestibule were divided by massive piers into three chambers, which were used as guardrooms. The top of this elongated gate-entrance was supported by huge beams and served as a platform for defenders. In short, massive gate-entries like those at Megiddo, Hazor, and Gezer bristled with troops and weaponry.

The inner gates swung open into the city. Inside this final pair of gates was where the defenders would make a last-ditch stand if the gates were penetrated by an enemy force; the area was therefore kept free of buildings of any sort. Here was also the place of public assembly. Adjacent to it were the markets and other places of business. (See section, THE INDUSTRIAL LIFE.)

Population Trends

An important reason for the enlargement and strengthening of the fortifications of cities was the increase in commerce among the nations of the Near East in which Solomon was a leader. Trade thrives in cities. It leads to a growth in the population of cities as against villages, and it undercuts agriculture as the basis of prosperity. Peace and prosperity in ancient times always resulted in an increase in population. Israel's population boomed under Solomon, and so did the percentage of those who dwelt in cities (i.e., walled, defensed towns of whatever population). The quality of life changed also, for the old tribal institutions and customs began to disappear or be ignored.

Solomon's Corvée

All this building of Solomon's (not forgetting his Temple and palaces in Jerusalem) took money and required labor. Despite the improvement in the standard of living of his people, Solomon was not able to finance and complete his private and public works program without mortgaging (and eventually losing) some cities in Galilee on the border of Tyre (1 Kings 9:10-14) and without coercing some of his subjects into forced labor (1 Kings 5:13-18). David had made forced laborers of males of conquered nations (e.g., 2 Sam. 12:31), and Solomon plainly continued that policy—a common one in the ancient Near East. But the enormous demands of his ambitious building program were so heavy that he ultimately resorted to a forced-labor draft of his own subjects. A young Israelite of c. 950 B.C. was in far less danger of being called up into military service than into Solomon's corvée, his unpaid labor draft. This system was probably administered by the prefect of each of the 12 administrative districts Solomon established (1 Kings 4:7-19). This officer of the king was responsible for collecting the stipulated revenues and payments in kind for the maintenance of the king's household, bureaucracy, and military establishment. This administrative arrangement probably intentionally ignored tribal boundaries and tribal organizations, so that the people would be bound to their central government rather than to their individual tribe, and be made to look to Jerusalem in all secular matters as they were now expected to do in religious matters, with the completion of the Temple.

In this rigorous domestic policy lay the seeds of the dissolution of Solomon's empire as soon as conditions changed or his own despotic hand was removed from the machinery. Within a few years of his death the United Kingdom would be a shambles.

THE MILITARY LIFE DURING THE DIVIDED KINGDOM

The military history of the period of the Divided Kingdom was to be quite different from that of the nearly 80 years (c. 1000-922 B.C.) of the United Kingdom. There are moments in the 9th and 8th centuries when the two nations, Judah and Israel, enjoyed independence of action, and even periods of territorial expansion and revival of trade, especially when their kings acted in friendly alliance. But for the greater part of the two centuries, 922–721 B.C., at the end of which Samaria, the northern capital, fell to the Assyrians, their military history is one of border skirmishings between themselves and with the Philistines; of loss of territory across the Jordan Valley to the Ammonites, Moabites, and Edomites; and of reacting to the military initiatives of the Egyptians, Syrians, and Assyrians.

The way the armies of the two kingdoms were organized and fought their battles can only be partly recreated. But archaeological excavations of fortifications and the monumental art, particularly of the Assyrian kings, tell us a lot about the advance in both offensive and defensive warfare. Each military innovation, each change in tactics, brought its corresponding change in the life of the men who bore the burden of the decisions and actions of their kings. The remainder of this section will be concerned only with major military events and innovations that directly affected the lives of those who experienced the warfare of the period or changed the methods of attacking and defending that have been described above (see especially THE WEAPONS OF DAVID'S ARMY).

Comparative Strengths of Judah and Israel

Judah was definitely the smaller and poorer country. In population, such scholars as W. F. Albright and Roland de Vaux have suggested that, at the time of the schism, the Northern Kingdom contained perhaps 750,000 Israelites, and Judah only 250,000. These figures by themselves dramatize the disastrous loss Rehoboam suffered in the defection of the northern tribes. Furthermore, Israel was larger geographically, was wealthier, and produced more food. The only compensating advantages for Judah were its more homogeneous population (far fewer Canaanites within its borders, for example); its less exposed position to invasion by the rising powers, Syria and Assyria; and its own distinctive geography, which limited the routes by which it could be invaded.

By the end of Solomon's reign conditions were in marked contrast to the days when Saul had risen to the kingship as a charismatic hero, a warrior-leader, raised to rally the tribes against Yahweh's foes, like the tribal judges before him. The heroic age of David was nearly 40 years past. The idea of a "holy war" had now long since disappeared, not to reappear fully in the history of the Hebrew people until the time of the Maccabees in the 2nd century B.C. War had become merely the business of kings. Kingship, not very different from that of the neighboring nations, was firmly in place over the people. Samuel's words (1 Sam. 8:10–18), warning of the ways of a king, may in fact be an after-the-event critique of Solomon's despotic methods of ruling. Before his death Solomon had lost the allegiance of the northern tribes (see 1 Kings 11:26–40), on whom the burden of the forced-labor draft had apparently been placed more heavily than on his own tribe, Judah. Revolt was in the air. That Solomon's successor was as witless a person as Rehoboam only brought the United Kingdom to its end sooner rather than later (see 1 Kings 12:1–20).

Rehoboam's Cities for Defense

The position of the passage 2 Chron. 11:5–12 suggests that Rehoboam "built cities for defense" *before* the invasion of the Egyptian Pharaoh Shishak (2 Chron. 12:1–12), but the strong probability is that Rehoboam's program of refortification came *after* the destruction of many cities in both Judah and Israel by the ambitious founder of a new Egyptian dynasty. Shishak (Egyptian: Sheshonk I) set out to reestablish Egyptian authority along the Fertile Crescent, specifically to bring to heel the Israelite nations. In a whirlwind campaign his armies ravaged scores of Palestinian cities and forts (on his monument to himself at Karnak he claimed 150 places by name) from the Negeb as far north as Beth-shan and Megiddo.

The reasons for believing that Rehoboam rebuilt his defenses *after* Shishak's invasion are two: First, at Megiddo, to cite one example, the walls destroyed by the Egyptians were, on the basis of archaeological investigations, casemate walls. But the walls of the next stratum, built on the ruins of the casemate wall, are the solid massive walls that are known to have made their appearance in Palestine c. 920 B.C., which fits Rehoboam's reign (922–915) perfectly.

The second line of argument for the building and rebuilding of fortifications *after* Shishak's invasion takes this line: Assyrian war reliefs begin, c. 900 B.C., to feature a new weapon, the battering ram (*see* Fig. 131). Shishak's tremendous success, it is held by some historians, was due to his introduction of this weapon and his successful use of it to break down the typical casemate walls of the cities of Judah and Israel. In short, the appearance on the military scene of a new weapon of attack drew forth in reaction a new design for a stronger wall for the defenders. The result was the construction of solid walls, as much as 20 feet thick at their base, of very large, faced stones, and with corner towers and with bastions in the faces of the walls to allow the defenders to fire sideways (parallel to the face of the wall) on those who approached the walls, as well as to strengthen them.

Both logic and the archaeological evidence of the walls, then, indicate that Rehoboam sought better protection for his cities, his troops, and his people by providing some of his cities—especially the larger places—with the stronger type wall after Shishak's invasion and not before it. Fortunately for king and people, the Egyptian proved to be a flash in the pan. The available evidence indicates that Egypt was simply not strong enough at that time to establish an expanded sphere of influence in Palestine of an ongoing sort, as for example, by maintaining enough troops in key cities to keep Judah in vassalage.

The fortified places on Rehoboam's list (2 Chron. 11:5–12)—by no means all built to the new specifications—are mostly on or near the S. and W. borders of Judah. To the E. Judah was protected by the Dead Sea. To the N. lay Israel. The routes by which foreign invaders might enter the central highlands of Judah with some ease if not attacked en route were from Beersheba via the road running N. to Hebron; from Lachish on a road running E. to Hebron; and up the pass E. from Aijalon and Beth-heron into Benjamin, N. of Jerusalem. Many of the places on Rehoboam's list are on or near these entry routes.

Rehoboam must have lost the larger portion of his professional soldiers with Jeroboam's revolt, and the larger portion of his chariots. Among the items of his inheritance from Solomon and David still intact were the administrative frameworks within Judah for calling up soldiers, for a forced-labor draft, and for collecting taxes and supplies for the royal household. This apparatus Rehoboam undoubtedly used to its full extent to obtain the labor and funds required to refortify destroyed cities and to build new border forts.

Asa's Fortifications on the Border with Israel

Rehoboam's build-up of border fortifications was continued by his grandson, King Asa of Judah, amid his frequent skirmishes in Benjamin, N. of Jerusalem, with Baasha of Israel. On one occasion Asa was given a significant assist by Ben-hadad, king of Damascus in Syria (1 Kings 15:16–22). As vs. 22 makes clear, Asa issued a summary command to all able-bodied men of Judah to come to Ramah, remove Baasha's building stones, and take them to Geba and Mizpah, cities in his control in the disputed area. The walls at Mizpah that resulted from Asa's decision averaged 13 feet thick, and in places were 20 feet. In height the wall may have reached 35–40 feet, all of stone (at Megiddo, Rehoboam's wall was of brick in its upper portion). Partly preserved portions of Asa's wall today stand 25 feet high, without their tops.

The fortifying of Mizpah by King Asa makes two points with regard to the life within Judah c. 890 B.C.: a king of Judah (and of Israel, too) had the unchallengeable power to call up what manpower his kingdom possessed for military or forced-labor duties; and secondly that the kings of Judah were developing a kind of siege mentality, placing emphasis constantly on defense fortification, perhaps sensing realistically that their nation—only 50 miles from its N. to S. borders, and but 20 miles wide—not only had no enthusiasm for aggressive wars but had no capability to sustain a major effort, and hence no other viable military option.

Assyria and Its Army

With the coming of Tiglath-pileser to the throne of Assyria in 745 B.C., the Indian-summer period of the reigns of Jeroboam II of Israel (786–746) and Uzziah of Judah (783–742) came to an end. Tiglath-pileser first resolved his problems in his homeland by reasserting the Assyrian power over the Chaldean people of Babylonia south of Assyria. Then he pushed back his borders on the north and east, and finally began operations in northern Syria, west of the great bend of the Euphrates River.

If "Azriau of Yaudi," mentioned in a text chronicling Tiglath-pileser's reign, is Uzziah of Judah, as some scholars believe, then Uzziah headed a coalition of states similar to the one in which Ahab participated earlier, and an indecisive battle or encounter of some sort seems to have taken place in Syria in 743 B.C. By 738 Uzziah was dead and Tiglath-pileser was receiving tribute from Syrian city-states, Tyre, and Israel. From now on the kings of Israel would rise and fall in quick succession, as anarchy set in, culminating in virtual civil war (2 Kings 15:8–28). The burning question dividing the people was whether Israel should continue to be subservient to Assyria and pay tribute, or join a coalition of states, hoping perhaps for support from Egypt (see Hos. 7:11).

But it was not just the new Assyrian vigor and drive toward empire that brought Israel down. The social fabric of the Northern Kingdom was rotten, as the prophets Amos and Hosea make abundantly clear (e.g., Amos 5:10–13; Hos. 4:1–3): as a locus of loyalty and leadership the kingship had been destroyed by a succession of coups; the religion, too, had become totally debased.

King Pekah of Israel (737–732 B.C.) brought disaster upon his country and little less than that on Judah. An anti-Assyrian, he attempted to force Jotham and then Ahaz of Judah, who followed a neutral policy, into a coalition he and Rezin, king of Damascus, had formed. To that end Pekah and Rezin attacked Judah and besieged Ahaz in Jerusalem. The Edomites and the Philistines seized the opportunity to take sizeable bites of Judah's lands in the Negeb and in the Shephelah. Not surprisingly, Ahaz appealed to Tiglath-pileser (2 Kings 16:7–8; see also Isa. 7:1–8:15). The Assyrian, probably delighted to have a legitimate excuse for a new initiative in the west, in 734–732 simply overran all the offending parties, including the Philistines and Damascus, whose King Rezin he summarily executed. He also destroyed

Megiddo and Hazor and other fortified cities in Israel. Samaria escaped, probably because Hoshea murdered Pekah and paid tribute immediately. Now most of Israel's traditional territory had been stripped from Samaria's control, and only a small, roughly rectangular block of hill country south of the Plain of Esdraelon, consisting of Ephraim and Manasseh west of the Jordan, remained to her. The captured territory Tiglath-pileser divided into three provinces under Assyrian governors.

The Israelites were now introduced to an Assyrian policy already in effect elsewhere in Tiglath-pileser's empire; designed to prevent nationalistic uprisings in conquered territories: he removed large numbers of Israelites, especially of the educated and moneyed classes, and relocated them in far-away regions of the empire. Those removed were then replaced by captives from another region. Thus began the infusion of foreign, non-Israelite blood into the people of the battered Northern Kingdom—a process that would later cause Samaritans to be looked upon as foreigners, suspected, and even despised by Jews returned from the Exile (see Neh. 2:10, 19–20, etc.; Jesus's conversation with the Samaritan woman, John 4:9; and the Parable of the Good Samaritan, Luke 10:30–37).

The final disaster now struck the tiny and impoverished Israel. Hoshea, against what seems now to be the dictates of experience and prudence, withheld tribute from Shalmaneser V, son of Tiglath-pileser, perhaps thinking that the change in kings afforded him an opportunity to break away. Instead Shalmaneser arrived with forces that quickly took or occupied all that remained of Israel except Samaria, which he laid under siege in 724 B.C. Though Shalmaneser died in 722, his brother and successor, Sargon II, continued the attack on the fortress and completed its destruction in 721 B.C. Sargon recorded that he deported 27,290 of Samaria's residents. Their replacements are referred to in 2 Kings 17:24. The Northern Kingdom thus came to an end.

Assyria's military might was the result, first, of maximum utilization of every arm known to military warfare: chariots (Fig. 126) and cavalry bearing bows and spears for battle in open terrain, coordinated with infantrymen, archers, and slingmen afoot (Fig. 127); infantrymen, archers, and slingmen for attacks on defended cities, assisted by ingenious forms of battering rams and tower-platforms on wheels that brought archers up to the level of the defenders on the walls of a city (Fig. 128)—these in turn supported by labor-gangs of infantrymen who built ramps, filled in moats, brought up scaling ladders, and wheeled the siege equipment into position after the ground had been leveled or the slope graded. To defend archers and infantrymen better, the Assyrians devised larger and curved shields and shields with hooded tops (Fig. 129). Their archers wore longer coats of mail. Tunneling

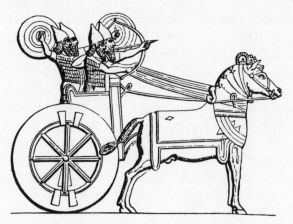

126. An Assyrian war chariot containing archers.

127. Assyrian slingers.

into cities, underground sapping of foundations of walls, assaulting gates and igniting their wooden doors, preventing food and military supplies from arriving—even psychological warfare, such as taunts, threats, and false promises of leniency upon surrender—were other Assyrian methods of breaking down the defenses of walled cities (Fig. 130).

The balance was heavily tipped in favor of the Assyrians by reason of their weaponry and their professionalism. They learned how to lay pontoon

128. This drawing from a relief in the palace of Sargon, Khorsabad (721–705 B.C.) shows spearmen, archers, shield bearers, battering rams of the four-wheel type being wheeled up artificial ramps.

bridges across rivers and how to enable an armed infantryman to swim across riding on an inflated goatskin bag. The small states of the west were forced into a purely defensive strategy: build strong city walls, assure a water supply, stock food supplies and arms, and defend the cities to such lengths that the attackers might find their capture too costly. For manpower, beyond a small professional corps, Israel's kings were now reduced to the inhabitants of the cities under attack and those who took refuge in them.

The walled-city strategy (combined with a more prudent foreign policy) might have worked tolerably well had it not been for the Assyrian version of the battering ram. But in the larger framework of time and geography the odds were almost hopeless that a little kingdom, through whose choicest land ran the greatest trade route of the ancient world, could stand up to—let alone stand off—the empires of richer, more populous lands, led by warrior-kings driven by pride and lusting for fame and riches.

The Battering Ram. When the battering ram made its first appearance in prehistory, it was nothing more than a large beam or a tree trunk carried forward to the object to be attacked on the shoulders of men; it was then lowered into their forearms, swung rhythmically, and finally crashed into a wall or door. In its next stage of development the beam was suspended like a pendulum within a frame which rested on rollers; when in position, the beam was swung by men toward the object of attack, and the blows repeated. Still later the battering motion was brought about by men pulling ropes, and

129. Types of shields. All are Assyrian except the Egyptian shield in the center.

the device was given a gable-shaped and finally domed roof that would absorb arrows fired from the walls of the city or deflect rocks dropped from directly above.

The Assyrian army was equipped with this last type of battering ram (*see* Fig. 130). But as Assyrian monumental art shows, it also employed a battering ram that *pried* instead of *battering*. Its function was to tear down rather than batter through. The forward or striking end of this second type was shaped like an axe-head (Fig. 131). This could be used to create or penetrate a chink in a wall, and then levered from side to side, gradually displacing mortar, a stone, a few bricks; and if allowed to operate for very long without counter-measures, ultimately destroying the fabric of a section of the wall, and hence causing its collapse. This might work not at all on the best-constructed section of a wall, consisting of carefully fitted, massive, faced stones, on whose parapet were soldiers well-supplied with stones and flaming brands to drop and arrows to rain down; but most cities had some older, weaker spots in their walls, or places where the defending soldiers could be brought under a withering fire of arrows, and these would be spotted and attacked at the right moment. The snout of this battering ram could apparently be rammed upwards at upper portions of walls. The upper halves or thirds of many city walls were constructed more flimsily or of less-

130. The attack of a city by the Assyrian army. Note the battering rams being pushed up the artificial ramps, the archers, the shield bearers, the slingers, the chariots, and the defenders of the city.

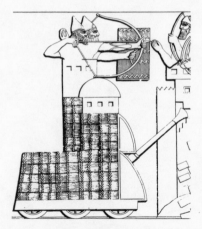

131. An Assyrian battering ram with an ax-shaped ram being used against a wall.

strong brick. In nearly all representations of the prying and levering battering ram it is shown working on a corner of the fortifications or near the top of a wall (presumably raised to such height by an earthen ramp constructed by infantrymen-laborers).

The battering rams of Tiglath-pileser and his immediate successors traveled (pulled by animals to the besieged city; pushed by men into position against the wall) on four wheels. From the turret hung ropes controlling the balance and action of the instrument. The domelike top of the turret, built to deflect rocks, was probably made of metal over a sturdy wooden frame. Inside a crew of men worked the ramming tool, sighting their target through small apertures. Some larger rams carried archers up in the dome who fired through small apertures.

To protect their battering rams and the men in them, the Assyrians designed movable towers that carried archers to a position facing the defenders on the parapets of the city. The function of these men was to take pressure off the battering ram by totally engaging the defenders.

Hunger and the gradual attrition of the strongest defending males worked on the side of the besiegers. Providing the commander of the attacking army could afford to keep his men on the site, he could expect the defense to become progressively weaker, until finally his men could almost literally pick the city to pieces. At the end the old and the maimed could expect to be put to death and the strong and intelligent survivors to be carried off into captivity.

Such was Samaria's fate.

The Fall of Jerusalem

The kingdom of Judah, after Assyria's destruction of the Northern Kingdom, escaped a similar fate twenty years later, when Sennacherib in 701 B.C. lifted his siege of Jerusalem after imposing harsh peace terms on King Hezekiah. This king, much praised for his piety (2 Kings 18:1–7; 2 Chron. 29:1–31:21), had joined in a general rebellion around the Assyrian Empire in an effort to end his vassalage after the death of Sargon II. For his rashness Hezekiah had forty-six of his fortified cities destroyed, if Sennacherib's own account can be trusted, with much loss of life; a strip of territory taken from Judah and returned to the Philistine city-states, which had not rebelled; and Temple treasures seized in partial payment of additional tribute.

Despite this lesson, Hezekiah apparently tried again to escape Assyria's grasp in about 690 B.C. when Sennacherib was in trouble in the eastern part of his empire. This time the Assyrian again destroyed many forts, but while besieging Jerusalem a second time, with Hezekiah determined on resistance, was diverted by the approach of an army under the Egyptian Pharaoh, Tirhakah. Sennacherib then went back to Syria, for reasons far from clear (see 2 Kings 19:7), where he lived another seven years.

Hezekiah's son, Manasseh, throughout his long reign (687–642 B.C.), prudently remained a loyal vassal to Assyria, which, under Esarhaddon, son of Sennacherib, destroyed Egyptian capability to make war or trouble outside its borders. Whatever else Manasseh may have done (2 Kings 21:1–17) his country enjoyed peace throughout his reign. To the small farmers, the raisers of sheep and goats, and the vine and fruit-tree husbandmen who made up the greater part of Judah's small population, peace, despite the social inequities of the times, as sketched in the previous century by the prophet Micah (e.g., 2:1–2), was no small blessing.

Now, however, the division within Judah that had existed since the time of Solomon between the people of the land and the city-dwellers—which meant Jerusalem—was becoming ever sharper. In the capital lived the princes, the king's bureaucrats, the powerful commercial figures, the great absentee landholders, and the priests who cared more for their Temple ritual and perquisites than for justice or mercy. It was in Jerusalem that men vied for wealth and influence, and formed pressure groups to urge this or that foreign policy on ineffective kings who dreamed of former royal glories. More and more the people of rural Judah were simply being used—and abused—by Jerusalem. The population of Judah, W. F. Albright estimated, had reached its peak about 750 B.C. at 250,000; it was now in rapid decline. The men called up to arms were spread among the border forts, walled cities like Lachish, and the royal city, Jerusalem. The days of Solomon's chariot army had long since passed. There is a colorful commentary on the shrinking size of the army back in the days of Hezekiah in 2 Kings 18:23, where the Rabshakeh (cupbearer of Sennacherib) taunts the men on Jerusalem's walls: "Come, now, make a wager with my master the king of Assyria: I will give you two thousand horses, if you are able to set riders upon them." At that time Judah could no longer afford to buy and keep the horses or train charioteers and riders. Her territory had shrunk back from the plains into the hills in which the Israelites had first found a footing in the days of Joshua. Furthermore, what with Hezekiah's disastrous attempts at rebellion and, later, Manasseh's docile tribute-paying, little Judah was continually strapped.

In a surprisingly short time, however, the built-in problems of an empire stretching in many directions and containing many conquered peoples awaiting an opportunity to settle old scores became more than the Assyrians could handle. In 626 B.C. Nabopolassar of Babylon managed to achieve independence and began what scholars call the Neo-Babylonian empire. In 612 B.C. the Medes and Babylonians together captured Nineveh (applauded in the book of Nahum) and the Assyrian domination of the region was shattered. The remnants of her former military might were now concentrated at Haran, in the region of the Upper Euphrates River.

While Assyria was fading, back in Egypt a new dynasty was beginning to hanker again for power along the trade route to Syria, and in Judah King Josiah managed to bring back under Judah's control much of the former Northern Kingdom, so weak had Assyria's presence there become. Josiah also introduced sweeping religious reforms. The foreign policy interests of Egypt and Judah clashed: Egypt wanted Assyria supported to prevent the further expansion of the new power in Mesopotamia and herself to control Syria and the Great Road to Egypt. Josiah wanted Assyria destroyed forever and dreaded being caught between an allied Assyria and Egypt. In 609 B.C., when Pharaoh Necho II was making one of his annual troop movements north on the Great Road to support the Assyrians in the region of Carchemish, King Josiah attacked him at Megiddo and lost his life. The details given in 2 Chron. 35:20–24 are meager, and those in 2 Kings 23:29–30 even more so. Perhaps Josiah had hoped to trap the Egyptian forces in the pass through the Carmel mountains which leads to the Plain of Esdraelon, but that is surmise. His being killed by an arrow while in his chariot suggests rather that the engagement was fought in open terrain. In any case, Judah's last chance to revive its long-term chances of survival perished with the beloved Josiah, and Judah now became vassal to Egypt.

Necho's forces were destroyed by Nebuchadnezzar at Carchemish in northern Syria in 605 B.C., one of the decisive battles of history. The entire southwest portion of the Fertile Crescent lay bare for the Babylonian taking. Jehoiakim, Egypt's puppet, fell in line, but about 600 B.C. thought he saw an opportunity for a revolt against Nebuchadnezzar (2 Kings 24:1)—a costly miscalculation. As Nebuchadnezzar was on his way west with an army in 597 Jehoiakim died, perhaps by assassination, perhaps in a military skirmish with marauders from the desert to the east who had been egged on by Babylon to harass Judah. Under the young King Jehoiachin, Jerusalem quickly surrendered to Nebuchadnezzar, and the royal family, soldiers, and leading citizens, 10,000 in all (2 Kings 24:14), were deported to Babylon. Jeremiah, in his account (52:28), sets the figure at "3,028 Jews" but this may refer to males only, which with wives and children might well come to the larger figure. The treasures of the Temple were again lost.

Nebuchadnezzar set on the throne of Judah the uncle of Jehoiachin and brother of Jehoiakim, giving him the throne name of Zedekiah. He was a weakling (Jer. 38:5, 19) and his advisors were soon plotting rebellion with Tyre and Sidon, Ammon, Moab, and Edom (Jer. 27:3), while Egypt as usual insinuated promises of help. Jeremiah, in chs. 27–29, details the follies of thinking and actions that he strove to prevent at the royal court. Without any observable consideration of the military risks or assessment of the manpower realities, rabid nationalists took the tiny nation down a suicide course.

In January 588 Nebuchadnezzar began his siege of Jerusalem and began destroying the outlying fortified cities. That summer he had to lift his siege for a while to turn back an Egyptian force, which promptly scurried back to Egypt. Eighteen months after his first appearance Nebuchadnezzar had reduced the city to the point of starvation and had simultaneously broken down enough of the walls by the skillful use of siegeworks and siege weapons to make an entry into the city in force.

Exactly which wall or walls of Jerusalem were breached cannot be determined today. Scholars are not certain exactly where the walls of the north stood at any specific period of Jerusalem's history. But since the slopes on the east and south sides are steep, an attack from those directions is ruled out. On the northern side, the slopes are gentle. This is the direction favored as the one used by the Babylonians.

The method used by the Babylonians to breach the walls was probably the same as that used by Sennacherib in his destruction of Lachish in 701 B.C., dramatically pictured on the walls of his palace in Nineveh, some slabs of

132. The siege of Lachish as drawn from the reliefs of Sennacherib's palace at Kuyunjik (Nineveh) (704–681 B.C.). Note the city gate, upper right, being attacked by battering rams, archers, shield-bearers, spearmen, and slingmen. The captives are being led out of a gate near the center of the drawing. Some of the city-dwellers have been impaled upon stakes outside the city.

which are now in the British Museum (Fig. 132). Preliminary to any all-out assault on a well-fortified city advantageously sited for defense was the filling in of a moat or fosse to create a level causeway leading to the selected points of attack, or the building of a wide ramp that would reduce the gradient and permit wheeled battering rams to be moved into position against the walls and remain there.

In either case, rocks and earth had to be brought in for fill, and when a roughly graded ramp had been made, wooden "tracks" for the battering rams and attack towers were laid on the surface. The most expendable labor-infantrymen were employed in this dangerous construction work. Shield-bearers provided them protection as best they could, using the large rounded and the top-angled shields that the Assyrians developed for such work. The wood for the surface came from trees cut down in the vicinity of the besieged city (see Jer. 6:6).

As the Lachish reliefs show, when the Assyrians (and the Babylonians also) began an attack using battering rams, they employed every weapon in their arsenal in support: archers and slingmen, from behind the action near the walls, would rain arrows and stones on defenders on the towers and walls, making it difficult for them to concentrate their counterattack on the battering rams. Though defenders had improved their own positions on the parapets by use of crenelated tops of walls and arrangements of metal shields to give them partial protection, nevertheless the battering ram and its partner, the movable tower bringing archers to close range, had tipped the balance in favor of the attackers.

At some point, on some day, a piece of wall would begin to come down, a gate would become weakened, and the defense would show a poor reaction to an attack somewhere on the perimeter. Now the Assyrians or Babylonians would throw assault troops into action. Scaling ladders would be set up against a part of the wall. Arrows and stones would fill the air above them, while infantrymen bearing swords or spears would race up the ladders. Once a few were over the top and engaging the defenders, the victory had been won. For the remaining defenders and inhabitants of the city—disaster.

In some such way, Jerusalem fell.

A SOLDIER IN THE ARMIES OF OMRI AND AHAB

It may help to visualize the life of a ninth-century soldier in Israel if the hypothetical career of one rather fortunate young man is described. Let him be a Benjaminite, born about 900 B.C., named Jarah. Let Jarah have no prospects for the future because his family has lost its property during the border skirmishes between Asa of Judah and Baasha of Israel. But Jarah had an uncle who once fought for Israel under an officer he admired named Omri, and Omri has become a general. So Jarah became a professional soldier under Omri's watchful eye, with prospects of becoming a member of Baasha's royal household troops, with barracks in the citadel at Tirzah, the northern capital.

But Baasha died (877 B.C.), and Jarah and many of the younger professional soldiers had only contempt for Elah, the drunkard prince who succeeded to the throne. So Jarah asked Omri to take him with him to the siege of Gibbethon, a strategic border outpost near the great coastal highway that had slipped back into Philistine hands since the United Kingdom split in two. While Omri, Jarah, and some Israelite troops were trying to capture Gibbethon, another officer, Zimri, who commanded that half of the king's chariot force that headquartered at Tirzah, murdered Elah while he was "drinking himself drunk in the house of Arza," his royal steward (1 Kings 16:9–10). Zimri then killed all of Baasha's family.

Jarah, devoted to General Omri, was among the first to declare loudly that if anyone deserved to be king over Israel it was the competent Omri, and soon the army at Gibbethon declared Omri king, with a great shout of acclamation and oaths of allegiance. So began the long fighting career of Jarah.

How Omri defeated Zimri at Tirzah and outlasted Tibni, another claimant to the throne, is told in 1 Kings 16:17–22. By the time Omri had full title to the kingship, Jarah was one of his staff officers and a friend of Prince Ahab, who was of about the same age. They both enjoyed driving Omri's new and improved chariots and practicing shooting their bows and arrows while careening down a highway or across a field.

Omri brought to the throne an intelligent and well-reasoned policy; he wanted domestic peace; friendly relations with Judah; commercial ties with Tyre, home of the great merchants of the Eastern Mediterranean; and he wanted those countries on his eastern borders—Ammon and Moab—to be subservient to Israel and break relations with the Arameans to the north. Now Omri was carrying his policy out. In a reign that probably lasted only eight years, with the help of patriotic and enthusiastic young men like Jarah, he accomplished so much that a hundred years later Israel was called by the Assyrians "the land of the house of Omri," even though his dynasty ended after only thirty-five years. The Book of Kings, which is interested only in the religious history of God's people, disposes of Jarah's hero in just fourteen verses.

Omri decided to build a new capital in a much stronger location. He picked "the hill of Samaria" (1 Kings 16:24) and built there a city so strong that the mighty Assyrians needed nearly three years to bring it to its knees (721 B.C.). Jarah by now had become a captain in Omri's palace guard. Very possibly Omri made Jarah an officer over one of the forced-labor gangs (mostly slaves captured in battles with Ammonites and Moabites) that were moving the huge blocks from the quarries into position in the walls or buildings of a brand-new city on a hilltop (see Fig. 108). Directing the technical aspects of the building were Phoenician masons, descendants of those first employed in Israel by Solomon in his Jerusalem building projects. Some of the walls of Samaria were the sturdiest ever built in Palestine. Ultimately, under Ahab, the city would be fortified by two enclosure walls, the inner one solid, the outer one in the casemate style, but with most of its chambers filled as solidly as possible with rubble.

Modern archaeologists have found traces of other walls on a terrace below the summit, and possibly another wall in Bible times surrounded buildings on lower slopes of the hill. The city has been rebuilt so often, from the time of Sargon of Assyria to the late Roman period, 4th century A.D. (when older stones were used as a quarry), that the reconstruction of Israel's capital is almost impossible.

Jarah, we may imagine, next became commander of a chariot company of fifty, sometimes quartered at Samaria, but more often at Megiddo or Taanach. In peacetime—which was most often now—Jarah's company patrolled the highways running from the border of Tyre near Acco, north of Mt. Carmel, across the Plain of Esdraelon to the fords of the Jordan and south into the hills of Manasseh to Samaria. One time he was part of the escort that brought Jezebel, daughter of the Sidonian king, Ethbaal, to Samaria, with her husband, Ahab, the heir apparent—a marriage Omri arranged to cement his friendship and commerce with the Phoenicians. Later Jarah would be disturbed by the presence in Samaria of so many strange-looking men, priests of Jezebel's god, Baal-Melkart; but as a loyal officer he would regard that as Ahab's business, not his.

Omri died suddenly of natural causes, and undoubtedly (as was the custom) his body, fully dressed in his royal robes, was carried on a bier, on the same day as his death, out of the city he had built. Our Jarah was one of the many officers who controlled the grief-stricken people as they pressed in upon the parade, led by wailing and chant-leading professional mourners. Jarah knew that Omri would be carried to the royal burial chambers he had had hewed from the easily cut limestone rock for family use, where he would be laid, uncoffined, on a slab in a niche dug horizontally into the far wall of the chamber. Jarah, too, mourned the passing of the great king; but Ahab had showed brains and energy, and so Jarah was unworried, not being perceptive enough to see the division within Israel being caused by the influence of Phoenicia, the new luxury for the upper class, and the ease with which many people—especially city folk—came to accept the worship of Jezebel's fertility gods, Baal and Asherah, or to tolerate that worship beside the worship of Israel's Lord.

For Jarah, wars under Ahab's leadership followed, first with Ben-hadad, king of Damascus, an Aramean city-state that was constantly annexing, whenever conditions allowed, as much of the farmland region across the Sea of Galilee as it could. Finally, after Ahab had defeated his rival twice, Ahab made a generous treaty with him which the prophets of Israel did not care for, thinking that Ben-hadad should be executed immediately in accordance with their revived concept of a "holy war." When this war was over, Jarah was promoted to commander of a contingent of 150 chariots.

Ahab, in his alliance with Ben-hadad, was warned of the westward movements of an Assyrian army under King Shalmaneser III. Ahab assembled all his chariots and ten thousand infantrymen and joined Ben-hadad and kings of other Aramean city-states such as Hamath, farther north than Damascus. Ahab's chariot force, inherited from Omri, had grown across the years until it was by far the largest among the allies. At Qarqar, not far from Hamath, on the Orontes River, perhaps 150 miles north of Hazor, Ahab's most northerly strong city, the allies intercepted Shalmaneser.

Ahab had used horses to pull some of his supply carts (as well as oxen and pack-asses), and had a few cavalrymen, controlling their horses by bridle only, without saddle and stirrups, mostly for scouting purposes. Jarah observed that the Syrian armies used their cavalry to carry fighting men—archers and spearmen. He noticed also that they could not do much fighting while the horses were moving at high speed or over rough ground because of the need to keep one hand always on the bridle. Still, he could not miss seeing that a horse carried a fighting man quickly from one part of the battlefield to another, and that, like a chariot advance, no infantrymen without heavy support from archers could possibly stand up to a massed charge of the cavalry.

The battle of Qarqar (853 B.C.) was joined in open terrain—one of the great battles of ancient history. Though Shalmaneser claimed a victory in his royal records, he did in fact turn back and busied himself for most of the rest of his reign in consolidating his enlarged lands east of the great bend of the Euphrates. From the point of view of the smaller western nations, this would be their high point in military might against the Mesopotamian nations, and never again would their alliance be so general. But the long view of history was not available to Jarah.

The Assyrian army at Qarqar contained (as did most armies of the era) three components: infantrymen, cavalry, and chariots. Their infantry had but two components: spearmen and archers, both also equipped with swords for hand-to-hand fighting. Slingmen do not appear in Assyrian war art until the time of Tiglath-pileser, who learned the uses of slingshot from his enemies, a hundred years later. The main firepower came from archers, who used a strong-looking composite bow (*see* Fig. 115) and wore long coats of mail to protect their bodies while their hands were occupied with their weapons. In an attack on a city (in contrast to a battle in open terrain) each archer was paired with a shield-bearer, also dressed in mail, who used a round shield to protect his archer's head and face. In hand-to-hand fighting in the open or scaling a wall, the spearmen bore the brunt of the fighting. Their straight two-edged sword was carried from the shoulder, but was also fixed to a belt. They did not wear mail, but carried a shield, small and round at this time, on their left arm. Shalmaneser's spearmen and archers wore conical helmets that came to a point. Their weapons and defensive equipment were not so much different from those used by David's infantrymen and archers, but were of a uniform and a higher quality, and of improved design.

Perhaps, after burying their dead, Ahab and his commanders, like Jarah, on the way home from Qarqar shared their impressions of the uses the Assyrians had made of their chariots and cavalry. The chariots of Shalmaneser were but little different from their own except in ornamentation, but the Assyrian cavalry were better trained fighting men than their counterparts in the allied army. At one point in the battle Jarah noticed that the Assyrians supported a hard-pressed infantry company by delivering, seemingly out of nowhere, a contingent of archers via horseback. This no doubt gave the battle-tired commanders something ominous to think about.

Now our chariot commander Jarah hoped for a long era of uninterrupted peace, but after only three years Ben-hadad and Ahab fell out again over territory both wanted to control in order to assure enough food for their growing populations—those lands east of the Sea of Galilee. The city of Ramoth-gilead, across the Jordan east of Beth-shan, in the one-time tribal territory of Gad, was the focus of action. In Solomon's day it had been the city of residence of the prefect of his sixth administrative region. It had slipped out of Israel's hands when Ben-hadad attacked King Baasha at King Asa's instigation (1 Kings 15:20). Probably Ahab thought it had been promised to him by the terms of his treaty with Ben-hadad (1 Kings 20:24) and doubly so for his help against Shalmaneser. Furthermore he seems to have been confident he could seize it without much trouble, especially if he could get his ally, King Jehoshaphat of Judah, to join him in the campaign. Jehoshaphat was willing, and their joint efforts to obtain a word of the Lord from all the prophets to sanction the campaign are told in 1 Kings 22:1–28. The battle took place on a plain near Ramoth-gilead, and during the furious action of the opposing chariot contingents, an arrow fired almost at random (vs. 34) pierced Ahab's chest where the separate parts of his coat of mail did not quite cover him. The wound was mortal, but his life lingered. Ahab ordered his chariot driver to drive from the battlefield to a slope in the rear, where, propped up, he could watch the action. In the afternoon, the battle still undecided, Ahab died. Word of his death soon spread throughout the forces of Israel. Commanders like Jarah were totally disheartened: they quickly ordered a cessation of the attack, and the entire army headed home, some of the veteran professional soldiers accompanying the body of their dead king to his burial place in the tomb with his father.

A faithful, brave soldier and charioteer like Jarah would naturally have been one of those who watched over the corpse of the king to the end. We may well imagine that, weary and heartsick and sensing that an era had ended, he sought the quiet of retirement from the army of Israel—in the home of a brother, or perhaps a widowed sister; and that the new king, Ahaziah, gave him a purse of money and a horse or a mule, as a reward for his some thirty years of distinguished military service to the house of Omri.

THE ROMAN PRESENCE

Before the Romans came to Palestine in 63 B.C. the Jews had known a succession of overlords. As a defeated, subject people, they enjoyed no military privileges whatsoever, but neither were they forced into military service by their masters. There was in effect no indigenous "military life" in Judea or elsewhere in Palestine from 538 to 168 B.C.

The Persians

In 539 B.C. Babylon fell to Cyrus, founder of the Persian Empire, and a year later Jews held in Babylonian captivity were allowed to return to their homeland and to rebuild the Temple destroyed nearly fifty years earlier (Ezra 1:1–4; 2 Chron. 36:22–23). The Persians were the most benign of the ancient conquerors, and the Jews back in Judea, though a subject people integrated into the empire, were allowed a large measure of participation in local government and given complete religious freedom. This government evolved into a theocracy headed by the High Priest, who held both religious and secular power and who of course, resided in Jerusalem. The only "army" consisted of the Temple police.

During this period the country once known as Judah came to be known as Judea, a Greek name meaning simply "land of the Jews." This name first appears in the Bible at Ezra 9:9. As a province within the Persian empire and later the Hellenistic Greek kingdoms of Syria and Egypt, Judea was essentially a geographical term, referring to a small area, hilly country, roughly a square in shape, with Jerusalem at its center. To the south it extended only as far as Beth-zur, a town lying between Bethlehem and Hebron, the historical capital of the territory of the tribe of Judah. Hebron and the Negev lands southwards were for a long period controlled by Idumeans (formerly known as Edomites). Later Judea would be greatly expanded by its Hasmonean priest-kings, and under Roman rule the province of Judea would have a still different configuration.

The Greek Seleucids and Ptolemies

After the Persians as overlords of the Jews came the Macedonian Greeks, following Alexander's victory at Issus in Syria in 333 B.C. On Alexander's death in 323 B.C., his empire was divided among his generals. The two who are of relevance to the life of the Jews were Seleucus and Ptolemy. Seleucus took the title of king in 305 B.C., his kingdom coming to be known as Syria, with its capital at Antioch. One of his policies, designed to help unify a kingdom comprised of many peoples, was to establish military colonies throughout its extent (Scythopolis built on the ruins of Beth-shan was one such; see "The Decapolis" below). Another policy was to introduce Greek philosophy, literature, and architecture in the form of such Greek institutions as the outdoor theater for dramas and the gymnasium for physical education and training in military skills as well as for public lectures. This Hellenistic culture, emanating from both Syria and Egypt, impinged very quickly on the Jewish tradition.

Egypt, after Alexander's death, fell to a general named Ptolemy. He also took the title of king in 305 B.C., calling himself Ptolemy I Soter ("the Savior"), and founded a new Egyptian dynasty known thereafter as the Ptolemies. He controlled Palestine from 320 to 311 B.C., when it was transferred in a peace treaty to Seleucus; but the Ptolemies regained control in 301 and maintained it until 198 B.C. During most of the 3rd century relations with the Jews were cordial and the control as benign as that of the Persians. It was at this time that the Egyptian city of Alexandria grew and flourished, both in international trade and in Hellenistic culture, and here a large colony of Jews prospered. It was during this period that the Septuagint, a translation of the Hebrew Scriptures into Greek, was prepared by Alexandrian Jewish scholars. That such a translation should be required for Jewish use is a major evidence of the extent of the influence of Hellenistic culture on Jewish life.

From 323 to 198 B.C. it may be said that the Greek kingdoms on either side of Palestine—whichever one ruled the country—attempted to Hellenize the Jews, to assimilate them, or to transform them into something "western" or "non-Jewish," but without resort to force.

The Maccabean Revolt

Before the end of the 3rd century B.C. the calm began to be broken by wars between the Seleucid king Antiochus III and Egypt, in which Judea was of necessity embroiled because of her geographical position. In secular terms, there were in Jerusalem pro-Syrian and pro-Egyptian partisans. There was an equally serious split in the religious fabric. One group was composed of people who regarded God as an ethnic god, to be worshipped in Jerusalem by means of the cult officiated over by the High Priest of the family of Zadok. On the other side were those who favored a civil ruler (a Davidic king) to a High Priest, who stressed a universal God, who gave greater devotion and sanction to the Law, the Torah (which, in Exile, they had turned to as their focal point), than they gave to the Temple. The former party became known as the Sadducees, a word derived from Hebrew *Zadukim*, meaning "adherents of the family of Zadok." The latter party became the Pharisees, a name derived from Hebrew *Perushim*, meaning "separatists," perhaps originally an epithet flung at them by their opponents as though they were traitors to the traditional faith of Israel.

In 176 B.C., Antiochus IV, calling himself "Epiphanes" ("God Manifest"), came to the Syrian throne. His foreign policy was to prevent Rome from penetrating the East. He thought to keep that expanding nation out by forcing Egypt into subjection and military support of himself and also by Hellenizing all the peoples of the region. He came very close to achieving his first goal in two campaigns, 169 and 168 B.C., but backed off when the Roman Senate sent an ultimatum telling him to leave Egypt or expect a war with Rome. Antiochus left.

On his way home from his 169 B.C. campaign in Egypt, Antiochus bullied the Judeans, entered the Temple, and took away its treasures. After his disappointment in 168 B.C., he dispatched a considerable force to Jerusalem, where Syrian troops looted the city, slaughtered several hundred Jews, and pulled down the walls. Antiochus then built a citadel, known at the Acra, within Jerusalem and installed a garrison there, which remained for twenty-five years, creating a small Greek city within the Holy City of the Jews. In these and other ways, Antiochus sought to impress on the Jews his desire to impose on them all things Greek.

During this period Jerusalem seethed with political partisanship, and the upper-class party composed of the high priestly caste and its wealthy trading-class supporters split over the high priesthood. Some wished only to perpetuate the focus of Jewish life on the Temple; others were content to give up traditional Judaism in an accommodation to Hellenistic culture and the financial benefits to be derived from the larger Greco-Roman world of trade. Factions connived for the high priesthood. One Joshua, who changed his name to the Greek Jason, supplanted his brother as High Priest by paying a large tribute to Antiochus, who, delighted to have a pro-Greek servant who would *pay* him for the position, thereupon set Jason in office. Three years later Jason lost his now-degraded office to another pro-Seleucid, Menelaus, who outbid him.

In December 168 B.C. Antiochus decided to force Hellenization upon the Jews. He decreed that any Jew found observing the Sabbath was thereby judged to be a traitor and subject to capital punishment He banned circumcision, on penalty of death. Scrolls of the Law were to be destroyed. Daily sacrifice in the Temple was abolished. To cap it all, Antiochus, with the knowledge of Menelaus, entered the Temple again, erected an altar to Zeus on the great altar and sacrificed a pig on it. His agents roamed Judea, attempting to enforce compliance and erecting altars to Greek gods.

Under such tyranny and in the face of such grave offense to everything held dear, the Jews—by no means all, but a large portion of them—resorted to revolt. The person who sparked the uprising was a Jerusalem priest named Mattathias, who in disgust at the debasement of the Temple removed himself from the capital city to live on his family's land in Modein, a town in the Shephelah on the road from Jerusalem to Jaffa. Here he was ordered by one of Antiochus' officers to offer a sacrifice to a Greek god. He refused. Another Jew stepped forward and performed the ordered sacrifice. Upon seeing this, Mattathias killed both Greek and Jew with a sword. He and his five sons then fled to the hills, much as David had done to escape Saul. Soon enough patriots responded to their call to arms to form a guerrilla army.

The story of the struggle for Jewish independence that lasted twenty-five years is well told in the Apocryphal book, 1 Maccabees. The word "Maccabees" came to be applied by Christian writers in the 2nd century A.D. to all of the family, male and female, of Mattathias. But in fact, "Maccabeus" was the nickname or distinguishing epithet given to Judas, the first of the sons of Mattathias to lead the guerrillas. Maccabeus comes from the Aramaic word *Maqqabai*, the meaning of which is uncertain: perhaps "the Hammer," after his hammering of Judea's enemies, or "the Hammer-headed," from the shape of his head. Though "Maccabeus" was therefore but the nickname of only one son, "Maccabees" (adjective, "Maccabean") came to cover the entire family, the four books (of quite different sort) about their wars, and the revolt that started Judea on the road to independence

Another name given to Mattathias and his sons and descendants is "Hasmoneans." The term "Hasmonean" is today used to designate the dynasty stemming from Simon, the last surviving of the five brothers, during whose leadership independence was gained in 142 B.C. The meaning of the term is very uncertain. It was first used by the 1st century historian Josephus, who thought that Mattathias was the great-grandson of one Asmoneus. But nothing is known of such a man.

Very little is known of the weaponry of the Maccabean army, but it probably varied little in design from the standard Greek weapons of the post-Alexandrian period: sword and shield, spear and javelin, bow and arrow. Much of it was seized from defeated Syrians (see 1 Macc. 6:6). Although 1 Maccabees makes more mention of armor and weapons than do the earlier books about the wars of the Israelites (Judges, Samuel, and Kings), there is available to us today no representational art from this war to tell us what the Syrian "coats of mail and . . . brass helmets" (6:35) or their "shield of gold and brass" (vs. 39) looked like.

What is clear from 1 Maccabees is that the brothers waged a guerrilla war for the greater part of the ongoing struggle and that they used their knowledge of the terrain of Judea to spring at the enemy when their troops were at a serious positional disadvantage. To a degree the Maccabeans returned to the principles of early Israelite "holy war" in that they "fought for Israel" (1 Macc. 3:2); they assembled at a holy site, Mizpah, for fasting, prayer, and the guidance of Scripture (3:46–48); and they applied the rules of Deut. 20:5–8 for the mobilization of a citizens' militia. But the comparison cannot be pushed far, for God is not an ever-present and active participant in 1 Maccabees as he was, for example, in Exodus, Numbers, and Joshua. Tactically the brothers followed in the tradition of Joshua, Gideon, and David in his early battles with the Philistines, compensating for lack of numbers and sophisticated weaponry with disciplined patriotism, canny use of advantageous terrain for battle, surprise, and speed of attack and retreat.

The Syrian forces opposite them used elephants in battle, as 1 Macc. 6:34–39 vividly describes. One of the Maccabee brothers, Eleazar, lost his life by fighting his way to one of these pachyderms which was bearing what appeared to be royal regalia and armor and carrying four warriors and an Indian driver on its back. Eleazar "got under the elephant, stabbed it from beneath, and killed it; but it fell to the ground upon him and there he died." The elephants in this battle were used to break the ranks of the Judeans by their brute strength and by creating panic. The Syrians also employed catapults, described below.

Judas Maccabeus led the Judean troops from 166 to 160 B.C., Jonathan from 160 to 143 B.C., and Simon from 143 to 135. They were abetted by Syria's dynastic problems after the death of Antiochus IV in 164 B.C., which led to debilitating struggles for power and to problems elsewhere in the sprawling Seleucid kingdom that prevented its giving full attention to the Judeans. Simon finally captured the Acra in Jerusalem and gained complete independence for Judea in 142 B.C. (1 Macc. 13:33–42), except for an apparently advantageous affiliation, through a treaty of alliance, with Rome. A grateful nation bestowed on Simon power, prestige, and the right of hereditary succession to the high priesthood (14:41–49). His death by murder in 135 B.C., along with that of two of his sons, ended a glorious period in Jewish history.

At a low point in the Judean struggle for independence, Judas Maccabeus had sent a delegation to Rome which drew up the treaty of alliance summarized in somewhat idyllic terms in 1 Macc. 8. That the Judeans had an idealistic concept of the Roman Republic is manifest especially in 8:11–16. Later, Jonathan renewed the connection (12:1–4), and Rome initiated a further renewal with Simon after Jonathan's death. Simon thereupon sent a gold shield worth a thousand minas (according to 14:24) to confirm the alliance, and Rome reacted positively to his gift by advising Ptolemy of Egypt and various Near Eastern kings that the Jews were Rome's friends and not to be attacked. So by the war's end Rome was looking upon Judea not as an ally but as a protectorate. In the next eighty years, as the Roman commitment in the East grew, Judea would become increasingly regarded as a vassal state.

The Hasmonean Priest-Kings

The successors of the remarkable Maccabean brothers, notably John Hyrcanus and Alexander Janneus, became progressively less idealistic, more secular, more interested in capturing cities and extending Judea's borders, and more tyrannical. Judea's borders became as extensive as those of the United Kingdom. By 100 B.C. Simon's descendants had taken the title and powers of king, while they simultaneously held in their blood-stained hands the high priesthood. Ultimately two sons of Alexander Janneus, Hyrcanus II and Aristobulus, waged a civil war for the two positions and for the power and perquisites that went with each. In their stalemate, each turned for arbitration to Pompey, the Roman governor in the East, fresh from victories in Pontus and Armenia. A third Jewish delegation urged the abolition of the monarchy.

The opportunity to intervene suited Pompey's purposes perfectly. His grand plan for the defense of Rome's eastern borders was to seal off the Parthians (successors to the Persians, southeast of the Caspian Sea) from all access to the Mediterranean and the vital land and sea routes to Rome from Asia Minor, Syria, Palestine, and Egypt. Rome had fallen heir to the Syrian kingdom, and now a stronger Roman presence in Palestine would complete the isolation of Parthia.

Pompey promised his decision on Judea after completing a campaign already planned against the Nabateans, east of Judea. However, while marching southwards with an army, he became suspicious of the intentions of Aristobulus and turned towards Jerusalem. Although Aristobulus quickly gave himself up to avoid a war, some of his adherents battled followers of Hyrcanus II in Jerusalem and then retreated inside the walled Temple. It took Pompey three months to break down the Temple walls on the north side with the aid of catapults. After a bloody mop-up, Pompey infuriated all Jews by entering the Temple and even the Holy of Holies. Thus Judea fell under Roman governance. It was also stripped of many of the cities and regions John Hyrcanus and Alexander had added to its territories.

The Decapolis ("Ten Cities")

One of Pompey's first administrative acts was to free ten Hellenistic (Greek) cities in Palestine built by Greek settlers during the 250-year period after Alexander's conquest of the East—some at new sites, others where Old Testament Israelite and Ammonite cities had once stood. All of these were in the region south and east of the Sea of Galilee, and all but one (Scy-

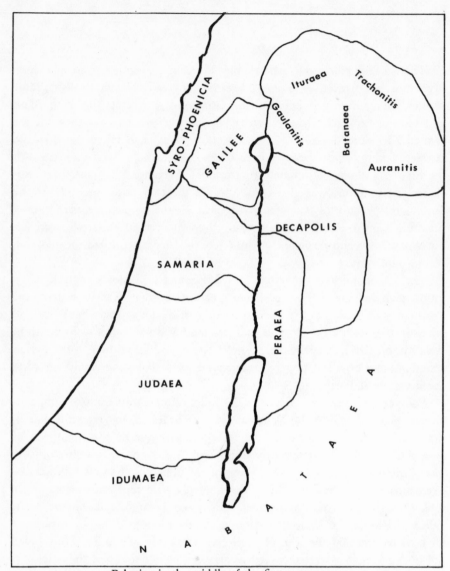

Palestine in the middle of the first century A.D.

thopolis, formerly Beth-shan in the Valley of Jezreel) were east of the Jordan Valley (see map). Pompey's idea was that these cities, non-Jewish in culture and fully content with Roman domination, would provide Rome with a stabilizing element—both military and cultural—along the edge of the Arabian desert. To assure the cooperation of these cities in promoting Roman interests, Pompey freed them from the province of Judea and gave them a nearly independent status under the overview of the Roman province of Syria. They were, however, subject to taxation and had the military responsibility of their own defense and of sealing the border to the east against marauding desert tribes. Since the ten cities were alike in cultural tradition and shared a common status vis-à-vis Rome, they formed a federation for mutual benefits. During Herod's reign some of these cities were placed under his rule, but after his death they again gained the large measure of independence enjoyed earlier, and the term "Decapolis" appears three times in the Gospels (Matt. 4:25; Mark 5:20; 7:31). Their location and federated status separated the two parts of the territory assigned by the Romans to one of Herod's sons, Herod Antipas—Galilee and Perea.

Herod the Great

The one person in Palestine who was canny enough to see which way the winds of history were blowing—and what Rome's wishes were—was an Idumean named Antipater, who had been forcibly converted to Judaism following his country's defeat by Judea. In the civil war which he instigated, Antipater backed Hyrcanus II and maneuvered him and himself to the threshold of power. In the Roman civil wars just ahead, prior to stabilization under Octavian, he would shift his allegiance and provide aid to the right party several times. He became governor of Judea under Julius Caesar and placed his two sons, Phasael and Herod, in key government positions in Jerusalem and Galilee, respectively. Though Antipater was finally poisoned and Phasael committed suicide during a bitter civil war in Judea after the death of Caesar, young Herod had so ingratiated himself with the Roman governor of Syria, and indeed with Octavian, the ultimate winner of power in Rome, that he, only nominally a Jew, emerged as king of the Jews and as a Roman "allied king."

As has been remarked by many historians of the classical world, the Roman emperor Caesar Augustus (Octavian) did not tolerate incompetence in the people he placed in power as kings or governors of the provinces directly under his control (as distinct from those controlled by the Roman Senate). Augustus constantly added to the territory Herod ruled, so that finally his kingdom was as large as it had ever been. Historians therefore conclude that these pragmatic evidences of the Emperor's approval of his rule justify Herod's being called "the Great."

After Herod's death Augustus divided his kingdom into three parts, as Herod had asked in his will, each to be ruled by a son: a much smaller Judea by Archelaus; Galilee and Perea by Herod Antipas; and regions east and northeast of the Sea of Galilee by Philip. (A Jewish delegation journeyed to Rome to ask, unsuccessfully, that Judea be joined to the province of Syria.) Within a decade Archelaus was governing so badly that Augustus removed him from office and banished him to Gaul. This marked the return of the governance of Judea to Roman officials—first called "prefects" and later "procurators"—appointed by the Emperor and directly responsible to him.

It is one of the ironies of Jewish history that Jewish leaders should, in the 100 years before the crowning of Herod the Great in 37 B.C., have regarded Rome first as a friendly power to whom it was helpful to be allied (see 1 Macc. 8; 12:1–4), and then as the settler of its own bitter internal disputes. In actuality there was much more peace and stability in Palestine after Rome had dictated its government—under Herod, his successors, and the Roman governors of Judea—than under the priest-kings of the Jewish Hasmonean dynasty. But to probably most Jews of New Testament times Roman over-lordship was an intolerable situation and a frustration of the glorious national destiny long expected. Some firebrands, called Zealots, wanted the people to choose the path of violence. More sober folk perceived the futility of revolt against so great a power as the Roman Empire, which, they knew from experience, brooked no upsetting of Roman law and order within its borders. Most Jews preferred to rely on the Messianic hope, taught by the later prophets, of a golden age sure to come in God's own time, to be ushered in by the destruction of their enemies, followed by His bringing His chosen people to their glorious destiny.

Herod's Building Program

Herod was one of the greater builders of history. Starting about 24 B.C. he accomplished an astonishing program within a period of about fifteen years. He undertook a complete rebuilding of the Temple on a magnificent scale that would have made Solomon jealous. (Though it was not entirely completed in Jesus' time, it was nearly so.) Adjacent to the northwest corner of the almost rectangular Herodian Temple platform, he constructed the Fortress Antonia, the highest tower of which provided the Herodian and the later Roman soldiers with a vantage point for watching what was going on inside the Temple walls in the Court of the Gentiles. On the higher, western hill, onto which Jerusalem had expanded, Herod built an immense palace of beautifully cut, massive stone. The Herodian masonry of the tower portion, the bases of the largest of the three towers at the northern end of the palace—a tower named for his brother—is one of the authentic archaeological remains of New Testament Jerusalem visible today. It is possible that Herod's royal palace surpassed the Temple in size and luxury.

Herod's building was by no means limited to Jerusalem. He constructed public buildings in Ascalon (the Philistine city Ashkelon), in honor of his family, who some scholars believe lived there. In Hebron he constructed a lovely building to mark the traditional site of the tombs of Abraham, Sarah, and Jacob. Of Herod's many buildings, this is the only one to survive to its

133. The remains of a Roman encampment just across a valley from Masada. This encampment has not been excavated and it remains as it has been since the first century A.D.

full height; today it is the Moslem Mosque of the Friend. Herod rebuilt Samaria with Greco-Roman buildings, including a temple dedicated to Caesar Augustus. He renamed the city Sebaste, the Greek word for Augustus. On the edge of the Plain of Sharon, the marshes of which he drained, Herod built the model agricultural town of Antipatris.

Militarily, Herod's program vastly extended and improved many of the hilltop forts erected by Judea's Hasmonean kings, most of which overlooked and guarded barren stretches near the Jordan River and west of the Dead Sea, along routes an invader would take to penetrate Judea's hilltop heartland. Among these forts were Alexandrium, Hyrcania, Machaerus, where later John the Baptist was beheaded, Gaba in Galilee, Esbon (Essebon) in Perea, and Masada, where last-ditch Jewish patriots would hold out tenaciously against the Romans at the end of the rebellion of 66 A.D. (Fig. 133).

Caesarea. Perhaps the most remarkable of Herod's building projects—almost breathtaking in concept and execution—was his creation of a new port-city built in the Hellenistic-Roman style. The site he chose was a Phoenician fortification site, twenty-three miles south of Mount Carmel, known as Strato's Tower, a fort built by a 4th-century Sidonian king of that name. As did Solomon nine centuries earlier, Herod built his personal wealth and Judea's prosperity on international trade. Palestine lacked a seaport on the

Mediterranean for the shipping of its agricultural products to Rome. Since the Palestinian coastline provided no natural haven for ocean-going boats, Herod constructed a long mole—a 200-foot-wide breakwater of massive stones, arc-shaped but interrupted on the north side to allow ships to enter, and with docking facilities on the landward side. Over a period of twelve years, culminating in dedicatory games in honor of Caesar Augustus, Herod constructed a city that would serve the Romans well as a provincial capital and seaport as long as the Empire held together. Herod gave Caesarea good communications (roads) into the interior of Palestine, especially to Sebaste, and he also gave the city a dependable supply of water, obtained from springs on the south slopes of Mount Carmel and led by an aqueduct to Caesarea (*see* Fig. 92). The city itself he laid out on a grid pattern similar to that of midtown New York City; underneath it he provided a vast drainage system.

Caesarea's buildings were of primarily two sorts. First there were those for commercial purposes: a massive seawall on the waterfront and quays at which smaller boats could tie up; and beyond this, oriented towards the waterfront, were a promenade, warehouses, mercantile buildings, lodging places for sailors, and a marketplace for buyers and sellers of the products of Palestine and the desert lands to the east. The second group of buildings consisted of public buildings typical of all Hellenistic-Roman cities of any significance: amphitheatre, hippodrome (or circus), theater, forum, a palace overlooking the harbor for himself, and a temple dedicated to Herod's patron, Augustus.

A Roman amphitheater was comparable to an American stadium. In the case of the Romans it was used for gladiatorial contests, wild-beast fighting, and athletic contests. Gladiatorial fighting was not necessarily to the death, but very often was. The gladiatorial participants were prisoners of war, deserters from the army, and men convicted of capital crimes; they also included slaves sold by their owners to a trainer of gladiators, and minor criminals who chose the profession as a way out of desperate financial straits or just because they liked fighting. Gladiators were trained by the gladiatorial producers as thoroughly as were Roman infantrymen, and there was normally a large enough supply so that no gladiator had to fight more than twice a year; some survived until released after they had passed their prime.

Wild-beast fighting could be either man vs. beast or animal vs. animal. The animals, collected by Roman generals in their foreign campaigns or sent to Rome as tribute or gift from the borderlands of the Empire, included the rhinoceros, crocodile, and elephant as well as lions, tigers, leopards, and bears. In at least some amphitheaters around the Empire, polar bears chasing seals was a popular attraction. So was a battle between an elephant and a bull. A hungry lion might be set loose to attack a grass-eating beast like a wild horse. In man-vs.-animal encounters, a gladiatorial animal-fighter armed only with javelins might be matched with a hungry leopard. The possible combinations were almost endless. Sometimes armed men atop an elephant would fight against a similar team on a second elephant. A strong streak of sadism running through Roman society has been noted by nearly all scholars of Roman civilization.

One part of a day's program at the amphitheater usually consisted of acts of trained animals, especially elephants, bears, and seals, which men have always been able to teach unusual skills. But little else about the Roman amphitheater's use of animals could be regarded today as family entertainment.

Athletic contests in a Roman amphitheater were not unlike those of the Greek Olympic games. As well as track-and-field events, they included wrestling and the Greco-Roman form of boxing, both amateur and professional. Those engaged did so naked, as was true of the ancient Olympic games. To the Jew the exposure of one's genitals was regarded as shameful (Isa. 3:17; 47:3; Ezek. 16:37; see also Gen. 9:22-23).

Some Roman amphitheaters of the period of Jesus and Paul were used for the performing arts—competitions in singing, instrumental music, poetry reciting, and original declamations; whether this was true at Caesarea is not known.

The hippodrome or circus was much larger than an amphitheater and was used for chariot racing, of which the Romans were inordinately fond. The most common types of race were those involving two or four horses per chariot and from two to four chariots in the race, sometimes two partners vs. two partners—a form of racing that produced ingenious strategies and "dirty tricks" to get one chariot of a team to the finish line first. The courses were the size of a small country-fair racetrack, but had sharp turns, requiring great skill in making a tight 180-degree turnabout at high speed. The Romans also liked to watch stunt riding—e.g., a rider standing upright on a horse or straddling two horses—such as is seen in a modern American circus. For some unknown reason they did not race horses with a jockey in a saddle, the usual form of horse racing today.

A Roman theater meant a permanent, stone theater, uncovered, usually with seats built in a semicircle on a steep hillside, natural or artificial. It could be used for plays, musical performances, pantomime dancing (acting out a plotted story in ballet), or crude, often obscene, burlesque-type mime. The plays at this time were mostly tragedies of martial subjects or Greek-type comedies, and the players seen in the provinces were generally troupes of strolling players (the ancient equivalent of "repertory road companies") from

Greece. Syrians loved the theater, and Syrian auxiliary troops in Roman uniform were probably the most regular spectators in the theater at Caesarea, the military headquarters of the Romans in Palestine. Very probably Herod and the later Roman prefects saw to it that such entertainment was provided to them periodically to keep them from boredom and troublemaking. But all such kind of entertainment was loathsome to the observant Jew. Those Jews who were attracted to such places found it almost incumbent upon them to wear Greek-style dress when attending, and the sight of such bowing to the dictates of foreign style further angered the patriotic Jew.

In summation, Herod, that Jew only by the accident of the forced conversion of his father, built Caesarea as a Roman city, geared for life as Romans knew it and as he, Herod, liked it. After Herod's son, Archelaus, was deposed by Caesar Augustus as incompetent to rule, Caesarea became the official seat of Roman governance under Roman prefects. Its population became more heavily Roman, or non-Jewish, though a substantial Jewish minority resided there, mostly for commercial reasons. Caesarea, so Roman in its physical manifestations and its cultural aspects, must have seemed to most Jews to be a totally alien intrusion into their life as well as a Babylon of wickedness in their midst.

The Antonia. Herod's total rebuilding and enlarging of the Antonia was another goad in the sides of wholehearted Jews.

At a high point on the eastern slope of the two hills on which Jerusalem sits, north of his city, David had had a fort. Nehemiah rebuilt the fort (2:8; 7:2), called "Baris" by Josephus, when the Persians allowed the Jews to rebuild the walls of Jerusalem. The Hasmonean kings had built a larger fort at the same site. Now, having enlarged the Temple area to the immediate proximity of the fort site, Herod so built the Antonia that it looked right down upon the people in the outer court, the Court of the Gentiles, from its position adjacent to the northwest corner of the Temple wall. To the people inside, looking up at it, the Antonia's tower must have seemed like an evil, spying foreigner impinging on their most precious institution. That Herod was rebuilding their Temple in a more glorious form than Solomon's counted not at all in his favor, once the Antonia's dominance was perceived. To make a bad matter worse, Herod named it after Mark Antony, his one-time Roman patron. Roman armies had twice entered the Temple precincts; the Temple treasuries had been emptied by Roman generals; civil wars with Rome backing one of the parties were all too familiar. Now here was the Antonia, symbol of militarism, of Roman authority, of Jewish loss of independence!

In physical terms, the Antonia rose 60 feet above the level of the rocky spur on which it stood. The four corner towers stood even taller, three of them 75 feet and the one at the southeast corner, facing the Temple, 100 feet above ground level. Thus the Antonia seemed to Jews not to be guarding the northern approaches to the city from external enemies but to be monitoring the religious activities of the inhabitants of the city, the Jews. In fact, during the Herodian and New Testament period civil disturbances were very likely to start in the Temple's Court of the Gentiles (see Acts 21:27–36), and thus policing it was a major function of the troops of Herod and later those of the Roman governors. Although this outermost court was a part of the Temple complex, it was—in the absence of any forum or central marketplace in Jerusalem—the center of much of the secular life in the city. Here men talked business, money was exchanged, and animals sold to pilgrims for sacrificial purposes within the more sacred precincts beyond. It was this court which Jesus attempted to cleanse of what he considered profane uses of God's Temple.

West of the Antonia ran the Tyropean valley, in a north-south direction, which almost cleaved the southern half of Jerusalem's site in two. Herod built his palace on the western hill, and the north wall of the city in Herodian and New Testament times ran in a generally west-east direction from the palace, with its own citadel facing north, to the Fortress Antonia.

The fortress provided barracks for a Roman cohort, 600 men, commanded by a tribune (Acts 21:37). (Additional troops were billeted at the citadel of the palace of Herod, later used as the residence of the Roman governors.) The Herodian improvements in what had once been a Hasmonean palace gave the Antonia apartments, courtyards, cloisters, baths in the Greco-Roman style, as well as barracks for soldiers. A flagstone paved court, probably dating from Herod's time, about 165 feet by 150 feet in size, can be seen today in Jerusalem under the convent of Notre Dame de Sion, which archaeologists agree is the site of the Antonia. Other remains at the site are stairways, the foundations of what was probably the northwest tower, and a flagstone pavement outside a guardroom on which are visible scratchings for a game apparently played by advancing markers from one position to the next, probably by casting dice. Whether this pavement dates to the period of Jesus is not quite certain, and the game scratchings may date from the time of Hadrian (2nd century A.D.), even if the pavement is earlier.

Herod's predecessors, the Hasmonean priest-kings, had used the Antonia as a palace, and quite naturally their vestments as the nation's High Priest were kept in the Antonia. Herod, ineligible to be High Priest because of his Idumean blood, in the words of Josephus (*Antiquities*, xviii.iv.3) "retained them in the same place, as believing that while he had them in his custody, the people would make no innovation against him." This practice was continued by his son Archelaus and by the Romans: the captain of the guard would hand over the vestments to the High Priest seven days before any festival (giving him enough time to purify them from contamination by contact with pagans) and requiring their return "the very next day after the feast was over." This practice continued until terminated by Vitellius, Roman governor of Syria, as a concession to Jewish public opinion following an incident that occurred a few years after the death of Jesus.

Stairs from the Antonia gave access directly to porticos inside the Court of the Gentiles. From these steps Paul made his defense to those Jewish leaders who opposed his views (Acts 22:1–21), and up these steps Paul was taken inside the Antonia by the Roman tribune for questioning. Again on the morrow Paul had to be taken into protective custody by the tribune up the same stairs (Acts 23:10). There was also a subterranean passage leading from the Antonia to the Court of Israel, presumably constructed by a Hasmonean priest-king for use in an emergency. By such impingement of military authority—and by non-Jews—the temper, the disposition of Jews towards secular power and the Roman presence was exacerbated.

The Antonia was captured from the Romans by Jews in the rebellion of 66 A.D. Titus recaptured it in 70 A.D. and used it to direct the fire of his catapults and finally the movements of his assault troops in the destruction of the Temple and of Jerusalem in 70 A.D. He leveled the city and slaughtered, delivered to the amphitheater at Caesarea for death at the claws and fangs of animals, or sold into captivity virtually the entire population. The Jews nevertheless continued to give the Roman emperors problems of governance until Hadrian put down another in a long series of rebellions (132–135 A.D.). He built a new Roman city atop the rubble of Jewish Jerusalem, naming it Aelia Capitolina; he forbade Jews to live there and colonized it with Romans. It remained a Roman city until the appearance of the great Moslem conquerors.

The Jews in Military Service in the Intertestamental Period

Judas Maccabeus and his brothers had no trouble raising and maintaining a strong guerrilla-type army for the revolt against Antiochus IV Epiphanes. The rebellion evoked a positive feeling of anger and of rekindled pride among the greater part of the populace, especially among those living outside Jerusalem. Men happily took up arms to rid their country of the oppressive power of the Seleucid kings. Idealism ran high. Even the first coins struck after independence had been gained reflect the democratic basis upon which the war had been fought, in their legend reading: "Commonwealth of the Jews."

But starting with Simon's son, John Hyrcanus, the rule of the Hasmonean priest-kings became absolute in their concentration of power in their own hands. The nation's independence having been won, conquest and personal aggrandizement of the priest-kings became the order of the day. Dissent and opposition were crushed. It is hard to find anything good to be said about Alexander Janneus (ruled 104–78 BC.). Josephus relates that he had 800 Jews who were opposed to him crucified and their families slain. The effective core of his army was composed of mercenaries, paid professional fighters: Greek commanders and soldiers of the forts he captured, men of conquered peoples who had no other trade or profession but fighting, and "loyal" Jews who believed in him in his lust for preeminence or who sought to win a share for themselves of wealth and property through seizure. The vast majority of common men and villagers in this period, the dream of a commonwealth having long departed, was apathetic toward the politics and effects of the wars of their kings, except for a deep-seated distaste for taxes, conscription, and forced labor that all too often landed upon their shoulders or their sons'. Well they knew that those who took exception risked a knife at their throats.

Under Herod the apathy toward military affairs among the people of the land continued. The civil wars that preceded his election by the Romans as their "client-king" were fought largely by rival parties for power within Jerusalem, supported by contingents of such interested outsiders as the Romans, Syrians, Parthians, Egyptians, and Nabateans. Julius Caesar, after Herod's father, Antipater, had saved his neck by breaking up an Egyptian siege by Ptolemy XI of Roman forces inside Alexandria with a small army composed of Jews and Idumeans, granted the Jews (among other favors) exemption from military service in the auxiliary forces in the Roman army. Though some of Caesar's favors were later retracted by Rome, military service in the Roman army was never required of Jews. The justification for the continued exemption, however, was the refusal of Jews to fight on the Sabbath or holy days (unless in defense of their own person); their refusal to salute or respect the legionary standards, which had images on them; their insistence upon ritual observances within the military life; and their refusal to eat pork, which was the standard meat rationed to the Roman armies.

Herod, however, was supplied a Roman contingent to help him gain actual possession of the throne of Judea in the period between his election as king by Octavian and Antony, confirmed by the Senate (40 B.C.), and his crowning in Jerusalem (37 B.C.). Thereafter Herod built an army of his own, owing its loyalty totally to him, of professional soldiers, mainly Idumeans like himself. These, it appears, formed his bodyguard but were also used in colonies along the borders of his kingdom. (By blood not a Jew, Herod feared the Jews, and employed a secret police force to report to him on their doings.) Herod also employed Greek-Syrian mercenaries, of which there were many available following the collapse of even the vestiges of Syrian power in the Near East. These latter were cruel and blood-thirsty, and greatly feared by the Jewish people of the land. The functions of the common man in Herod's system was to pay taxes and provide the conscript labor required to carry out his grand building and construction plans (see "Herod's Building Program").

After Herod's death and Rome's removal and banishment of his son, Archelaus, Roman soldiers returned to Judea as a part of the Roman rule of the province under Roman governors owing their appointment to the emperor, not the Senate. A Roman army replaced Herod's army. The Roman soldier was a disciplined fighting man, and law and order in Judea was more efficiently and fairly enforced than it had been in a long time. The Jews of Jesus' day lived in a peaceful province of a well-organized and well-run empire. Neither war nor military service interrupted their lives. Still, the very presence of a Roman soldier was a constant daily reminder of lost independence, of frustrated dreams, of servitude to a pagan authority. Jews were made to feel alien in their own land. With such emotions prevalent, the scene was being prepared for firebrands and irreconcilable nationalists who would ultimately take Judea down the path of revolt, against impossible odds, to total destruction.

The Roman Soldier

In Jesus' time, Roman soldiers would be seen in Palestine (normally) only in the province of Judea, which included Samaria and Idumea. Herod Antipas and Philip had their own troops; only in case of an emergency would they request Roman troops from the governor of the province of Syria at Antioch. The Hellenistic cities that formed the Decapolis (see "Decapolis" above) ruled themselves in a federation supervised by Antioch and in exchange defended and policed themselves and their region. The Roman presence in the form of troops within their territories would be minimal and temporary.

In Judea in the first half of the first century A.D., however, there were normally 3,000 Roman troops—auxiliaries and not regular legionaries—assigned to the province by the Roman governor of Syria. Their headquarters in Judea were at Caesarea. Of these 3,000 soldiers there was usually one cohort (approximately 600 men) in Jerusalem at the Antonia and the citadel at the governor's palace, supplemented as needed at times of unrest in the city and at the high festivals when crowds were large, by additional contingents from Caesarea. Other locations where Roman soldiers in significant numbers were stationed were Sebaste (the former Samaria) and Masada. From such major military centers units would be detailed to man the smaller forts and police the roads and ports of entry of trade caravans from Egypt,

South Arabia, Damascus, and the Syrian desert, and to oversee the collection of transit taxes. They were also employed in the construction and repair of roads and bridges. Upon the Roman troops fell the responsibility to keep moving the orderly flow of commercial traffic from the outskirts of the Empire to its heart at Rome. From Judea this traffic moved into Caesarea for forwarding by ocean-going ships or, especially in the winter months, when ships could not navigate the stormy Mediterranean, northward in horse-drawn wagons by roads to Antioch and then west on the great land route across what is modern Turkey and Greece, with transshipments by boat to Philippi and again across the Adriatic Sea to Brundisium on the east coast of Italy. With their orderly minds the Romans determined that their carriages could manage twenty-five miles a day, and that a team of horses should be asked to work only one-third of that distance. Therefore along this main route they established overnight resting places every twenty-five miles, approximately, with additional posts for changing horses roughly every 8⅓ miles.

The basic unit of the Roman army was the legion. Its size varied from 3,000 to 6,000 men under the command of a legate, assisted by a prefect, legionary tribunes, and assorted officers performing specialized functions. A legion's actual size at any one time depended on the success of recruiting efforts, the military need of the moment, recent losses suffered, the state of the imperial coffers, and other factors. Theoretically a legion contained 6,000 men. Organizationally it was divided into ten cohorts, each commanded by a professional officer called a tribune, almost always a Roman citizen and a member of the equestrian (middle) class who intended to make a career of public service. The cohort was comprised of six centuries, each commanded by a centurion (see below).

The Roman legion was basically a heavy infantry force. It was supported by "wings" of cavalrymen, 500 in number, commanded by officers who took orders only from the field officer in command. A legion also had assigned to it other specialist forces required by the military situation: for example, a company of Syrian slingers or Arabian archers to assist in an attack on a strongly defended city.

Each cohort included among its specialists men trained as secretaries and judicial assistants; clerks to keep the soldiers' records, including their savings accounts; standard bearers; messengers (scouts and dispatch riders); orderlies; interrogators, torturers, and executioners. A cavalry wing included men who stabled and groomed the horses wherever the wing was based.

The Roman army was divided in another way, into legionary troops composed of Roman citizens and auxiliary troops recruited in conquered provinces. (In either case they were professional soldiers, trained and disciplined.)

The legionary troops were headquartered in provinces bordering on lands of potential enemies, but at a distance from actual borders and in an easily supplied base. Syria, with its Roman provincial capital at Antioch, was such a headquarters. From two to four legions (out of about twenty-five in all) were always stationed there in New Testament times.

Pontius Pilate as Roman governor of Judea, was not a legate but a prefect appointed by the Emperor (in his case, Tiberius) and personally responsible to him. The normal quota of Roman troops for Judea was five cohorts, assigned to the province by Antioch from auxiliary troops raised by the legate there, and one cavalry wing—about 3,000 men in all. Probably all of the auxiliaries who served in Judea were pagan Syrians or Samaritans, the latter of mixed racial stock going back to the deportation and replacement policies of the Assyrian kings. These auxiliaries—and nearly all Jews too—could speak the common language of the region, Greek in its Eastern Mediterranean form or dialect called *koine*, which means simply "common."

One of these cohorts of auxiliaries was called the "Augustan Cohort of Sebastenians," a unit from Sebaste (Samaria) which perhaps for its performance in quelling a nationalistic uprising some years earlier had been honored by Caesar Augustus and allowed to use his name in its designation and to carry in its identifying colors a medallion bearing his image. It was very likely these troops and their ensigns that got Pontius Pilate off to a bad start in his prefecture when he allowed this auxiliary cohort to take its standards into Jerusalem and place them on the battlements of the Antonia, where they fluttered above the Court of the Gentiles. Observable also were the golden disks, with their embossed effigies of Augustus, and Tiberius too, attached to the unit's ceremonial spears. In no time at all a riot was underway, and Pilate ultimately backed down and removed the offensive insignia to Caesarea, his provincial capital. Jewish distaste for graven images, no matter who made them, was powerful (see Exod. 20:4-5). Equally offensive was *worshipping* them (so claimed by the Jews) or introducing the cult of emperor-worship inside their Holy City and almost within the Temple itself. To the Roman soldier his standards were a focal point of loyalty: he regarded them as symbols to be preserved with his life in battle and to lose them to an enemy was a disgrace removable only by their recapture. Standards were held in considerable awe by Roman soldiers because they played a symbolic role in pitching and striking a military camp, held a key position near the battle front of a cohort, and were used to signal the troops, by swaying movements, to change the direction of attack, to close ranks, etc. Finally—in a way not known in American military experience, but to a degree in the history of British regiments—Roman standards were honored on special occasions by being anointed with precious oils and decorated with flowers or laurel wreaths. They were treated with greater awe than is the American flag when it is saluted by troops on parade or at a flag-raising ceremony. Standards, however, were not literally worshipped. But the line of distinction was one the Jews were unable to draw: they regarded the ensigns and the place they were kept as numinous, spirit-filled, and consequently a challenge and an insult to the Lord.

The Roman soldier was the most carefully selected, best trained, and most honestly treated fighting man in the ancient world. A sturdy physique was a prerequisite. Recruits were trained in individual combat techniques and in group maneuvers as rigorously as college football players or United States Marines. They were kept in top-notch condition by periodic marches and exercises, and by a sensible, plain diet. Every permanent military installation had its bath house, with siderooms of different temperatures and humidity, and latrines with drains that worked and lessened disease. Even when in the field the Romans took particular care to assure their camp an ample water supply for hygienic and sanitary purposes.

The diet of the Roman soldier provided him with the necessities for maintaining health and strength. In the field wheat that could be baked in the form of hard biscuits or made into a porridge; salt, olive oil, vinegar, and wine were staples. Great quantities of coarse, healthful wheat bread were issued. When in season, vegetables were served in camp. The meat ration was commonly salt pork. However, meat was never regarded as a daily need, but was reserved for the conclusion of a mission or for special occasions in the calendar. No doubt when away from their home base, while marching or patrolling a road, Roman soldiers helped themselves to whatever caught their eye, such as fruit and vegetables; a terrified farmer would hardly protest, lest something worse befell him.

The Roman Governor

The responsibilities of the Roman governors of Judea were those of fiscal agent, provincial judge, and commander-in-chief of the military. As fiscal agent (i.e., collector of provincial revenues), he saw to it that all eleven toparchies or districts into which Judea was divided for tax-collection purposes came through with the tax revenues expected of them. As provincial judge he heard appeals, conducted trials involving crimes punishable by death, and settled disputes in the thorny legal areas involving a Jew and a Gentile. He might "hold court" wherever he was acting in his official capacity, by setting up his portable judgment seat—a platform and a chair for him to sit on, symbols of his magisterial authority. As a military commander it was his duty to insure peace and stability, assure a sufficiency of food and supplies for the troops under his control, be sure that the garrisons were adequately manned and properly officered, and rotate the troops to distribute fairly both pleasant and unpleasant kinds and locations of duty.

The Roman prefects (apparently called procurators for the first time under Emperor Claudius, after the death of Jesus) had by necessity one further responsibility in Judea: maintaining a working relationship with the High Priest, who headed the Jewish Sanhedrin or council, which had those powers of government not specifically reserved to Rome. None of the Roman governors performed in this area with much success. The reigns of Herod the Great and his grandson, Herod Agrippa I (41–44 A.D.), were freer of violence and complaints because these Palestinian monarchs were more successful acting as buffers between "hard-line" officials in Rome and uncompromising Jews than were the appointees of the Roman Emperors. In this regard, Pontius Pilate was by no means the worst of Rome's governors in Judea.

Roman Weapons

The *javelin* was a weapon to be thrown. It was six to seven feet long, the top three feet of which was made of iron, provided with a socket to which the shaft was attached by rivets, and came to a pyramidal-shaped point of hardened steel, usually about six inches long (Fig. 134). The point was barbed so that it would remain stuck in the the shield of an enemy, forcing him to cast his shield away. A javelin was hurled at the enemy before hand-to-hand fighting began.

The *sword* was double-edged and about two feet long. Many that have been found were fitted with a corrugated grip. The sword was used like a bayonet for thrusting when at close grips with an enemy. It was carried in a scabbard hung from a shoulder strap around the neck and attached also to the girdle worn around the waist (Fig. 134). The sword was hung high on the *right* side of the infantryman's body, where it would not interfere with his leg action in marching or running, or limit the defensive movement of his shield-bearing left arm. Officers did not carry a shield; hence they wore the sword on their left side, in the more usual position.

The *dagger* was about nine inches long, a personal weapon acquired by a soldier to suit his preference in design. It was carried in a scabbard attached to the left side of his belt, the scabbard also reflecting the owner's taste in metallic decoration (Fig. 135). A sharply honed dagger had many uses beyond military ones, as a cutting tool.

The Catapult. Catapults were brought to a peak of efficiency under Roman engineering skills. The *scorpiones* (scorpion) variety hurled several small javelins at one time, sometimes carrying flaming tow; the *onager* (wild ass), so named for its violent "kick" when fired, hurled very heavy stones;

134. The uniform of a Roman soldier.

135. A pyramid of ballistae found at Herodium.

the *ballista* hurled lighter stones, weighing fifty-five pounds, as far as 440 yards, Josephus reported (Fig. 135). It is the last-named that the Romans used with such deadly effect in the siege of Jerusalem by Titus in 70 A.D. They could be used to create weakness in the walls of a city or as anti-personnel weapons, directed at homes.

The stone was set in a kind of sling affixed to a wooden spar set in a heavy wooden frame, the whole assembly of a ballista weighing about four tons. The power came from the tension created by twisting heavy skeins of rope fibers on a windlass. When the windlass was released by a trigger, the spar slammed forward against the forward frame of the catapult and the projectile continued on its way (*see* Fig. 134).

Defensive Armor. The *shield* was a bit larger, more oval, and more curved than that employed by Assyrian and Babylonian infantrymen in their conquests of Israel and Judah (see Fig. 135). It was constructed of thin sheets of wood, glued together, with the grain of the successive layers running in opposite directions. Its edges were bound with bronze or wrought iron. In the center, on the inside, was a handgrip, while a metal boss on the outer side provided extra protection at this point. The rest of the exterior was usually covered with leather and decorated in various ways in bronze, sometimes gilded or silvered. It is thought that each cohort had its own distinctive coloring for its shields, but this may have been true only of legionaries or of ceremonial shields as distinct from those used in the field. Each shield bore the name of the soldier and of his centurion.

The *helmet* of the infantryman showed an exterior of bronze, but on the inside it had an iron skull-plate. An extension protected the neck in the back, and a ridgelike projection in front partially shielded the face from a downward blow. At the sides hung hinged cheek-guards that dropped below the jaw bones. The helmets of legionaries were provided with plume-holders across the top, plumes being useful in identifying troops of the same cohort, as well as being decorative in parades. Whether plumes and plume-holders were part of the uniform of auxiliary infantrymen, is improbable. We know much less about auxiliaries than about legionaries, for most monumental art depicts only legionaries in action or standing in full uniform. We also know more about Roman military dress of the early second century A.D. than we do about the first century A.D.

The *cuirass* or corselet was protective armor for the trunk, extending from the neck to the top of the hips (see Fig. 135). These were sleeveless jackets made of hardened leather, with strips of metal or extra pieces of leather added where most needed, as for example, from neck to shoulder and over the region of the heart. Sometimes a cuirass was made of two pieces of metal, front and back, joined by clasps or buckles. Some centurions probably wore chain armor instead of either of the simpler forms.

No greaves were worn by infantrymen; mobility was preferred to protection of the legs. However, they were part of the equipment of centurions and higher-ranking officers.

Clothing. In addition to his armor the Roman soldier in normal climes wore a linen undergarment and a short-sleeved woolen tunic, gathered at the waist and falling to the knees. Exactly how it was fastened by soldiers wearing armor and equipment so that it fell in graceful folds front and back is not clear from Roman art. In this era trousers were worn only by orientals. (How Roman soldiers countered the intense heat of summer in Palestine by adapting their clothing is not known.)

On his feet the Roman soldier wore a very heavy sandal, virtually a boot, consisting of several thicknesses of leather sole studded with hobnails, fitted to leather thongs long enough to run well up the shin, where they were tied. The Latin word for these military boots is *caligae*. (The successor of Emperor Tiberius, Gaius, who spent his boyhood among soldiers in army camps, was nicknamed Caligula, meaning "little boot." The name stuck.) In cold weather the soldier would lay wool or fur atop the leather soles and also bind wool around his ankles and legs as he wound and tied the thongs. Centurions wore boots with nails driven into the soles to give longer wear.

All generalizations about the clothing and protective armor of auxiliary troops are subject to the further qualification that the auxiliaries of the various outer provinces of the Empire did not dress very much alike. The Roman military establishment permitted locally recruited troops to incorporate into their Roman uniforms some of the features of the uniforms worn by their country's fighting men before the advent of Rome. This accounts for much of the variation in armor and clothing that scholars have encountered in their search for accurate descriptions.

Terms of Service in Auxiliary Forces

The enlistment period was twenty years. At the end of that period, Roman citizenship was conferred upon the retiring soldier. Hence for a non-Roman an enlistment was a step onto the ladder of upward mobility in the Roman world. Marriage during the period of service was forbidden, for the Roman government wanted no responsibility toward dependents and felt that unmarried soldiers fought more whole-heartedly.

Camp-following women were tolerated by the authorities, who even established camps for them near the major bases. Sometimes these liaisons resulted in marriages after the period of service had been completed. Children of such liaisons, if marriage ensued, were legitimized by the State and were then Roman citizens.

The pay of the auxiliary infantrymen is not known. Legionaries during the first half of the first century A.D. received 225 denarii per annum, paid three times a year, 75 denarii every four months. Auxiliaries certainly received less, and 150 denarii per annum is the figure suggested by some scholars. Men of the cavalry wing were better paid than infantrymen; so were slingers and archers. The usual wage of a civilian laborer without craftsman's skills was one denarius a day in Palestine; hence the annual wages of both legionaries and auxiliary troops were considerably less than that. The soldier, however, had almost no expenses beyond his personal clothing and the cost of replacement weapons, which was subtracted from his account. He was even supplied with ample rations of *posca*, the cheap wine drink of soldiers, when he was at his station. A new emperor might, to curry favor with the troops, declare a bonus to all hands, and there was always the hope of acquiring valuable booty after a battle, or by confiscation.

The Centurion

The gap between a Roman infantryman, whether of the legionary or auxilary variety and the centurion was considerable—in appearance, capability, responsibility, and pay.

To treat the last-named first, exact pay scales for centurions at any one period are not known. Scholars estimate that the centurion's base rate was about five times the annual wages of a legionary infantryman, which would be about 1,200 denarii annually. But all centurions in a legion and a cohort were graded according to seniority: the top-ranked centurion in each cohort received more than the lowest, and the top centurion of a legion, *primus pilus*, was paid as much as 3,750 denarii, as well as having many perquisites and the opportunity to accept bribes from subordinates for relief from unpleasant camp duties. And upon retirement a centurion was given a substantial grant, in money or land, sufficient to lift him into the equestrian class and put him into business, if he chose, in the city where he made his home in his retired status.

There was also a sharp distinction between a centurion's uniform and that of the men under his command. While the dress of this remarkable Roman military officer varied from century to century, from region to region within the Empire, and perhaps from legion to legion, it is always considerably more splendid than that of the ordinary infantryman's. Fortunately for modern students, some excellent depictions of centurions' dress have been preserved in tombstone monuments and tablets found in widely separated places, and in these centurions stand before us today as they might have stood for a parade-dress inspection long ago—except for the absence of color.

If it is permissible to synthesize from these monumental delineations, the centurion wore a brightly gilded or silvered helmet and normally wore his crest of plumes on top. It seems not determinable whether each centurion was free to create his own individual crest; whether the crests varied according to the wearer's rank among centurions within the legion; or whether legions had their own crest style.

A centurion's corselet was beautifully ornamented and decorated with crafted metal shoulder pieces. (Some wore fine coats of mail; a considerable freedom seems to have prevailed in the choice of protective armor for those who could afford to follow their own preferences.) Equally eye-catching ornamentation was found on his wide belt. The ordinary tunic of the infantryman was replaced by a pleated garment that reminds one of the dress-uniform kilts of the British Highlands regiments. The centurion wore his sword on the left, unlike the infantryman, and in his right hand he carried the symbol of his rank and responsibility, the twisted vine-stick, with which on occasion he meted out harsh punishment to recalcitrant or disobedient soldiers. Decorated greaves, made of light, thin metal, seem to have been used by centurions when formally dressed, but shields were not carried.

The horse was the centurion's method of conveyance when on the march, and he was provided with a groom for his steed. There were not yet stirrups for the rider of horses, but the centurions knew the comfort of a saddle with projections to help him remain steady, and he controlled his mount by reins and a bit. Affixed to his left shoulder—if we may generalize from the monuments—was his cloak, made of whatever fine woolen materials he could find or chose to purchase.

In general, then, the centurion's uniform was brighter and more eye-catching, and of finer quality and workmanship in every respect. In turn, the centurions were surpassed in elegance by the officers above them—in Palestine most notably by the tribune of each of the cohorts stationed there—in the fineness and color of their cloaks. Each rank was entitled to use its own color in its cloak, and more individualistic defensive armor was permitted. So, too, was the wearing of decorations—gold and silver necklaces, armlets, bracelets, etc.—awarded for personal or unit bravery. But little such military ostentation would have been seen in Judea, except in Caesarea, a very Roman city.

In his capabilities and responsibilities the Roman centurion may be thought of as a combination of the master sergeant of the U.S. or British armies before the advent of the airplane and the vast technology of weaponry and communications, mixed with the qualities of leadership associated with a captain of the infantry who has earned his commission in the field.

Most centurions were Roman citizens, but it was possible for non-Romans to emerge from the ranks of the auxiliaries to this level. In any case, the centurion was an officer who had earned his rank and was a thoroughly tested fighting man and commander of others. Theoretically his company consisted of 100 men, as his title states; but for much of this period a century consisted of only eighty men, plus perhaps a half-dozen specialists of a staff-sergeant sort. These eighty men were divided into ten sections of eight men each (comparable to U.S. infantry squads), who shared two rooms in their regular barracks and a tent when in the field.

The Centurions of the New Testament. The centurions who are mentioned more than briefly in the Gospels and Acts are four: the centurion of Capernaum (Matt. 8:5-13; Luke 7:1-10; cf. John 4:46-53); the centurion at the cross (Matt. 27:54; Mark 15:39; Luke 23:47); Cornelius (Acts 10:1-33); and Julius (Acts 27:1—28:16).

Luke reports of the centurion in Capernaum that "he loves our nation, and he built us our synagogue." Apparently, then, he was a proselyte to Judaism. In Matthew and Luke it is his servant-slave that he wishes Jesus to heal. In John he is referred to as "an official" (RSV; literally, "king's officer"), and the slave has become his son. No Roman garrison in Capernaum is known. Furthermore, Capernaum lay in the territory of King Herod Antipas, who had his own military. The centurion clearly is well established in the town. The best answer to the puzzle is that this centurion (perhaps not a Roman but a Samaritan or Syrian) was living there in retirement.

The centurion at Calvary was one of Pilate's men, probably a Roman who commanded one of the centuries quartered in the Antonia.

Cornelius was certainly a Roman; his name shows it. Furthermore, he is a centurion of the Italian Cohort, a name indicating that its members had been recruited in Italy of Roman citizens and freedmen. (This cohort is known positively, by inscriptions, to have been stationed in Caesarea only in 69 A.D. and after, but there is no evidence that it was not there earlier.) The description given of Cornelius in Acts 10:2 fits that of a man who worships the God of the Jews but has not formally adopted their religion—i.e., has stopped short of circumcision. He too is well established in his community: he has a "household" (vs. 2) and "is well spoken of by the whole Jewish nation" (vs. 22). The question whether centurions might marry has been given no definitive answer by scholars. Some believe that they might only if they reenlisted, at which time their terms of service were softened and a permanent residence was possible to them.

The centurion who accompanied Paul to Rome belonged to the auxiliary unit from Syria designated the Augustan Cohort. The Augustan Cohort was assigned to Caesarea for at least two periods in the first century A.D. The name Julius is Roman. Centurions, most of whom were Roman, were transferred from cohort to cohort, and from legion to legion, as they rose in seniority. Julius may have been on temporary duty in Caesarea and was being returned to his regular post by the governor of Judea, Festus, simultaneously conducting Paul "and some other prisoners" (Acts 27:1) to Rome.

THE INDUSTRIAL LIFE

Industrial life in the ancient world was a natural outgrowth of various crafts and jobs performed in the home. As society grew and became more complex and the technical skills became more refined, there arose the necessity and the opportunity to specialize and to learn a particular trade. Initially these trades were plied in the home or in a small shop set up adjacent to the home. The trade was passed on from father to son generation after generation. Social and economic considerations eventually led to the organization of guilds, or professional associations of craftsmen. These craftsmen frequently worked in a particular area of the city. Jerusalem had a baker's street (Jer. 37:21), a fuller's field (Isa. 7:3), a potter's area (see Jer. 19:1-2), and a goldsmith's district (Neh. 3:32).

Manufacturing plants often were located near the natural resources or raw materials from which the goods were produced. An industrial center based on the dyeing and weaving of wool, dated to the time of the Judean monarchy, was excavated by W. F. Albright at Tell Beit Mirsim. Professor Albright noted that the site was situated in an area well suited for raising sheep and goats. Royal pottery workshops were established in Netaim and Gederah, located in the Shephelah of Judah in an area rich in fine clay (1 Chron. 4:23). There was a "house of linen workers" located at Beth-ashbea (1 Chron. 4:21) and a "valley of craftsmen" around Lod and Ono (Neh. 11:35).

The Bible provides some information about carpenters, potters, jewelers, workers of metal, weavers, and other craftsmen. This is supplemented by archaeological evidence from numerous sites in ancient Palestine. Entire workshops have been excavated, while at other times individual pieces of ivory, pottery, jewelry, metal, and carved stone have revealed how the craftsman worked his raw material.

The combined evidence is sufficient to be able to draw a picture of several industries in existence during the biblical period, especially during the time of the Hebrew monarchy. Little is known about the craftsman's social or economic standing or about his education. More is known about his work, his skill, and the products he manufactured. It is often assumed that the craftsman made little profit from his work, and that his education was limited to the training he received as an apprentice. The craftsman's skill, however, is known to have been excellent—in many cases he was as much an artisan as a craftsman.

THE CONSTRUCTION INDUSTRY

In the formative stages of civilization, man had to provide his own labor and construct his own dwellings. As society became more complex and technology more advanced, the need arose for specialists who could cut stone and shape wood quickly and accurately and erect brick or stone walls with skill and craftsmanship. Many individuals continued to construct their own homes, but by the time of the United Kingdom professional craftsmen were available who could be hired to lay a brick wall, cut a tomb out of solid rock, or erect a public building. Biblical and archaeological evidence combine to provide an indication of the main features of the construction industry in ancient Israel. In addition to looking at the bricklayer, the stonemason, and the carpenter, attention will be given to a related member of the construction trade, the shipbuilder.

The Bricklayer

Mud-brick buildings were one of the earliest forms of housing in the ancient Near East. This type of construction was relatively inexpensive and simple to fashion. It was frequent in river valleys, coastal plains, and other areas where stone was scarce and clay or moist earth readily available. The earliest bricks were molded by hand, were oval or rounded in shape and varied in size. When wooden molds were introduced, the bricks became more standardized and wall construction more uniform.

Although brickmaking was a simple process, it required an available source of clay, a sufficient supply of water and straw, and a large labor force. A shallow pit was dug and filled with clay and water. Chopped straw wás added as a binder to retain the strength and form of the bricks (see Exod. 5:6–21), and the ingredients were mixed by treading through the mire with the feet. When thoroughly mixed to the right consistency, the solution was compressed into rectangular or square wooden molds and the resulting bricks set out in the sun to dry: "go into the clay, tread the mortar, take hold of the brickmold!" (Nah. 3:14).

When sufficiently baked by the sun, the bricks were laid in courses, generally on a stone foundation, by a bricklayer (see Fig. 15). He relied on simple tools—a trowel, a stretched string to mark the line of the wall, a wooden square, and a plumb line—which, together with his trained eye, assured the accuracy of his construction. The entire process—from mixing the clay to laying the brick—is depicted on a wall painting in an Eighteenth Dynasty Egyptian tomb at Thebes (Fig. 136).

The Stonemason

Stone provided a more permanent building material than mud-brick. The construction of stone walls and the cutting of stone blocks was the trade of the stonemason (see 1 Kings 7:9–12). In addition to buildings constructed of stone, the stonemason might also carve rock-cut tombs (see Isa. 22:16) or excavate water conduits such as that constructed in the time of Hezekiah (see 2 Kings 20:20). A stonemason was highly prized for his skill, and frequently worked for the king (Fig. 137).

One type of wall construction in ancient Israel consisted of simple, uncut rubble. Considerable skill was required, since the shape of each stone had to be chosen with care and fitted accurately within the framework of the other stones to assure stability of the wall. Rubble walls constructed without mortar which have survived for well over two millennia attest to the skill of the ancient stonemason.

The stonemason's craft is best represented, however, in the distinctive masonry style introduced into Israel during the Solomonic period and apparently of Phoenician origin. Solomon hired Phoenician craftsmen to construct the palace and Temple at Jerusalem, and possibly to train Israelites

136. Captives making bricks in an Egyptian tomb painting of the fifteenth century B.C.

137. A modern Arab stonemason at work.

as well (1 Kings 5:6; 2 Chron. 2:7–8, 13–16). Nothing remains of the Solomonic architecture of Jerusalem, but the masonry of this period can be observed in contemporary archaeological levels at other sites, such as Megiddo, one of the cities Solomon rebuilt (1 Kings 9:15).

Preserved sections of a number of the walls from the Solomonic period at Megiddo were constructed of well-cut blocks of ashlar masonry (hewn or squared stones). This ashlar masonry was laid in a distinctive "header-stretcher" pattern, with blocks set lengthwise along the wall ("stretchers") alternating with blocks laid across the width of the wall ("headers"). The exterior face of the blocks was dressed with narrow borders (on one to three, and occasionally all four, sides) leaving a raised boss in the center. Such masonry construction is referred to in the description of Solomon's palace in Jerusalem: "All these were made of costly stones, hewn according to measure, sawed with saws, back and front. . . . The foundation was of costly stones, huge stones, stones of eight and ten cubits." (1 Kings 7:9–11; cf. 5:15–18; 6:7).

The same skilled craftsmanship is even more apparent in the architectural remains of the royal citadel at Samaria (see Fig. 108), built by Omri and Ahab, kings of Israel who had close ties with the Phoenicians (see 1 Kings 16:23–33). Only the foundation courses of this well-planned citadel survive, but they were constructed of exceptionally well-dressed ashlar masonry, fitted closely together—without mortar—and laid in "header-stretcher" fashion. The exterior faces of the lower courses of stone were worked smooth to a marginal draft (a depressed border along the joints). The draft appears to be the remains of edges smoothed to receive guidelines drawn by masons to indicate how the stone should be cut. The guidelines, portions of which can still be seen on excavated remains, were drawn by snapping a taut cord smeared with red paint against the stone. The tool marks of the chisels and adzes used by the masons frequently are preserved on the ashlar blocks. In laying a wall, a string would be stretched between two cornerstones to act as a guide (see 2 Kings 21:13; Isa. 28:16–17). Throughout the construction, the wall would be measured for accuracy (see Ezek 40:5 ff.) and checked for vertical alignment with a plumb line (see Amos 7:7–8).

The Carpenter

Phoenician craftsmanship also was used by Solomon for the carpentry work of the royal palace and Temple in Jerusalem (see 2 Chron. 2:13–14). Indeed, fine wood was one of the main exports of the Phoenicians (1 Kings 5:8–10; 9:11), and, declared Solomon, "There is no one among us who knows how to cut timber like the Sidonians" (1 Kings 5:6). Nevertheless, Israelite carpenters supplied most of the necessary skills.

Various kinds of wood were available to the carpenter. Some of the more expensive kinds were imported, such as cedar and cypress from Phoenicia (1 Kings 5:8; Ezra 3:7) and almug wood from Ophir (1 Kings 10:11). Other kinds of wood were common to Israel, such as sycamore (1 Kings 10:27) and olive wood (1 Kings 6:31). Wood was used for a variety of purposes. Hewn beams for ceilings and support columns were cut from wood (1 Kings 6:9), as were window frames and doors (1 Kings 6:31–35). Wooden furniture was constructed, some of which was exceptionally elegant, such as the royal throne and beds inlaid with ivory (the sense of 1 Kings 10:18–20 and Amos 6:4). Parts of some musical instruments were also made of wood (1 Kings 10:12).

The roof paneling, doors, and ceilings of the Jerusalem Temple, made of wood, were carved in intricate patterns of open flowers, gourds, cherubim, and palm trees (1 Kings 6:18, 29, 32, 35). Normal house construction was less elegant. Simple Israelite family dwellings, such as those discovered at Tell Beit Mirsim and ancient Tirzah (Tell el-Far'ah, near Nablus), had flat roofs formed over horizontal wooden beams. The beams were overlaid with a matting of reed, cane, or small branches, which was in turn paved with a watertight surface of hard-packed clay. Similar roof construction is found in many areas of the Middle East today (*see* Fig. 20).

The finer work of the Israelite carpenter is described by Isaiah in reference to the carving of idols: "The carpenter stretches a line, he marks it out with a pencil; he fashions it with planes, and marks it with a compass;

he shapes it into the figure of a man, with the beauty of a man to dwell in a house" (Isa. 44:13). Besides the tools referred to by Isaiah—the (chalked) measuring line, the pencil, the plane, and the compass—the carpenter's tool kit included metal saws, adzes, chisels, awls, and files, examples of which have been recovered from archaeological excavations. The biblical carpenter worked in his shop, or on the site of a major construction such as the Jerusalem Temple. He was skilled and deft—an artisan as well as a craftsman.

The Shipbuilder

Related to the carpenter was the shipbuilder, who could construct a masterful ship capable of sailing across the Mediterranean Sea. Vessels varied in size, from the simple, locally made fishing boat (Luke 8:22) to the large Phoenician merchantman or "ship of Tarshish" made by expert craftsmen (1 Kings 10:22; Jon. 1:3). The Israelites themselves had few sailors and lacked the expertise and skill to build large ships. Solomon used Phoenician ships (Fig. 138) and sailors in the Red Sea (1 Kings 9:26–28; 2 Chron. 8:17–18).

The Phoenicians were renowned for their ability to sail deep waters and vast distances, and to construct beautiful ships (Isa. 2:16). Phoenicians at Tyre constructed their merchantmen and fleet fighting ships with planks of fir, masts of cedar, oars of oak, and decks of pine (Ezek. 27:5–6). The sails were cut from fine embroidered Egyptian linen, while the awning or deck cover was made from cloth dyed along the Phoenician coast (Ezek. 27:7). The ship was caulked, probably with bitumen, by men from Byblos ("Gebal," Ezek. 27:9).

Phoenician ships were mainly of two types. One type, the so-called "round" ship, had a rounded hull and raised prow and stern. It was used for normal commerce, plying along the coastal waters of the Levant (see 1 Kings 5:9). The other type of Phoenician ship, the so-called "long" ship, was larger

138. A Phoenician merchant vessel.

139. A slow wheel for making pottery. It is made of two units, an upper stone onto which the clay is centered, and a lower stone which has a conical protrusion that is inserted into the socket.

and more streamlined with a pointed ram at the prow and a high, curved stern. It was equipped with two banks of oars on each side, two steering oars extending from the stern, a central mast, and a high upper deck from which warriors' shields hung over the side. The "long" ships were large, seaworthy vessels—the "ships of Tarshish" mentioned in the Old Testament—armed and considerably faster than the ordinary "round" merchantmen. Both types of Phoenician ships are depicted on numerous reliefs from the ancient Near East, including one from the palace of Sargon II, king of Assyria (c. 722–705 B.C.), at Khorsabad (Iraq).

THE POTTERY INDUSTRY

The Israelite potter belonged to a long, developed tradition of craftsmanship in Palestine. The earliest pottery—crude, handmade and sun baked—dates to the sixth millennium B.C. (Pottery Neolithic Jericho) and was made in the home. By the time of the United Kingdom (c. 1000 B.C.) ceramic traditions were well developed and the potter's craft was a well-established specialization. Professional guilds or "workshops" were in existence and royal workshops were located in the Shephelah at Netaim and Gederah (1 Chron. 4:23). Pottery kilns were skillfully constructed, and the slow wheel and probably the fast wheel also were in general use. The slow wheel, or "tournette," was a simple turntable of stone or wood rotated by hand or foot (Fig. 139). The fast or "kick" wheel consisted of a throwing head (probably of wood) connected by a wooden shaft or axle to a large, heavy flywheel (either of stone or wood). The clay to be thrown was placed on the throwing head and turned counterclockwise (assuming a right-handed potter) by rotating the flywheel with the foot. The kick wheel provided the speed, momentum, and control by which the clay on the throwing head could be shaped by centrifugal force. It gave the potter greater versatility and control, allowed a much faster production rate, and resulted in more symmetrical shapes and greater uniformity between pots.

Although it appears that the fast wheel was in general use during the period of the Divided Monarchy, further research is necessary before the date of its introduction can be established with certainty. The difficulty arises from the fact that the distinction between a vessel turned on a slow wheel and one "thrown" on a fast wheel rarely can be determined by visual inspection alone. Visual traces of the manufacturing technique by which a pot was made frequently were erased when the vessel was finished, either by wet-smoothing (wiping the clay surface with a damp cloth or hand), coating with a slip (a thin, highly levigated, watery clay applied over the surface of a pot either by dipping or by painting with a brush or cloth), or burnishing (compressing the clay surface and sealing its pores by rubbing the surface of the vessel with a small, smooth tool such as a pebble or sea shell). The potter's wheel referred to by Jeremiah (Jer. 18:3) is not necessarily a fast wheel, even though the Hebrew term is in the dual. What is represented is a stone socket and a circular stone platform that fits into and rotates on the socket. Several examples of such pairs of stones have been found in archaeological excavations. In all cases, however, both stones are approximately the same diameter, and it would have been impossible to turn this type of potter's wheel with any speed. Each pair of stones is a slow wheel, or "tournette," indicating the possibility that the potter in Jeremiah's description was using a slow rather than a fast wheel (see Fig. 97). The earliest literary reference to the kick wheel dates to the early second century B.C., in a description of the potter's craft in the apocryphal book Ecclesiasticus (38:29–30):

> So too is the potter sitting at his work
>   and turning the wheel with his feet;
> he is always deeply concerned over his work,
>   and all his output is by number.
> He moulds the clay with his arm
>   and makes it pliable with his feet;
> he sets his heart to finish the glazing,
>   and he is careful to clean the furnace.

Even though workshops accounted for most of the pottery, certain vessels continued to be made in the home.

The Potter's Craft

The Old Testament makes wide use of the potter's technical vocabulary and refers to pottery in a variety of contexts. In outlining the potter's craft, five basic steps can be distinguished: obtaining the clay, preparing the clay, shaping the clay, drying and finishing the vessel, and firing the vessel. In the description that follows, no attempt has been made to cover all aspects of the potter's craft as it was known during the Israelite monarchy; the primary intention is to impart a feel for the craftsmanship and skill of the ancient potter.

Clay and Its Handling

The clay used by the biblical potter generally was obtained in the vicinity of his workshop. Only rarely was it shipped over long distances. Clay is a product of the natural weathering of rocks and occurs freely in nature. It is relatively easy to obtain, inexpensive to use, and a highly versatile art form. Clay is plastic when moist and can be formed into any number of shapes. When fired, clay becomes rigid and retains, throughout its use, the shape it took in the potter's hands. Even when broken, the sherds (fragments of broken pottery) are virtually indestructible and remain a constant testimony of the potter and culture that produced them.

Few natural clays can be worked directly. Biblical potters had to weather (age) and prepare their clay for use. Weathering was accomplished by allowing the clay to be exposed to the elements of nature so as to break the clay down into a usable form (Fig. 140). The process was aided by periodic cutting, turning, and treading. Clays of different grades were obtained by mixing the clay with water and allowing the particles of clay to settle out in a series of basins or settling tanks. The clay in each successive tank was of a finer consistency and therefore more plastic. The remaining mixture consisted of an extremely thin, watery clay or "slurry," which was used as a slip.

Another step in preparing the clay for use was treading, or walking through the clay with a measured step and rhythmic pace. The water was thus distributed throughout the clay to effect an even consistency. Large stones and other intrusive materials were also removed. Treading required skill and was referred to by Isaiah in describing impending disaster (Isa. 41:25).

Frequently a clay was too plastic and required the addition of a "temper"

140. A pile of raw clay exposed to the elements for weathering.

or "filler" (any substance added to clay to reduce plasticity). Fillers included fine sand, crushed pottery, chopped straw (see Exod. 5:6–21), and ground flint. The filler acted as a binder to retard the drying process, reduce excessive shrinkage, and prevent cracking. If the clay was too stiff, small amounts of water or a more plastic clay could be added.

The final preparation of the clay before forming, called "wedging," was usually done by hand. This consisted of folding, beating, and kneading the clay—over and under, in and out—in order to mix it evenly and remove pockets of air (Fig. 141). Failure to remove all air would result in steam being produced in the air pockets during firing, which would explode and shatter the vessel. The filler was added at this stage. In all, proper wedging demanded a considerable effort on the part of the potter. The feel of the clay in the potter's hands would indicate to him when the clay was fully prepared.

Forming the Vessels. A pot could be formed in a variety of ways, depending on the clay, the type of vessel to be manufactured, and the potter's skill. Vessels were hand-molded (formed from a ball of clay held in the hand), coiled on a slow wheel (built up in a series of sausage-shaped strips of clay), pressed in open molds from rolled-out sheets of clay, or thrown on a fast wheel (formed from a single lump of clay by the potter's hands as the clay rotates continuously on the wheel). To throw a pot the potter

141. A modern potter wedging the clay by kneading it over and over again.

positioned a mass of prepared clay on the throwing head and centered it by moving the clay up and down between his wet hands as the wheel turned until there was no distinguishable wobble (Fig. 142). Constantly keeping his hands wet by periodically dipping them in an adjacent bowl of water, the potter then thrust his left hand down into the center of the clay mass and with his right hand on the exterior surface of the clay, formed the vessel between his two hands (Figs. 143, 144, 145).

In addition to the intended shape of the vessel, its size also determined the procedure followed. A large vessel, for example, might be completed in three stages so that the clay would not become overworked. Vessels with a long, narrow neck were made in two or more pieces and then joined. Several small bowls or juglets could be fashioned out of a single mass of clay, working from the top and cutting each vessel off at the base with a thin string as it was formed (Figs. 146, 147). (Village potters in Lebanon today can form twenty small vessels from the same mass of clay in less than ten minutes.) A potter's skill was determined by the aesthetic form of his vessels, the thinness of his pieces, and the speed at which he could produce them.

Finishing Off the Vessels. When formed, the vessels were allowed to "set up," or dry, to a leather-hard state. They were then finished off. Excess

142. The potter first places clay on the wheel and shapes it with his hands until it is symmetrical and balanced.

143. The potter then makes an indentation in the center of the clay to begin the shaping of the vessel.

144. With each hand exerting pressure—one on the inside and one on the outside—the potter pulls his hands upward gradually to form the sides of the vessel.

145. The bowl is shaped into the desired form.

146. If the vessels are intended to be fairly
small, several may be shaped from a single
piece of clay.

clay could be removed and the vessel trimmed down with a metal blade or
sharp flint ("shaving"). The vessel could be decorated with incisions, with
various combinations of paint, or by coating the vessel with a thin, watery
clay solution which has the consistency of cream (called a "slip"). The vessel
also could be burnished (rubbing the surface with a smooth, hard, round-
faced tool such as a water-worn pebble or sea shell). A particularly fine class
of pottery in use during the period of the Divided Monarchy was coated
with a red slip and carefully burnished to a smooth, high luster. Known as
"Samaria Ware" in archaeological circles, it demonstrates the outstanding
skill and craftsmanship of the biblical potter.

After the vessels were carefully dried, the potter would "stack" or load
the pots into a two-story kiln attached to his workshop, enclose the stacked
pottery with a brick or clay cover, and bake them. At least three full days
were required to fire the pottery, since it was necessary to raise the temperature in stages, hold the fire at its peak for a time, and lower the temperature
gradually. This prevented any sudden temperature change that would shatter
the vessels. A number of excavated pottery kilns are contemporary with the
period of the Israelite monarchy. Examples occur at Megiddo, Tell en-Nasbeh

147. Once the smaller vessels are shaped, they can be cut from the clay mass by a string.

(Mizpah?), and in particular at Sarafand (biblical Zarephath), Lebanon, where an entire potter's quarter dating from the 15th century down to the 7th century B.C. has been uncovered.

Pottery Workshops. Pottery workshops generally were located within a specific area outside the city. The potter's quarter at Sarafand was located on a promontory along the shore overlooking the ancient harbor. Pottery kilns discovered at Megiddo lay outside the city wall on the eastern slope of the tell within the necropolis area. Biblical evidence suggests that the potter's quarter of Jerusalem lay outside the city. Jeremiah was directed to smash a "potter's earthen flask" at the "Potsherd Gate" (Gate of Potsherds) along the Hinnom Valley (Jer. 19:1–2). The "Gate of Potsherds" probably received its name from the discard or "waster" piles of the Jerusalem potters. The "waster" piles would have been primarily from vessels broken during firing, and so the kilns, and the potter's workshops as well, would have been located near the gate outside the city wall. The same area appears to be mentioned in Nehemiah's account of the rebuilding of the walls of Jerusalem, where "Tower of the Ovens" is perhaps to be taken as a reference to pottery kilns (Neh. 3:11; 12:38). The potter's quarter of Jerusalem, therefore, should be located somewhere to the south of the present Old City, perhaps in the vicinity of the Zion Gate.

The "potter's house" visited by Jeremiah (Jer. 18:2–4) should be located in the same area as the "Gate of the Potsherds." This shop was probably one of a number of workshops in the same vicinity. The workshop would have been centered about a small room where the potter sat at his wheel forming the vessels and where the most recent vessels—those awaiting finishing— were placed. A small room where the prepared clay was stored until ready for use would have been located to one side. A long narrow room where the leather-hard vessels were stored before firing perhaps would have been located adjacent to the kiln. The final part of the workshop would have been the kiln itself whose blackened upper surface dominated the area. The area surrounding the kiln and workshop would have been taken up by a "waster" pile, a basin or well for water, and piles of new clay in various stages of weathering. Potsherds, pottery slag from the kiln, ashes, and various pottery tools would have been scattered about. Off to one side rows of recently fired pottery would have been sitting waiting to be sold or to be transported to another market.

The Potter's Role

The potter served a major role in Israelite society. Clay from which he formed his pottery was also used for bricks, tiles, figurines, plaster, household ovens, and many other articles. He supplied society with the essential containers, plates, jugs, mugs, and pots of daily life. Vessels which he made were used for cooking (Lev. 6:21), for the storage of liquids (Num. 5:17), and even as containers for scrolls (Jer. 32:14). Some 34 Hebrew and Aramaic terms in the Old Testament refer to the ceramic vessels made by the potter. Moreover, the potter's wares were put to use after they were broken. A broken fragment of pottery could be used for dipping water or transferring live coals from one hearth to another (Isa. 30:14). Job used a sherd to scrape his sores (Job 2:8). Pottery fragments were also used to write on, as is evident from the ostraca of Samaria and Lachish.

The potter's craft and skill also suggested a number of Old Testament metaphors. Potsherds were symbols of dryness (Ps. 22:15), and the breaking of a pot was a symbol of total destruction (Jer. 19; Isa. 30:14; Rev. 2:27). A pottery vessel was also a place to store items of value (2 Cor. 4:7). In the minds of Israel's poets, the potter above all was a skilled craftsman who could take a formless mass of clay and fashion the most elegant vessel with his hands (Isa. 29:16; 45:9).

THE METAL INDUSTRY

There are few explicit biblical references to the actual processes by which metals were refined and metal objects formed. According to Genesis, the first smithy was Tubal-cain: "he was the forger of all instruments of bronze and iron" (Gen. 4:22). The statement suggests a great antiquity for the history of metallurgy, a fact confirmed by modern research. Archaeological excavation has recovered tools and other objects of copper which were in use as early as the Chalcolithic period (4th millennium B.C.). Indeed, recent survey work and excavation has shown that copper was being mined at this early date in the Timna region of the Wadi Arabah, about 20 miles north of Ezion-geber. The same area was mined by the Egyptians during the Ramesside period (end-14th to mid-12th century B.C.), and later still by the Romans.

Despite the statement that the home of the Israelites was a land "whose stones are iron and out of whose hills you may dig copper" (Deut. 8:9), there are no known copper or iron deposits in ancient Israel. Both had to be supplied through trade or conquest, but the Bible is relatively silent on the actual sources of Israel's metals. "Silver, iron, tin, and lead" were supplied by Tyrian ships from "Tarshish," probably Spain (Ezek. 27:12). Copper ore may have come from Cyprus, but this is unattested in the biblical narrative. It may also have come from the Wadi Arabah, although there is no evidence that these mines were worked during the period of the Israelite monarchy. It may simply be that a considerable amount of the copper and iron used by Solomon to form the Temple furniture was obtained by trade or taken in booty: "And from Tibhath and Cun, cities of Hadadezer, David took very much bronze; with it Solomon made the bronze sea and the pillars and vessels of bronze" (1 Chron. 18:8).

Metalworking in Israel

Evidence suggests that Israel did not have a native tradition in the working of metals but instead derived that knowledge from her neighbors. The earliest smelting of iron in the ancient Near East seems to have occurred in the 14th century B.C. in the Hittite area of Asia Minor (Turkey). It would appear that the Philistines introduced iron into Palestine and monopolized its use, as well as other aspects of metallurgy, down to the time of Solomon (1 Sam. 13:19–21):

Now there was no smith to be found throughout all the land of Israel; for the Philistines said, "Lest the Hebrews make themselves swords or spears";

but every one of the Israelites went down to the Philistines to sharpen his plowshare, his mattock, his axe, or his sickle; and the charge was a pim for the plowshares and for the mattocks, and a third of a shekel for sharpening the axes and for setting the goads.

Only after the power of the Philistines had been broken by Saul and David did iron come into common use in Israel, a factor attested by archaeological evidence as well.

A variant tradition traces the origin of metallurgy into Israelite society through the Kenites (literally "smiths") and Midianites, who probably were itinerant smiths in the area of Edom and the Wadi Arabah (see Num. 10:29–32; 24:20–22; Judg. 1:16; 4:11, etc). According to the biblical narrative, the events associated with the Kenites are placed in the time between Moses and the Judges, which would fit the working of the Arabah copper mines during the Ramesside period. It is quite probable that the Israelites came into early contact with itinerant smiths along the Jordan Valley and in the area to the south of the Dead Sea. However, there is no evidence that there were smiths among the Israelites during the days of their wanderings, and although the Wadi Arabah deposits were worked immediately prior to the time of the Israelite settlement in Canaan, they apparently were not worked during the time of the Israelite monarchy.

Additional evidence is provided by the statement that Solomon hired a craftsman from Tyre—Hiram, "a worker in bronze"—to provide the metal-work for the Jerusalem Temple (1 Kings 7:13–14, 40–44). The conclusion is that the working of copper, bronze, and iron were foreign to Israel at least down to the time of Solomon. Bronze and iron working were introduced into Israelite society during the reign of Solomon through the Philistines, Phoenicians, and possibly the Kenites, as the biblical narratives suggest.

In a list of the family of Judah appears "Joab the father of Ge-harashim" —i.e., guild of craftsmen—"so-called because they were craftsmen" (1 Chron. 4:14). The community of craftsmen was located northwest of Jerusalem along the Shephelah at the southern end of the Plain of Sharon and appears to have been in existence throughout the period of the Divided Monarchy. It has been suggested that the "craftsmen" were "smiths" who preserved a tradition in metallurgy from the time of the Philistine iron monopoly. The same area was resettled after the return from Exile (Neh. 11:35). "Workers in iron and bronze" were hired to help repair the Jerusalem Temple during the reign of Josiah (c. 640–609 B.C.; 2 Chron. 24:12). Israelite "smiths" or metalworkers were carried into Exile along with craftsmen and other important groups of people following the Babylonian destruction of Jerusalem in 587 B.C. (2 Kings 24:14; cf. Jer. 24:1).

The metals known and used in Palestine were gold, silver, "bronze" (i.e., copper), iron, tin, and lead (see Num. 31:22). Numerous objects were made from copper or bronze and iron. From bronze were made armor (1 Sam. 17:5-6), shields (2 Chron. 12:10), doors (Isa. 45:2), and all the bronze objects for the Temple including pots, basins, shovels, and the large "molten sea" (1 Kings 7:15-47). From iron were forged door bolts (Isa. 45:2), spearheads (1 Sam. 17:7), picks and axes (2 Sam. 12:31) and nails (1 Chron. 22:3). All of these objects required skilled craftsmen: smelters and refiners, forgers and smiths.

The Four Phases of Metalworking

The work of the metal industry can be divided roughly into four phases: mining, smelting, refining, and forming. Mining required little skill and was commonly performed by slaves or captured enemies. Job provides a vivid though general description of the mining process (Job. 28:1-11), where workers

> . . . search out to the farthest bound
>   the ore in gloom and deep darkness.
> They open shafts in a valley away from where men live; . . .
> Man puts his hand to the flinty rock,
>   and overturns mountains by the roots.
> He cuts out channels in the rocks,
>   and his eye sees every precious thing.
> He binds up the streams so that they do not trickle,
>   and the thing that is hid he brings forth to light.

Smelting is the process of separating the metal from its ore. The ore would first be prepared and broken up into workable chunks which were then smelted over a fire, rendering them into copper or iron and a waste product, slag, which would be discarded. The liquid metal—copper or iron—was cast into ingots for transportation to the smith's forge or shop. Smelting was usually done near the mines themselves. Slag heaps are very noticeable today in areas where smelting once took place. Numerous copper smelting furnaces and slag heaps have been found in the southern Arabah. Iron smelting furnaces were known in biblical times (see 1 Kings 8:51; Jer. 11:4), and iron slag occurs at Ashdod.

Refining was done at the craftsman's shop in association with forming. Copper (or bronze) was generally reheated in a clay crucible (a deep cup-shaped container) for refining. The copper in the crucible either was covered with charcoal or placed over a charcoal fire and brought to a high temperature in a liquid state. To achieve the temperature, the fire was fanned by use of a bellows attached to a clay pipe, or *tuyere*. Air forced through the *tuyere* by the bellows would fan the charcoal and bring the copper (or bronze) to a sufficient temperature, the purpose being to remove impurities and consolidate the copper (see Jer. 6:28–29).

The refined metal was either hammered into shape, or else poured in a liquid state into a mold, or forming die, constructed of stone or clay. Several types of stone molds have been recovered from archaeological excavations in Palestine. Some were of the open type, consisting of a depression cut into the surface of a block of stone or other suitable material. Such molds were easy to make and functioned very well in casting simple shapes such as dagger blades and axes. These objects had to be finished by hammering or annealing. More complex shapes, such as jewelry and arrowheads, required the use of a closed mold. This type of mold was constructed in two pieces which could be fitted together leaving a cavity in the shape of the object in the center, much like the principle of sand casting used today. The liquid metal was poured into the closed mold through filler holes, and allowed to harden. The mold was then broken open (either separated in the case of stone, or broken away in the case of clay) and the object removed and finished off by filing and polishing. Even more complex shapes, such as hollow statues, could be formed with the use of an additional clay or sand core. Bronze objects for the Jerusalem Temple were cast in the "plain of the Jordan . . . in the clay ground between Succoth and Zarethan" (1 Kings 7:46).

Iron in its smelted state is rather spongy and interwoven with impurities. To form iron, it had to be forged, that is reheated to a red-hot state and hammered into its final shape on an anvil while still hot. The process is described in two places in the book of Isaiah: "the ironsmith fashions an axe and works it over the coals; he shapes it with hammers, and forges it with his strong arm" (Isa. 44:12; see also Isa. 54:16).

The ancient smith was familiar with his raw material and knew its strengths and its limitations. He himself became from his labors strong and sinewy, and was capable of forming the crudest nail or the most refined bronze wine-service. From iron he could forge a bolt or a long sharp sword. From bronze he could mold a knife blade or hammer a very thin sheet to form a cauldron.

THE TEXTILE INDUSTRY

The textile industry is one of man's earliest crafts. Spinning and weaving were initially done in the home by the women of the family. In time, home-shops were formed and weaving became specialized and industrialized. Guilds were formed and distinct parts of a town or city—even entire villages—became the centers of a textile industry. Phoenician cities were famous for their rich purple cloth, the "royal" or "Tyrian" purple of antiquity (see

Ezek. 27:7). From Egypt, "fine embroidered linen" was a constant delight (see Prov. 7:16) and Damascus produced "white wool" (Ezek. 27:18).

Two basic fibers provided cloth for the ancient Near East: wool and flax (linen). Wool was predominantly a product of Palestine and Syria, a fact illustrated by the frequent mention of sheep and shepherds in the Bible. Mesha, king of Moab—"a sheep breeder"—was required "to deliver annually to the king of Israel [Ahab] a hundred thousand lambs, and the wool of a hundred thousand rams" (2 Kings 3:4). Linen, on the other hand, came primarily from Egypt. Some flax came from the area around Jericho (Josh 2:6), and linen was a valuable article of trade from Edom (Ezek. 27:16). Both cotton and silk were introduced relatively late into the textile industry of Palestine. King Sennacherib (c. 705–682 B.C.) appears to have introduced the cotton tree into Assyria. It was also produced in southern Egypt and the Sudan about the same time, as illustrated by a reference in Isaiah to "the weavers of white cotton" (19:9). Silk, which originated in China, may have been imported in the time of Ezekiel (see Ezek. 16:10, 13), but was still considered a treasured article of trade in Rome (Rev. 18:12). Cotton and silk, therefore, were not a part of the textile industry of the ancient Israelites.

There were various qualities of wool and linen, and a variety of products were woven from their fibers. White wool was especially prized (Ezek. 27:18), and was a symbol of purity and whiteness (Isa. 1:18). Ordinary garments were of wool or bleached linen, the latter especially good in summer because of its coolness. Linen was also used for bed clothing (Prov. 7:16), curtains, swathing the dead, sails of ships (Ezek. 27:7), and wrappers for scrolls. The wealthy and prominent often had garments of "fine embroidered linen," which was especially prized (see the priestly garments, Exod. 28:39, etc.; the veil of the tabernacle, Exod. 26:31; Prov. 7:16). Joseph was "arrayed . . . in garments of fine linen" by Pharaoh as a sign of his status (Gen. 41:42).

How were these textiles made and what were the processes of manufacture and the tools utilized? Some information can be gleaned from various biblical passages, coupled with artifacts and information from archaeological excavations. Four basic processes can be distinguished, and these will be discussed briefly in turn: Fullering, Dyeing, Spinning, and Weaving.

Fullering

Fullering is the process of washing, bleaching, and thickening the various fibers prior to dyeing and spinning. Normally this would be done with the fiber—the wool or flax—but there was also the necessity of finishing newly woven cloth and of cleansing and bleaching soiled garments. Preparation of wool for spinning was mainly done in the household in antiquity, with woolen garments made in the home for household use. The process consisted of washing in hot water, drying, beating the dry wool to detach fibers, plucking, and finally carding. Preparation of flax was a related, but lengthier process, and often done by professionals. The cut flax was tied and set up to dry (see Josh. 2:6), then soaked in water from five to fifteen days to loosen the fibers, after which the fibers were drawn over the edge of a stone or board and beaten with a wooden mallet, and finally refined by combing.

Fullering and bleaching, as well as the cleaning of old garments, were the tasks of professional fullers and launderers—usually men. There are several representations of the process in Egyptian wall reliefs and tomb paintings. Linen was first soaked in cold water in stone vats or pottery jars. It was then boiled in a vat or kettle over a fire in a mixture of water and an alkaline cleansing agent, borith (see Mal. 3:2; Job 9:30), beaten and scraped with wooden clubs on a stone or wooden base, and rinsed either in tubs or in flowing water. The new or clean cloth was then wrung to remove excess water, laid in the sun to dry and bleach, and finally smoothed and folded. It was necessary for the industry to be near a source of water (see Isa. 7:3; 36:2), as well as to be located outside the city wall because of the foul smell given off by the process. Such was the location of the "Fuller's Field" of Jerusalem (2 Kings 18:17; Isa. 7:3), which lay along the road south of the eastern hill, or "city of David," beyond the "conduit of the upper pool."

Dyeing

The dyeing of wool, like fullering and bleaching, was normally the task of a professional. Dyeing is a very ancient art, and the dyes themslves were derived from a variety of sources. Among the most widely used colors was red, taken from the bodies of certain female insects, or the cheaper "madder," extracted from a herbaceous perennial native to Syria, Palestine, and Egypt. Blue and yellow dyes were also used. The most highly prized dye, however, was purple or scarlet in color and extracted from the murex shell. It was produced along the Phoenician coast and referred to as "Tyrian Purple," the color of royalty (see Ezek. 27:7; Judg. 8:26; Luke 16:19). Depending on the time of soaking and drying, various shades could be achieved ranging from crimson red to deep, dark purple and even an approximation of our modern black. The Tyrian hired by Solomon to furnish the Temple was a "man skilled in purple, crimson and blue fabrics" (2 Chron. 2:7).

The dyeing process is not referred to in the Bible, although there are frequent references to dyed materials (e.g., Exod. 35:23, 25, 35; Judg. 5:30). A dyeing and weaving center was identified at Tell Beit Mirsim by the late W. F. Albright, who excavated the site. In the latest stratum (designated A) a half-dozen dyeing installations were discovered. Each consisted of a room containing two round stone vats with small openings on the top and a shallow channel around the rim, masonry basins and benches in front of or between the vats, and storage jars containing lime or potash for fixing the dye. Thread, rather than cloth, would have been dyed here, as indicated by the narrow openings of the vats. The cloth-bath process included two baths, after which the dye would have been squeezed out and the dyed thread set out to dry.

Spinning

Spinning is the process of forming continuous threads by drawing out and twisting the fibers. The process is of great antiquity, originating in the household as a predominantly female occupation, as is evidenced in expressions such as "spinster" and "distaff side" (see Prov. 31:13, 19). Men, however, also spun thread after the industrialization of the textile industry, as indicated on Egyptian wall reliefs and paintings. Spinning was generally done by rotating a spindle in the hand while feeding the threads in a regular manner. These threads were fed from a staff or an open bowl with interior "handles." The "handles" prevented the threads from becoming entangled. A number of clay "spinning bowls" have been found in various archaeological excavations in Palestine and Egypt. Spindle whorls (small flywheels positioned at the lower end of a spindle for momentum) of various shapes and sizes have been recovered as well. Spindles, usually made of wood, are less frequently preserved. The process is depicted on a number of Egyptian monuments, a particularly good scene occurring on the wall of a Middle Kingdom tomb at Beni Hasan.

Weaving

Weaving was the final stage in the process of manufacturing cloth and garments and did not differ considerably from the present method of weaving cloth with a hand loom. Weaving is essentially the interweaving of two series of threads called the warp (threads lengthwise in the loom) and the woof (threads which run at right angles to the warp). The warp threads are stretched on a loom, and the woof threads are passed over and under the warp threads. Various models of looms and the weaving process—some excellently detailed—have been recovered from Egyptian tombs.

Weaving was done by both men (Exod. 35:35) and women (2 Kings 23:7). Initially, it met the immediate needs of a particular household, but later was developed as an industry to serve the needs of society as a whole. One workshop was located at Beth-ashbea, where there were "families of the house of linen workers" (1 Chron. 4:21). As with the other aspects of the textile industry, there is little specific information on weaving in the Bible,

148. Egyptian women crouching to weave at a horizontal loom.

although there are numerous general remarks. The shaft of Goliath's spear, for example, was compared to a weaver's beam (1 Sam. 17:7). Job claimed that his days were "swifter than a loom" (Job 7:6), probably alluding to the speed of the shuttle that passed the woof through the warp. The woof was compressed by means of a reed or stick (see Judg. 16:13–14).

Three different types of loom were used in antiquity. One was a horizontal loom easily transported by nomads, which consisted of two beams secured to the ground by four pegs (Fig. 148). This type of loom is still used by Bedouin today and is the type portrayed in the story of Samson and Delilah (Judg. 16:13–14). A second type of loom consisted of two vertical beams inside of which the warp was stretched between crossbars at both ends. The third type of loom also had two vertical beams, but was slanted toward the rear and had a single crossbar located at the top (*see* Fig. 98). The warp threads were attached to the crossbar and weighted at the bottom by "loom-weights." The "loom-weights" were objects of stone or clay pierced with a hole through which the warp threads were tied. This type of loom was most common in Palestine during the period of the monarchy. Although neither the looms themselves nor the woven garments have been preserved, "loom-weights" have been discovered in a considerable number of archaeological excavations in the Levant.

THE JEWELRY INDUSTRY

Jewelers, goldsmiths, silversmiths, engravers, and workers in ivory had a number of traits in common and for this reason are treated as a group. All of these artisans worked with precious or semiprecious materials and shared similar tools and techniques. Personal ornaments frequently were made from a variety of different materials necessitating a close association and even overlap among the various specialists (*see* Fig. 27). Such a relationship is apparent in the description of Bezalel, the artificer of the tabernacle, who was filled "with ability and intelligence, with knowledge and all craftsmanship to devise artistic designs, to work in gold, silver, and bronze, in cutting stones for setting, and in carving wood, for work in every craft." (Exod. 31:3-5).

Objects of gold, silver, precious stones, and ivory are rarely found in archaeological excavations in Palestine, and when they are, their location is nearly always the tomb of an important official, a king's palace, or a shrine. Household utensils and personal ornaments associated with the majority of the people of ancient Israel were readily available and relatively inexpensive, made as they were from such raw materials as clay, bone, limestone, wood, and leather. Indeed, many of the objects probably were made in the home rather than by professional artisans.

Since Palestine lacked precious natural resources such as gold or silver, raw materials for elaborate and expensive jewelry or silver table settings had to be imported or acquired through conquest. As a result, the jewelry industry probably was controlled by a limited number of families or shops that operated in favored localities. Many jewelers may have shared the same shop while others worked within guilds attached to the royal palace. Goldsmiths in Jerusalem formed a guild following the Return (Neh. 3:8, 31-32), and a guild of silversmiths in Ephesus organized a protest against Paul's preaching (Acts 19:24 ff.). These craftsmen were highly skilled and knew both the limitations and properties of their raw materials, such as the melting point of different grades of metal or the resistance to abrasion of various stones.

Some raw materials were received through tribute or as diplomatic gifts (2 Sam. 8:10-12). In many cases, however, Phoenician merchants were the intermediaries (see Ezek. 27:12-25). Silver was obtained from Tarshish (Spain?, 2 Chron. 9:21; Jer. 10:9) and gold from Ophir (East African coast?, 1 Kings 9:28; Job 22:24). Gold and precious stones came from Arabia (1 Kings 10:2; Ezek. 27:22). An ostracon (document written on a pottery fragment) dating to the 8th century B.C. was discovered at Tell Qasile (near Jaffa) and reads: "Gold of Ophir to Beth Horon, Forty Shekels."

Goldsmiths and Silversmiths

Goldsmiths and silversmiths refined, worked, and shaped precious metals (see Job 28:1; Zech. 13:9; Mal. 3:2-3). Refining was carried out in a brazier filled with charcoal. The brazier consisted of a pottery bowl on a stand, examples of which are common in archaeological excavations throughout the Levant. Gold or silver was melted over the charcoal in a small, porous crucible held by a pair of bronze or iron tongs. A reed tipped with a clay nozzle was used as a blowpipe. Gold, which occurs in its pure state, could be refined easily. Silver was obtained by refining silver-rich lead ore (see Jer. 6:29–30; Prov. 25:4). Because of their value, both gold and silver objects were remelted and reused when discarded or broken (Ezek. 22:20–22). The quality of the gold or silver would depend on its source, the refining process, and the number of times refined (see Ps. 12:6).

Once refined, the liquid metal could be poured into stone molds to form pieces of gold or silver jewelry (Judg. 17:3–4). A number of stone molds have been recovered from archaeological sites in Palestine. Gold and silver also could be beaten or hammered into various shapes (Jer. 10:9). The tools usually utilized consisted of: polished pebbles held in the hand and hammered against the metal; copper or bronze chisels for cutting the metal; bronze or stone hammers with one flat end and one tapered end; sharp awls for punching holes; wooden blocks and stakes for beating and shaping. Particularly fine gold leaf for overlay (see Isa. 40:19) was achieved by hammering and then pressing. Silver bowls decorated in raised relief or *repoussé* were pressed out with tools of bone or bronze. Other techniques included filigree work and granulation. Filigree was the technique of forming designs in open style from very thin wire. In granulation the design was formed by soldering tiny droplets or granules of gold into a gold base (see Isa. 41:7).

Jewelers

Lapidaries and beadmakers worked with precious or semiprecious stones. They were required also to be familiar with ring settings of gold or bronze and with the art of inlay in stone and wood. Some of the tools used in antiquity included: various abrasive stones for filing; fine quartz sand for smoothing; wool or fiber pads for polishing; bronze or iron chisels and knives for cutting and shaping; awls and "graving tools" for engraving designs or inscriptions (see Exod. 32:4); and various copper or flint bits and a bow drill for boring. In boring a hole through a cylindrical bead for attachment to a necklace, the stone would be drilled from both ends, the cuts meeting approximately in the middle. Various designs and inscriptions were frequently engraved on settings and seals (Exod. 28:9–11; 39:6). An iron style might have been used for this work (Jer. 17:1). See section, JEWELRY.

Ivory Workers

Carved ivory was a luxury in the ancient world and was considered an obvious sign of wealth (Amos 3:15; 6:4). Three major collections of carved ivory have been discovered in archaeological contexts contemporary with the period of the Divided Monarchy of Israel, including a fine collection of figures and inlays from Israelite levels at Samaria (*see* Fig. 109). Ivory was carved in panels, in the round or in open work. The finer pieces were carved in low relief with the details of the design deeply grooved, filled with colored insets and set off with gold leaf. Ivory was used as inlaid decoration on furniture (1 Kings 10:18; Amos 6:4) and wall paneling (1 Kings 22:39; Ps. 45:8), and for figurines, jewelry, and various objects of a personal nature such as combs, small boxes, and cosmetic dishes.

Some ivory was obtained from elephants native to northern Syria, mentioned in Egyptian and Assyrian texts dating to the 2nd and beginning of the 1st millennium B.C. Additional ivory was obtained from distant lands by way of Phoenician ships (1 Kings 10:22; Ezek. 27:15). The tools and techniques used by the worker in ivory were similar to those used by gem cutters and jewelers: scribers, files, bow drills, scorpers (hand-held chisel-like tools), awls, and wooden mallets. Ivory's strength and homogeneous nature were considered worthy qualities by the artisan. Its lack of grain allowed freedom in carving, and its hardness permitted intricate and delicate designs. Although the natural color of ivory was appealing in itself, some finer pieces were inlaid and gilded.

THE FISHING INDUSTRY

Fishing was a limited but intensive industry in ancient Palestine. Only the Sea of Galilee and the Mediterranean coast were fished extensively. The waters of the southern Jordan River valley and the Dead Sea were too saline for fish to survive. A number of fishing communities were located along the shores of the Sea of Galilee during the New Testament period, as attested by many references. Information is lacking, however, during the Old Testament period, which simply may indicate that the Sea of Galilee lay outside of Israelite control. A similar situation prevailed along the Mediterranean coast. For much of the Old Testament period the coastal waters were under Philistine or Phoenician control. Consequently, these peoples, Phoenicians especially, rather than the Israelites, monopolized the Mediterranean fishing industry (see Neh. 13:16). As a matter of fact, with the exception of the waters off the mouth of the Nile, the Mediterranean was less rich in fish than other seas. Sea fishing was further limited by the straight, harborless, and often rugged coastline of Palestine.

Despite the restricted areas in which the Israelites might fish successfully, there are numerous references to fishing and the fishing industry in the Bible. Men fished either along the shore or from small boats. Fishing was a full-time profession for those engaged in it, and involved long hours. Fishermen frequently worked at night (John 21:3–4) and cooked a portion of the catch over a fire for breakfast (John 21:9–13). Often the efforts were unproductive (Luke 5:5), but at other times a considerable catch was made (Luke 5:6–7; John 21:11).

Methods of Fishing

Several methods of fishing were used in biblical times, none of which was highly industrialized. The three main methods were the fishing line and hook, the large dragnet, and the smaller net or seine (see Hab. 1:15). Fishhooks were used in Palestine since the preagricultural Natufian age, the 9th millenium B.C. archaeological sites of which have produced hooks and spearpoints of bone and antler. Fishhooks of copper, bronze, and iron are known from the period of the Israelite monarchy (see Amos 4:2), and hooks were still in use during the early Christian era (Matt. 17:27). The description in Job of the mythological sea monster Leviathan mentions fishhooks, fishing spears, and barbed harpoons (Job 41:1–7). The latter may have been used for large sea fish in the Mediterranean and Red Seas, such as sharks.

Fishing with a net was used more widely and was more efficient. The smaller net or seine was worked by hand, generally from the shore (Ezek. 47:10). The larger, heavier net (the "dragnet") was played out from a boat and dragged through the water, frequently in conjunction with other boats (Luke 5:4–7; Matt. 13:47–48). The ancient Egyptians fished on the Nile with either hooks or a dragnet stretched between two boats (see Isa. 19:8). A model from an Eleventh Dynasty (c. 2135–2000 B.C.) tomb at Thebes consists of two canoelike boats of papyrus dragging a large net between them. On each boat are oarsmen, workers tending the net, and another worker cleaning and stacking the fish.

In addition to catching the fish, fishermen had to perform a variety of other tasks that included washing (Luke 5:2) and repairing the nets (Matt. 4:21). In order to be able to manage the large nets and for social and economic reasons fishermen usually worked in groups or guilds (Luke 5:7, 10; John 21:2–3). Fishermen also had to sort and clean the fish (Matt. 13:48). Moreover, the fish had to be dried and salted if they were not to be sold immediately or were to be transported to a distant market. The fish would be split open with a sharp knife, salted, and suspended by ropes to dry in the sun. Fishermen either sold the fish along the shore where they caught them or carried them in baskets to a village market (Fig. 149). There was a Fish Gate, and probably an associated fish market, in Jerusalem (2 Chron. 33:14; Neh. 3:3; Zeph. 1:10).

149. A woman buying fish in an open fish market in modern Jerusalem.

MISCELLANEOUS INDUSTRIES

There are a number of additional "industrial" activities which were performed almost exclusively in the home or for which there is little specific information in the Bible. Several of these industries were not native to Israel, and biblical contact with them is only through the actual products. Other industries functioned only within the royal court of the king; the laborers in them therefore were more like servants than craftsmen. Almost any activity could in one way or another become a man's specialty and in this sense be interpreted as a part of the industrial life of the Bible. A few of the miscellaneous specialties should be noted.

The Baker

Baking was normally a household chore performed by women in ancient Israel (see section, FOOD). Because of the necessity of feeding large gatherings of people and therefore of baking large quantities of bread, it appears that professional bakers were attached to royal courts in the ancient Near East. A "chief baker" was a member of the royal court in Egypt in the time of Joseph (Gen. 40:2). The Egyptian royal bakery is depicted on reliefs and represented by wooden models. That royal cooks and bakers were a part of palace life in the days of the Israelite monarchy is suggested by

Samuel's description of the burdens of kingship (1 Sam. 8:13). However, the statement should be taken as referring to royal servants rather than to a specialized trade. The rise of city life under the monarchy favored commercial development; hence commercial bakeries. Hosea appears to allude to a specialist when he uses the baker's oven as a metaphor (Hos. 7:4). In the time of Jeremiah (c. 600 B.C.), professional bakers were located in a specific area of Jerusalem, the "Baker's Street," from which area the prophet received a daily ration of a loaf of bread while imprisoned (Jer. 37:21) (*see* Fig. 21).

The Miller

Grinding grain into flour was done in the Israelite household. There are no references to professional millers in the Old Testament. However, a related process, threshing, appears to have been handled by specific individuals, at least by the time of the Israelite monarchy. The reason may have been that threshing required a larger area than grinding: large quantities of straw could not be threshed conveniently in the home. Araunah, the Jebusite, from whom David purchased the "threshing floor" (2 Sam. 24:18-25), appears to have been a professional thresher. His "factory" was a large expanse of virtually flat rock on the crest of the hill north and outside of the City of David (early Jerusalem), where the Temple was eventually built. Araunah threshed the grain by driving a sledge pulled by two yoked oxen over grain spread out on the rock (2 Sam. 24:22) (*see* Fig. 70). The sledge was constructed of planks of wood turned up at the front with sharp stones or pieces of metal affixed to the bottom (see Isa. 41:15). A roller set with sharp cutting edges was also used to thresh grain (see Isa. 28:27-28). Araunah's sledge was pulled by oxen; the "cart" mentioned by Isaiah was pulled by horses. As payment for his services Araunah probably would have received a portion of the threshed grain, in addition to that eaten by the oxen. Since threshing and milling are related operations, it is possible that threshers later worked as millers when the opportunity arose. However, milling does not seem to have been done outside the home during the Old Testament period.

By the time of the New Testament the situation had changed. In his discourse on humility, and to explain the consequences of harmful influence, Jesus drew a picture of a man drowning in the sea because of the weight of a "great millstone" tied around his neck (Matt. 18:6 and parallels) (*see* Fig. 73). Heavy, circular stone mills appear to have been introduced into Palestine during the Hellenistic period (4th-2nd century B.C.). The wheel-shaped millstone revolved about a vertical wooden beam in a trough cut out of a rigid stone base. The millstone was turned by means of a horizontal

axle attached to a blindfolded mule or donkey. This type of millstone, however, was more commonly used to crush olives. Jesus' association of "millstone" and "sea" in Matt. 18:6 probably reflects the use of millstones and
weights, used in the production of olive oil in antiquity, as anchors on ships.

The Barber

A barber shaves and trims beards and cuts and dresses hair. Whether or
not this was a separate vocation in ancient Israel is uncertain, but professional barbers are known in Egypt from an early period. An Egyptian wall
painting from Thebes portrays a barber attending to army recruits in the
service of Pharaoh Amen-hotep II (15th century B.C.). The barber is depicted tying a soldier's hair in a knot and fixing the hair below the knot
into strands with fat taken from a bowl. Early biblical references to the
cutting of hair imply little more than that the hair should or should not be
cut (Num. 6:5). Later references indicate that there were professional barbers in Israel by the time of the Exile (Ezek. 5:1; cf. Isa. 7:20). Based on
Egyptian practice, the barber appears to have worked in the open. There is
little information as to a barber's style or technique. His only tool seems
to have been a razor, hand-held and shaped like an axhead. Egyptian razors
were frequently decorated.

The Glassmaker

No evidence exists of a glass industry in Palestine prior to the Hellenistic period. There are, however, numerous examples of faience and glasslike objects from Palestinian archaeological contexts dating to the Late
Bronze Age (16th–13th century B.C.). It appears that the material was not
made locally, but imported, primarily from Egypt, but also from Mesopotamia. A few authorities contend, nevertheless that at least some of the faience beads and other objects were produced in Palestine. If so, they were
made either by Egyptian craftsmen, or under their direction.

Three main periods can be distinguished during which glass or glasslike
materials were used in the ancient Near East. The first period covers the
15th through the 13th century B.C. Two principal centers of the industry were
Egypt and Mesopotamia (including northern Syria, where some scholars
suggest originated glass techniques). Whether all of the material from this
period is "imitation colored stone" (faience or frit), or whether there are
some examples of true glass, arouses controversy still to be resolved by sci-
entists. Faience, used for beads, figurines, and some small vessels, is a porous
body of finely ground quartz grains. The grains are held together by a
vitreous (glassy) coating, but the material is still crystalline—not true glass.
Glass is noncrystalline and is hon. ngeneous throughout with a liquidlike

structure. Faience was never completely melted like glass, but only "sintered" (i.e., cemented together). The purpose of faience, and any glasslike materials made in this initial period, was to replace and imitate rare precious stones. It was a method of producing cheap beads.

The method of manufacturing vessels from faience and glasslike materials at this time (15th–13th century B.C.) is readily visible in the spiraling lines of their various color patterns. A core was first made around a metal rod in the intended shape of the vessel. Softened "glassy" canes were then wrapped around the core in spiral fashion, compressed together, and the vessel shaped by rolling the wrapped core on a smooth surface. The vessel could then be removed from the core (i.e., the core was withdrawn) and decorated by winding threads of the same material around the vessel. Handles and other auxiliary pieces were also added.

The second period in which glass or glasslike containers were popular is during the 8th through the 6th century B.C., or approximately the second half of the Israelite monarchy. Again, there is no evidence that glass was manufactured in Palestine, and all of the very few examples known are imports, primarily from Mesopotamia (Assyria and Babylonia). It is possible that some pieces were imported from Phoenicia, since the Greeks attributed the origin of glass to the Phoenicians, but such importation cannot be proven.

150. Glassware dating from the Roman period (Rockefeller Museum, Jerusalem).

That glass was an expensive luxury item at the time is made clear not only by the archaeological record but also the only reference to glass in the Old Testament, where it is considered on a par with jewels, silver, and gold (Job 28:17). The reference may be to the luxuriant molded and cut glass vessels then appearing in the ancient Near East.

The third period in which glass vessels were used—and in this case true glass—was the Hellenistic-Roman age. Initially, the glass vessels were molded in a very thin form, but from the middle of the 1st century B.C. glass vessels were blown (Fig. 150). In this period there appears for the first time evidence for glass workshops in Palestine. Quantities of glass slag are known, as are several glass furnaces. An unparalleled number and variety of Hellenistic molded glass bowls from the end of the 2nd century B.C. has recently been recovered from the site of Tel Anafa in Upper Galilee, suggesting to its excavator that the glass must have been locally made. Even more recently debris from a glass workshop was excavated in the Jewish Quarter of the Old City of Jerusalem. Dating to the middle of the 1st century B.C., the debris marks a transition point from the molding of glass to the initial stage of blowing from glass tubes. Allusions to glass in Revelation clearly signify that blown glass is meant (Rev. 21:18, 21), and the image presented may even have been based on a glass furnace, where there would be a "sea of glass mingled with fire" (Rev. 15:2).

❧ Suggestions for Further Reading

THE FOLLOWING list is selective, and represents a small portion of the many references available for further research. In addition to the works cited under specific headings, attention is called to such journals as *The Biblical Archaeologist, Catholic Biblical Quarterly*, the *Israel Exploration Journal*, the *Journal of Biblical Literature*, and the *Palestine Exploration Quarterly*, and to similar periodicals which provide up-to-date information on subjects of current interest in the fields of biblical archaeology, research, history, and the daily life of the peoples of the Bible and the ancient Near East. General information on specific topics (e.g., "Dress," "Jewelry," "Marriage," and "Medicine") is also available from the four-volume *The Interpreter's Dictionary of the Bible* (Nashville: Abingdon Press, 1962) and its *Supplementary Volume* (1976), together with more compact Bible dictionaries such as John L. McKenzie's *Dictionary of the Bible* (Milwaukee: Bruce Publishing Co., 1965) and *Harper's Bible Dictionary* (8th ed., New York: Harper & Row, Publishers, 1973). For more detailed study the reader is referred to the bibliographies provided in the works listed under the individual headings below.

GENERAL

Bouqet, A. C. *Everyday Life in New Testament Times.* New York: Charles Scribner's Sons, 1954.

Everyday Life in Bible Times. Washington, D. C.: National Geographic Society, 1967.

Heaton, Eric W. *Everyday Life in Old Testament Times.* New York: Charles Scribner's Sons, 1956.

Pritchard, James B. *The Ancient Near East in Pictures Relating to the Old Testament.* 2nd ed., with supplement. Princeton, N.J.: Princeton University Press, 1969.

Pritchard, James B., ed. *Ancient Near Eastern Texts Relating to the Old Testament.* 3rd ed., with supplement. Princeton, N.J.: Princeton University Press, 1969.

de Vaux, Roland. *Ancient Israel* (Vol. 1, *Social Institutions*; Vol. 2, *Religious Institutions*). New York: McGraw-Hill Book Company, 1965.

I. THE WORLD OF THE BIBLE

Aharoni, Yohanan. *The Land of the Bible: A Historical Geography.* Philadelphia: The Westminster Press, 1967 (new edition in preparation).

Aharoni, Yohanan and Avi-Yonah, Michael. *The Macmillan Bible Atlas.* New York: Macmillan Co., 1968.

Baly, Denis. *The Geography of the Bible.* 2nd ed. New York: Harper & Row, Publishers, 1974.

Baly, Denis and Tushingham, A. D. *Atlas of the Biblical World.* New York: World Publishing Co., 1971.

Bright, John. *A History of Israel.* 2nd ed. Philadelphia: The Westminster Press, 1972.

Hillers, Delbert R. *Covenant: The History of a Biblical Idea.* Baltimore, Md.: The Johns Hopkins Press, 1969.

May, Herbert G., ed. *Oxford Bible Atlas.* 2nd ed. New York: Oxford University Press, 1974.

Mayes, A. D. H. *Israel in the Period of the Judges.* London: SCM Press Ltd., 1974.

Noth, Martin. *The Old Testament World.* Philadelphia: Fortress Press, 1966.

———. *The History of Israel.* 2nd rev. ed. New York: Harper & Row, Publishers, 1960.

Wiseman, D. J., ed. *Peoples of Old Testament Times.* Oxford: At the Clarendon Press, 1973.

II. HOW THE PEOPLE OF THE BIBLE LIVED

HOMES

Beebe, H. Keith. "Ancient Palestinian Dwellings," *The Biblical Archaeologist* 31 (1968), pp. 38–58.

———. "Domestic Architecture and the New Testament," *The Biblical Archaeologist* 38 (1975), pp. 89–104.

de Schauensee, Maude. "Portable Architecture," *Expedition*, Vol. 10, No. 3 (Spring, 1968), pp. 32–9.

Ussishkin, David. "King Solomon's Palaces," *The Biblical Archaeologist* 36 (1973), pp. 94–101.

de Vaux, Roland. "Tirzah," in D. Winton Thomas, ed., *Archaeology and Old Testament Study.* London: Oxford University Press, 1967, pp. 376–78.

FOOD

Bouqet, A. C. *Everyday Life in New Testament Times*, pp. 69–79.

Forbes, R. J. *Studies in Ancient Technology*, Vol. III. 2nd ed. Leiden: E. J. Brill, 1965, Chapters II–III (pp. 51–110).

Heaton, Eric W. *Everyday Life in Old Testament Times*, pp. 81–115.

Pritchard, James B. *The Ancient Near East in Pictures*, nos. 149–58.

———. *Gibeon, Where the Sun Stood Still.* Princeton, N.J.: Princeton University Press, 1962, Chapter IV.

CLOTHING

Pritchard, James B. "Syrians as Pictured in the Paintings of the Theban Tombs,"

Bulletin of the American Schools of Oriental Research, No. 122 (April, 1951), pp. 36–41.

——. *The Ancient Near East in Pictures*, nos. 1–66 and 770–72.

JEWELRY

Aldred, Cyril. *Jewels of the Pharaohs: Egyptian Jewelry of the Dynastic Period*. New York: Praeger Publishers, Inc., 1971.

Maxwell Hyslop, K. R. *Western Asiatic Jewellery c. 3000–612 B.C.* London: Methuen & Co. Ltd., 1971.

MEDICINE

Forbes, R. J. "Cosmetics and Perfumes in Antiquity," *Studies in Ancient Technology*, Vol. III, Chapter I (esp. pp. 1–26).

Majno, Guido. *The Healing Hand: Man and Wound in the Ancient World*. Cambridge, Mass.: Harvard University Press, 1975.

Neufeld, Edward. "Hygiene Conditions in Ancient Israel (Iron Age)," *The Biblical Archaeologist* 34 (1971), pp. 42–66.

Van Beek, Gus W. "Frankincense and Myrrh," *The Biblical Archaeologist* 23 (1960), pp. 69–95; reprinted in *The Biblical Archaeologist Reader*, Vol. 2. (1964), pp. 99–126.

FAMILY EVENTS

Mendelsohn, Isaac. "The Family in the Ancient Near East," *The Biblical Archaeologist* 11 (1948), pp. 24–40; reprinted in *The Biblical Archaeologist Reader*, Vol. 3. (1970), pp. 144–62.

Schauss, Hayyim. *The Lifetime of a Jew*. New York: Union of American Hebrew Congregations, 1950.

de Vaux, Roland. "Family Institutions," Part I in *Ancient Israel*. Vol. 1, *Social Institutions*, pp. 17–61.

RELIGIOUS EVENTS

Andreasen, Neils-Erik A. *The Old Testament Sabbath: A Tradition-Historical Investigation*. "SBL Dissertation Series," No. 7. Missoula, Mont.: Society of Biblical Literature, 1972.

Gray, George Buchanan. *Sacrifice in the Old Testament: Its Theory and Practice*. Oxford: At the Clarendon Press, 1925, Chapters XVIII–XXV (pp. 271–397).

Kraus, Hans-Joachim. *Worship in Israel: A Cultic History of the Old Testament*. Oxford: Basil Blackwell, 1966.

Rowley, H. H. *Worship in Ancient Israel: Its Forms and Meaning*. Philadelphia: Fortress Press, 1967.

Safrai, S. "The Temple and the Divine Service," Chapter IX in *The Herodian Period*. The World History of the Jewish People, Vol. VIII, edited by Michael Avi-Yonah. New Brunswick, N.J.: Rutgers University Press, 1975, pp. 282–337.

de Vaux, Roland. *Ancient Israel*. Vol. 2 (Part IV). *Religious Institutions,* esp. Chapters 15–18.

III. HOW THE PEOPLE OF THE BIBLE WORKED

THE LIFE OF THE NOMAD

Coon, Carleton S., et. al. "Badw," in *The Encyclopaedia of Islam*. Vol. I, rev. ed. Leiden: E. J. Brill, 1960, pp. 872–92.

Seale, Morris S. *The Desert Bible: Nomadic Tribal Culture and Old Testament Interpretation*. London: Weidenfeld and Nicolson, 1974.

Van Seters, John. "The Nomadism of the Patriarchs," Chapter 2 in *Abraham in History and Tradition*. New Haven, Ct.: Yale University Press, 1975, pp. 13–38.

de Vaux, Roland. "Introduction—Nomadism and Its Survival," in *Ancient Israel*. Vol. 1. *Social Institutions*, pp. 1–15.

THE LIFE OF THE FARMER (see also under *Food*)

Albright, William F. "The Gezer Calendar," *Bulletin of the American Schools of Oriental Research*, No. 92 (1943), pp. 16–26.

Anati, Emmanuel. *Palestine Before the Hebrews*. New York: Alfred A. Knopf, 1963, pp. 137–314, esp. pp. 217–33.

Baly, Denis. *The Geography of the Bible*, esp. Chapters 4–7 (pp. 43–90).

Pritchard, James B. *The Ancient Near East in Pictures*, nos. 84–96.

Stager, L. E. "Climatic Conditions and Grain Storage in the Persian Period," *The Biblical Archaeologist* 34 (1971), pp. 86–8.

———. "Farming in the Judean Desert During the Iron Age," *Bulletin of the American Schools of Oriental Research*, 221 (Feb. 1976), pp. 145–58.

de Vaux, Roland. "Palestine During the Neolithic and Chalcolithic Periods," Chapter IX(b) in *The Cambridge Ancient History*. Vol. I, Part 1. Cambridge: Cambridge University Press, 1970, pp. 498–538.

THE PROFESSIONAL LIFE

Cody, Aelred. *A History of Old Testament Priesthood*. Analecta Biblica, 35. Rome: Pontifical Biblical Institute, 1969.

Huffmon, Herbert B. "Prophecy in the Mari Letters," *The Biblical Archaeologist* 31 (1968), pp. 101–24; reprinted in *The Biblical Archaeologist Reader*, Vol. 3. (1970), pp. 199–224.

Mantel, H. D. "The High Priesthood and the Sanhedrin in the Time of the Second Temple," Chapter VIII in *The Herodian Period*, pp. 264–81

Millard, A. R. "The Practice of Writing in Ancient Israel," *The Biblical Archaeologist* 35 (1972), pp. 98–111.

Pritchard, James B. *The Ancient Near East in Pictures*, nos. 103–11, 191–211, 229–89, 597–629, 794–97, and 803–12.

Sellers, Ovid R. "Musical Istruments of Israel," *The Biblical Archaeologist* 4 (1941), pp. 33–47; reprinted in *The Biblical Archaeologist Reader*, Vol. 1. (1961), pp. 81–94.

de Vaux, Roland. *Ancient Israel*. Vol. 2. *Religious Institutions*, Chapters 5–8 (pp. 345–405).

———. *Archaeology and the Dead Sea Scrolls*. Rev. ed. London: Oxford University Press, 1973, esp. Chapter III.

THE CIVIL LIFE

Avi-Yonah, Michael, ed. *The Herodian Period*, Chapters I–V (pp. 1–205).

Heaton, E. W. *Solomon's New Men: The Emergence of Ancient Israel as a National State*. New York: Pica Press, 1974, esp. Chapter 3 (pp. 47–60).

Macdonald, John. "The Status and Role of the Na'ar in Israelite Society," *Journal of Near Eastern Studies* 35 (1976), pp. 147–70.

McKenzie, John L. "The Elders in the Old Testament," *Biblica* 40 (1959), pp. 522–40.

Mettinger, Tryggve N. D. *Solomonic State Officials*. Lund, Sweden: CWK Gleerup, 1971.

Ussishkin, David. "The Necropolis from the Time of the Kingdom of Judah at Silwan, Jerusalem," *The Biblical Archaeologist* 33 (1970), pp. 34–46.

de Vaux, Roland. "Civil Institutions," Part II in *Ancient Israel*. Vol. 1. *Social Institutions*, pp. 63–209.

THE MILITARY LIFE

David, William Stearns. *A Day in Old Rome*. Boston: Allyn and Bacon, 1953.

de Vaux, Roland. "Military Institutions," Part III in *Ancient Israel*. Vol. 1. *Social Institutions*, pp. 211–67.

———. "Singular Combat in the Old Testament," Chapter 7 in *The Bible and the Ancient Near East*. Garden City, N.Y.: Doubleday & Company, 1971, pp. 122–35.

Watson, G. R. *The Roman Soldier*. Ithaca, N. Y.: Cornell University Press, 1969.

Webster, Graham. *The Roman Imperial Army*. New York: Funk and Wagnalls, 1969.

Yadin, Yigael. *The Art of Warfare in Biblical Lands*. 2 vols. New York: McGraw-Hill Book Company, Inc., 1963.

———. "Warfare in the Second Millenium B.C.E.," Chapter VII in *Patriarchs*. The World History of the Jewish People, Vol. II, edited by B. Mazar. New Brunswick: Rutgers University Press, 1970, pp. 127–59.

THE INDUSTRIAL LIFE

Dever, William G. "The Water System of Hazor and Gezer," *The Biblical Archaeologist* 32 (1969), pp. 71–8.

Forbes, R. J. *Studies in Ancient Technology*, 9 vols. 2nd ed. Leiden: E. J. Brill, 1962–74.

Hodges, Henry. *Technology in the Ancient World*. Baltimore: The Penguin Press, 1970.

Jerusalem Revealed: Archaeology in the Holy City 1968–1974. Jerusalem: The Israel Exploration Society, 1975, pp. 75–84.

Johnston, Robert H. "The Biblical Potter," *The Biblical Archaeologist* 37 (1974), pp. 86–106.

Kelso, J. L. and J. P. Thorley. "The Potter's Technique at Tell Beit Mirsim, Particularly in Stratum A," in W. F. Albright, *The Excavation of Tell Beit Mirsim*. Vol. III. The Iron Age (AASOR, Vols. XXI–XXII) (New Haven, Ct.: The American Schools of Oriental Research, 1943), pp. 86–142.

Kenyon, Kathleen. *Royal Cities of the Old Testament*. London: Barrie & Jenkins, Ltd., 1971.

Pritchard, James B. *The Ancient Near East in Pictures*, nos. 112–16, 122–48, and 778–87.

Roebuck, Carl, ed. *The Muses at Work*. Cambridge, Mass.: The MIT Press, 1969.

Rothenberg, Benno. *Timna: Valley of the Biblical Copper Mines.* London: Thames and
    Hudson, 1972.
Yadin, Yigael. "The Fifth Season of Excavations at Hazor, 1968–1969," *The Biblical
    Archaeologist* 32 (1969), pp. 63–70.

❧ Index of Scripture References

OLD TESTAMENT

Genesis

1:28	89
2:12	82
2:24	100
3:7	48
3:16	91
4	133
4:1	69
4:10	136
4:21	230
4:22	373
4:25	92
4:26	92
9:1	89
9:20	183
9:22–23	341
11:3	33
12–50	9
12:3	13
12:6	169
12:16	128
13	162
14:14–16	271
14:18	191
15:1	135
16:4	91
17:10–14	95
17:12–13	96
17:25	95

18:1–8	138
18:1–15	30
18:4	85
18:4–8	42
19:1–8	138
19:2	85
19:30	26
20:7	203
21:3	92
21:4	92
21:8	98
21:14	125
22	134, 191
22:1–4	97
23:10	242
23:18	242
24	42
24:2ff	237
24:13	100
24:22	58
24:28–32	138
24:31–33	42
24:32	85
24:53	64
24:60	102
24:65	101
25:8	105
25:25–26	92
26:15–22	134
26:17–33	162
26:20	31
27:28	156

28:18	75
29:6	100
29:6–10	141
29:18–21	99
29:23–25	101
29:27	103
29:27–28	99
30:24	92
30:32	130
31:14–16	99
31:38–40	142
31:42	135
31:45	135
31:54	191
32:14	133
33:18–20	169
34:4	98
34:12	99
34:14–16	96
34:25	96
35:14	75
35:16	91
35:17	90
37:7	179
37:14	143
37:22	125
37:25	81
38:27–30	73
38:28	90
40:2	385
40:12	206
41	150

Genesis (con't.)

41:8 204
41:35–36 149
41:39–57 258
41:42 377
41:45 .... 190, 191
41:47–49 149
41:51–52 92
41:55–57 149
43:11 .... 81, 159
43:24 85
44:5 204
44:15 204
46–47 149
46:1 191
46:4 104
47:22 .... 190, 191
47:29–31 237
49:24 135
50:2–3 105
50:10 106
50:26 105

Exodus

1:8–14 264
1:11 149
1:15–19 73
1:15–21 90
1:16 90
1:21 89
2:7–9 97
2:16 190
2:16–19 141
2:22 92
3:5 196
3:17 270
4:24–26 95
6:26 271
7:1 203
7:11 204
12:1–28 .... 112, 146
12:8 181
12:12 69
12:17 271
12:22 35
12:24–27 209
12:43–49 96
12:47–48 96
13:2 96
13:14–16 96
14:2 279
14:6–9 278

14:13 271
15:3 .... 270, 271
15:20 203
17:9 280
17:16 ...... 270, 271, 279
18:21 293
18:21–22 241
19:16–19 270
20:4 63
20:4–5 348
20:18 270
21:7 134
22:16 99
22:18 .... 70, 205
22:29–31 96
23:12 109
23:14–17 115
23:16 .... 182, 188
23:22 270
23:27–28 271
25:6 74
26:31 377
27:20 .... 74, 186
28:1 190
28:4 196
28:6–14 196
28:9–11 382
28:15 192
28:15–30 ... 192, 193, 196
28:28 192
28:30 ...... 191, 192, 206
28:31 196
28:36–38 196
28:39 .... 196, 377
28:39–40 196
28:42 196
29:35–36 190
29:38–42 196
29:39–43 194
30:34 82
30:34–38 80
31:2–6 63
31:3ff 189
31:3–5 381
31:12–17 109
31:14–15 110
32:4 382
32:13 270
32:25–29 190
32:32–33 292
34:20 97
34:22 ...... 146, 181, 188
34:31 109

35:6 132
35:23 378
35:25 378
35:35 ...... 189, 378, 379
36:14 132
38:8 233
39:2–7 196
39:6 382
39:8–21 .... 192, 196
39:22–26 196
39:27 196
39:28 196
39:30–31 196
40:18–35 30

Leviticus

1:3–17 196
1:10 132
2:1–7 75
2:15–16 80
4:13–21 241
4:15 241
4:23 132
7:28–36 193
8 190
8:30 75
9:3 132
9:15 132
11–15 72
11:24–25 95
12:2–8 95
12:3 95
13 71
13:33 86
13:45 52
14:8–9 86
15:5–8 95
15:10–11 95
16 118
16:4 196
16:8–10 206
17:12–13 136
17:14 136
18:3 53
19:9–10 179
19:10 184
19:26 .... 70, 205
19:27 .... 52, 86
19:28 104
19:31 .... 70, 205
20:2–5 97
20:6 .... 70, 205

Leviticus (con't.)

20:27	....	70, 205
21:1–4	....	105
21:5	....	86, 104
21:7	....	233
21:9	....	233
22:4	....	105
22:7	....	95
23	....	115
23:10–11	....	181
23:15	....	114
23:15–17	....	181
23:16–17	....	182
23:22	....	179
24:2	....	186
25:25	....	238
25:47–49	....	238
26:5	....	174

Numbers

1:4–15	....	135
3:13	....	96
3:41	....	97
3:46–51	....	97
3:47–48	....	96
5:2–3	....	69
5:17	....	372
6:5	....	387
6:7	....	69
6:9	....	86
6:18	....	86
8:16–18	....	97
8:17	....	96
8:18	....	97
9:2–14	....	181
10:8–9	....	270
10:29–32	....	374
11:7	....	82
11:8	....	75
11:12	....	97
11:16–25	....	243
18:16	....	97
19:1–22	....	69
19:11–16	....	105
21:2–3	....	271
21:8–9	....	70
21:14	....	279
22	....	129
22–24	....	199
24:6	....	81
24:20–22	....	374
27:21	....	191, 206

31:1–12	....	280
31:3	....	270
31:22	....	375
32	....	162
35:9–34	....	137
35:33	....	137
35:34	....	137

Deuteronomy

1:13	....	241
1:15	....	293
3:12–20	....	162
4:9–10	....	209
5:12–14	....	109
5:14	....	129
6:3–23	....	270
6:4–9	....	35
6:7	....	209
6:10–11	....	162
6:20–25	....	209
7:13	....	158
8:7–8	....	158
8:7–12	....	40
8:8	....	159
8:9	....	373
8:10–11	....	70
8:15	....	125
9:3–5	....	270
10:16	....	95
11:10–11	....	150
11:14	......	154, 158, 174
12–26	....	194
13:9–10	....	190
14:1	....	104
14:22–29	....	146
14:29	....	190
16	....	115
16:1–8	....	146
16:9–10	....	181
16:9–11	....	181
16:9–12	....	146
16:13	....	188
16:13–15	....	146
17:5–6	....	137
17:9	....	190
18:1	....	190
18:4	....	131
18:9–14	....	205
18:15–22	....	201, 203
19:1–13	....	137
19:11–12	....	241
19:14	....	146

20:2	....	270
20:3	....	271
20:5–8	....	333
20:5–9	....	272
20:7	....	101
21:18–21	....	241
21:19	....	242
21:22–23	....	105
22:8	....	40, 171
22:9–10	....	146
22:10	....	177
22:12	....	52
22:15	....	242
22:23–27	....	101
22:28–29	....	99
23:9–14	....	271
23:17–18	....	**233**
23:24–25	....	146
24:6	....	146
24:19–21	....	179
24:20	....	185
24:21	....	184
25:4	....	180
25:9	....	89
26:11–13	....	190
27:9	....	190
28:15–24	....	156
30:6	....	95
31:9–13	....	194
32:39	....	69
32:46	....	209
33:8–11	....	190
33:10	....	194
33:28	....	156
33:29	....	271
34:10	....	203

Joshua

2:1ff	....	233
2:1–6	....	279
2:6	....	179, 377, 378
3:5	....	270
5:2–3	....	95
1:12–15	....	162
5:8	....	96
5:11	....	181
5:15	....	196
6:22–25	....	233
6:24	....	296
7:1–2	....	271
8	....	279
9:21–27	....	264

Joshua (con't.)

10:8	271
10:10	271
10:13–14	270
10:25	271
12:21	309
13:1–19:51	238
15:21–62	262
17:7–11	169
17:12	309
18:10	206
19:17–18	239
20:1–9	137
22:8	296
22:10–34	242
22:16	241
22:30	241
24	169, 239
24:12	271
24:13	162
24:29–30	244

Judges

1:12–13	99
1:12–15	99
1:16	33, 374
1:19	163, 279, 296
1:21	279
1:23–25	279
1:27	309
1:27–35	279
1:27–36	163
1:28	264
1:30	264
1:33	264
1:35	264
2:8–23	272
3:1–6	241
3:8	241
3:9	245
3:9–10	244, 245
3:10	272
3:12–14	241
3:15	245
3:16	274
3:27	272
4	273
4:4	203
4:4–5	245
4:5–6	238
4:7	273
4:10	241

4:11	374
4:13	273
5	273
5:4	270
5:8	273
5:10–11	162
5:11	163
5:14–15	241
5:15	241, 273
5:16	162
5:21	273
5:23	271, 272
5:24–25	162
5:30	49, 378
5:31	271
6:1–8:12	280
6:1–8:32	239
6:2	26
6:2–5	163
6:11	163, 180
6:25–27	163, 191
6:34	272
6:35	272
6:36–40	156
6:37	163
7:1–23	239
7:9–14	270
7:24	272
8:1–3	245
8:2	163
8:14	241
8:16–17	43
8:22–23	245
8:23	32
8:26	378
9	169
9:4	281
9:8ff	32
9:37	169
10:1–5	245
10:4	129
10:6–12:7	245
10:7–9	241
10:18	242, 245
11	134
11:5–11	245
11:26	238
12:8–15	245
13:15–23	191
14:2	98
14:8–9	140
14:10–18	102
14:12	49

14:17	103
14:20	102
15:4–5	163
15:5	158
15:18	95
16:13–14	380
16:20	272
17–18	191
17:1–5	163
17:7–13	190, 191
17:10	193
17:10–12	163
18:3–6	191
18:5–6	192
18:14–20	191
18:30–31	191
19:1	190
19:16–26	138
19:21	85
19:29–30	272
20:8	31
20:27–28	191
20:16	301
20:27–28	191
21:1–5	272
21:8–15	272
21:19–21	188
21:25	238

Ruth

2:2–3	100
2:17	180
3–4	163
3:2	181
4:1–12	242, 252
4:14–17	91
4:15	103

1 Samuel

1–3	210
1–4	191
1:3	191, 271
1:6–10	91
1:19–20	91
1:19–28	97
1:21	191
1:24–28	97
2:5	98
2:8	241
2:10	270
2:13–14	193

1 Samuel (con't.)

2:22 233
4 271
4:1–11 .... 246, 280
4:1–7:1 192
4:3–4 191
4:21 92
5 .... 71, 271
5:5 190
5:6 69
6:2 190
6:5 230
7:5–11 245
7:10 270
7:15–17 245
8:1–22 245
8:4 198
8:4–5 246
8:4–11:15 246
8:10ff 32
8:10–18 311
8:11–17 248
8:12 293
8:13 386
8:14–17 .... 179, 254
8:19–20 246
9:5ff 198
9:6 198
9:7–8 203
9:9 198
9:11 100
9:11ff 198
9:12–13 203
9:19 203
9:22–24 203
10:1 .... 75, 199, 246
10:1–26 244
10:5 ... 198, 199, 231, 246
10:8 198
10:17–24 246
11:1–11 246
11:7 272
12:1ff 32
13:2 .... 31, 280
13:3 272
13:3–4 246
13:6 27
13:11–18 163
13:19–22 246
13:19–22 296
13:20–21 178
13:21 176
14:2 .... 159, 280

14:6 95
14:26–27 161
14:32–34 136
14:37–42 206
14:36–42 192
14:50 246
14:52 .... 246, 281
15:2 271
15:6 33
16:1 75
16:4 272
16:13 ...... 75, 199, 255
16:16 231
16:16–23 230
16:18–21 281
16:21 257
16:23 231
17:4–7 246
17:5–6 375
17:7 .... 375, 380
17:12–18 295
17:18 293
17:22 296
17:26 95
17:28 125
17:36 95
17:45 270
17:50 301
18:7 287
18:13 293
18:21 100
18:25 99
19:13 132
19:18 198
19:18–24 198
19:20 198
19:24 203
20:21–22 285
20:34 48
21–22 191
21:4 285
21:4–5 270
21:7 281
22:1 .... 26, 285
22:1–2 282
22:2 286
22:7 .... 281, 293
22:9–10 192
22:13 192
22:14 283
22:15 192
22:18 281
23:6–12 192

24:1 125
25 42
25:1 231
25:2 133
25:5 285
25:6 285
25:20 129
25:28 .... 271, 279
25:29 302
25:41 85
27:8–12 282
28:3 206
28:6 .... 206, 270
28:6–25 206
28:9 206
28:18 271
28:19 270
30:7 270
30:7–8 192
30:12 184
30:26–31 241
31:1–7 280
31:1–13 246
31:13 106

2 Samuel

1:10 .... 59, 258
1:11 232
1:11–12 .... 104, 231
1:12 108
1:17–27 231
1:21 .... 75, 156
2:1–4 246
2:4 242
2:14 285
2:28 231
3:27–30 137
3:31 ..... 104, 105, 232
3:33–34 231
3:39 286
4:4 97
5:1–3 246
5:3 242
5:6–9 247
5:6–10 290
5:8 217
5:17–25 ...... 246, 290
6:1–19 247
6:5 231
7:1–3 255
7:4–17 199
8:2 307

2 Samuel (con't.)

8:2–12 254
8:3–4 288
8:4 303
8:8 296
8:10–12 ...._... 381
8:15 253
8:15–18 .... 193, 247, 253
8:16 261
8:17 .... 215, 255, 260
8:18 283
9:7 48
10 293
10:6 294
10:6–14 .... 254, 290
10:8 294
10:9–14 287
10:15–19 ...... 253, 254
10:17 294
11 305
11:1 8
11:9 283
11:11 270
11:13 283
12:16–23 69
12:20 .... 75, 106
12:26–31 .... 253, 305
12:31 .... 179, 264, 296,
       307, 310, 375
13:29 293
14:2 .... 75, 106
14:25–26 86
14:26 52
15:1 .... 257, 284
15:2–6 245
15:14 283
15:18 ..... 282, 283, 285
16:1 .... 43, 184
16:2 285
17:28 161
18:1 293
18:9 .... 289, 293
18:15 285
19:35 257
20 287
20:1–22 290
20:23 283
20:23–26 .... 247, 253
20:24 .... 261, 264
20:25 .... 210, 255
23:8 287
23:8–11 287
23:8–39 .... 257, 282

23:18 287
23:18–39 286
23:20 286
23:21 286
24:1–9 .... 247, 262, 292
24:2 292
24:11 .... 199, 203
24:16 180
24:18 180
24:18–25 386
24:22 .... 180, 386
24:25 255

1 Kings

1:5 .... 257, 284
1:8 .... 199, 203
1:22ff 199
1:30 258
1:32 203
1:32–40 199
1:32–48 258
1:33 293
1:38 283
1:39 .... 75, 258
1:39–40 230
1:40 231
1:44 283
1:46 258
1:47 258
2:10 105
2:19 .... 256, 261
2:26–27 255
2:35 207
3:1 .... 61, 247
3:16–28 253
4:1–6 .... 247, 253
4:2 255
4:3 .... 210, 215, 260, 261
4:5 262
4:6 .... 258, 264
4:7 .... 182, 252, 254
4:7–19 .... 247, 253, 262,
       310
4:7–28 163
4:12 252
4:20 163
4:20–28 247
4:21 254
4:22 182
4:22–23 ... 48, 252, 262
4:22–28 254
4:25 159

4:26 .... 262, 308
4:27–28 .... 252, 262
4:28 .... 48, 182
5–7 216
5:1–12 247
5:1–6:38 255
5:1–7:12 ...... 254, 265
5:6 .... 360, 361
5:6–11 226
5:8 361
5:9 362
5:10–11 .... 164, 168
5:11 186
5:13–14 .... 252, 264, 265
5:13–18 .... 163, 247, 310
5:14 264
5:15 265
5:15–18 360
6:7 360
6:9 361
6:18 361
6:29 361
6:31 361
6:32 362
6:35 361
6:38 216
7:7 253
7:8 247
7:9–11 360
7:9–12 359
7:13ff 216
7:13–14 374
7:14 189
7:15–47 375
7:40–44 374
7:46 376
8:37 174
8:51 375
8:62–64 .... 193, 255
9:10–14 310
9:15 ...... 216, 249, 307,
       308, 309, 360
9:15–19 .... 254, 265
9:16 .... 61, 247, 253
9:17–18 307
9:17–19 216
9:19 .... 164, 262, 307
9:20–21 264
9:20–22 264
9:24 247
9:25 255
9:26–27 226
9:26–28 ... 247, 253, 362

1 Kings (con't.)

9:27	226
9:28	381
10:1–15	253
10:2	225
10:4–5	257
10:11	226, 361
10:12	231, 361, 381
10:14–15	254
10:15	309
10:18	383
10:18–20	361
10:22	253, 362, 383
10:26	308
10:26–29	254
10:27	159, 361
10:28	309
10:28–29	226
11:1	247
11:3	256
11:14–25	308
11:26–40	312
11:27	308
11:29ff	203
11:29–39	199
11:41	260
12:1ff	169, 252
12:1–20	163, 236, 264, 312
12:16	31
12:18	264, 265
12:25	169
12:26–33	255
13:4	71
13:30	231
14:1ff	194
14:2–3	203
14:11	105, 144
14:13	231
14:17	248
14:19	260
14:25–26	304
14:25–28	257
15:12	233
15:16–22	265, 313
15:20	329
15:22	153, 163, 265
15:23	261
16:8	258
16:9	258
16:9–10	325
16:11	258
16:17–22	325

16:20	261
16:23	258
16:23–33	360
16:24	164, 254, 326
16:28–33	254
17–18	156
17:9ff	203
17:12	75
17:21	206
18:17ff	199, 206
18:26–29	199
18:30–39	206
19	146
19:9	26
19:15–16	199
19:16	198, 210
19:19	176
19:19–21	202, 210
20:13ff	199
20:14–21	262
20:15–20	288
20:16–21	200, 254
20:24	329
20:29–34	200
20:34	224, 226
20:35	198
20:35ff	199
21:1–16	164, 253
21:2	168
21:8	242
22	200, 201
22:1–4	200
22:1–28	329
22:5ff	194, 198
22:5–8	270
22:5–10	200
22:6	200, 203
22:7–9	200
22:8	200
22:10	180, 199, 203
22:11–12	200
22:13	200
22:17–23	200
22:24	200
22:26–27	200
22:29–35	254
22:34	329
22:34–35	200, 305
22:39	261, 383
22:48	254
26:34	254

2 Kings

1:8	203, 204
1:11ff	293
2	210
2:3	198
2:3–7	198
2:8	203, 204
2:12–15	203, 204
2:14	206
2:24	206
3:11	194
4:3–6	206
4:7	224
4:8–10	203
4:10	40
4:18–20	154, 179
4:22–37	70
4:23	109
4:38ff	203
4:38–41	206
4:42	181, 203
6:25	129
8:7–9	203
8:7–13	194
9:1	75
9:1–13	199
9:3	75
9:6	75
9:13	258
9:21–25	257
9:22	205
9:25	257
9:30	88
10:1	210, 256
10:1–11	242
10:5	258
10:6	210, 256
10:15–17	32
10:19	190
11	109
11:1–3	256
11:2	97, 256
11:4	284
11:4–12	257
11:12	258
11:12–20	258
11:14	230
11:19	258, 284
12:2	210
12:4–15	255
12:10	215
12:10–12	261

2 Kings (con't.)

12:18	255
13:13	258
13:21	105
14:28	261
15:5	258
15:8–28	314
15:15	261
15:19–20	262
16:7–8	314
16:8	255
16:10–16	255
16:15	194, 196
17:24	315
18:1–7	321
18:15–16	255
18:17	378
18:17–37	261
18:18	215, 258, 261
18:18ff	259
18:31	157
18:32	158
18:37	261
19:7	321
2:19–22	206
19:35	72
20:20	217, 261, 359
21:1–17	321
21:5	205
21:13	361
22:3–4	215
22:3ff	261
22:3–7	255
22:3–23:25	194
22:8	210
22:8–10	261
22:11–20	192, 194
22:12–20	204
22:45	261
23:1–2	242
23:1–25	255
23:5	205
23:6	105
23:7	233, 379
23:8	153
23:29–30	322
23:33–35	262
24:1	323
24:14	323, 374
25:1–4	197
25:8ff	197
25:12	165
25:18–21	197
25:19	215
25:22–26	259
33:4	377

1 Chronicles

2:55	215
4:14	228, 374
4:21	228, 357, 379
4:23	228, 357, 363
6:31–48	230
11:4–7	287
11:4–8	247
11:10–41	282
11:11	287
11:11–14	287
11:15	288
11:20–47	286
11:22	286
11:23	286
12:40	74
13:1	293
13:14	230
14:8–17	246
15:1–16:43	247
15:16ff	230
15:16–16:6	230
18:3–4	288
18:8	373
18:14–17	253
18:17	357
19:6–20:3	293
19:7	294
19:17	294
22:3	179, 296, 375
25:1	199
25:1–16	203, 230
25:1–31	230
25:2–6	199
25:8	210
27:1–15	291
27:16–22	291
27:25–31	168, 253, 262
27:26	179
27:27	185
27:28	159
27:32	210, 215, 256
28:4–8	257

2 Chronicles

1:2	293
2:7	378
2:7–8	360
2:7–10	164
2:13–14	216, 249, 361
2:13–16	164, 360
2:15	226
2:16	226
2:17–18	265
3	216
5:12–14	231
7:6	194
8:13	182
8:17–18	226, 362
9:11	361
9:21	227, 253, 381
11:5–12	312
11:11–12	288
11:13–14	190
11:21	256
11:23	257
12:1–12	312
12:10	375
13:9–10	190
15:3	190
16:12	69
16:14	105
17:2	262
17:5	262
17:8–9	210
17:12	165, 262
17:14–19	264
19:5–7	245
19:8–11	194
20:28	230
20:35–37	254
21:3	257, 258
24:12	374
25:5	264
26:8	254
26:10	157, 164, 165, 168
26:15	216
26:20	69
27:26–31	164
29:1–31:21	321
29:25–30	231
29:30	199
32:1–3	217
32:3–4	217
32:27–29	264
32:28	158, 262
33:6	70, 206
33:14	384
34:8	261
35:15	203

2 Chronicles (con't.)

35:20–24 322
35:25 231
36:22–23 330

Ezra

1:1–4 330
2:36–40 .... 190, 197
2:66–67 129
3:7 361
3:10 231
4:8–6:18 14
4:10–11 266
4:16–17 266
4:13 268
5:3 266
5:6 266
5:14 266
6:6 266
6:17 132
7:6 215
7:10 215
7:12–26 14
7:24 .... 230, 268
8:15–20 190
9:9 330
10:8 265

Nehemiah

1:3 165
2:7 266
2:8 342
2:9 266
2:10 315
2:17 165
2:17ff 265
2:19–20 315
3:3 384
3:8 .... 228, 381
3:11 371
3:15 217
3:15–16 224
3:16 217
3:31–32 .... 228, 381
3:32 357
5:1–5 165
5:11 158
5:14 266
5:14–15 268
5:18 266
6:14 204

7:2 342
7:39–43 .... 190, 197
7:68–69 129
8:7–9 210
11:35 .... 357, 374
12:38 371
12:46 230
12:47 230
13:12 158
13:15 111
13:16 383
13:19 111

Esther

1:1 266
1:6 36
2:12 85
4:3 104

Job

1:2 103
1:3 128
1:20 .... 86, 104
2:8 372
5:26 179
7:6 380
9:30 .... 85, 378
10:9–11 69
16:18 136
22:24 381
24:3 128
24:11 184
28:1 381
28:1–11 375
28:12–19 64
28:18 57
28:17 389
29:7 243
29:7–25 242
30:1 144
38:26–27 125
41:1–7 384
42:15 99

Psalms

12:6 382
22:1 94
22:15 372
22:16 144

23:1 144
23:5 75
24:8 270
32:3–5 69
32:4 154
38:1–11 69
42:4 231
45:6–7 255
45:8 383
45:14 102
48:6 74
58:6 189
60:8 85
65:12 125
69:28 292
78:52 144
78:55 31
78:63 101
80:9 183
80:9–11 183
80:12–13 183
89:19–21 255
104:2 31
104:15 158
105:34–35 174
107:27 189
108:9 85
126:5–6 179
127:3 91
128 92
129:3 175
129:7 179
133:3 156
139:13–16 69
147:14 158
147:16 130

Proverbs

1:8 209
3:15 57
4:1 209
6:20 209
7:16 377
8:11 57
20:4 175
20:15 57
23:1–3 47
24:3 189
25:4 382
27:9 83
27:27 132
31:1 209

Proverbs (con't.)

31:10 57
31:13 379
31:18 39
31:19 379
31:23 242

Ecclesiastes

12:5 159

Song of Solomon

1:5 31
1:8 31
1:10–11 64
1:14 85
2:10–14 103
2:13 183
2:15 159
3:6–8 101
3:9–11 102
4:1 101
4:3 101
4:13 159
5:11 86
5:14–15 64
6:7 101
8:2 159
8:11 184

Isaiah

1:5–6 76
1:8 161
1:11–15 .... 190, 201
1:13 109
1:16–17 201
1:18 377
1:28 130
2:4 184
2:16 362
3:2–3 .... 70, 205
3:16 .... 59, 64
3:17 341
3:18 59
3:18–24 .... 53, 64
3:24 87
4:3 292
5:1 .... 159, 183
5:2 .... 183, 184
5:5 183
5:6 159

5:8 164
5:12 231
6 202
7:1–8:15 314
7:3 .... 228, 357, 378
7:20 387
7:25 178
8:3 204
8:6 217
9:3 179
13:8 74
13:20 31
15:2 86
16:10 184
17:5 179
17:6 185
18:4 .... 154, 156
18:5 183
19:8 384
19:9 377
20:2–6 203
21:5 75
22:12 231
22:15 260
22:15–25 259
22:16 .... 259, 359
22:20–22 260
22:21 259
23 .... 225, 226
24:8–9 231
24:13 185
26:17 91
28:1 183
28:16–17 361
28:23–26 146
28:24–25 175
28:25 .... 161, 177
28:27 .... 161, 180
28:27–28 ...... 180, 386
29:16 372
30:14 372
30:24 .... 176, 181
31:8 264
32:11 232
32:11–12 231
33:20 31
34:13–14 125
36:2 378
36:3 .... 259, 260
38:1–6 69
38:12 31
40:19 .... **382**
40:20 189

40:22 31
41:7 382
41:15 .... 180, 386
41:15–16 180
41:25 .... 364, 365
42:14 74
44:12 376
44:13 362
44:25 205
45:2 375
45:9 372
47:3 341
47:9–15 204
47:13 205
51:8 131
54:16 376
55:1 41
56:11 144
58:13 109
61:10 102
63:3 184

Jeremiah

1:1 202
1:4–10 202
1:6 202
1:11–12 161
2:2 .... 125, 201
2:6 125
2:8 192
2:20 233
2:22 86
2:32 102
4:20 31
4:30 88
5:15–17 41
5:24 154
6:16 201
6:20 201
6:24 74
6:26 232
6:28–29 376
6:29–30 382
7:21–22 201
7:23 201
7:29 231
7:30–34 201
7:34 101
8:22 81
9:9–11 202
9:16 189
9:17 231

Jeremiah (con't.)

9:25–26 95
10:2 206
10:9 ...... 189, 381, 382
10:11 14
10:20 31
11:4 375
14:1–6 156
14:1–10 232
15:3 144
15:7 181
16:4 105
16:6 232
16:7 108
16:9 101
17:1 382
17:21–22 110
18:2 228
18:2–4 372
18:3 364
18:18 ...... 190, 192, 194
19 .... 202, 372
19:1 224
19:1–2 .... 357, 371
19:5 201
19:13 40
20:15 91
22:13–17 248
22:18 231
22:23 74
23:1–4 144
23:10 125
24:1 374
24:1–10 46
24:2 159
26:23 105
27:3 323
27:9–10 205
27:16 198
27–29 323
29:1 197
31:5 .... 159, 183
31:10 144
32:6ff 203
32:6–7 238
32:10–14 215
32:14 372
32:35 201
33:13 144
34:5 231
35:2–4 32
35:6 33
35:6ff 31

35:6–10 32
36:4 215
36:10 215
36:12 .... 215, 260
36:20–23 260
37:21 ...... 228, 357, 386
38:5 323
38:6–13 157
38:19 323
39:1–3 197
39:11–41:18 259
40:5 266
41:1–3 266
41:4 232
41:9 157
48:7 190
48:33 184
48:37 .... 86, 104
50:8 132
52:12ff 197
52:24–27 197
52:28 323

Lamentations

2:20 197

Ezekiel

1:3 .... 197, 202
4:9 161
5:1 387
7:26 194
8:1 265
8:11–12 243
8:16 117
9:2–3 215
12:1–16 202
13:17–20 205
13:18–20 70
14:1 243
16:4 73
16:8 100
16:8–14 102
16:10 377
16:10–14 64
16:11 58
16:13 .... 74, 377
16:28 233
16:37 341
19:1–14 202
20:1 .... 243, 265
22:20–22 382

22:21 205
23:5 233
23:40 88
23:42 .... 58, 102
26:17–18 202
27 .... 225, 226
27:2–9 232
27:5–6 362
27:7 .... 362, 377, 378
27:9 362
27:12 373
27:12–25 381
27:15 383
27:16 377
27:17 164
27:18 377
27:19 82
27:22 381
27:26 226
27:30 .... 104, 232
27:30–32 232
27:32–36 232
27:34 227
28:12–19 202
29:5 105
32:2–8 202
32:28 232
33:21 197
33:32 101
34:17 132
39:18 132
40:3 179
40:5ff **361**
42:14 196
43:13–17 195
44:4–31 197
44:11 .... 195, 196
44:15 190
44:17–18 179
44:17–19 196
44:18 .... **196**
45:8 164
46:18 164
47:10 384

Daniel

2 206
2:4 to 7:28 14
8:5 132
12:1 292

Hosea

1:2–9	233
1:4	92
1:6	92
1:9	92
2:5	131
2:8	158
2:9	131
2:11	109
2:13	64
2:14–23	201
2:22	158
4:1–19	233
4:6	194
6:4	156
7:4	386
7:11	314
9:10	46, 159
10:8	201
10:11	180
10:11–12	175
13:3	156
13:15	174
14:7	183

Joel

1:4	174
1:10	158
1:20	125
2:18–19	74
2:22	125
2:28–29	204
2:23	154, 174

Amos

1:1	202
3:5	382
3:15	250
4:2	384
4:9	174, 185
5:1–2	202
5:10–13	314
5:11	248
5:12	252
5:15	242
5:21–23	201
5:21–24	190
5:24	201
6:1–8	248
6:4	250, 361, 382, 383

7:7–8	361
7:9	201
7:12–14	198
7:12–15	200
7:14	159, 202
7:15	202
9:13	159, 184

Jonah

1:3–5	226
1:3	362

Micah

1:8	203
1:16	86, 104
2:1–2	164, 321
3:11	194
4:3	184
4:4	159
5:7	156
6:6–7	201
6:8	201
6:15	186
7:1	159

Nahum

3:12	159
3:14	358

Habakkuk

1:15	384

Zephaniah

1:8	53
1:10	384

Haggai

1:1	266
1:10–11	156
1:11	158
2:13	105

Zechariah

3:10	159
8:12	156
8:16	242
9:9	129

10:2	205
10:3	132, 144
13:4	203
13:9	381

Malachi

1:2–3	166
3:2	86, 378
3:2–3	381
3:5	205
3:16	292

NEW TESTAMENT

Matthew

1:1–16	93
2:11	77
3:4	203, 204
3:7–10	208
4:21	384
4:23	211
5:15	39
6:17	75
6:19–20	131
6:25	54
6:28–33	55
7:6	57
7:16–20	47
8:4	73
8:5–13	356
9:9	269
9:10–11	269
9:11–12	47
9:20–22	54
9:33	232
9:35	211
9:37–38	179
11:7ff	204
11:21	213
12:2	111
13:3–8	177
13:45	57
13:47–48	384
13:48	384
15:2	243
16:1–4	206
16:1–12	208
16:6–12	206
17:24	268

Mathew (con't.)

17:27	384
18:6	187, 386, 387
20:1ff	184
20:1–6	167
21:11	204
21:23	190, 265
21:33	183
21:33ff	184
21:33–41	167
22:2	102
22:17–21	269
23	207
23:2	206
23:2–12	216
23:5	54
23:7–8	211
23:23	161
23:37	166
25:3	74
25:4	158
25:32	143
25:25–36	42, 46
26:3	265
26:26–28	47
26:57–68	198
26:59–68	190
27:1–26	268
27:46	94
27:54	356
27:59	105

Mark

1:21	212
2:4	40
2:22	158
2:27	111
3:1–5	71
3:2	111
4:25	337
4:26–29	178
5:20	337
5:41	20
6:4	204
7:1–5	243
7:31	337
12:38–40	207
13:28	159
14:12ff	114
15:1–5	268
15:34	20
15:39	356

Luke

1:8	190
1:58	91
1:76	204
2:1–7	269
2:22–24	95, 97
2:36	204
2:46	211
3:1	266, 268
3:11	55
3:17	181
4:25	156
5:2	384
5:4–7	384
5:5	384
5:6–7	384
5:7	384
5:10	384
5:27–30	269
6:1	158
6:4	198
7:1–10	356
7:14	105
7:24–28	204
7:46	75
8:22	362
9:62	175
10:30–37	315
11:37–54	207
12:13–21	166
12:54	5
12:55	5
13:1	268
13:14	111
14:8–14	47
15:3–4	144
16:19	378
19:1–8	166
19:1–10	269
20:22–25	166
22:12	40
23:10	216
23:47	356

John

1:49	211
2:1–10	102
3:2	211
3:20	39
3:26	211
3:29	102

4:9	315
4:13–14	8
4:20	169
4:31	211
4:34	46
4:46–53	356
5:10	111
6:35	46
10:4	144
10:11–16	144
11:44	105
11:49–53	198
12:3	83
13:5	75
15:1–2	183
16:21	91
18:13–24	198
18:19–24	190
19:22	119
19:23–24	54
19:39	81
19:39–40	105
21:3–4	384
21:11	384
21:9–13	384

Acts

2:1	115, 181
2:5	115
2:14ff	204
4:1–2	207
5:17–18	190, 198
5:34	207
6:7	190
10:1–33	356
10:2	356
10:9	40
10:22	356
11:27–28	204
11:30	244
13:1	204
13:6–11	206
13:7	268
14:1	211
14:13	190
14:23	244
15:2	244
15:4	244
15:5–11	96
15:6	244
15:22–23	244
16:3	96

Acts (con't.)

16:4 244
16:35–39 266
18:12–17 268
19:14 103
19:24ff 381
20:16 181
20:17 244
21:9 204
21:18 244
21:27–36 343
21:37 343
22:1–21 344
22:28 266
23:6 207
23:8–10 208
23:10 344
23:12–26:32 268
23:25 268
24:27 268
25:10–12 266
26:5 207
26:14 176
26:32 266
27:1—28:16 .... 227, 356
27:1 357
27:9 118

1 Corinthians

5:7–8 114
11:14–15 52
12:28 204
12:28–31 211
14:1ff 204
15:37 158

2 Corinthians

4:7 372

Galatians

2:10 96

Ephesians

4:11 211
5:21–33 100

1 Timothy

2:9 57

2 Timothy

1:11 211

Hebrews

4:14ff 190
10:21 190
11:9–10 31
13:2 42

James

3:1 211
5:14 244
5:17 156

1 Peter

3:3 .... 53, 87
5:1–5 244

Revelation

2:27 372

5:10 190
15:2 389
18:12 377
21:18 389
21:21 389

APOCRYPHA

1 Maccabees

3:2 333
3:46–48 333
4:36–59 120
6:6 333
6:35 333
6:34–39 334
6:39 333
8 .... 334, 338
8:11–16 334
9:37–39 101
12:1–4 .... 334, 338
13:33–42 334
14:24 334
14:41–49 334

2 Maccabees

4:12 54
7:27 98
12:39–46 108
12:43–44 108
15:36 120

Sirach (Ecclesiasticus)

48:17 217

Index of Names and Subjects

Abel, 133
Abigail, 42–43
Abishai, 285, 286, 287, 290, 291, 294
Abner, 137, 246, 281, 285
Abraham, 9, 31, 42, 98, 124, 131, 135, 136, 138, 225
  covenant between God and, 96
  rescue of Lot by, 271
Absalom, 43, 52, 137, 284, 289, 291
Achan, 49
Achish, 282
Acts, book of, 21
Adamah, 294
Adoram (Adoniram), 264
Adullam, 281, 285
Agabus, 204
agriculture
  in ancient Near East, 148–57
  greater efficiency in Roman period, 167
  See also Farming.
Ahab, 200, 226, 254, 262, 327–29
  chariots of, 289
  construction at Megiddo by, 308
  "ivory house" of, 261
Ahaz, 314
Ahijah, the Shilonite, 199, 203
Ahimelech, 281
Akiba, Rabbi, 18
alabaster, 62, 84
Albright, William F., 41, 85, 255, 311, 321, 357
  findings of, at Tell Beit Mirsim, 387–79
Alexander Jannaeus, 335, 345
Alexandria, 84, 331
almonds, 43, 159
  bitter, 84
aloes, 81, 82
alum, 76
Amalek, 280
Amalekites, 128, 282
el-Amarna, 260
amethyst, 61
Ammonites, 264, 266, 288, 290
  Joab's campaign against, 293–95
Amos, 23, 200, 202, 314
amphitheatre, at Caesarea, 340–41
amulets, 60–61, 62, 72
angels, 207
animals, domestic, 36
  used in amphitheatres, 340–41
  wild, 143
anklets, 59, 62
Anna, 204
Antioch, 330
Antiochus IV "Epiphanes," 16, 331–33
Antipater, 337, 345
Antonia, 342-44
Aphek, 246
apocalyptic literature, 16, 21
"appeal to Caesar," 266, 268
aqueducts, 221, 223, 340
Arabah, 309, 373, 374, 375
Aramaeans, 128
Aramaic (language), 14, 16, 94
  language of Jesus, 19–20
Archelaus, 337, 342, 343, 346

archer(s), 278, 293, 301, 306
  Assyrian, 315
architects, 216, 218
aristocracy, city-dwelling, 235
Ark, 30, 246
armlets, 59
armor, 277–78, 303–305
  Roman, 352–53
army, 248
  of Assyria, at Qarqar, 328
  biblical references to professional troops,
    290-91
  of citizen-soldiers, 272–73, 280, 291ff.
  code-words for elements of, 294
  of Deborah and Barak, 272–73
  defensive armor of, 277–78
  leadership of, 271–72
  offensive equipment of, 297–303
  organization of Roman, 347–48
  professional, of David, 280, 281–91,
    293–95
  protective equipment of David's, 303–
    305
  recruits for professional, 289–90
  standing, organized by David, 288–90
  supplies for, 295–96; under Solomon,
    307–308
  weapons of Israelite, 274ff.; of David's
    296–305
arrow(s), 300–301
Asa, 69, 153, 313
Asahel, 137, 285
Ashdod, 284, 375
Ashkelon, 283, 338
ass, 123, 125, 128–29
ass-nomad(s), 123, 133
Asshur, 68
Assyria, army of, 314–20, 328
  defeat of, by Babylon, 322
  deportation policy of, 315
  siege equipment of, 315-16
Assyrians, 11, 86
  scribes among, 213
astrology, 205, 206
Augustus, Caesar, 337, 339, 345, 348
ax, 274–75
Azazel, 119

Baal, 117, 145; prophets of, 199
Baalath, 307
Baal-peor, 141
Baasha, 153, 313

Babylonians, 11, 41, 44, 93, 94, 314
  attack method of, 324–25
  capture Ninevah, 322
  magic among, 204–206
  See also Mesopotamia.
Balaam, 199
balm, 81
balsams, 76ff.
Baly, Denis, 295
barley, 7, 127, 157, 158, 174; bread, 43
  See also Grain.
barrenness, 91
Bashan, 162, 167
bathing, 84; of feet, 75
battering ram, 312, 315, 317, 324
  Assyrian, 318–20
bdellium, 56, 82
beads, 59, 62, 63
beans, 45, 161
beauty treatments, 89
bed(s), 30, 36
Bedouin, 30, 121
bees, 44
beets, 45
Ben-hadad, 313, 327, 329
Benaiah, 285, 286
Beni-hasan, tomb-paintings at, 49, 50
Beth-ashbea, 379
Bethel, 153, 191
Beth-shan, 75, 288, 307, 312
betrothal, 100–101
Bible, as a book, 12ff.
  arrangement of, 12–18
  copying of, 18–19
  Hebrew, 14–16
  history covered by, 8–9
  insipration in writing of, 23–24
  translation of, 19
  unique nature of, 22–24
bier, 105
birth, of a child, 90–91
birthstool, 90
bitumen, 33, 362
blanket(s), 50
blessing(s), prayer of, 112
  of relatives, 102
blood, 134, 136
  mystical qualities of, 136–37
blood relationship, 237
blood-vengeance, 136–37, 237
bodyguard, of David, 284, 285, 288
bone, used in jewelry, 62
booths (sukkoth), 116

Booths, Feast of, 41, 115–17, 146
"borders," *see* Tassels.
borith, 378
bow(s), 276, 277, 300
bracelets, 58, 62
bread, 43, 172; unleavened, 43
breastplate, 63, 192–93
brick(s), making of, 358
  use of, in houses, 33–34
bricklayer(s), 34, 358–59
bride, 99, 100, 101, 102
bridegroom, 100, 101, 102
bronze, 179, 374
building trades, 358–62
bull, sacrifice of, 119
burial, 104–108
butter, 44

Caesar, Julius, 345
Caesarea, 221, 267, 347
  built by Herod, 339–42
Cain, 133
calamus, 82, 84
Caleb, 99
caligae, Roman, 353
camel(s), 30, 45, 78, 133, 225
  drivers, 43
Canaanites, 28, 32, 33, 41, 162, 240, 311
  chariots of, 273, 278
  civilization of, 147
  commerce of, 225
  influences of, 234
  slipping of Israel into ways of, 271
  used as forced labor, 264
candles, 119
carbuncle, 61
Carites, 284
carnelian, 59, 62, 63
carpenter, 361–62
castor oil, 68
cassia, 82, 84
catapult, Roman, 350–51
cattle, 124. *See also* Oxen.
cavalry, 289, 293
  Assyrian, 315
caves, 105; used as homes, 25–27
census, of David, 292; of Augustus, 268
centurion, Roman, 347, 354–57
Ceylon, 57, 78, 82
chair(s), 30, 37
chariot(s), 226
  Assyrian, 315
  Canaanite, 273, 278

of David, 288–89, 294, 302–303
  Egyptian, 278
  of Solomon, 290, 307–308
charioteers, 279, 293
chariot racing, 341
chalcedony, 61
cheese, 44, 140
Cherethites, 283–84
chickens, 45, 166
child, children, 89, 134, 139
  birth of, 90–92
  naming of, 92–94
  redemption of firstborn, 96–97
  weaning of, 97–98
childbirth, 73–74
cinnamon, 82, 84
cistern(s), 44, 123, 125, 156–57, 165, 269
circumcision, 95–96
cities, defense of, 306–307
  See also Gates, Walls.
cities of refuge, 137
cities, rise of, 238–39
cities, walled, 305–307
  attack on, by David, 306–307; by Sargon, 315–16; by Nebuchadnezzar, 323–25; by Pompey, 336
  Solomonic gates to strengthen, 309
citizenship, Roman, 265–66
clan, 134–35, 234
clay, 355–56
cleanliness, of clothing, ceremonial, 52
climate, of Palestine, 4–7, 154
cloak, 50, 54
clothing, 48ff.
  everyday apparel, 45–52
  in Mosaic law, 52–53
  in N.T. times, 53–55
coat of mail, 277, 279, 296, 300, 304–305
cohort, in Roman army, 343, 347, 348
  Italian, 356
  Augustan, 348
construction industry, 358ff.
cooking, 26, 37
  use of olive oil in, 74–75
copper, 62, 373, 375
copper acetate (verdigris), 76
Cornelius, 356
corpse, 106
cosmetics, 74ff.
  cases for, 59
  ingredients used in, 84–85
costus oil, 83
cotton, 76, 377

couches, 36
council, clan, 134–35
Court of the Gentiles, 338, 342, 343, 344, 348
Court of Israel, 344
covenant, 12, 109
  between God and Israel, 201
  new, 12, 47
craftsmen, 188–89, 227–29
cremation, 80, 105
cucumbers, 45, 161
cuirass, Roman, 352
cups, 59
curds, 140
Cyrus the Great, 11, 93

dagger, 274, 350
Damascus, 78, 266, 314
"Dan to Beersheba," 2
Daniel, book of, 16, 94, 206
dates, 43, 44, 45, 161
daughters, low state of, 138
David, 11, 42, 43, 47–48, 99, 242, 246–47, 281, 284
  abandons "holy war" tradition, 292
  Achish employs, 282
  Ammonite war of, 293–95
  as commander, 291
  forced labor introduced by, 264
  mourning of, 104
  music of, 230
  organizes a professional army, 288–90;
    a citizen-army, 291–93
  royal troops of, 282ff.
  "Thirty" and "Three" of, 286–88
Dead Sea Scrolls, 19, 208
death, 103ff.
  burial, 104–108
  by stoning, 137
Deborah, 203, 272–73
Decapolis, 335, 337, 346
demons, belief in, 70
desert, true, 133
  as known to Hebrews, 125
  desert and sown land, 4, 150–51, 234
Deuteronomy, book of, 9, 52
dew, 156
diadem, 102
diamonds, 56, 61
disease, demonic theory of, 65, 70
  Hebrew concept of, 69
  Old Testament kinds of, 70–71

plague among Philistines, 71–72
diviners, 204–206
Doeg, 281
donkey, see Ass.
doors, 34
dowry, 99
dreams, 205, 206, 270
drought, 44, 150, 155–56, 179
dyeing, of fabrics, 378–79

"early rain," see Rain.
East Africa, 77
Edom, Edomites, 288, 309, 314, 374
eggs, 45, 166
Egypt, 3, 42, 56, 76, 209, 312, 313, 314, 322, 323, 373
  army of, depicted, 279, 293
  chariots of, 278
  cosmetics used in, 84
  irrigation farming in, 148–50
  jewelry of, 61–63, 65
  magic in, 204, 205
  medicine in, 66–67
  musicians of, 230
  Ptolemy gains rule of, 331
  royal herald in, 261
  scribes in, 213
  Vizier in, 258
Ehud, 274
Ekron, 284
elders, 238, 241–44
Eleazar, brother of Judas Maccabeus, 334
electrum, 63
elephants, 334
Elijah, 32, 146, 199, 203, 206, 210
Elisha, 32, 40, 70, 71, 199, 202, 206, 210
Elkanah, 97, 191
embalming, 79, 105
emeralds, 56, 61
emerods, 72
Endor, witch of, 206
engineers, 216–23, 218, 221
engravers, 380
ephod, 50
Esarhaddon, 321
Essenes, 202, 204, 208–209
Esther, 85
evil spirits, 60
Exile, 206
Exodus, 35, 146
  book of, 9
  commemoration of, 112
  date of, 9

exorcism, 67, 68
eye paint, 87–88
Ezekiel, 202, 205
Ezion-geber, 226, 307, 308
Ezra, 18, 94, 206

faience, Egyptian, 62, 63
family, 30, 134, 234
    events in life of, 89ff.
    head of, 134, 234, 241
    typical, 239–41
farmer(s) 127, 144ff., 163
    household of, 170–73
    life of typical, recreated, 168ff.
    seasons of agricultural year of, 174
farming, 144–45
    appearance of large-scale, 163
    effect of Rome on Palestinian, 166–67
    history of biblical, 161ff.
    irrigation, 148–50
    rain-fed, 150–51
    See also Agriculture.
father, 89, 91, 96, 97
    as head of family, 134, 139, 234, 241
    performed rite of circumcision, 95
    role of, in marriage, 98, 99, 100
    as teacher, 209
feldspar, 56, 61
Felix, Antonius, 268
Fertile Crescent, 3–4, 128, 323
festivals, pilgrimage, 112ff.
    celebration of harvest, 181–82
Festus, Porcius, 268, 357
figs, 45, 46, 159
firstborn, sacrifice or dedication of,
    96–97
First Fruits, Day of, see Weeks, Feast
    of.
fish, 45
flax, 76, 377
flute, 232
foods, 40ff.
    everyday, 43–46, 172–73
    in Jesus' teachings, 46–47
    royal meals, 47–48
foot-washing, 85
forced labor (corvée), 247, 252, 264–65,
    310
frankincense, 77–81
fringes, see Tassels.
fullering, 377–78
fullers, 85–86, 377–78
Fuller's Field, 228, 378

Gad, 199, 202
galbanum, 80, 82, 83
galena, 87
Gallio, 268
Gamaliel, 207
garlic, 45
garnet, 63
gates, city, 306
    of Hazor, Megiddo, Gezer, 242,
    309
Gath, 282, 284
Gaza, 78, 284
Geba, 153, 313
Gedaliah, 259, 266
Gederah, 357, 363
gems, see Jewelry.
Gezer, 61, 307
    calendar, 40, 173–74
    gate at, 242, 309
    walls of, 254
Gibbethon, 325
Gibeah, 281
Gibeon, 217, 219
Gideon, 43, 163, 191, 270, 272
    victory of, over Midianites, 280ff.
Gilead, 81, 162
girdle, 49
girls, 100
gladiators, 340
glaze, Egyptian, 62
gleaning, 179
goat(s), 45, 123, 131–33, 135, 142
    breeders of, 123
    hair of, 28
    milk of, 132
    sacrifice of, 119
    skin of, 30
God, and the Bible, 23–24
    names for, 135–36
gold, 58, 59, 61, 62, 63, 77, 374
goldsmiths, 380
Gospel, of the New Testament, 14
gospels, 13, 20
governors, of province of Judah, 266
    Roman, 348, 349–50
grain, 74, 158, 166
    cultivation of, 174–78
    grinding of, 182–83
    See also Barley, Wheat.
grapes, 159, 184, see also Vine.
grave, 105
Great Trunk Road, 63, 64, 78
greaves, Roman, 353

guilds, professional, 209, 228, 357
  of metalsmiths, 374
  of weavers, 376
gum arabic, 43
gums, 76ff.

Habiru, 128
hair, normal style of Israelite male, 52
hairdressing, of women, 86–87
hairnets, 59, 63
Hammurabi, Code of, 67
Hannah, 97
Hanukkah, Feast of, 119–20
harem, 256
Harvest, Feast of the, see Weeks, Feast of.
harvest, festivals of, 181–82
harvesting, 178–79
Hasidim, 206, 208
Hasmoneans, 333, 335ff., 344–45
hats, 50. See also Helmets, Turbans.
Hazor, 217, 218, 273, 288, 307, 315
  gates of, 242, 309
  walls of, 254
headbands, 50, 102
heber, 33
Hebrews, 13, 128, 131, 133–34, 135
  and hygiene, 72–73
  See also Israelites, Jews.
helmets, 278, 296, 304
  Roman, 352
henna, 88
herald, royal, 261
Herod Agrippa I, 350
Herod Antipas, 337, 346, 356
Herod the Great, 218, 337ff., 350
  building program of, 338–44
Hezekiah, 259, 261, 263, 290, 322
  peace terms imposed on, 321
High Priest, 119, 330, 331, 350
  vestments of, kept in Antonia, 343–
    44
Hilkiah, 261
Hiram, king of Tyre, 226, 253
hippodrome (circus), of Caesarea, 341
hoeing, 178
Holy of Holies, 335
"holy incense," 82–83
"holy oil," 82
Holy Spirit, 115
"holy war," 271, 292, 311, 327, 333
  ideology of, 270ff.
homes, 25ff.
  cave-homes, 25–27

furnishings of, 250
houses, 33–36, 39–40
tent-homes, 27–30
See also Houses.
honey, 43, 76, 161
horse(s), 129, 278
See also Cavalry.
Hosea, 45, 233, 314
hospitality, 41–43, 75, 137–38, 237
houses, 34, 35–36, 89, 361
  of rich vs. people of the land, 248
  of typical farmer, 170–73
household, constituents of, 89
householder, 239–41
Huldah, 203
hygiene, in Old Testament, 72–73
Hyksos, 128
Hyrcanus II, 335, 337

Imhotep, 66, 67
incense, 74, 77, 80
Incense Route, 78
India, 45, 56, 78, 82
industry, biblical, 357ff.
infantrymen, 279, 293, 315
Ingathering, Feast of, 188
inlay work, 62, 63, 65
inns, 43
institutions, Hebrew civil, 233ff.
  effect of monarchy on, 246ff.
instruments, musical, 231, 232
iron, 373, 375
  farm tools of, 164
  forming of, 376
  Philistine monopoly of, 373–74
irrigation, 151, 165
Isaac, 9, 31, 42, 98, 124, 134, 135, 136
Isaiah, 203, 205
Ishbaal, 285
Ishtar, 68, 232
Isis, 66
Israel (an ethnic group, "the people of
    God"), 241–42, 269, 271
  civil life of, 233ff.
  circumcision in, 95, 96
  as complex nation, 247
  covenant between God and, 12, 201
  decorative arts in, 63
  end of national existence of ancient, 265
  family's importance in, 89–90
  geography of, 2–4; geographical in-
    fluence on, 8
  medicine in, 68–70

Israel (con't.)
"new," 13
redemption of, 112
scribes in, 213–15
Twelve Tribes of, 235–36
See also Army, Holy war.
Israel (Northern Kingdom), 153, 236
compared with Judah, 311–12
decay of, 314–15
evidences of administrative methods in, 263–64
Israelites, 48, 64, 96, 125
agricultural society reflected in laws of, 146
burdens of monarchy upon, 247–48
civil institutions of, 236ff.
family events among, 89ff.
food of, 41ff.
forced labor among, 264
"holy war" concept of, 270–72
methods of tribal armies of, 279–80
structure of society of, 234
as tent dwellers, 27
and true Bedouins, 133–34
typical homes of, 33–36, 39–40, 170–73
See also Army, Family Events, Religious Events, Temple.
ivory, 62
"ivory house" of Ahab, 254
workers in, 380, 381

Jacob, 9, 75, 101, 103, 105, 124, 131, 135, 136, 142
Joel, 33
jasper, 59, 61
javelin, 278, 298–99, 350
Jehoash, 210, 261
Jehoiachin, 323
Jehoiakim, 260, 323
Jehoshaphat (king of Judah), 254, 262, 329
Jehoshaphat (royal herald), 261
Jehu, 32, 199, 242
Jephthah, 134, 245, 272
Jeremiah, 16, 23, 32, 40, 46, 202, 203, 205, 260, 371
figures of, on deportees to Babylon, 323
structures of, on abuse of Sabbath, 110
Jeroboam I, 11, 71, 313
Jeroboam II, 263, 314
Jerusalem, 4, 40, 65, 113, 344, 357
becomes royal capital, 247
captured by Pompey, 335

Fall of, 321–25; after-effects of, 235
Herod's construction in, 338–39, 342–44
partisan rivalries in, 332
rainfall in, 155
Solomonic walls for, 308
water supply of, 217–18
women of, 53
worship centralized in, 194
See also Josiah, Temple.
Jesus, 5
acclaimed as a prophet, 204
attitude of, toward clothing, 54–55
name of, 94
food in teachings of, 46–47
need for accounts of life of, 20
opposition of, to Pharisees, 207
presentation of, at Temple, 97
as teacher, 211
jewelers, 380
jewelry, 55ff., 99
among "The people of the land," 58
Egyptian, 61–63
industry of making, 380ff.
jewels, 55; of kings, 56–57
Jews, 11, 344–45
canonization of Bible of, 16–18
and Romans, 334ff.
war of independence under Maccabees, 331ff.
Jezebel, 242
Joab, 137, 285, 286, 289, 290, 305
campaign of, against Ammonites, 293–95
commander-in-chief, 287
Job, 99
John the Baptist, 204, 208, 211
John, gospel of, 21
John Hyrcanus, 335, 344
Jonadab (Jehonadab), 32
Jonathan (son of Saul), 48, 281, 285
Jonathan (Maccabean), 334
Jordan River, 45, 75, 153
fords of, 294
Joseph (son of Jacob), 9, 105, 206
Josheb-basshebeth (Jashobe-am), 287
Josiah, 233, 242, 261, 291
centralization of worship under, 113, 114, 116
foreign policy of, clashes with Egypt, 322
killed at Megiddo, 322
Joshua, 280

Joshua, book of, 9, 136
  list of provinces of Judah in, 262
Judah (Southern Kingdom), 11, 153, 236
  compared with Israel, 311–12
  last years of, 321–23
  population of, in 7th century, 321–22
  routes into, 313
  siege mentality of kings of, 313–14
  social division within, 321–22
Judaism, rabbinic, 207
Judas Maccabeus, 119, 333, 334, 344
Judea, 267, 330
  falls under Roman governance, 335
  functions of Roman troops in, 346–47
  placed under direct Roman governance, 338, 346
  responsibilities of Roman governor of, 349–50
  Rome's intrusion into affairs of, 334
judges, 11
  "major" and "minor," 244
  period of, 238–42
  as seen in Book of Judges, 244–45
Judges, book of, 9, 136, 235–36
judgment seat, 349
Julius, 356

Kenites, 33, 374
kid, 132, 133
king, centralization of authority under, 246ff.
  children of, 256–57
  enthronement of, 257–58
  functionaries and officials of, 257ff.
  as head of state, 253
  as religious head, 255
  wealth and power of, 253–58
Kings, First and Second Books of, 11
koine, 348
kohl, 87, 88

Laban, 42, 99, 101, 103, 138, 142
labor, compulsory, 264–65, 310
Lachish, 215, 288, 306, 307
ladanum, 85, 89
lament, to honor the deceased, 231
lamps, 37, 39
lapis lazuli, 59, 61, 62, 63
"latter rains" See Rains.
Law, 15, 86, 105
  on occult practices, 205
  rabbis as teachers of, 211

scribes as recorders and interpreters of, 215–16
  tablets of the, 30
  written and oral, 207
  See also Torah.
lead, 375
lead oxide, 76
Leah, 99, 101, 103
leeks, 45
legate, of Syria, 267
legion, Roman, 347, 353–54
lentils, 45
leprosy, 71, 73
lettuce, 45
Levites, 191, 195, 210
  duties of, 190
Leviticus, book of, 9, 72
life after death, 91–92, 106, 207
linen, from Egypt, 377
  sails of, 362
lint, 76
loincloth, 49
loom, 379, 380
lots, sacred. See Urim and Thummim.
Lower Beth-horon, 307
Luke, 20, 87
Luther, Martin, 18
lye, 85

Maccabees, Revolt of, 331–34
mace, 274, 275
magic, 65, 68, 70
  and medicine, 72
magicians, 204–206
makeup, feminine, 87–88
malachite, 87
mamre, 42, 124, 138
manna, 43
mantle, 49–50
Marduk, 68
Mark, 20
marketplace, 224
marriage, 89, 98ff.
  bridal procession, 101–102
  feast culminating, 102–103
  levirate, 237–38
  negotiations leading to, 98–99
Mary (mother of Jesus), 95, 269
  purification of, 97
Masada, 346
Masoretes, 19
Mattathias, 111, 332–33
Matthew, gospel of, 20

Matthew, customs official, 269
meat, 44–45
medicine, 65ff.
  exorcism in, 67, 68
  gods of, Egypt, 66; Mesopotamia, 68
  use of oil in, 75–76
Mediterranean Sea, 3, 4, 45, 273, 335, 347
Megiddo, 64, 65, 217, 219, 251, 273, 288, 307, 312, 315
  defensive walls of, 254
  described, 249
  gates of, 209, 242
  masonry at, 360
  so-called "chariot stables," 308
melons, 45
Mephibosheth, 48
mercenaries, 281, 282, 283–85
  of Hasmoneans and Herod, 345
merchants, 223–26
Merneptah, stele of, 9
Mesha, 13
Mesopotamia, 3, 56, 209
  exorcism in, 67, 68
  gods of, 68
  irrigation farming in, 148–50
  medicine in, 67–68
  scribes in, 213
Messianic hope, 338
metals, known and used in Palestine, 374–75
metalsmiths, 58; guild of, 374
metalworking, 373–76
Micah, 163
Micaiah, 200
Midianites, 30, 128, 280
midwives, 73–74, 90
militia ("army of Israel"), 273, 287, 288, 294
  organization and structure of, 291–93
  used at siege of Rabbah, 295
milk, 44, 140
millstone, 146, 167, 168
  as used in crushing olives, 186–87
mining, 375
Miriam, 203
Mishnah, 116, 119, 211
Mizpah, 153, 313
monarchy, administrative organization of, 252ff.
  effect of, on independent farmers, 163–64
  rise of cities under, 234–35
  shaped under David, 246–47

money, coined, 58
Moses, 9, 18, 206, 280
  circumcision of, 95
mother, 90, 91, 96, 97, 98
  ritual uncleanness of, 94–95
moths, 131
mourners, professional, 104, 231–32
mourning, 104ff.
  gestures of, 232
  manifestations of, during period of, 106–108
  See also Family Events, "Death."
mule, 129, 289, 293
murder, 136
music, 230; musicians, 210, 230–31
myrrh, 77–81, 89

Naaman, 49, 71
Nabal, 42
Nabataeans, 335
Nahum, 322
names, 92–94
nard, 82, 83
Nathan, 109, 203
Nazirites, 52
Nebuchadnezzar, 323–24
Necho II, Pharaoh, 262, 322, 323
neck collar, 63
necklaces, 57, 62, 63
Negev (Negeb), 4, 153, 158, 164, 167, 330
Nehemiah, 204, 266, 268
  on the Sabbath, 110–11
Netaim, 357, 363
New Testament, 12, 19ff.
  canonization of, 21–22
New Year (Rosh ha-Shanah), celebration of, 117–18
Nicodemus, 81
Nile River, 148, 149–50
Noadiah, 204
nomadism, 128; institutions of, 123ff.
nomads, life of, 121ff.
  seminomads, 124–25
  Semitic, 127
Numbers, book of, 9

Obadiah, 27
occult, arts of the, 204–206
offering, burnt, 196
oil, castor, 76
oil, olive, 74–76, 158, 167
  production of, 185–88
oil, "pure," 186

oil, sesame, 76
ointments, 74ff.
Old Testament, 12–16, 19
    reward of life as seen in, 106
olive(s), 153, 166
    celebration of harvest of, 146
    cultivation of, 185
olive trees, 157, 158–59
Omri, 325, 326, 327
onions, 45
onycha, 80, 83
onyx, 59
Ophir, 253
Othniel, 99, 272
oxen, 45, 175, 176, 177

palace, minister of the, 258–59
Palestine, 25, 55
    beginnings of agriculture in, 146–47
    civil life in, during periods of foreign
        domination, 265–66
    climate and rainfall of, 75, 152, 154–57
    diversity of land of, 153
    geography of, 3–4, 150–53
    harvest products of, 74
    land use and crops, 157
palms, 120
partridge, 140
Passover, 7, 35, 41, 96, 146
    foremost annual celebration, 112–14
    in Jesus' day, 113
pasturage, 123, 127, 142
Patriarchs, 9, 133, 191, 224–25
Paul, 20, 21, 28, 206, 207, 244, 357
    in the Court of the Gentiles, 344
    imprisoned at Caesarea, 268
    on long hair, 52
    on prophets and prophecy, 204
    use of two names by, 94
    voyage to Rome of, 227
Paulus, Sergius, 268
pearls, 57–58
peas, 45
Pelethites, 283–84
Pentecost (Feast of Weeks), 7, 114–15
    Christian celebration of, 115
Peoples of the Sea, 283
Perea, 337
perfumes, 74ff.; ingredients for, 84
Persia, 11, 82, 330
Petra, 27
Pharisees, 54, 111, 206–207, 331
Philip, Herod, 337, 346

Philistines, 11, 246, 280, 282, 283, 288, 314
    army of, 281, 291, 293, 296–97
    monopolized use of iron, 373–74
    origins of, 283
    plague among, 71–72
    "uncircumcised," 95
Phoenicians, 32, 65, 226, 361
    commerce of, 225
    purple cloth of, 376
    as shipbuilders, 362
physicians, in Egypt, 66–67; in Israel, 69;
        in Mesopotamia, 67, 68
pig, 73. See also Swine.
pilgrim festivals, 112ff.
    historicization of, 117
Pilate, Pontius, 221, 267, 268, 350
    Roman prefect, 348
pistachio nuts, 43, 159
plague, bubonic, 71–72
planting, of grain seed, 177, 178
plowing, 174–77
pomegranates, 44, 45, 159
Pompey, 335, 336
population, of United Kingdom, 309–10
    of Israel and Judah, 311–12
potter, 363ff.; in Israelite life, 372
pottery, steps in production of, 363–70
    location of workshops for, 371–372
prefect, Roman, 266–67. See also Pilate.
priest(s), 210
    chief, 193
    duties of, 190
    garments of, 196
    and Levites, 190–98
    lifestyle of, under David, 193
    role of, in curing illness, 69
    Temple activities of, 195–96
priesthood, history of, in Israel, 190
    and medicine, 65, 66, 67
    sacrificial ritual reserved to, 194
priest-kings, Hasmoneans, 335ff.
procurator. See Prefect.
prophecy, after Jerusalem's fall, 204
    in the Church, 204
prophets, 198ff., 206, 270
    classical, 200–202
    early, 198–99
    female, 203–204
    functions of, 199–200
    manner of life of, 202–203
    name of section of Hebrew Bible, 14ff.
prostitution, 232–33
pruning, 183–84

Psalms, book of, 230
Ptolemy I "Soter," 330
Ptolemy XI, 345
purification, 72; of mother, 94–95

quail, 43, 140
Qarqar, 289, 327, 329
quern, rotary, 168; saddle, 167, 182–83
quiver, 278, 301, 302
Qumran, 208–209, 216

Rabbah (Rabbath-Ammon), 294, 295, 305, 307
Rabbi, title of respect for Jesus, 211
Rachel, 90, 91, 99, 101
Rahab, 233
rainfall, 125, 126, 127, 135, 150, 151
   minimum needed for farming, 123
   in Negev, 164–65
   of Palestine, 4–7, 154–57
rains, winter ("early"), 5, 125, 146, 154, 174; spring ("latter"), 154
Ramah, 313
Rameses II, Pharaoh, 278, 279
Rameses III, Pharaoh, military depiction of, 279, 296
rape, penalty for, 99
razor, 52
Rebekah, 42, 102
Rechabites, 32
refining, 375–76
Rehoboam, 11, 288, 311, 312
   cities for defense of, 312–13
Rephidim, 290
resins, 76ff.
resurrection, 207
Revelation, book of, 21
Rezin, 314
rice, 166
rings, 59, 62
ritual, at the Temple, 194–96
roads, Roman, 221
Rome, functions of troops in Judea, 346–47
   places Judea under direct governance, 338
   presence of, in Palestine, 329ff.
   required no military service of Jews, 345
   Simon's alliance with, 334
   soldiers of, 346–49
   troops of, under Pompey, 335
roof, 39–40
rouge, 88

rubies, 61
rugs, 50

Sabbath, 109–12; in Exile, 110
   increasing restrictions about, 111
   laws of, 91
sack cloth, 232
sacrifice(s), at the Temple, 194–96
   attached by prophets, 201
   of firstborn, 96–97
Sadducees, 206, 207–208, 331
saffron, 83
sailors, 226–27
sails, 377
salt, 91
Samaria, 11, 254, 266, 326
   fall of, 315
   masonry at, 360
   rebuilt by Herod, 339
Samaritans, infusion of non-Israelite blood into, 315
Samson, 272
Samuel, 199, 203, 210, 245
   warning of, on "ways of kings," 248, 311–12
Samuel, First and Second Books of, 11
sanctuaries ("high places"), 191, 198, 201
sandals, 50; Roman military, 353
Sanhedrin, 243, 350
sapphire, 59, 61, 62
Sarah, 98
Sargon II, 315
satrap, 266
Saul, 11, 48, 206, 246, 270, 272, 280, 284
   first king, 246
   initiates standing army, 281
scarab, 59, 63
scribes, 54, 210, 213–16
Sea Peoples, 283, 296
Sea of Reeds, 9
seal, 63
Sebaste, 339, 340, 346, 348
secretary, royal, 260–61
seed, 177
seer, 199
Seleucus, 330
seminomads, Hebrews as, 124–25, 133, 134
Sennacherib, 72, 259, 261, 321
Septuagint, 16, 331
seven, a symbolic number, 103
Shalmaneser III, 327, 328
Shalmaneser V, 315
Shaphan, 261

shaving, 86
shearing, of sheep, 131
Sheba, Queen of, 48, 79, 225, 253, 287, 290
Shebna, 259
sheep, 45, 123, 129–31, 135, 142
shell, used in jewelry, 62
Shephelah, 153, 357, 363, 374
shepherd, 131, 141–44
Sheshbazzar, 266
shield, in pre-monarchy era, 276
   as used by David's Army, 303–304
   of Philistines, 296
   of Romans, 352
Shiloh, 193, 233
ships, Phoenician, 362–63
Shishak (Sheshonk II), Pharaoh, 312
shoes, 50. See also Sandals.
shops, retail, 224
siege equipment, Assyrian, 315–16
silk, 377
Siloam tunnel, 217–18, 259
silver, 58, 59, 61, 374
silversmiths, 380
Simon, brother of Judas Maccabeus, 334
sin offering, 94–95
Sinai, Mount, 9
Sisera, 273
sling, 275, 301–302
slingers, 293, 301, 306, 315
Smith, Edwin, Surgical Papyrus, 67, 76, 80
smelting, 375
soap, 85, 86
society, institutions of biblical, 233ff.
   Israelite, 234–36, 245–48
soldiering, under David, 280ff.
   in Roman occupation army, 346ff.
Solomon, 11, 48, 61, 153, 193, 225, 226, 253
   building program of, 307–309
   chariots of, 289, 308
   forced labor under, 264–65, 310
   as a military man, 290
   national complexity under, 247
   population trends under, 309–310
   taxes, transit of, 79
   wealth and power of, 253–54, 256–57
Song of Solomon, 101
sons, 91, 238
South Arabia, 77, 78, 82
sown (land), 127
   desert vs., 150–51
spear, 276, 296, 298
spices, 161

spies, 279
spinning, 376, 379
stacte, 80, 82–83
staff, shepherd's, 143
standards, Roman, 348–49
stonemason, 359–60
stoning, death by, 137
storehouses, 263
stove, 30
straw, 366
Succoth, 43, 288, 294, 376
sugar, 43, 45, 161
summer, in Palestine, 7, 154
superintendent of the district prefects, 262–64
superintendent of the forced levy, 264–65
swaddling cloth, 74, 91
swine, 45, 175
swords, sickle, 274, 279
   two-edged Philistine, 296
   of David's army, 298
   Roman, 350
synagogues, 207, 211
Syria, 45, 288
   Joab and David's battles with, 294, 295
   under Persian rule, 266
   under Seleucid rule, 330ff.

Tabernacle, 30, 80
table, 30, 37
taboo, 73
Tabor, Mount, 273
Tamar (mother of twins), 73, 190
Tamar (town), 307
tambourines, 101
Tarshish, ships of, 227, 253, 363, 373
tassels, 52, 54
tax, taxes, 164, 169, 182, 247, 248, 262, 347
   collection, Roman system of, 269
   under Persian rule, 268
   receipts for, 263–64
   Roman, in Judea, 268–69, 349
   types of, 254
teachers, 209–11
Temple, 109–10, 208, 254, 285, 308, 330, 331, 335, 344
   centralization of sacrifices at, 113, 114, 116
   despoliation of, by Antiochus, 332
   half-shekel tax for, on Jews, 268
   music of, 230–31
   sacrifice at, 194–96
   treasure of seized as tribute, 321

"tent of meeting," 30
tents, 28–31; imagery of, 31–32
textile manufacture, 376–77
theatre, Roman at Caesarea, 341–42
Three, the, 277–78
threshing, 180
threshold, 34–35
Thirty, the, 286–87
Tiglath-pileser III, 262, 314
timber, 226
timbrels, 100
tin, 375
Tirhakah, Pharaoh, 321
Tirzah, 325
tithe, 146
Titus, 344
toilet kit, 88
tombs, 105, 106
tools, of carpenter, 362
Torah, 14, 15, 16, 18, 194, 207, 331
tower-platforms, Assyrian, 315, 324
trade, 224; international, 224–26
tribe, 134, 135, 234
    disintegration of tribal regime, 238–40
    "twelve tribes," 235–36, 239
Tubal-cain, 373
tumors, 72
tunic, the colobium, 49, 50, 54
turban, 50
turquoise, 56, 61, 63
Tyre, 65, 226, 314
    "Tyrian purple," 376, 378
    See also Phoenicians.

uncleanness, ritual of mother, 94–95
    of a corpse, 105
Unleavened Bread, Feast of, 112, 114–15
Uriah the Hittite, 282, 305
Urim and Thummim, 191–92, 194, 206, 270
utensils, housewife's, 30
Uzziah, 71, 164, 258, 314

Vaux, Roland de, 208, 248, 301
vegetables, 45
veils, 100, 101
vine(s), 153, 166
    cultivation of, 183–84
vineyards, 159; tending of, 183–84

walls, 359; casemated, 306
    solid, replacing casemated, 312
war, 8, 269ff., 311
    Israelite strategems in, 279–80
    of Jewish independence, 333–34
    sanctification of, 270–71
water, 123, 131, 135, 158
    See also Rainfall.
water bags, 133
weapons, of David's army, 297ff.
    in era before Philistines, 274ff.
    of Roman army, 350
    See also Sword, etc.
weather. See Climate, Rainfall.
weaving, 28, 376, 379–80
wedding, 101–103
Weeks, Feast of, 41, 114–15, 146
wells, 44, 123, 124, 269
wheat, 7, 127, 157, 158, 174
    celebration of harvest of, 146
    See also Grain, Harvesting.
windows, 37
wine, 44, 74, 158
    production of, 184–85
winnowing, 180–81
wood, kinds and uses of, 361
    fine, 62
wool, 13; of Damascus, 377
women, 73; as mourners, 231
    work of nomadic, 139, 140
    See also Mother.
Writings, section of Hebrew Bible, 15ff.

Yadin, Yigael, 285, 287, 291, 294
Yahweh, 112, 119; attributes of, 270, 271
yeast, 43
Yom Kippur, 118–19

Zacchaeus, 269
Zadok, 207
Zarephath (Sarafand), pottery finds at, 371
Zealots, 338
Zedekiah, 323
Zephaniah, 53
Zerubbabel, 266
Zeruiah, 286
Ziba, 43
Zipporah, 95